Social Policy in Britain

Second Edition

Pete Alcock

Consultant Editor: Jo Campling

palgrave
macmillan

First edition 1996
Second edition 2003

Published by
PALGRAVE MACMILLAN
Houndmills, Basingstoke, Hampshire RG21 6XS and
175 Fifth Avenue, New York, N.Y. 10010
Companies and representatives throughout the world

PALGRAVE MACMILLAN is the global academic imprint of the Palgrave
Macmillan division of St. Martin's Press, LLC and of Palgrave Macmillan Ltd.
Macmillan® is a registered trademark in the United States, United Kingdom
and other countries. Palgrave is a registered trademark in the European
Union and other countries.

ISBN 0333-99334-9

This book is printed on paper suitable for recycling and made from fully
managed and sustained forest sources.

A catalogue record for this book is available from the British Library.

10   9   8   7   6   5   4   3   2   1
12   11   10   09   08   07   06   05   04   03

Printed and bound in Great Britain by
Creative Print & Design (Wales), Ebbw Vale

For Sandra

Contents

Part II

Structure

Part III

Context

Part IV

Issues

List of Figures and Tables

Figures

Tables

Preface to the Second Edition

This book is intended to provide a general introduction to social policy for students studying the subject at all levels of further and higher education. The main intended readership is students in higher education on the first year, or at the first level, of undergraduate degree courses in social policy. However, the book will be equally valuable to students studying social policy as part of a broader undergraduate programme in the social sciences, as part of NVQ, BTEC or A level courses in further education or as part of professional education courses in areas such as social work or nursing. It also aims to provide a comprehensive and up-to-date guide to the subject for students first encountering social policy at postgraduate level, or wishing to re-examine previous studies as part of a new postgraduate course.

The book adopts a comprehensive and yet topical approach, and aims to provide a clear and comprehensive guide to all the major issues that are likely to be encountered in the study of social policy. The primary focus of the book is on Britain and on the development and analysis of British social policy. Its primary intended readership, therefore, is students in British universities and colleges. However, as is argued in the text, it is no longer feasible to restrict the study of social policy to the context and actions of only one nation state. The international context of British social policy is thus discussed, and in particular the growing impact of the European Union (EU) upon policy development in Britain. This provides a framework for the coverage of British policy development, however, rather than an extensive focus on comparative study or on the EU in particular detail. Students seeking a textbook on comparative social policy or on social policy in the EU should look to some of the increasing numbers of specialist texts now focusing on these issues and discussed in Chapter 14.

It is also no longer possible to deal comprehensively with the provision of social policy across Britain. The devolution of political and policy-making powers to Scotland, Wales and Northern Ireland since 1999 has led to significant and growing diversity in welfare provision across these separate subnations (see Chapter 15). This is especially important in certain policy areas, such as education, health and social care, where devolved powers have led to major departures in policy and practice. There is not the space in this book to cover all of the details of these differences; and readers will have to look elsewhere for these in the publications on devolution that are now emerging and on the websites of the devolved administrations referred to in Chapter 15. In a number of places therefore the policy developments referred to here are those taking place in England only, but where there are significant departures from these within the devolved administrations these are mentioned in the text.

These caveats should not be taken to suggest, however, that this book is likely only to be of interest to students of social policy in Britain – or even England. The policies and issues within British social policy discussed here are situated within a broader international and theoretical context; and this is likely to make the book of interest to students in other countries too, who wish to find a comprehensive and accessible guide to the development and analysis of policy within the UK that could provide a basis for comparative study.

Readers of this book may start at the beginning and carry on through to the end; however, many students of social policy following a course, or courses, of study will probably want to move backwards and forwards between the sections and chapters in order to find out about the specific themes or issues that they are studying at any particular time. With this in mind, the contents of the book have been carefully divided between sections and chapters addressing different issues, and have been written so that any one chapter could be read in isolation from those around it, but in the expectation that the others would probably be used or referred to at another time. This is a book, therefore, that can either be read or used as a source of reference (or, perhaps most commonly, both).

The chapters have also been divided into subsections, with subheadings listed in the contents. These are intended to help readers to find quickly the particular issue on which they want to focus at any one time. However, where issues – or particular terms or concepts – are not listed in the contents, readers should use the index at the end. This provides page references to the detailed coverage of all specific concepts and empirical policy developments and is perhaps the quickest way of all to gain access to the book in order to find the answer to a particular question. To help the book to work as a tool for learning as well as a source of information, this new edition includes boxed summaries of the key points at the beginning of each chapter and suggestions of useful sources of further reading (including some key websites) at the end. Direct links to these key websites can be found on the book's own companion website, **www. palgrave.com/socialpolicy/alcock**. The text is also interspersed with questions to help readers to assimilate the material covered and to reflect on some of the broader issues involved. These are distinguished as questions for *comprehension* and questions for *reflection*; and, as well as providing a stimulus for individual readers, they could also be used as learning tools by tutors or student groups.

Chapter 1 is a general introduction to the subject of social policy, the history of its development and some of the major changes in emphasis and focus that have been experienced within it. The term 'social policy' of course refers not only to an academic subject but also to the empirical basis of that subject, the policies that have been developed within society to meet welfare needs. The chapter also summarises the development of British social policy in the context of the academic study of it. However, there is no comprehensive coverage of the history of British social policy here; and again readers wanting such coverage should look elsewhere.

Part I of the book provides a summary of the main areas of social policy provision in Britain. There is additional coverage compared to that provided in the first edition of this book and this means that the text now provides a comprehensive introduction to the substance of social policy as well as to the themes and issues underlying its development and operation. Part II outlines the structural context of policy delivery and highlights the different sectors which provide welfare services. Part III explores the major contextual factors which influence social policy development, including a summary of the different ideological perspectives which inform both academic debate and practical policy making. Finally Part IV discusses some of the key issues which feature in current debates about social policy practice, including the questions of who should pay for social policy and how we should deliver it, and concludes with a short overview of major developments and future prospects.

Inevitably in an introductory text there are limits to what can be covered, even in an expanded framework such as this second edition. Readers wishing to look in more detail at particular issues or debates, or particular areas of service development or delivery, will need to move on to more specialist texts within these areas, such as those listed in the further reading; indeed, it is likely that they will be directed to do so by tutors. So, although this could be the first and most comprehensive text that students of social policy use, it will almost certainly not be the only one.

PETE ALCOCK

Acknowledgements

I should like to take this opportunity to thank a few people who have supported me in the production of this new extended edition of the book. Jo Campling encouraged me to write the first edition, and assured me that a revised second edition (much needed) would be worth the additional work involved in producing it. Catherine Gray at Palgrave Macmillan was equally encouraging, and understanding in recognising the time it would take to do this on top of my other commitments at Birmingham. I hope that their support has proved well founded. I should also like to thank the three anonymous reviewers who commented on the fist draft of the text for Palgrave Macmillan. They made many helpful suggestions, and the book has undoubtedly been improved as a result of their comments; although I must, of course, remain responsible for its final content. Finally, and most importantly, I am grateful to Sandra Cooke for her continuing support and encouragement, and for her helpful advice in places on both content and presentation.

PETE ALCOCK

The author and publishers wish to thank the following for permission to reproduce copyright material: Bills (1989) *The Theory of the Voluntary Sector: Implications for Policy and Practice*, reproduced with permission of Billis; Bonoli, George and Taylor-Goody (2000) *European Welfare Futures: Towards a Theory of Retrenchment*, reproduced with permission of Bonoli, George and Taylor-Gooby; Crown copyright material is reproduced with the permission of the Controller of HMSO and the Queen's Printer for Scotland; Glennerster and Hills (eds) (1998) *The State of Welfare: The Economics of Social Spending* (2nd edition), reproduced with permission of Glennerster and Hills, and Oxford University Press; Guardian News Service Limited for Figure 5.2; Ham (1999) *Health Policy in Britain* (4th edition), reproduced with permission of Christopher Ham and Palgrave Macmillan; Hantrais (2000) *Social Policy in the European Community* (2nd edition), reproduced with permission of Hantrais and Palgrave Macmillan; Hills (2000) *Taxation for the Enabling State*, CASE paper 41, reproduced with permission of Hills and London School of Economics; Malpass and Murie (1999) *Housing Policy and Practice* (5th edition), reproduced with permission of Malpass and Murie and Palgrave Macmillan. Every effort has been made to trace all the copyright-holders, but if any have been inadvertently overlooked the publishers will be pleased to make the necessary arrangement at the first opportunity.

List of Abbreviations

ABI	Area Based Initiative
ACU	Active Community Unit
ASI	Adam Smith Institute
BMA	British Medical Association
BUPA	British United Provident Association
CAB	Citizens Advice Bureau
CAF	Charities Aid Foundation
CCETSW	Central Council for Education and Training in Social Work
CDF	Community Development Foundation
CPAG	Child Poverty Action Group
COS	Charity Organisation Society
CPS	Centre for Policy Studies
CSE	Certificate of School Education
CSP	*Critical Social Policy*
CSR	Comprehensive Spending Review
CVS	Council for Voluntary Services
DES	Department of Education and Science
DfEE	Department for Education and Employment
DfES	Department for Education and Skills
DG	Directorate General
DHSS	Department of Health and Social Security
DoH	Department of Health
DTLR	Department of Transport, Local Government and the Regions
DWP	Department for Work and Pensions
DSS	Department of Social Security
EAPN	European Anti-Poverty Network
EAZ	Education Action Zone
EEC	European Economic Community
EPA	Educational Priority Area
ERM	Exchange Rate Mechanism
ESRC	Economic and Social Research Council
ET	Employment Training
EU	European Union
FE	Further Education
FEFC	Further Education Funding Council
GCE	General Certificate of Education
GCSE	General Certificate in School Education
GDP	Gross Domestic Product
GHS	General Household Survey
GLC	Greater London Council
GNP	Gross National Product
GOR	Government Office for the Regions

GP	General Practitioner
GREA	Grant Related Expenditure Assessment
GSCC	General Social Care Council
HAT	Housing Action Trust
HAZ	Health Action Zone
HEFC	Higher Education Funding Council
HImP	Health Improvement Programme
ICA	Invalid Care Allowance
IEA	Institute of Economic Affairs
ILO	International Labour Organisation
IMF	International Monetary Fund
JSA	Jobseekers' Allowance
JSP	*Journal of Social Policy*
LEA	Local Education Authority
LETS	Local Exchange and Trading Scheme
LMS	Local Management of Schools
LSE	London School of Economics
LSP	Local Strategic Partnership
MP	Member of Parliament
MSC	Manpower Services Commission
NACAB	National Association of Citizen's Advice Bureaux
NCVO	National Council for Voluntary Organisations
NDC	New Deal for Communities
NGO	Non-Governmental Organisation
NHS	National Health Service
NI	National Insurance
NICE	National Institute for Clinical Excellence
NPM	New Public Management
NSPCC	National Society for the Prevention of Cruelty to Children
NVQ	National Vocational Qualification
ODPM	Office of the Deputy Prime Minister
OECD	Organisation for Economic Co-operation and Development
OFSTED	Office for Standards in Education
OPCS	Office of Population Census and Surveys
OPEC	Organisation of Petroleum Exporting Countries
PCG	Primary Care Group
PCT	Primary Care Trust
PFI	Private Finance Initiative
PSBR	Public Sector Borrowing Requirement
PSNCR	Public Sector Net Cash Requirement
PSS	Personal Social Services
QAA	Quality Assurance Agency
quango	Quasi-autonomous non-governmental organisation
RAWP	Resource Allocation Working Party
RDA	Regional Development Agency
RPI	Retail Price Index
RSG	Rate Support Grant

RSL	Registered Social Landlord
SAT	Standard Attainment Test
SEU	Social Exclusion Unit
SMR	Standardised Mortality Ratio
SPA	Social Policy Association
SRB	Single Regeneration Budget
SSA	Standard Spending Assessment
SSD	Social Services Department
SSRC	Social Science Research Council
TEC	Training and Enterprise Council
TVEI	Technical and Vocational Education Initiative
UGC	University Grants Committee
UN	United Nations
VAT	Value Added Tax
VSU	Voluntary Service Unit
WHO	World Health Organisation
WRVS	Women's Royal Voluntary Service
YOP	Youth Opportunities Programme
YTS	Youth Training Scheme

Introduction: The Development of Social Policy

SUMMARY OF KEY POINTS

- Social policy is a unique subject, but is closely linked to the other social sciences.
- It has broadened its sphere of analysis and debate and moved from *administration* to *policy*.
- Academic study of social policy has always been closely linked to policy practice, with leading academics sometimes acting as advisers to government.
- The creation of the 'welfare state' by the post-war Labour government established public services to meet welfare needs. This was a major achievement for social policy reformers, but was also criticised by social policy academics.
- Criticisms of state welfare from the *New Left* and the *New Right* have argued that the continued expansion of state welfare is not sustainable. In the last quarter of the last century this seemed to be borne out as an economic crisis led to retrenchment in social policy planning and welfare expenditure.
- At the beginning of the twenty-first century a *Third Way*, between the left and the right, has been championed by government in the UK, and elsewhere.
- Social policy can no longer be studied within national boundaries.
- Comparative analysis of welfare in different countries has revealed that in different countries there are different *mixes* of welfare services.
- It is how this welfare mix operates, and changes, in Britain that is the core concern of students of social policy.

What is social policy?

It is probably true that there will always be argument and debate about what constitutes an academic subject and how to define particular subjects. In the area of social science, in particular, there has been debate about the overlap between subjects such as sociology, economics, politics and social policy, and about what should be the core concerns of each. This debate has not just been an academic one: it has a political significance, too. For instance, in the early 1980s the Conservative government in Britain, under the influence of the Secretary of State for Education and Science, Sir Keith Joseph, required the major state body providing research funding for the social sciences to change its name from the *Social Science Research Council* (SSRC) to the *Economic and Social Research Council* (ESRC) in a direct attempt to shift the focus of research in the social science field towards economic issues and applied policy research.

Students of social science must recognise therefore that what they study, and how they study it, is consequently the subject of continual academic and political debate (and, indeed, disagreement). Of course, in general this is no bad thing. We cannot, and should not, take for granted that we are working only within a limited field where we alone are experts and everyone is agreed what it is we are experts on. If this were the case academic knowledge would not advance very far, and it would not have much impact on the broader social world.

However, recognition that the boundaries of our study are never closed and that the focus of our concern is subject to external influences does not mean that we cannot find distinctive features of research and debate within social policy that make it possible, and desirable, to separate out this work from the different, although related, concerns of sociology, economics, politics and other social sciences. If we examine the development of the subject of social policy, we can see clearly how the attempt to provide a specific focus for study was embarked upon, how this led to boundary disputes with other subjects, how it was subject to external political influence and to internal theoretical debate, and how these events changed the nature of social policy itself. In fact, debates over the nature of social policy even resulted in a change in name for the subject from *social administration* to *social policy*, symbolised by the change of the professional association from the Social Administration Association in 1987. It was a change, however, that was not without conflict and disagreement (see Glennerster, 1988; G Smith, 1988; Donnison, 1994). Many university departments and qualifications are still called social administration, and the ESRC only recently changed its description of research in the area to social administration and policy.

What is more, in most British universities social policy in fact often shares departmental status with other cognate social sciences such as sociology, or with professional education such as social work, and the teaching of these is generally closely related. And in research institutes specialists in social policy often work alongside sociologists, economists, statisticians and even lawyers. Nevertheless social policy *is* a discrete academic subject with its own specific theoretical and empirical foci; and the boundary disputes, the theoretical arguments, and even the change of title, are evidence of healthy self-criticism and self-reflection, rather than self-doubt. There are undergraduate and postgraduate degrees in social policy, academic journals publishing the findings of social policy research, and a professional association representing social policy practitioners (now the *Social Policy Association*, or SPA). As a history of the development of the subject reveals, social policy has an important and unique contribution to make to our understanding of the social world and its future development.

From social administration to social policy

Where social policy differs from sociology is in its specific focus upon the development and implementation of policy measures in order to influence the social circumstances of individuals rather than the more general study of those social circumstances themselves. Where it differs from economics is in its focus upon welfare policies, or policies impacting upon the welfare of citizens, rather than those seeking to influence the production of goods, materials and services. Social policy is also different because the title of the subject is also the substantive focus of study. Social policies are developed within societies to meet the needs for welfare and wellbeing within the population, and it is theories and practices that underlie these social policies that students study. Thus while sociology students study *society*, social policy students study *social policies*.

Within the British social policy tradition in particular, what has also distinguished social policy from some other social science subjects has been its specific, and driving, concern not merely to understand the world, but also to change it. In this tradition social policy is not only a *descriptive* subject, it is also a *prescriptive* one. This is in part because the early academic development of social policy in Britain was closely allied to the political development of *Fabianism*. The Fabians were both academics and politicians, and they wanted to utilise academic research and analysis in order to influence government welfare policy. Throughout much of the early part of last century the development of British social policy was often synonymous with the concerns and perspectives of the Fabians; and the subject largely shared Fabianism's benign view of the role of state provision within welfare policy. Social policy also shared the empirical focus of Fabianism, in particular its concern to measure the need for, and the impact of, state welfare provision.

The ideological and empirical alliances with Fabianism were, however, associated most closely with the social administration perspective of the subject, and with a concern with *what* is done by policy action, and *how* it is done, rather than *why* this is done, or indeed *whether* it should be done. This narrower focus has come under critical scrutiny as the academic subject has developed over the last 50 years or so. Of particular importance in this process of development was the work of Richard Titmuss, the first Professor of Social Administration, who was appointed at the London School of Economics (LSE) in 1950. In his inaugural lecture at the LSE Titmuss described social policy as 'the study of the social sciences whose object ... is the improvement of the conditions of life of the individual in the setting of family and group relations' (1958, p.14). This included a commitment to prescription (improving living conditions) and to an understanding of social context. These concerns were taken up by Titmuss in his later work, which remains the most influential legacy of conceptual reflection and empirical analysis within the subject, both within the UK and beyond (see Alcock *et al.*, 2001). Titmuss was especially concerned, however, to argue that the role of academic study was to explore the values which lay behind policy decisions and the research evidence that should shed light on these, rather than to extol the virtues of particular policy changes. It is this reflective approach which led him to challenge some of the narrower perceptions of the achievements of the Fabian-inspired welfare reforms of post-war Britain, and which still provides an inspiration to critical judgement amongst students of the subject today.

In the latter half of the twentieth century the narrow focus of the Fabian tradition upon how to improve existing welfare services thus began to come under increasing criticism and attack from different perspectives which sought to widen the questions asked by the subject and to challenge the underlying assumption of the benign role of the state in welfare provision. Furthermore, the narrow focus and assumptions of the social administration tradition have also been called into question by the increasing academic and political concern with *international* comparisons of welfare policy. For what international comparisons quickly reveal, as Titmuss again was influential in pointing out, is that welfare policies have not developed elsewhere as they have done in Britain; that different political assumptions in different countries have led to different patterns of provision; and, therefore, that different political assumptions could lead to different patterns of provision in Britain too.

The cumulative effect of these questions and challenges has been to bring about a significant shift in the focus of academic debate and political influence within the subject, which has been represented by the change in title from administration to policy. This has resulted in a shift from a subject that was, in Mishra's (1989, p.80) terms, 'pragmatic, Britain-centred, socially concerned and empirical', to one that is characterised by ideological division, theoretical pluralism and a growing internationalism. However, this shift, significant though it is, should not deter us from recognising the continuities, as well as the discontinuities, in the development of social policy that in particular its concern with policies for welfare provides.

Fabianism

The concern of social policy to contribute to the development of political change – as well as to analyse it – is generally credited with providing for its birth as a subject in Britain, at a time when state policy towards the welfare of citizens was undergoing a radical revision and Fabian politics were seeking both to understand and to influence this. The Fabian Society was formed in 1884, under the leading guidance of Sidney and Beatrice Webb. The Webbs were firm believers that collective provision for welfare through the state was an essential, and inevitable, development within British capitalist society; Sidney Webb also held strong views on the moral values of social (or socialist) provision (Headlam, 1892; Ball, 1896).

One of the early examples of the influence of Fabian thinking was within the Royal Commission on the Poor Laws and the Relief of Distress, of which Beatrice Webb was a member. The Commission was established by the government, in 1905, to review the old Victorian approach to support for the poor. It signified a recognition by government of the need to overhaul welfare policies and of the importance of social policy debate in shaping this process, and it increased the pressure on government to bring about the major changes in social security and other policies that were introduced in the ten years before the First World War.

Debate about the future direction of welfare policy was a central concern of the work of the Commission, and when it reported in 1909 the Commission produced both a Majority and Minority Report, as the members could not all agree about the role that the state should play as provider of welfare services. The *Minority* Report was largely written by the Webbs and argued for an extensive role for state provision. The *Majority* Report envisaged a greater, continuing, role for charitable and voluntary action. Nevertheless, both argued for significant reform and in retrospect there was as much in common across the two reports as there was in conflict between them; and, as we shall see in Part II in particular, both state and voluntary action have in practice played significant roles in the subsequent development of social policy.

Influential in the drafting of the Majority Report were Charles Booth and Bernard and Helen Bosanquet, leading members of the Charity Organisation Society (COS), which coordinated much of voluntary sector provision of social work and social services and the training of social workers. In December 1912, however, the COS's School of Sociology was merged with the LSE, founded by the Webbs, to form the LSE's new Department of Social Science and Administration. This was arguably the first academic base for the study of social policy and it provided a significant academic forum for the debates rehearsed in the deliberations of the Poor Law Commission to be continued and developed. The first lecturer to be appointed to the new department in 1913 was Clement Attlee, demonstrating almost immediately the close link that the Fabians were concerned to secure between academic analysis and political change because, after the Second World War, Attlee became the Prime Minister of the Labour government which introduced many of the far-reaching state welfare reforms that the Fabian reformers had been calling for throughout the intervening period.

During the early part of the twentieth century the LSE Department of Social Science and Administration also received significant financial support from the private trusts of an Indian millionaire, Ratan Tata. This money was specifically tied to support for empirical research on policies for the prevention and relief of poverty and destitution. It therefore provided an impetus for the development of another significant aspect of the subject: its concern with empirical work on the need for, and impact of, social policy. In particular, the research funding supported the work of academics such as Tawney, and Bowley and Burnett Hurst, who were early pioneers in the theoretical and empirical investigation of poverty and inequality in Britain (Harris, 1989).

During the period following the First World War, therefore, the department at the LSE contained the main themes of the subject of social policy in its early form. The department was informed, and directed, by a strong ideological commitment to Fabianism, in particular the use of academic knowledge and research on social problems to create pressure on the state to introduce welfare reforms. The continuing influence of the old COS, however, also maintained a concern with the role of the voluntary sector in social service and, although diminished by the statism of the Fabian approach, this broader concern with non-state welfare provision has always remained a vital feature of political as well as academic debate in social policy.

Teaching at the LSE, although also informed by sociology and economics, remained firmly tied to the education and training of social services workers, however; and research work focused on the detailed investigation of the problem of poverty. Despite the high-profile political context of its birth in the early twentieth century, when the Webbs and the Bosanquets were influential in shaping the reform of Victorian welfare policy in Britain, social policy soon became more concerned with the pragmatic issues of education for practice and empirical research on established social problems (the social administration tradition).

The welfare state

In the period following the Second World War this tradition reached what was perhaps its high-water mark with the creation of what has often been referred to as a 'welfare state' in Britain. The development of this welfare state owed much, in principle at least, to the influence of the Beveridge Report in 1942. Beveridge (himself Director of the LSE during the interwar period) had been appointed by the wartime government to conduct a review of social security policy. However, when his report appeared, at around the time of one of the earliest allied victories at El Alamein, it included, alongside a detailed blueprint for the reform of benefits, a vision for a much broader role for the state in meeting collective welfare need, captured in his famous reference to the need for public action to remove the 'five giant evils' that had haunted the country before the war: *disease, idleness, ignorance, squalor* and *want*.

Beveridge's report was a best-seller, and it set the scene for debate about policy development after the war. Reforms were introduced by the post-war Attlee government to combat Beveridge's evils through state action:

- the National Health Service to combat disease
- full employment to combat idleness
- state education to fifteen to combat ignorance (actually introduced in 1944 by the wartime National Government)
- public housing to combat squalor
- the National Insurance and Assistance schemes to combat want.

At the same time local authority Children's and Mental Health Departments introduced comprehensive social service provision too. All of these policy changes are discussed in more detail in Part I.

This was probably the most intensive period of social policy reform ever experienced in the UK. The head of the LSE Department of Social Science and Administration during this period was T H Marshall. In a famous treatise on citizenship (1950) he argued that the earlier development of civil and political citizenship in British society had been complemented in the mid-twentieth century by the creation of *social citizenship*. With the expansion of public funding for comprehensive state services it is easy to see how this embodiment of social citizenship and the new role which it included for the state as the provider of social services came to be seen as the creation of a welfare state.

Furthermore, the post-war welfare state appeared to have widespread political and ideological support. Although most of the reforms were introduced by the Labour government elected in 1945, when Labour were replaced by the Conservatives in 1951, the state welfare services were maintained in almost exactly the same form. The general assumption was that there was a political consensus over the desirability of state welfare provision within a capitalist economy. In 1954 *The Economist* magazine coined the phrase *Butskellism* to refer to this consensus, which was an amalgamation of the names of the Labour Chancellor of the Exchequer, Gaitskell, and his Conservative successor, Butler (also the author of the 1944 education reform: Dutton, 1991, ch.2). This consensus seemed to represent an accommodation in Conservative thinking to the role of state intervention, referred to by Macmillan as *The Middle Way* (1938), and a recognition in Labour thinking of the abandonment of the need for a future socialist revolution (Crosland, 1956; Addison, 1975).

The welfare state and the post-war consensus may be seen as significant achievements for social policy but they also presented the subject with something of a challenge, for in a sense they removed the need for further academic and ideological debate and therefore the main basis for future political influence. In the period following the introduction of the welfare state, social work practice and training became more and more concerned with the individualistic, psychoanalytical approach to social problems; voluntary sector activity began relatively to decline; and policy research became restricted to the narrow role of gathering facts to support the case for the gradual expansion and greater effectivity of the now-established agencies of state welfare. The success of Fabianism therefore meant that social policy debate ran the risk of being restricted to analysis and improvement of existing welfare services.

Such a narrow consensual approach was not without its critics, however (see Lowe, 1990). In particular the work of Titmuss challenged the supposed comprehensive nature of the new state services and their assumed egalitarian consequences, pointing out that support also took place outside state services and frequently selectively benefited the rich rather than the poor, and directly questioning the concept of the 'welfare state' itself (see Alcock *et al.*, 2001). Evidence of the limitations of state welfare was also developed by Titmuss's colleagues at the LSE. For instance, Townsend and Abel-Smith conducted research which showed that, despite the welfare reforms to combat want, many people were still living in poverty in Britain in the 1950s and 1960s (Abel-Smith and Townsend, 1965; Townsend, 1979).

Influential though these criticisms were in questioning the success of the welfare state in meeting all the goals of its Fabian protagonists, they remained to some extent within an overall Fabian framework of academic and political debate which continued to dominate social policy. Titmuss and his colleagues were staunch supporters of the principles behind the state welfare services introduced after the war and their criticisms were intended to create pressure to improve these rather than to question their basic desirability. By the 1970s, however, changes in Britain's welfare capitalist economy were beginning to create the climate for a challenge to the assumed desirability of the maintenance and gradual expansion of the post-war welfare state; and more critical voices were beginning to develop within social policy debate to challenge the Fabian domination of debate and research.

QUESTIONS: COMPREHENSION

- Why did social administration change its name to social policy?
- What is 'Fabianism', and to what extent did Fabian thinking dominate the development of British social policy in the last century?

QUESTION: REFLECTION

- What are the implications for students and practitioners of the recognition that social policy is a *prescriptive* subject?

The New Left

Towards the end of the 1960s and the beginning of the 1970s, the rapid expansion of higher education saw social policy becoming established as an academic subject in most British universities and expanding its research base with increased state and charitable support for an ever wider range of projects on the implementation of state welfare. In 1967 the professional association was established, and in 1971 a major academic journal for the subject was launched: the *Journal of Social Policy* (*JSP*).

However, the expansion of social policy also brought into the subject a wider range of academics and practitioners, not all of whom shared the Fabian perspective or the LSE roots of its earlier members. The late 1960s and early 1970s was a period of the renaissance of Marxist and other radical debate within the social sciences in most welfare capitalist countries, referred to by many of the leading protagonists as the *New Left*. The expanding base of social policy brought this debate into the politics and ideology of welfare too.

Marxist theorising covered a range of different, and disputed, approaches to social structure and social policy but, in general, there was agreement among many that the achievement of the welfare state in post-war Britain and the Fabian-supported consensus on the gradual and unilinear growth of welfare protection were neither as successful, nor as desirable, as had been assumed.

Pointing to the empirical work of Titmuss, Townsend and others, the Marxists argued that the welfare state had not succeeded in solving the social problems of the poor and the broader working class and, in practice, operated to *support* capitalism rather than to *challenge* it (Ginsburg, 1979). They argued, therefore, for a rejection of the consensual, Fabian, approach to the understanding of, and support for, state welfare and its replacement with a *political economy of the welfare state* (Gough, 1979), which situated the explanation of the growth of state welfare in the needs of the capitalist economy for healthy and educated workers and the struggle of the working class for concessions from the capitalist state (sometimes referred to as the *social wage*).

By the 1980s the influence of the left was no longer a 'new' feature of the subject; theoretical debate between Marxists and Fabians about the desirability, or the compatibility, of their different approaches to the subject ranged widely (Taylor-Gooby and Dale, 1981; Lee and Raban, 1988). In 1981 a new journal, *Critical Social Policy (CSP)*, was launched to provide a forum for such debates and for other alternative approaches to theory and research in social policy.

The New Left critics challenged the theoretical assumptions of the post-war consensus approach to state welfare, arguing for a conflict model that saw welfare reforms as the product of struggle and compromise rather than gradual enlightenment (Saville, 1983). They also challenged the assumed desirability of state welfare services, arguing that for many working-class people welfare services such as council housing or social security were experienced as oppressive and stigmatising. These criticisms were not only informed by Marxism: the pages of *CSP*, in particular, were also filled with academics and practitioners arguing that state welfare was also failing women, ethnic minorities and other oppressed or marginalised social groups (an issue to which we shall return in Chapter 16).

It is perhaps no coincidence that the New Left challenge to the Fabian domination of social policy was occurring at more or less the same time as the welfare state itself was also under threat from Britain's changing economic and political fortunes. The failure of economic growth in the 1970s to continue to provide a platform for expanding state welfare was argued by Marxists to be an inevitable consequence of the inability to reform capitalism from within and was evidence that the process was beginning to experience a 'crisis' in which stark choices would have to be faced by social policy planners and politicians (see Mishra, 1984). However, the crisis – if crisis it was – in state welfare of the 1970s not only attracted a critical reappraisal of the Fabian domination of social policy from the left, but it also provoked a counter-attack from right-wing theorists.

The New Right

Despite the overriding influence of Fabianism within social policy, especially during the immediate post-war period, right-wing critics of state welfare had always argued against the interference of state provision with the workings of a capitalist market economy (Hayek, 1944). During the 1950s, through the work of organisations such as the Institute of Economic Affairs (IEA), the appeal for a 'return' to the classic liberal values of a *laissez-faire* state and self-protecting families and communities was kept alive, if rather marginalised from mainstream social policy debate. In the 1970s, however, the crisis in the welfare state created circumstances in which such right-wing critics of state welfare could present a more cogent attack on Butskellism. What is more, this academic attack was accompanied by a shift to the right in politics too, exemplified by the election of Margaret Thatcher as leader of the Conservative Party in 1975. Together these changes provided an opportunity towards the end of the last century for a new liberalism (neo-liberalism) to rise to a prominence in academic and political debate that it had not achieved at any time in the previous 80 years.

Drawing on the work of right-wing American theorists such as Friedman (1962) and Murray (1984), the IEA and others began to develop a neo-liberal critique of state welfare and Fabian politics that both they, and their left-wing critics, began to refer to as the *New Right*. Not of course that these views were that new either, as we shall discuss in Chapter 12: they drew on classical liberal thinking from the nineteenth century and before. Their main argument was that state intervention to provide welfare services, and the gradual expansion of these which Fabianism sought, merely drove up the cost of public expenditure to a point at which it began to interfere with the effective operation of a market economy (Bacon and Eltis, 1976). They claimed that this was a point that had already been reached in Britain in the 1970s as the high levels of taxation needed for welfare services had reduced profits, crippled investment and driven capital overseas.

Like the New Left, the New Right also challenged the desirability of state welfare in practice, arguing that free welfare services only encouraged feckless people to become dependent upon them and provided no incentive for individuals and families to protect themselves through savings or insurance (Boyson, 1971). Furthermore, right-wing theorists claimed that state monopoly over welfare services reduced the choices available to people to meet their needs in a variety of ways and merely perpetuated professionalism and bureaucracy (Green, 1987).

After 1979, once the Conservative Party under Thatcher's leadership came into power, these academic arguments found a sympathetic hearing from government ministers such as Keith Joseph and Rhodes Boyson. However, the more extreme forms of New Right thinking never completely dominated the Conservative governments of the 1980s and 1990s. Even under Thatcher the influence of the right (dubbed the *dries*) was to some extent counter-balanced by those more sympathetic to a continuing role for the state (the *wets*); and although, as we shall see in Part I, significant reforms were made to many public welfare services, the basic principles of comprehensive public services for health, education, social security and social services remained largely intact. Thatcher herself was removed from power in 1990 by challengers within the Conservative Party and replaced by the more pragmatic approach of John Major.

The Third Way

By the 1990s, therefore, the domination that Fabianism had enjoyed over social policy had been overturned from two contradictory directions and, at the same time, its influence on government through support for the Butskellite consensus had been displaced by a political climate in which controversy was widely preached and the value of traditional academic analysis and empirical research openly questioned.

Furthermore, it was not just those from the left and right of the political spectrum who were challenging the consensual approach to welfare: other critical perspectives too were questioning the central role of Fabianism and the benign view of the state welfare. Feminist writers began to question what they claimed was the male domination of academic social policy and the assumptions about unequal gender roles that were contained in much practical social policy provision (Wilson, 1977; Dale and Foster, 1986). In a critical reappraisal of social policy analysis throughout the post-war period F Williams (1989) argued that both the gender and racial (or racist) dimensions of policy practice had been largely ignored by mainstream debate; and, as we shall see in Chapter 16, the importance of other social divisions has also now come to influence academic argument and policy development. This wider range of critical perspectives has also opened up a debate about the extent to which complex social organisations and social processes can ever be captured within the simplistic left/right dichotomies which had had such a dominant influence over policy debate throughout much of the last century. Within a modern (or perhaps a 'post-modern') society it is argued there are many contradictory and conflicting influences on social policy and that no one approach can meet all needs in all circumstances (see Chapter 12).

The abandonment of old certainties had also influenced political and policy development by the beginning of the twenty-first century. When Tony Blair became leader of the Labour Party in 1994 he began a thorough review of past policy priorities, which led to a rebranding of the party as *New Labour* and a rejection of many of the state welfare commitments of past Labour governments. Drawing on a distinction developed by a Commission on Social Justice (Borrie Commission, 1994) appointed by his predecessor John Smith, Blair argued that New Labour should reject both right-wing pro-market approaches and old left support for monopolistic state services in favour of a *Third Way* for policy development, located between the state and the market (Blair, 1998). When Labour came to power in 1997 this new approach quickly came to dominate both political debate and policy practice.

In part Labour's embrace of a third way was recognition of a changed understanding of the more complex make-up of modern societies, drawing on the work of Giddens (1998), Director of the LSE and an adviser to Blair. In part, however, it was also a product of a more pragmatic approach to policy making and service delivery, captured by the government slogan 'what counts is what works'. Rather than assuming that services are best provided by the state (the old, Fabian, left) or the market (the New Right), the new Labour government claimed to be concerned only with what was the most effective way to meet social needs; and this was a practical judgement based on empirical evidence of effectiveness. There has been much debate about the extent to which the Third Way *is* based upon a new philosophy for welfare provision in (post)modern society or is merely an eclectic pragmatism within which any mix of provision and organisation might be supported and no clear principles underlay policy development; and this is a debate upon which social policy academics take both sides (see Powell, 1999 and 2002).

However, it is not just within the UK that a third way for welfare reform has been promoted at the beginning of the new century. Many of Labour's new policy prescriptions owe much to the reforms developed by the Clinton administration in the USA in the 1990s, and Blair himself was strongly influenced by Clinton. In Europe, too, Third Way principles have been espoused, most notably by the Social Democratic government in Germany under Schröder, which refers to this as *Die Neue Mitte* (the new middle). And in practice different examples of policy provision, drawing on different mixes of state, market and other providers, can be found in most other advanced capitalist countries, as comparative analysis of social policy has increasingly begun to reveal.

QUESTIONS: COMPREHENSION

- To what extent were the New Left and the New Right critics of state welfare arguing that public provision for welfare was incompatible with the effective operation of a capitalist market economy?
- Is the Third Way a Labour government invention?

QUESTION: REFLECTION

- Does the Third Way mean that politicians and policy makers no longer believe that the state can provide for the welfare needs of all citizens?

Comparative perspectives

Throughout much of its early development, however, social policy had remained, like many other academic subjects in the social sciences, concerned almost exclusively with policy change and policy implementation in Britain. This is perhaps understandable, for Britain has had a more or less self-contained social and legal order and a government with the power to introduce policies affecting the lives of all people in Britain. British social policy students thus studied Britain, and the description of, and the prescription for, welfare policy focused primarily on Britain and its government. However, as we are all now very much aware, the lives of people in Britain are not only affected by the decisions and actions of the British government.

In the twenty-first century we live in what is an increasingly globalised world order, where the power and influence of major international companies is greater than that of many individual nation states. As we discuss in Chapter 13, no government, including the British one, can now operate independently of such global forces. Furthermore, as we shall see in Chapter 14, major decisions on economic and social development, affecting people in many countries, are taken on an international scale by bodies operating over and above the remit of national governments, such as the World Bank and the International Monetary Fund (IMF). Of particular importance for us is the European Union (EU) of which Britain is a member, and within which the decisions taken by the representative bodies of the EU have a direct impact upon policy development in its member nations. Social policies in Britain are thus no longer exclusively British – if indeed they ever really were – and the subject of social policy has been required to recognise, and to analyse, this broader international dimension.

Both left- and right-wing critics of Fabian social policy were, of course, able to point to the lessons that could be learned from policy development in other countries. Some of those on the left looked to the socialist countries of the Soviet bloc although, even before the collapse of Soviet socialism, others were drawing attention instead to the social democratic countries of Scandinavia as models for welfare reform in Britain. Those on the right used the Soviet bloc as a negative example, and argued rather for policy changes modelled on the market-oriented welfare provisions found in the USA. What was clear to all was that the welfare policies, or the welfare states, of other countries demonstrated that social policies did not *have* to be as they were in Britain.

Recognition of the importance of international comparison radically changes the focus of debate within social policy; but it, too, is not without its problems and disagreements. For a start, much of the early development of social policy in Britain had been presented as a gradual extension of state welfare, as if driven by a kind of inexorable law of progress, and tempered only by questions of speed, not direction. International comparisons initially tended to be dominated by similar assumptions. The expectation was that other countries would be following the same pattern of state welfare growth as Britain, albeit perhaps at a different pace. This assumption of international congruity is sometimes called a *convergence* thesis, because all nations are assumed to be converging towards one common goal.

Although it is true that most capitalist and socialist countries have developed policies to make some provision for the welfare of citizens, this convergence thesis can, however, only be sustained at a level of massive simplification. More detailed study of the welfare policies of other countries, even of Britain's nearby neighbours in the EU, reveals significant differences in the form, and the extent, of social policies, and in the political pressures that have given rise to them (George and Taylor-Gooby, 1996; Bonoli, George and Taylor-Gooby, 2000). By the 1980s social policy scholars in Britain and elsewhere were increasingly concerned to make such international comparisons, not merely in order to argue for the importation into Britain of models of welfare provision from other countries, but rather to demonstrate, at a more general theoretical and empirical level, the widespread diversity within welfare states. They sought, in effect, to challenge the convergence thesis with a celebration of difference, or a *divergence* thesis (Mishra, 1990; and see Alcock and Craig, 2001).

The development of comparative analysis in social policy can be traced back in particular to the work of Titmuss, who did much to promote policy development in other countries and developed an approach to comparative study of welfare states using three models drawn from the different value positions underlying their development (Titmuss, 1974). Perhaps the most influential contribution to comparative analysis, and to the divergence thesis, however, has come from the Swedish academic, Esping-Andersen (1990). Esping-Andersen carried out a detailed study of the welfare states of a number of developed welfare capitalist countries, from which he concluded that the different developments could be roughly grouped into different types of *welfare regime*. Esping-Andersen identified three major welfare regimes, somewhat similar in practice to Titmuss's three models:

- the *Liberal*, exemplified by the USA
- the *Corporatist*, exemplified by Germany and the rest of continental Western Europe
- the *Social Democratic*, exemplified by Scandinavia, in particular Sweden.

Esping-Andersen's analysis was based upon extensive empirical example of the development of welfare services across a number of advanced capitalist nations which he has also developed further in later work, as we discuss in more detail in Chapter 14. However, critics have argued that his *Three Worlds of Welfare Capitalism* (the title of the book), although demonstrating divergence in the international development of social policy, are even themselves something of a simplification of the range of differences that can be found within and between the regimes (see Alcock and Craig, 2001). Nevertheless Esping-Andersen's regime approach has dominated comparative social policy study over the past decade or so, and has revealed that comparative analysis can draw on both theoretical analysis and empirical data to help us to understand better the different ways in which policy develops in different contexts.

The welfare mix

What the different forms of welfare regime to be found in other countries reveal, of course, is that welfare policies develop in different ways in different social, economic and political contexts. These differences also reveal a varying balance within different regimes between the role of the state in the provision of welfare, for example, with public welfare playing a major role in social democratic regimes such as Sweden and the private market playing a major role in liberal regimes such as the USA. It is not, however, only the balance between the state and the market which varies between different regimes. In corporatist regimes such as Germany, considerable emphasis is placed on the informal role of family structures in providing welfare support (for instance, in the care of children or the long-term chronically sick). In other regimes, such as the 'welfare societies' of some Mediterranean countries including Greece and Spain, many welfare services are provided by voluntary agencies including churches and other religious organisations.

In other words, in different welfare states there is a variation between the roles of different *sectors* in the provision of welfare services. We shall return in Part II to look at the roles of these different sectors, in Britain in particular, in more detail. However, it is important to recognise here that it is not just that the balance between the different sectors varies between different welfare states, or welfare regimes, but also that this balance may vary within any one welfare state over time (especially, of course, if that welfare state is experiencing a move from one regime to another). Indeed, it is primarily upon the balance between the roles of the different sectors of welfare that the nature of the welfare regime in any one country at any one time can be determined; and in all regimes there will inevitably be such a balance.

Despite the public welfare reforms which established the 'welfare state' in Britain in the 1940s and pro-market reforms of the New Right in the 1980s, welfare services in this country have in practice remained a mixture of state, market, voluntary and informal provision. Furthermore, the balance of this mixture has changed over time, with private market and other non-state forms of welfare growing in importance in the 1980s and 1990s. The general point is, however, that there has always been a balance between the providers of services. Some commentators have referred to this as a *mixed economy* of welfare, and argued that this welfare mix is actually a more accurate term to describe the overall nature of provision in Britain, and elsewhere, than the welfare state.

The welfare mix has also now received formal political recognition in the Third Way pragmatism of the Labour government's policy planning. The government's concern to base policies upon an assessment of what works in practice has led to recent support for new forms of market provision (for private pensions), voluntary activity (delivery of community care by non-profit organisations) and informal welfare (continuing reliance upon family support for vulnerable citizens). Blair himself has championed the objective of 'a strong civil society enshrining rights and responsibilities... where government is a partner to strong communities' (1998, p.7); and the government has openly preached the values of public/private partnerships in the development of welfare services, and has entered into a 'compact' with the voluntary sector.

Most commentators would probably now agree with the government that welfare services in Britain, as in all other welfare capitalist societies, are best described as a welfare mix, with different elements delivered in different measure by different means. The role of social policy analysis, therefore is to study the development and operation of these measures and these means and to use theoretical argument and empirical research to seek to influence them. This requires:

- knowledge of the structure and development of the major welfare services
- knowledge of the role and structure of the different sectors providing these
- analysis of the ideological, economic and international context within which they are situated
- understanding of important issues affecting use of services such as social divisions and inequalities, the costs of providing services and the means of ensuring access to them.

It is these different dimensions of analysis that will be taken up in the next four sections of this book.

QUESTIONS: COMPREHENSION

- Why have comparative scholars argued that it is no longer possible to study social policy within a national context?
- What is a 'mixed economy of welfare'?

QUESTION: REFLECTION

- To what extent have recent critical perspectives undermined the desirability and feasibility of the 'welfare state'?

FURTHER READING

There is no book dealing directly with the development of the study of social policy. However, Bulmer, Lewis and Piachand (1989) provide an interesting history of the development of the work of the academic department at the LSE; and Alcock *et al.* (2001) collect together (with commentaries) the key works of its leading scholar Titmuss. Powell and Hewitt (2002) is a good overview of changing conceptions of the welfare state. There are a number of books which aim to provide a history of the development of social policy provision in the UK. Fraser (2003) goes back to the early roots of policy before the nineteenth century, whereas Glennerster (2000) focuses in more detail upon developments since 1945. Timmins's (2001) discussion of post-war welfare policy in the UK is a fascinating study of some of the politics behind the policy process. A useful website providing introductory material on the subject is maintained by Paul Spicker at **www2.rgu.ac.uk/publicpolicy/introduction/index**.

Part I

Welfare Services

Social Security

2

SUMMARY OF KEY POINTS

- Social security involves the redistribution of resources within society. This takes place through market, voluntary and informal transfers as well as through the provision of state benefits.
- Public expenditure on social security has been gradually rising despite the attempts by recent governments to contain it.
- Social security is administered by independent agencies under the overall control of the Department for Work and Pensions (DWP).
- Redistribution through benefits may be *horizontal* or *vertical*, and the difference between these also leads to different principles for benefit provision based on *insurance* or *assistance*.
- The development of social security policy has seen shifts between insurance and assistance benefits, with means-testing becoming more prevalent since the last quarter of the twentieth century.
- Entitlement to benefits varies for different groups of claimants including pensioners, the unemployed, the long-term sick and disabled and those on low wages.
- Non-take-up of benefits is a significant problem, especially for means-tested benefits.
- Means-testing of benefits also leads to the unemployment and poverty traps.
- The new Labour government instituted wide-ranging reviews of social security and has made some limited moves to increase benefits, especially for families with children.

What is social security?

Social security is the term normally used to refer to the range of policies aimed at transferring cash resources between individuals and families in the UK. In practice, however, these transfers cover a wide range of public and private redistribution and social security is not necessarily always used to cover all of them. It is worth reflecting first briefly on the term itself, however, for the words used convey something of the means and ends which govern policy in the area.

1. *Social* implies that what is going on here is collective, or at least collaborative; it is an activity which is intended to involve and impact upon individuals in their relations with others.
2. *Security* implies that what is being provided is intended to secure people's position within those social relations, and indeed to secure social structures for all more generally.

These are powerful and positive connotations and to some extent they have provided the underpinning for ideological support for social security policy over the last century or so. However, in more recent times these connotations have sometimes taken on a more contradictory tone: for example, with social security criticised as a heavy cost upon the public purse, and the position of 'being on the social' being seen as having devalued social status.

It is perhaps obvious, and inevitable, that social security should have negative as well as positive connotations, for in practice some may see it as a benefit and some as a cost. But the negative images conjured up by some critics of social security – most starkly perhaps in some elements of the popular press – can make the development and implementation of policy in this area more difficult: for instance, opinion poll evidence which has consistently over recent years demonstrated strong support for public spending on health and education does not elicit such support for increased social security transfers (Taylor-Gooby, 1999).

In the USA a number of public income transfers are referred to as *welfare*; and there it is generally the case that welfare policies and welfare receipt are viewed in negative terms, with recent attempts being made by government there to cut dependency upon welfare. These negative connotations have in the last two decades been imported into Britain too, with social security policy now frequently referred to as 'welfare policy', and often with a more disparaging tone. In fact there is a distinction in the USA between welfare policy, which technically refers to certain benefits targeted on poor families, and social security, which is a form of income insurance to which the majority of employees contribute. In Britain, and in the rest of Europe, there is a similar distinction between targeted *social assistance* support and contributory *social insurance* provision, and we will return to discuss this in more detail shortly. There has also generally been more public support for insurance-based protection, although both are still referred to as social security (and sometimes now welfare).

Whatever form it takes, however, social security is concerned with policies governing cash transfers, or the *redistribution* of resources within society. Such transfers take place across all dimensions of social activity. In Part II we distinguish between the state, market, voluntary and informal sectors of welfare. In all four sectors redistribution is taking place.

1. Informally money is passed across generations and within communities.
2. Voluntary organizations operate to redistribute cash and goods, from Oxfam's international aid to the soup kitchen for local rough sleepers.
3. Private companies provide for investment and protection for pensions, sickness, mortgage costs and other contingencies.
4. Government provides cash benefits and other forms of support both nationally and locally.

There is also a significant amount of financial support and protection provided by employers for their employees, including company-based pension schemes and sick pay. These could be regarded as part of private market protection, although the government and other public employers are some of the major providers of these; and they are generally referred to as *occupational* provision.

The redistribution occurring within the different sectors of the policy landscape is an important element in the provision of 'social security' for all members of society, for all of us at various points in our lives depend upon support from a number of these different sources. However, in social policy debate social security is usually taken to mean state, or public, provision for protection through redistribution. It is mainly state provision, developed by government, that we will discuss in the rest of this chapter. Nevertheless it is important to note that social policy planning increasingly focuses upon the interrelationship between the protection provided within different sectors: for instance, future planning for pension provision is based upon an explicit partnership between state benefits and private and occupational pension protection, with most future pensioners being expected to invest in private pensions which they will receive alongside support from the state on retirement.

Organisation and administration

Public provision of social security is now the major part of social expenditure organised through the state to provide for the needs of citizens. Of course, in one sense social security provision is not public *expenditure*, as money is not spent by government officers but is merely *transferred* between citizens. As we shall discuss shortly the nature and direction of these transfers is extremely complex and overlapping, with almost all people receiving benefits at some points in their lives and many people currently receiving benefits at the same time as paying contributions through National Insurance and taxation. And when the impact of taxation transfers as well as social security payments is taken into account, which as we shall see is generally not the case in British social policy planning, this picture becomes even more convoluted. Nevertheless the provision of social security benefits is recorded as public expenditure and, as such, it is now by far the largest element of public expenditure at around 33 per cent of the total, greater than health and education together, and accounting for around 11 per cent of gross domestic product (GDP: see Figure 17.1). What is

Table 2.1 Benefit expenditure in real terms
(1999/2000 prices, £billion)

	1990/1	1993/4	1996/7	1999/00	2003/04
Total	74.3	96.3	100	99.1	103.9
Insurance benefits	40.1	46.2	45.7	46.7	50.5
Means-tested benefits	21.8	33.2	34.8	30.4	29.7

Source: Adapted from DSS (2000a), Annex B.

more, social security expenditure has been growing in real terms for the last two decades or so, as Table 2.1 charting growth since 1990/91 reveals.

Expenditure figures such as these need to be treated with some caution for what is counted in a total benefit expenditure can include (or not) a number of different elements. For instance, some totals exclude support for housing benefit paid through local, not central, government; and since 1997 the replacement of some means-tested benefits with tax credits paid through the Inland Revenue has removed the cost of support in this area from the social security budget. Furthermore, increases in expenditure are the product of a wide range of different factors. In recent times these include the growing numbers of pensioners, the rise (and then fall) in unemployment levels and the growing numbers of lone parent families. They are not, by and large, however, a product of higher levels of benefit payment for, as we shall discuss later, levels of benefit payment have largely been held constant or even declined.

In part the pressure to contain the levels of benefit is a product of concern over the overall growth in social security expenditure which results from these other factors. In the 1980s the Thatcher governments sought, largely unsuccessfully, to contain most areas of public expenditure, including in particular social security; and in 1993 the (then) Department of Social Security published a paper (DSS, 1993) focusing on past and projected future growth in social security expenditure which formed the basis for further strategies to curb these expansive tendencies, including measures to restrict entitlement to some benefits, notably those for unemployment and invalidity/incapacity. Despite this, total expenditure passed the £100 billion mark in the late 1990s, and the Labour government elected in 1997 continued to seek to contain the social security budget through shifting some expenditure to tax credits, through encouraging unemployed claimants back into work and through further changes to benefits for lone parents and long-term incapacity. The pattern of expenditure thus seems to be fairly well set with a so far inexorable growth in the scale of expenditure due largely to increased demand for support, and with governments seeking to restrict this expansion through measures to reduce demand where possible or to restructure provision to shift costs from the social security budget.

Formal responsibility for the management of both budgets and benefit delivery lies with the Department for Work and Pensions (DWP). This replaced the previous Department of Social Security (DSS) and the employment parts of the Department for Education and Employment (DfEE) in 2001, although there is a long history of departmental changes of name and responsibility predating this most recent restructuring (see McKay and Rowlingson, 1999, ch.3). However, the Department no longer has direct control over the delivery of benefits to claimants, as a result of the organisational changes which followed the 'Next Steps' initiative in the late 1980s and early 1990s. The aim of these changes was to place the administration of some public services in the hands of quasi-autonomous non-governmental organisations (quangos). In the case of social security this meant primarily the Benefits Agency, initially the largest of these bodies, which took over the delivery of most social security benefits through local offices in each town or urban district; although there were others, notably the Child Support Agency (administering maintenance payments from absent parents) and Information Technology Services Agency (providing technical support). There was also the Contributions Agency, which merged with the Inland Revenue in 1999, and the War Pensions Agency, which joined the Ministry of Defence in 2001. The Benefits Agency was itself replaced in 2002 by Jobcentre Plus, providing benefit and employment services to claimants of working age, and the Pensions Service, administering benefits for pensioners.

To most claimants these quasi-independent agencies may feel no different from government offices, and they are staffed by government officers working to the same procedures and regulations as previously operated within the Department. However, there have been significant moves over the last decade or so to improve customer relations within benefit delivery. From a time when claimants waited for hours in seats bolted to the floor and then shouted through plastic screens to nameless officers who did not have access to their individual files, administration of most benefits has moved to embrace a model of personal contact, backed up by computer-based information storage in national and regional centres. Under an initiative called ONE the agencies have sought to provide one source of contact for each claimant with the aim of simplifying the process of claiming all benefits through one base. For claimants of working age this is now referred to as the 'single gateway' and it aims to incorporate advice and assistance on training and job search as well, together with the opportunities available under the New Deal (see Chapter 7).

However, such simplicity is contradicted by the fact that the responsibility for administering some benefits, notably housing benefit and council tax benefit, lies with local, rather than central, government. Here administrative procedures are quite different, and sometimes much slower. Local authorities are also responsible for the provision of a range of other forms of cash transfers (such as free school meals) and subsidised access to local services (such as public transport and leisure facilities). These benefits and services are in practice aimed at those claimants also in receipt of some of the major national social security benefits, and so the experience of many claimants remains one of confusion and disjuncture in the pursuit of their rights to public support.

For the most part now, however, claimants do have a right to the benefits which they are claiming through the public agencies. There has long been a debate about the extent to which social security support should be provided as of *right*, subject to clear written rules and regulations, as opposed to under *discretion*, where social security officers are required to make an individual judgement about the financial needs of each claimant. The earliest form of social security provision in the UK, the Poor Law, was based upon discretionary payments related to individual assessment of need, and this continued to play a central role in the delivery of many means-tested benefits until the last two decades of the twentieth century. Discretionary payments create administrative and budgetary problems, however (how should different needs be assessed and how can spending be anticipated and controlled?), and they have now largely been removed from mainstream social security provision. The one exception to this is access to lump sum payments for exceptionally costly items of need under the Social Fund, although here most payments are provided as loans only (repaid by deductions from future benefit payments) and the total amount of payments is constrained by cash limits set for each local benefits office.

The existence of rights to social security benefits means that potential claimants can be given clear advice about their entitlement. This is primarily done through publicity leaflets prepared by the DWP. However, as we shall see, the rules governing entitlement to the wide range of benefits available are very complex, with detailed regulations running into hundreds of pages, which officers themselves require specialist training to understand. Most claimants are likely to have only a vague idea of their legal rights, and ignorance and confusion over rights is one of the major reasons for the failure of some to claim all the benefits to which they may be entitled, to which we shall return briefly below. Advice can be sought from social security officers, of course, including now via telephone information lines. However, help may also be available from specialist *welfare rights* workers.

Welfare rights workers are employed by local authorities or by advice agencies in the voluntary sector to provide an independent advice and assistance service for benefit claimants, and many advice agencies also include volunteer advisers. Most welfare rights workers are not lawyers, and there are few lawyers who specialise in social security law as it is not a lucrative area of legal practice; but specialist welfare rights workers have become an important source of independent support for social security claimants and have developed a range of strategies to support and encourage the claiming of benefits (see Alcock, 1997, ch.15).

The rights base of current benefit provision does provide an important legal foundation for the delivery of social security policy (see Dean, 1996). It means that if claimants are unhappy with the decisions taken about their benefit entitlement by social security officers then they can challenge these through a legal appeal. Claimants have a right to an appeal against most benefit decisions to a Social Security Appeal Tribunal, although many cases may be resolved before reaching the stage of a formal hearing; and then, subject to the ordinary rules about appeals, there can be further recourse to the courts in the UK and European Union. Pursuing an appeal certainly requires some understanding of legal rules and procedures, and here welfare rights workers may also offer assistance, and even advocacy, to claimants who wish to challenge benefit decisions. Not surprisingly, perhaps, relatively few social security cases make it into the court process; but on occasions important issues have been subject to appeals in the courts and judicial decisions have altered the interpretation of regulations to the benefit of claimants, underlining the symbolic importance of the role of rights in the delivery of policy.

QUESTIONS: COMPREHENSION

■ How has the balance of social security expenditure changed over the last 50 years and what have been the main implications of this for claimants?
■ What are the advantages and disadvantages of the idea of *rights* to benefits?

QUESTION: REFLECTION

■ Should we be concerned about the gradual rise in social security expenditure?

Principles

At the heart of social security policy are the principles which underlie the payment of benefits, and more generally the transfer or redistribution of resources which these aim to achieve. In broad terms we can distinguish between two fundamental principles which might inform cash transfers within society.

1. *Horizontal redistribution.* This is the transfer of resources across the life cycle of members of society. It is based on the assumption that at different points in our lives we may be more likely to need income support. This is particularly the case in childhood (and for the parents of children) and in retirement, as during working age most people are likely to be in paid employment and therefore able to make contributions and/or pay taxes. Thus horizontal redistribution provides support at these times of need (child benefit and pensions) paid for by contributions made at times of (relative) plenty, and it is a form of support from which we all may expect to benefit and towards which we all may be responsible for contributing.
2. *Vertical redistribution.* This is the transfer of resources from rich to poor within society. Within an unequal distribution of income and wealth there may be those at the bottom who do not have enough resources to support themselves and their dependents adequately, and those at the top who have more than they need. Resources can (and arguably should) therefore be transferred from those who have more than enough to those who have too little. Unlike horizontal redistribution, however, there is a difference between those who pay, and may never benefit, and those who benefit, and may never pay.

There are important ideological, political and economic differences between these two approaches to social security policy, and they result in very different ways of financing and delivering benefit support. However, in practice both

Table 2.2   Distribution of income through taxes and benefits, 2000/01

	Bottom quintile	Next quintile	Middle quintile	Next quintile	Top quintile	All
Original income*	3,090	8,820	18,570	29,950	55,740	23,320
Income* with benefits	8,420	14,290	22,080	32,000	56,850	26,730
Income* after direct taxes	7,440	12,200	17,960	25,060	43,550	21,240
Income* after indirect taxes	4,970	9,100	13,730	19,770	36,690	16,850

* Average household income.
Source: Adapted from Social Trends 33, Table 5.17 (Summerfield and Babb, 2003).

have informed the development of social security in Britain and both remain at the centre of provision today. As research carried out at the London School of Economics (LSE) has revealed, social security does redistribute from rich to poor with the value of cash benefits received being highest for the those at the bottom of the income distribution, and it also redistributes across the life cycle with all income groups benefiting from some element of redistribution over their lifetime (Hills, 1997). The effect of both forms of redistribution together means that all benefit from life-cycle transfers to a similar extent, but that those at the bottom of the income scale (the lifetime poor) benefit much more from publicly funded transfers through social security benefits whereas the better-off are more likely to pay for their own transfers through taxation and self-financing (Hills, Gardner et al., 1997, p.20). This is confirmed by Table 2.2 which reveals that, although all benefit from the redistribution effects of taxes and benefits, those in the lowest quintiles of the income scale benefit most.

The principles governing redistribution lead to different methods of financing social security payments, and determining entitlement to benefits. These too can be divided into two broad approaches, as outlined below.

1. *Social insurance.* This is linked to horizontal redistribution and the idea that those in work make contributions which are then redistributed to those at other stages in their life cycle. Workers therefore pay social security contributions, and these are collected together into a national insurance fund from which benefits are paid to those unable to work. Social insurance benefits typically cover such circumstances as retirement, sickness or disability, and unemployment (usually conceived of as a temporary period whilst seeking further work). Entitlement to benefits is linked to payment of contributions, with only those meeting specified contribution conditions able to apply. It has some similarities to private insurance therefore, although in most social insurance schemes contributions are used to meet current benefit needs rather than being invested to cover the demands which might be made by future claimants (sometimes referred to a 'pay-as-you-go' funding). Because

of this funding base, social insurance payments are sometimes referred to as contributory benefits.

2. *Social assistance.* This is linked to vertical redistribution and the idea that benefits should be targeted only on those who need support because they are poor. Here provision is paid for by taxes on those with adequate incomes (usually including some element of progression with those on the highest incomes paying the most) and benefits are paid to those who can demonstrate that they are in need. This involves the application of 'means-tests' in which the financial circumstances of potential claimants are investigated to make sure that they do not have sufficient other sources of support. Means-tests mean that these benefits are income-related, and they can be used to redistribute resources across a range of different income levels within society, but within social security provision is generally limited to those at the very bottom of the scale only. Assistance benefits are therefore also referred to as selective or targeted social security provision.

Social insurance and social assistance provide the ideological and organisational basis upon which most social security provision is founded throughout most of the developed world. In most countries, however, both insurance and assistance schemes can be found operating alongside each other. This has been the case in Britain since the early part of the twentieth century, and the very different principles informing the two forms are a source of much complexity and confusion, in particular for claimants, many of whom in practice rely on support from both insurance and assistance benefits.

There have also been changes in the balance of coverage of these different types of provision with insurance becoming more widespread in the middle part of the last century and assistance becoming more dominant towards the end of it, as we shall discuss briefly below. However, there is another form of benefits operating within Britain, known as *universal* benefits, which are paid to everyone falling within a designated social group. The main such benefit is child benefit, which is paid to all parents or guardians of young children, although there are some others paid to people with specific disability needs. Table 2.3 summarises these different principles and their implications for social security provision.

Table 2.3 The principles behind social security provision

	Who should pay?	**Who should benefit?**
Universal	All	All
Social insurance	Employers and employees	Contributors
Social assistance	Taxpayers	The poor

The development of social security

The history of the development of social security provision in Britain is a long and complicated one. We can only hope to provide a brief overview here therefore (for a more detailed summary, see Alcock, 1999). Most commentators trace current policy back to the Poor Law which dominated British social policy provision before the twentieth century. The Poor Law was basically a locally administered social assistance scheme providing support on a discretionary basis to those who could establish that they were effectively destitute. Poor Law provision aimed to control and discipline the poor, and the support it provided was deliberately designed to be below that enjoyed by the lowest-paid workers; this is referred to as the principle of 'less eligibility' (see Jones and Novak, 1999, ch.4). The effects of this, amongst other things, were to give dependence upon social security support an undesirable and stigmatised status within society and to reinforce a negative image of the role and scope of public support.

In the early part of the twentieth century the Poor Law was gradually replaced by social insurance-based protection for unemployment, sickness and pension support (see McKay and Rowlingson, 1999, ch.3). However, not all those in need of support were covered by these schemes and so assistance-based Poor Law provision remained, renamed Public Assistance in the 1930s (Deacon and Bradshaw, 1983). In 1942 a fundamental review of social security provision, commissioned by the wartime government, was produced by William Beveridge. The Beveridge Report (1942) is still the only comprehensive review of social security in Britain; it was influential throughout the developed world, and formed the basis of the post-war reforms of the system which remain the fundamental structural features of provision to the present day.

In essence Beveridge proposed that social security should be organised and delivered on a social insurance model, called in Britain National Insurance (NI). However, he recognised that the contributory model might leave some in need who did not fulfil the NI criteria and so he recommended that assistance provision be continued as a 'safety net' for those outside the NI scheme. Renamed National Assistance, the intention was that this means-tested support would play a minor and declining role within the social security system, but this has proved to be far from the case. In the 1950s some 1 million claimants remained dependent upon National Assistance. This rose to 2 million in the 1960s, 4 million in the 1970s, 8 million in the 1980s; and in the 1990s the numbers dependent upon income support, as assistance support had now become called, reached 10 million. And, as Table 2.1 reveals, means-tested benefits now constitute nearly one-third of social security expenditure.

One of the reasons for the expanding role of social assistance provision in the latter part of the twentieth century was the limited protection in practice provided by the NI scheme. However, means-tested provision was itself expanded both in scale and scope. In the 1960s National Assistance became supplementary benefits, and in the 1970s new means-tested benefits to provide assistance with housing rents and support for low-income families in work were introduced. In the 1980s the Thatcher governments embraced the principle of means-testing, or targeting as they called it, as a more effective form of social security protection focusing state support only upon those in proven need. And in 1988 extensive reforms to means-tested benefits were introduced following a review of provision led by the Secretary of State, Norman Fowler. This led to the retitling of these benefits as income support, housing benefit and family credit, and to an integrated model for the administration of them under a single means-testing framework.

At the beginning of the twenty-first century the Labour government has continued many of the trends that had emerged at the end of the previous century, albeit within the rhetoric of the need to 'renegotiate' the contract between the individual and the state which underpins social security provision (DSS, 1998a). The extended role for means-testing has thus been retained, and is now justified as ensuring that resources go to those most in need. Support for low-income families in work has been converted from a social security benefit into a tax credit, but has been extended to a wider range of low incomes and extended to cover child care costs, and to provide support for those without children. At the same time NI provision for state pensions remains a key feature of support for all in old age, and insurance benefits for short-term unemployment and long-term sickness and incapacity have been retained.

Entitlement to benefits

Current social security provision in Britain is a product of this history and the shifting balance of the different principles which underlie benefit entitlement. This is a complex and contradictory history, and as a result benefit provision itself does not follow a logical framework but rather reflects these different historical trends. Determining individual entitlement and calculating potential weekly benefit payments is therefore a specialist task for social security officers and welfare rights workers, and the best sources of accurate advice on this are the various handbooks produced each year by the Child Policy Action Group (CPAG). The benefit rates also themselves change on annual basis in order to maintain their value against inflation, with the new rates coming into effect at the beginning of the tax year in April.

National Insurance remains the major feature of social security in expenditure terms (see Table 2.1). This is primarily because it includes the basic state pension which is paid to all those over pension age who have a record of contributions to the NI scheme. One of the reasons this expenditure remains high is because the number of older people is growing both absolutely and in relation to the rest of the population. This is a phenomenon common to most developed countries, and indeed is less pronounced in the UK than in some others; it has led many governments to seek to control potential future public expenditure on pensions (Bonoli, 2000). The cost of state pensions is also rising, however, because increasing numbers of pensioners are entitled to an earnings-related supplement to their pension based on contributions made since 1978, when this was introduced. In the 1980s the government sought to contain this growth in pension expenditure by linking the annual rise in the basic pension to inflation in prices only rather than earnings (previously increases had followed the higher of these). At a time of wage inflation this had the effect of reducing the relative value of the basic pension, and although since then the Labour government has on occasion increased pensions beyond price inflation, there is no commitment to return to a regular link with wages as this would result in a significant rise in pension levels and thus expenditure commitments.

The Conservative governments also tried to reduce pension costs by encouraging the growth of private and occupational pensions, which would mean that those with such protection could opt out of the state earnings-related scheme. This is a policy which is to some extent shared by Labour who are now developing a partnership between public and private pension protection with state earnings-related support being restricted to those on low incomes whilst in work, and the majority of working people being expected to take out private or occupational protection, under *stakeholder* schemes tightly regulated by government (DSS, 1998b). For those pensioners who do not have private or occupational protection and are not covered adequately by the basic NI pension there is now the Minimum Income Guarantee, which in effect is the promise that all those over pension age should be entitled to an income equivalent to means-tested income support levels. Such provision is means-tested and is not paid in full to those with other sources of income or capital support, although the pension credit to be introduced in October 2003 will ensure that those with additional income living near the Minimum Income Guarantee level can retain some benefit from this.

Pensions account for the vast bulk of NI expenditure, but contributory benefits still remain for unemployment and sickness. Unemployment is now covered by the Jobseekers' Allowance (JSA), which provides six months' non-means-tested support for those who meet the NI contribution conditions and, as the name suggests, is linked to agreements by claimants to take steps to secure a return to the labour market (see Chapter 7). Sickness cover was once a major feature of social security protection; but in the 1980s support for short-term sickness, up to six months, was transferred to employment, with all employers required to provide at least a minimum level of payment for workers off work sick. Beyond six months, however, claimants with chronic sickness or disability move on to NI protection through incapacity benefit, providing that they meet the contribution conditions and a medical test that requires that they are incapable of 'all work'. The numbers claiming incapacity benefit were rising at the end of the last century, from around 400,000 in 1981 to 800,000 in 1991 and 1,200,000 by 1996, at which point they began to level off (Alcock *et al.*, 2003, p.112). In part this is because many long-term unemployed claimants do also have health problems; and so it is perhaps debatable whether these people should more accurately be regarded as incapacitated or unemployed, although their claiming of a sickness benefit means that they do not appear on the official register of unemployment.

The Jobseekers' Allowance for the unemployed is no longer only an insurance benefit, however. After six months, claimants remain on the benefit and subject to the same job search requirements, but their benefit moves on to a means-tested basis, so that then any other resources (including the income of a spouse or cohabitee) will have the effect of reducing overall entitlement. In practice this means-tested JSA is merely a retitling of income support, which has for some time been payable to unemployed claimants not covered by NI benefit. And for those out of work and not required to seek work under the JSA rules, such as lone parents or people with certain disabilities, income support is still available.

Income support is in effect a minimum income scheme for British citizens. It is only payable to those out of full-time employment (defined as 16 hours a week) and is reduced if there are any earnings over £5 or £15 a week (depending on circumstances) or any capital over £3,000 in total. It does not cover housing costs although, subject to some restrictions, interest payments on mortgage debts are covered. Claimants paying rent, however, can claim housing benefit, administered by local authorities, together with council tax benefit as this too is outside the nationally administered scheme. Income support (and means-tested JSA) claimants are also entitled to free school meals for their children and to a range of other local authority and health benefits (such as free prescriptions), although whether all claimants realise the full extent of their entitlements is questionable, as we shall shortly discuss. Further, these claimants may be able to receive discretionary loans from the Social Fund to purchase expensive items which they cannot afford from their weekly benefit. However, there is no right to these and they are subject to strict cash limits. They have to be repaid by deductions from future benefit payments, pushing claimants then below even these minimum income levels.

For those in low-wage employment means-tested support is also available, including housing benefit for rent payments. However, support for those on lower pay now generally takes the form of *tax credits* payable through employers and set against tax liability by the Inland Revenue, which administers this aspect of social security support. This has been a significant shift in the operation of means-testing under the Labour government since 1997. Initially the previous provision of family credit was replaced by working families tax credit, which was made available to a much wider range of low-income families. This acted as a supplement to the wages of workers with dependent children, and was intended to make low-paid work more attractive in order to encourage labour market participation as part of the government's more general commitment to promote employment, as discussed in Chapter 7. Similar credits were made available to cover some of the costs of child care for parents and to support low-paid disabled workers. In 2003 these were amalgamated and extended into a generic working tax credit for all low-paid workers, together with a new child tax credit, which includes the child elements of the working families tax credit, a contribution to child care costs and more general means-tested support for children. From October 2003 there will also be the pension credit mentioned above.

Also, as mentioned earlier, there are some universal benefits available in Britain. The most important of these is child benefit, which provides a contribution towards the costs of rearing children paid to all parents or guardians. Critics have argued that, as with all universal services, child benefit is 'wasting' public resources in paying benefits to wealthy parents as well as poor ones, and on occasions governments have considered clawing back child benefit by taxing it for higher-paid earners. However, the great value of the universal benefit is that all do claim it and that no stigma is associated with its receipt, and of course some contribution towards the costs of rearing future generations could be regarded as a valuable public investment for all citizens.

Certain benefits to meet the needs of some disabled people are also universal, in the sense that they are not subject to contribution conditions or means-tests. These include primarily the Disability Living Allowance paid to cover costs associated with attendance needs (help with feeding, dressing and so on) and mobility needs (help to get around). Payments under this scheme are generally set at very low levels, however, and are only paid after a medical assessment of need. Thus in practice only small numbers of people do claim these benefits.

QUESTIONS: COMPREHENSION

■ What are the relative advantages and disadvantages of social insurance and social assistance as the basis for entitlement to social security support?
■ In what ways has the Labour government expanded the role of means-testing within social security?

QUESTION: REFLECTION

■ What are the arguments for and against means-testing or taxing of universal child benefit?

Problems with benefits

It is perhaps no surprise to discover that the operation of social security does experience some problems in meeting its aims of horizontal and vertical redistribution; although, of course, quite what constitutes a problem rather depends upon one's point of view. There are some critics who argue that the whole system itself operates to control and discipline citizens rather than to support and protect them (see Jones and Novak, 1999). Few in social policy would take such an oppositional stance, but most commentators do recognise that the system, perhaps inevitably, has negative and as well as positive features. And many would agree that some of the problems which claimants or administrators experience do pose significant challenges to any claims for social security to be an effective form of security for all.

The first, and perhaps most worrying, problem is that of non-take-up. Because social security benefits are so varied and entitlement regulations so complicated many potential claimants do not understand or realise their full entitlement: that is, they do not take up their right to benefit. This has been a longstanding problem within social security, and it is not unique to Britain (see Van Oorschot, 1995). It also varies between different types of benefit with high take-up levels for universal and contributory benefits, such as child benefit and pensions, and lower levels for means-tested benefits, such as income support and housing benefit. Of course, estimating levels of take-up is a rather inexact science; we can only guess at what those who do not claim might be entitled to. However, the DWP does make regular attempts to estimate the levels of take-up for the major means-tested benefits, calculating these by caseload (numbers claiming) and expenditure (amount of money claimed); and for income support these generally hover around 80–90 per cent and 90–95 per cent respectively, although they are below this for income-related JSA (DSS, 2000b). These may look like high figures, but they mean that one-fifth or more of the poorest claimants are not getting the benefits to which they are legally entitled; and for other means-tested benefits, especially smaller payments such as school meals, the proportions of non-claimants are much higher.

The reverse of the problem of non-take-up is that of fraudulent claiming: that is, people claiming money to which they are not entitled. Such fraud, where proven, is a criminal offence and can lead to prosecution and even imprisonment. However, very few criminal cases are actually brought. Much more significant is the more general concern with relatively minor cases of unreported overpayment or concealment of circumstances by claimants. In recent years the government has been concerned that levels of minor benefit fraud have been increasing and adding significantly to the overall social security bill. As with non-take-up, of course, these figures are only estimates, and although the government sometimes claims that billions of pounds are lost through fraud, the various attempts that have been made to 'crack down' on fraudsters and tighten up delivery have not generally resulted in significant savings in benefit costs (Sainsbury, 1998).

Both non-take-up and fraud are particularly associated with means-tested benefits. So, too, is the other major problem in social security practice, that of perverse incentives. Because means-tested income support is paid for family needs, including housing costs, the amount of benefit to which a family may be entitled could be greater than the wage that the potential breadwinner might be able to earn, especially in times of economic decline. This is called the 'unemployment trap', because it may have the effect of removing the positive incentives to take work and trapping claimants on unemployment benefits. For most families in Britain this is now unlikely to be the case because the tax credits paid to those on low wages should ensure that overall income in work is above income support benefit levels.

However the supplementing of low wages by means-tested tax credits creates another problem: the 'poverty trap'. This is a result of the withdrawal of such means-tested support when wages rise, coupled with the increasing liability to tax and NI contributions on additional wages. The effect of these deductions is to impose a high 'marginal tax' on additional income; in other words, loss of means-tested support together with other liabilities can mean that as much as 80 or 90 per cent of any increased wages are lost by those who receive them. This can also create perverse incentives, so that it may be better (or little worse) to remain on low wages rather than seek to increase these (for instance, by undertaking more work or seeking promotion). It also has the effect of trapping those on low wages in poverty, and across a wide range of low incomes the effect of credits means that take-home pay is more or less the same whatever the initial income might be. What is happening here is a kind of flattening of wage differentials at the lower end of the income scale, and hence it is sometimes now referred to as the 'poverty plateau'; it is a significant by-product of current policies to support low-wage employment, as we shall discuss in Chapter 7.

It is significant that all of these problems with social security provision occur in the delivery of means-tested benefits. It is also no coincidence. Because means-tested benefits are targeted on the poor they must be subject to complex regulations aimed to ensure that only those who need support receive it. These rules are difficult for many of those in need to understand, and they are also easier to abuse (perhaps not always maliciously). They also require that support be withdrawn when circumstances improve, leading to the poverty trap. Many of these problems do not apply in the same way to contributory or universal benefits; and in a sense therefore the solution to them is an obvious one (although, of course, there are other implications which would flow from adopting alternative principles within social security protection).

The policy context

Social security policy in Britain at the beginning of the twenty-first century is in large part the product of past policy commitments developed over the previous century. Past policies constrain future developments. And in social security this is perhaps particularly the case, for those currently relying on benefits may have had no opportunity to make alternative provision for support. Introducing change into policy is therefore a complex, and inevitably a gradual, undertaking. However, this does not mean that change cannot be attempted; and in fact social security is one of the areas where policy change remains a significant and high-profile feature of government agendas.

Shortly after coming to power in 1997 the Labour government instituted a review of the key principles of social security policy, published in a wide-ranging Green Paper, *New Ambitions for our Country*, in 1998 (DSS, 1998a). This outlined a vision for policy development over the next 20 years based in particular upon a 'new contract' between the individual and the state for social protection. In practice much of this new contract relies upon individuals of working age seeking employment in the labour market in order to avoid, or escape, dependence upon social security support. This is referred to by government as a strategy to move people from 'welfare to work' and it is discussed in more detail in Chapter 7. It also requires a shift to a new partnership in pension protection between public and private provision, as discussed in a second Green Paper, *Partnership in Pensions* (DSS, 1998b).

Alongside these broader, and more long-term changes, the Labour government has also introduced a series of reforms to other benefits: for instance, reducing the scope of incapacity benefit and removing some of the benefits for lone parents. It has also restructured means-tested benefits to replace some with tax credits, and extended the scope of these. There is no doubt therefore that, like their predecessors, the Labour governments are committed to retaining a mix of insurance and assistance support, albeit a mix that is still moving towards greater means-testing. In broad terms this is line with developments in many other advanced industrial countries. In continental Europe and North America insurance benefits operate alongside assistance support, although the balance between the various elements is very different in different countries. International pressures, not least in Western Europe from the EU, do influence national social security policy; but in practice the current policy framework here is very largely a UK affair.

This is particularly the case for what is for many people, and claimants especially, one of the key elements of social security policy: the determination of the levels of benefit payment. How much is paid ultimately determines the budgets of individuals and governments; and yet there is actually relatively little policy debate about the levels of benefit payments themselves. There is no agreed policy base for the setting of benefit levels in Britain, although this is not the case in all other countries (see Veit-Wilson, 1998); and, although for some benefits there is a requirement to uprate existing levels in line with price inflation, this does not apply to all, and does not prevent improvements beyond this. There is much research evidence arguing that current benefit levels, most importantly within the basic minimum income support scheme, are insufficient to meet the needs of the individuals and families who depend on them and lift them out of poverty (see, for instance, Gordon *et al.*, 2000). However, this raises controversial questions about what families need and what constitutes poverty, which are subject to unresolved political and academic debate (Alcock, 1997).

The setting of benefit levels is thus a political issue rather than a matter of specific social security policy; and this has continued to be the case under the current Labour governments. Since 1997 Labour has increased the value of the basic state pension and also made increases to some elements of child support in child benefit and income support. In both cases these changes followed political commitments to improve the circumstances of these claimants; and, albeit marginally, this is what has been achieved. However, there has been pressure on government from some quarters to do more, particularly in order to extend vertical redistribution to help the poor.

Despite the above changes, the government has not been keen to make high-profile policy commitments on redistribution. It has, however, made significant promises to tackle poverty. The government has set itself (and future governments) a target of halving child poverty by 2010 and eradicating it by 2020, although there is some dispute as to the progress that has been made towards this (see Kenway and Palmer, 2002). And it has instituted the publication of an annual report on the broader progress in combating poverty and social exclusion, initially under the title of *Opportunity for All* (DSS, 1999). These are important policy commitments, and they are backed by a wide range of further initiatives to tackle the broader problem of social exclusion in modern British society, including the establishment of a *Social Exclusion Unit*, reporting direct to the Cabinet Office. They also make it clear that the goal of combating poverty and exclusion requires policy-makers to go beyond the cash transfers which are made within the social security system; this acts as a reminder that social security is about more than just poverty relief, and that the relief of poverty will require more than social security reform.

QUESTIONS: COMPREHENSION

■ Why is non-take-up of means-tested benefits so prevalent?
■ What are the 'unemployment trap' and the 'poverty trap', and why is it argued that these create perverse incentives for low-paid workers?

QUESTION: REFLECTION

■ How should we decide on the level at which to set social security benefits, and what role should this play in the prevention or reduction of poverty?

FURTHER READING

The most comprehensive current text on social security in the UK is McKay and Rowlingson (1999), although Ditch (1999) also provides a useful collection of papers on key issues and a new collection edited by Millar (2003) will be available soon. Alcock (1997) is the main academic text on poverty and anti-poverty policy; but for up-to-date figures on poverty levels it is best to look to the most recent CPAG pamphlet, *Poverty: The Facts* (Howard et al., 2001). The website of the DWP carries most government documents and reports: see **www.dwp.gov.uk**. A useful website for new data on poverty is **www.poverty.org.uk**.

Education

3

SUMMARY OF KEY POINTS

- There are two contrasting views of education: *liberal education* and *training*.
- Education is a major contributor to the development of *human capital* and is now regarded as a continuing need for all citizens.
- There are different levels of education provision: nursery, primary, secondary, further, higher and adult.
- Public education in England is administered by the Department for Education and Skills (DfES) with separate administration in Scotland, Wales and Northern Ireland.
- Private schools still provide for a small minority of children from wealthy backgrounds.
- Universal state education up to 15 was introduced in the Butler Act in 1944.
- After the 1960s the *tripartite* system of secondary education was replaced by *comprehensive* schools.
- In 1988 a national school curriculum was introduced and more power devolved to schools to manage their affairs.
- Further and higher education both expanded significantly in the last quarter of the twentieth century, and there is a future target of 50 per cent of young people in higher education.
- Concerns over equality of opportunity in education have led governments to target extra resources on to certain schools or categories of pupils.
- Quality assurance is now provided within education by public inspection agencies such as OFSTED (the Office for Standards in Education).

What is education?

Education is about learning and teaching; and education policy is concerned with the ways in which learning and teaching are organised and delivered in order to ensure that all citizens have the appropriate opportunities to learn. However, at the heart of education policy debate is a distinction, and perhaps a conflict, over what should be the primary aims or functions of individual learning. This is the distinction between education as the acquisition of knowledge (liberal education) and education as the acquisition of skills (training).

Liberal education, sometimes presented as the 'traditional' basis for education policy, is the notion that education should be provided to equip citizens – and especially children – with knowledge for its own sake (we should all have the opportunity to know something about the world in which we live), and in order to develop cognitive capacity (learning, and testing, helps us to develop our minds). In such a model knowledge is based upon a traditional curriculum (history, geography and science), and achievement is measured by the levels of understanding reached, with the undergraduate degree being the ultimate goal (at least for some). In the most extreme form of this approach the content of education is of little importance compared to the level of qualification reached: for instance, the study of Latin and Ancient Greek at private school and Oxford and Cambridge universities was once widely considered evidence of high academic achievement, despite the fact that virtually no one speaks or writes in these languages and knowledge of them is therefore useless for practical purposes.

Education as training stresses in contrast the content of education and the practical utility of the knowledge acquired. In this approach education should be geared to providing citizens with skills and competences that will be of value to them later in life, and will be of value to society more generally by ensuring that the workforce is equipped to perform the tasks needed to sustain and enhance economic and social development. In such a model the content of the curriculum is as important as the level of ability reached, and greater emphasis is placed upon vocational knowledge, such as technological, financial and organisation skills. Vocational training may be of value to adults as well as children and may be linked to labour market experience. In part because of this link with employment, training has traditionally had a lower profile, and priority, within public education policy (although, as we shall see, there have been moves to raise the profile of vocationalism in recent times).

In fact the distinction between liberal education and training is far from clear cut, and to a large extent the different approaches are compatible and can be pursued in tandem: for instance, one could study Latin alongside computer science. What is more, supporters of both models are agreed about the importance of some core elements of educational knowledge and skills, in particular the role of the 'three Rs' (Reading, wRiting and aRithmetic – not in fact all Rs at all), in underpinning all learning and teaching. Nevertheless within educational debate there have been changes in the balance of emphasis upon educational knowledge and practical skills, and this has had consequences for the development of education policy.

Of most recent significance here were the policy debates and changes which were fostered in the UK in the 1970s. At the beginning of the decade a series of documents were published by right-wing critics of education policy, collectively known as the *Black Papers* (Finch, 1984, pp.43–4), which argued that basic literacy and numeracy skills (the three Rs) were being neglected in educational provision and that policies should change in order to address this problem. The issue was taken up a few years later by the Prime Minister, James Callaghan, who initiated what he called a *Great Debate* about the future direction of education policy, in which he claimed that there were: 'complaints from industry that new recruits from schools sometimes do not have the basic tools do to the job that is required ... [and that] there is no virtue in producing socially well-adjusted members of society who are unemployed because they do not have the skills' (Callaghan, 1976, quoted in Finch, 1984, p.222). Following this a Green Paper (1977) was issued outlining the case for more attention to be paid in school education to developing an understanding of industry and the economy, and providing pupils with practical skills.

The Thatcher governments of the 1980s shared many of these concerns with the practical and technical focus of education. They sought to promote this through specific initiatives to extend the provision of technical skills such as the establishment of City Technology Colleges directly supported by industry and through funding the Technical and Vocational Education Initiative (TVEI) to supplement the traditional curriculum in schools. In practice, however, these debates and initiatives did not lead to any fundamental changes within education policy (for instance, few technology colleges were actually established); and the regulation of the school curriculum introduced in 1988 (see below) confirmed the continuing centrality of many traditional subjects and approaches.

Nevertheless the concern to raise the profile of training and skills within education did have an enduring effect and has shifted education policy towards the enhancement of skills as well as knowledge. This is captured in the focus upon education as investment in *human capital* (the idea that high standards of education, which raise both knowledge and skills, are of benefit to individuals and to the society in which they live and that public investment in such 'capital' is therefore an essential priority for government). In a speech to the Labour Party conference in 1996 Tony Blair claimed that the three social policy priorities for the future Labour government would be 'education, education, education', because investment in improved educational standards was of such importance to broader economic and social development. Under Blair the government since 1997 has continued with the concern to raise basic standards, with the requirement for 'literacy hours' and 'numeracy hours' in all schools, and with continued emphasis upon regulation and inspection to ensure that goals were met, as we shall discuss later. At the beginning of the twenty-first century the government has also more openly embraced the commitment to support for education for adults as well as children, with a commitment to the promotion of what is now called *lifelong learning*. Education is now about both knowledge and skills, therefore, and ensuring high standards in both is in the interests of individual learners and their fellow citizens.

The structure of provision

Education is provided for a range of different learners at a range of different institutions within all societies, and within the UK these can be classified into six broad levels, each with rather different aims and organisational frameworks.

Nursery education

This is the provision of school-based learning for children before the commencement of formal compulsory education, which begins in the year in which a child is five, and for this reason it is sometimes referred to as pre-school education. Attendance at nursery schools is therefore voluntary and in the past places at nursery schools were few in number and sometimes hard to obtain. It is now policy to require local authorities to ensure that places are available for all three and four year olds who want to attend, and a significant investment has been made in expanding publicly funded nursery provision. However, many pre-school children also attend private or workplace nurseries or playschools, or are cared for at home; and so public nursery provision is far from comprehensive.

Primary education

From the age of five and up to 16, school education is compulsory in the UK (it starts later in some other countries), although occasionally parents can make arrangements for their children to be educated at home. For the first seven years, up to the age of 11, this is called primary education and it takes place in separate schools, usually divided into infant schools (5–7) and junior schools (8–11), with children entering in the school year (September to September) in which they reach this age. The vast majority of children go to the primary school nearest to their home and most schools admit all local children although, as we shall see shortly, there are some specialist schools and some private schools. Primary education is geared to providing children with basic skills, particularly in literacy and numeracy, and teachers in these schools are trained specifically in such primary work.

Secondary education

At the age of 11 children move from primary into secondary education, and this almost always involves a change of school. Secondary schools also generally take local children, but they are normally larger and cover a wider area. There is also a wider range of more specialist secondary schools. At one time, as we shall see, children were selected for different secondary schools on the basis of an assessment of ability, and such selection still continues to some extent in some areas. Secondary education is geared towards the preparation of children for public examinations, which they sit at the age of 16 and which are in effect a standard measure of their abilities and achievements. These examinations are called General Certificate in School Education (GCSE) and 'pass' marks are graded from A* to E, with A* to C being regarded as evidence of ability to continue with further study. Some secondary schools also provide further education (in 'sixth forms') up to the age of 18 in order for children to sit 'AS and A level' examinations, a higher standard of public examinations also graded from A to E which are used by universities as entry criteria for undergraduate study. Such attendance is not required, and many children leave school at 16, although the numbers who 'stay on' have been rising significantly in recent years.

Further education

Children leaving school at 16 do not necessarily end their education at this point. From the ages of 16 to 19 (and indeed beyond this) they can transfer to a further education (FE) college. FE colleges also provide A level education; indeed, there are some sixth form colleges which specialise in this, and for those in secondary schools without sixth forms this is the only route to A level study. However, colleges also provide a range of other (more vocational) courses, as we shall discuss shortly.

Higher education

Higher education is more specialist education provided for adults in universities and colleges of higher education. Most higher education students study for an undergraduate degree (usually called a Bachelor of Arts, BA, or Bachelor of Sciences, BSc, which represents a throwback to what was once a largely male preserve) in a specialist area, such as social policy. An undergraduate degree course generally lasts for three years if completed on a full time basis. Most universities also provide higher, and more specialist, postgraduate awards (at Masters level, either MA or MSc) and also research-based awards (in partic- ular the Doctor of Philosophy, or PhD, which is a generic term for research in any area). Many 18 year olds who achieve sufficiently high passes in their A level exams go on to study university degrees, although universities also admit students at all ages and with a range of different educational backgrounds; as we shall see, the numbers of these students within higher education has been growing.

Adult education

Adults in higher, or further, education are studying for specific awards or qual- ifications, usually linked to current or future employment careers: for instance, a degree in law can be a stepping stone towards a career as a professional lawyer. However, there is some educational provision for adults which is not geared to such instrumental goals, but rather aims to provide an opportunity for adults to continue learning after school age, in order to enhance their general knowledge and understanding. Such adult education is mainly provided within FE colleges and has sometimes been geared to leisure activity (for instance, art or music classes); but in recent times adult education has focused more specifically on the (re)learning of basic literacy and numeracy skills, which may have been missed at school, or on preparation for further or higher education through part-time

GCSEs and A levels or alternative 'access' qualifications which may be recognised by universities as equivalent entry criteria.

* * *

In keeping with the policy commitments to education as an investment in individual and social development, school education provision in the UK (and, in particular, compulsory education) is provided by the state free at the point of use and funded out of general taxation; and this has been the case for over a hundred years. Some higher education students are currently required to contribute towards the fees paid to universities for their education and, as we shall see, this is set to expand further; but most of further and higher education is also provided and funded by the state.

State education in England is formally the responsibility of the Department for Education and Skills (DfES), which replaced the previous Department for Education and Employment (DfEE) in 2001, when responsibility for employment was transferred to the new Department for Work and Pensions (DWP). Education is one of the policy areas where devolved powers have been given to the separate administrations in Scotland, Wales and Northern Ireland; and since then some significant departures in education policy have been pursued in the devolved administrations. For instance, in Scotland the charging of fees to university students has been abandoned and improved conditions introduced for teachers in schools, and in Wales children are not tested at the age of seven, and league tables of school performance are not published.

Further and higher education are administered nationally through separate agencies (quangos) established by the DfES – the Learning and Skills Councils and the Higher Education Funding Council – and in the devolved administrations separate bodies with similar functions have been established. In contrast school education (including nursery schools) is largely administered locally by Local Education Authorities (LEAs) which are departments of local government, except in Northern Ireland where is it the responsibility of five education boards. LEA management of school education was established in the early part of the twentieth century; but, at the end of the century, as we discuss in more detail below, more powers were taken by central government and schools were given the opportunity to 'opt out' of LEA control. LEA management is still the predominant form of administration, but it is no longer comprehensive; and this has created divisions within the state school system.

Not all education in the UK is provided and funded by government, however. There are also a number of private schools, which charge a fee to pupils and operate outside the state education system. The private or independent schools are sometimes, misleadingly, called 'public schools', although in practice most will only admit pupils who meet their internal selection criteria and whose parents are able to pay the necessary fees. Private schools operate at primary (sometimes here called preparatory) and secondary level, and they are frequently single sex (either for girls or boys only). Some also permit pupils to live at the school during term time, referred to as 'boarding'. Some private schools have a long history and have a high public profile, such as Eton and Harrow boys' schools on the outskirts of London. Many also have high standards of pupil achievement in GCSEs and A levels, in part because they can afford to have small classes and pay high salaries to teachers. They have also, of course, traditionally been the preserve of the middle and upper classes, who can afford to send their children there. And there is an element of self-selection going on here with many private school children later becoming wealthy adults, whose children also then attend these private schools.

Despite a number of measures to reform and expand state education, private education has always remained as a significant sector of school provision; and on occasions policy interventions have sought to use public finds to intervene in this middle-class preserve. In the middle of the twentieth century some fee-paying schools could also receive public funding under what was called the 'direct grant' scheme and could admit (usually the brightest) local children who would be supported by scholarships from the LEA (Sanderson, 1999, p.138); but this was abolished in 1975. A similar provision was introduced in the 1980s under which children from poorer backgrounds could attend private schools on 'assisted places' funded by the government, although again this was in effect restricted to those meeting high academic entry requirements. However, this too was abolished by the Labour government after 1997. For those who can pay the fees (and wish to) private schools still remain, and overall around 6 per cent of pupils attend them, although this proportion varies significantly in different parts of the country. They are now subject to many of the regulatory and accountability procedures which are applied to state schools to ensure that pupils attending them are receiving adequate and appropriate education.

QUESTION: COMPREHENSION

■ Why has vocationalism become so important in determining education policy?

QUESTION: REFLECTION

■ Should private education be permitted when state-funded places are available for all pupils?

Education in schools

Public provision of school education in Britain can be traced back to the nineteenth century, when local schools for what would now be classed as primary education were established in many local areas. Often these schools were linked to local churches who provided the financial support for building and maintaining them, and also influenced the curriculum to promote the teaching of Christian beliefs and values. Some, however, were small independent enterprises supported by local parents. After 1870 local School Boards were established and could raise public funds for schools from local rates; and after 1880 attendance at school from the ages of 5 to 10 became compulsory. In 1902 one of the earliest of the twentieth-century welfare reforms transferred responsibility for the management of schools to Local Education Authorities, and gave them responsibility for developing secondary education in grammar schools for some pupils.

In the early part of the twentieth century, secondary school education within the state sector did expand, although it did not provide a comprehensive service for all children. This was changed in 1944 in one of the most important policy and legislative reforms of school education in the UK. The 1944 Education Act was introduced by R A B Butler, a Conservative minister in the wartime coalition government, and is sometimes referred to after him as the Butler Act. It was supported by the Labour Party, however, and maintained by them as a part of their major reforms of state welfare in the 1940s; and it reaffirmed the role of the state as the provider of free education for all children.

The Butler Act involved a 'nationalisation' of much of the previously disparate publicly supported school provision, although the links between some schools and local churches remained (see Finch, 1984, p.15). It also confirmed LEAs as the agencies for the management and development of school provision. Most importantly, it extended compulsory school attendance to the age of 15 (extended in 1972 to 16) and established a system of separate secondary schools to provide this. This new secondary school system was called the *tripartite system*, as it envisaged three different kinds of secondary school providing different sorts of secondary education to different groups of pupils.

The principle behind the tripartite system was one of selection. In the last year of primary education, at the age of 10 or 11, pupils would undergo an examination (called the *11 plus*), and on the basis of the results from this would be selected for one of three local schools.

1. Grammar schools, hitherto the traditional secondary provision, would take pupils with academic ability and would prepare them for public examination at 16 (then GCEs) and 18 (A levels).
2. Secondary Technical Schools would take pupils with more technical abilities and prepare them for a more vocational career.
3. Secondary Modern Schools would take pupils with 'practical' abilities and provide them with a mixture of educational knowledge and work-related or domestic skills.

The notion of allocating pupils to schools according to aptitude or ability had an obvious notional attraction. However, the system was dogged by fundamental problems of both principle and practice, and quickly began to attract criticism from policy-makers and parents.

In principle the idea of selection at the age of 11 was problematic. The 11 plus examination, based on English, mathematics and 'intelligence testing', was not a satisfactory basis for determining the future abilities of young children, as the later progress of many children confirmed: some grammar school children left school at 15 or 16 without public qualifications and growing numbers of secondary modern school pupils sat and passed the public General Certificate of Education (GCE) examinations (Lowe, 1999, p.216). There was also considerable disquiet, not least among parents and children, that future life chances and career opportunities should be so heavily dependent upon the testing and selection of 11 year olds.

In practice the notion of distinctive, and yet equivalent, secondary provision did not materialise. As the continuation of pre-war secondary education in many areas, the grammar schools inherited buildings, resources and staff which the newer technical and modern schools could not match. They attracted the best teachers and it quickly became clear that in most respects they were the 'best' schools. Thus attendance at grammar school was a coveted goal and attendance at secondary modern a sign of failure. This was compounded by the failure to develop technical schools in many areas, so that the third leg of the scheme was not really available for a lot of pupils. The 11 plus examination therefore became a pass or fail hurdle to achieve access to grammar school education, with middle-class parents coaching and encouraging their children to ensure higher pass rates, or sending their children to private schools where this did not succeed. This reproduced something of a traditional class divide within what was purportedly a meritocratic regime, undermining the supposedly egalitarian goals of state education. What is more, access to grammar schools varied geographically with, in 1959, 35 per cent of pupils in grammar schools in the South West compared to 22 per cent in the North East (Lowe, 1999, p.218), and also by gender, with girls doing on average much better in the 11 plus examination than boys.

By the 1960s therefore the tripartite system was not working as its architects had intended, and it was subject to increasingly widespread criticism by policy makers and politicians. One of the leading critics was the Labour politician, Anthony Crosland, who believed that social development required non-selective secondary education (1956), and when he became Secretary of State in 1965 he required LEAs to draw up plans to replace the existing schools with *comprehensive* secondary schools. The aim of comprehensives was to provide the same educational opportunities for all secondary-school children in single (large) local schools, although within these pupils could be 'streamed' into separate classes according to ability for particular subjects. And over the next decade or so most secondary schools were converted to comprehensives, mainly through a redesignation and restructuring of existing schools, although this did not happen in Northern Ireland.

However, some LEAs were opposed to the loss of grammar schools and resisted comprehensivisation; and after the election of the Thatcher governments in the 1980s the requirement was removed. Thus state grammar schools and selection at the age of 11 still continue in some areas, notably Buckinghamshire; and since the 1988 school reforms some secondary schools have opted out of LEA control to establish themselves as state grammar schools (for instance, in Birmingham); and, of course, private grammar schools have remained for those who can afford to pay. But for the vast majority of children in mainland Britain secondary education is now provided in comprehensive schools catering for all children from 11 to 16 or 18 in a local area or neighbourhood.

In the 1960s there was also a reawakening of concern with a wider range of educational issues, prompted by the publication of a series of reports by government committees examining different aspects of provision.

1. The *Crowther* Report of 1959 focused on the later years of secondary schooling and recommended a extension of the school leaving age and the introduction of a new range of public examinations at 16 which all pupils could take: the Certificate of School Education (CSE). This was later merged with the GCE which had primarily only been taken by a minority of the brightest pupils to create the current GCSE.
2. The *Newsom* Report in 1963 looked at secondary pupils with lower abilities and recommended that more effort be made to promote and develop their learning, including changes in teacher training provision to improve teaching methods.
3. The *Plowden* Report of 1967 focused upon primary education and in particular the concern that some primary children in some schools were not doing as well as their peers. The report argued that this was due to cultural and social factors as well as school provision and proposed 'positive discrimination' to target additional resources to schools in deprived areas to boost performance, a policy which we will discuss in more detail shortly.

These relatively formal reviews of the 1960s were followed in the 1970s by the more controversial Black Papers and the Great Debate, discussed earlier; and the latter were to provide a more direct backdrop to the policy reforms of the 1980s.

In keeping with their more general assault on local government (see Chapter 15) and their concern to promote vocationalism, the Conservative governments of the 1980s aimed to reduce the power and control of LEAs over the provision of state education. They also wished to introduce marketisation and, where possible, privatisation into school education. These policies reached their peak in the Education Reform Act of 1988, a change as momentous as the Butler Act 44 years earlier. The 1988 reforms undermined the role of LEAs from two directions. From *above* more direction was provided by central government, most notably the imposition of a national curriculum to govern the content and structure of school education, backed up by national attainment tests for all pupils at the ages of 7, 11, 14 and 16. From *below* more power was given to schools to manage their own affairs, most notably the devolution of financial management to head teachers and governing bodies, under what was called the Local Management of Schools (LMS).

Local management did not only include budgetary control; schools were also freed up from LEA allocation of pupils. This was part of a more general attempt to introduce market principles of choice and competition into state education (or rather quasi-markets as commentators now call them: see Chapter 9). Parents can in theory send their children to any school of their choice and schools are required to publish information about the performance of their pupils in order to inform parent choice, although this has been dropped for primary schools in Scotland and for these and secondary schools too in Wales. The system does not quite work like this in practice, however, for schools can also take decisions over which pupils to admit; and the effect is that some (better) schools become oversubscribed and other (poorly performing) schools cannot attract sufficient pupils. Because public funds are distributed to schools on a per capita basis this means that poorer schools get poorer still and can get trapped in a downward spiral of falling rolls, poor results and inadequate budgets.

The situation is further complicated by the fact that the 1988 reforms also permitted those schools that wished to (and were able to attract the support of the governing bodies and parents for the project) to opt out of LEA involvement altogether and receive state funding direct from Whitehall. In practice only a minority of schools did this; but the situation varied across different local areas, and in some cases it led to a return to selective secondary provision by schools seeking to escape local comprehensive provision and return to the grammar school ethos.

The 1988 reforms thus significantly altered the principles and the practice of school education, with more control now devolved to individual schools within a centrally prescribed curriculum and a significant element of competition introduced into a system which was previously based on local education in LEA controlled schools. One of the highest-profile examples of parents exercising the right to choose a school for their child was that exercised by the Labour leader, Tony Blair, who opted to send his son to a Catholic selective school rather than the local comprehensive in the early 1990s. Not surprisingly perhaps, therefore, the Labour government has retained this, and most of the other, elements of the 1988 reforms.

However, in keeping with the pre-election promises to prioritise education policy, Labour has provided more public money for schools with the aims in particular of reducing class sizes (all infant school classes are now 30 or below) and raising the levels of performance of the lower-achieving schools. Where they exist, grammar schools remain, however; and private education still retains an important share of (especially secondary) provision.

Further education

Further education, particularly for 16–19 year olds, has traditionally been associated with the acquisition of vocational qualifications: the skills and qualifications needed for particular jobs within the labour market. Throughout much of the twentieth century such work-based skills were primarily acquired through the *apprenticeship*, under which young workers received on-the-job training and part-time education leading to specific, industry-based, qualifications. In the latter part of the century such training and education became more widely available in FE colleges, and the apprenticeship model began to decline in significance. This decline was accelerated by more general economic changes which reduced the scale and importance of traditional manual skills in manufacturing and introduced a range of new information technology and financial management skills which were not covered by apprenticeship training.

Vocational provision therefore began to be concentrated within FE colleges, and this trend was accelerated with the establishment of the Manpower Services Commission (MSC) in the 1970s. As we discuss in Chapter 7, the MSC was primarily designed to support the entry into employment of specific groups of unemployed workers, notably school leavers and the long-term unemployed. However, for school leavers in particular, this support generally included training courses provided by FE colleges, and the effect of this was to extent the range and scale of vocational training within FE for this age group.

The expansion of FE vocational education continued after the MSC was replaced by local Training and Enterprise Councils (TECs) in the 1980s; and in the 1990s much of this provision was incorporated into what was relabelled the 'modern apprenticeship'. The rapid growth of vocational provision in FE had left a vast and complex range of different courses with different structures and purposes, however; and following the establishment of the National Council for Vocational Qualifications in 1986 moves were made to introduce a more consistent National Vocational Qualification (NVQ) framework into which all provision could be fitted on a comparable basis. FE college provision is now dominated by NVQ courses, together with the provision of A level education for those young people (and adults) who are not able, or do not want, to study in secondary schools.

The Labour governments since 1997 have sought to extend further the provision of vocational education in FE colleges as part of a more general drive to raise the skills and qualification levels of the UK workforce, and have in particular expanded training provision for young people under their New Deal programme (see Chapter 7). They have also endorsed the recommendations of the Kennedy Report (1998) to expand FE provision in order to widen participation in education and 'draw back into learning those who have not traditionally taken advantage of education opportunities' (para. 1.2).

FE colleges themselves were originally established and managed by LEAs as part of the range of local educational provision for which they were responsible. However, the moves to centralise control over education in the 1980s and 1990s, and the concern to establish a national framework for FE provision, led in 1992 to the transfer of FE to a new national funding body, the Further Education Funding Council (FEFC), putting FE, like higher education, on to a national footing, with devolved control in Scotland, Wales and Northern Ireland. In 2001, however, the FEFC itself was replaced by a Learning and Skills Council, incorporating also the work of the local TECs on the modern apprenticeship. Thus FE provision is now in effect a comprehensive national provision of vocational and work-related education for adults of all ages, but directed specifically at 16–19 year old school leavers, many of who are undertaking training as part of a government-sponsored programme such as the New Deal.

Higher education

University education has a long history in the UK, dating back to the Oxford and Cambridge university colleges, first created in the thirteenth and fourteenth centuries, and the four universities established in Scotland. Until the end of the nineteenth century, however, attendance at university was a privilege largely restricted to upper-class young people who had attended private schools. Around the turn of the century a number of new universities were established in the major English provincial cities, such as Birmingham, Manchester and Leeds; these are sometimes called 'redbricks' because of the architectural style of their major buildings. These new institutions encouraged an extension of provision of higher education both numerically and geographically, although university study remained a largely middle-class preserve, not least because of the financial support that young people needed to complete their degrees.

Entrance into university was also restricted to those who could meet entry criteria established by the universities, based primarily upon academic merit and achievement as measured by A level examinations. Following the expansion of secondary education after the Second World War, the numbers able to achieve these standards was growing and the government sought to encourage a growth in attendance at university to meet the aspirations of this expanding cohort of young people. This was facilitated in particular by the introduction in 1962 of LEA funding (maintenance grants) for all students gaining a university place; and in 1963 a government Committee on Higher Education (the Robbins Committee) recommended that more places should be made available to provide degree study for all those capable of undertaking it, including an expansion from 8 to 17 per cent of the 18–21 age group in higher education.

Such a massive expansion would require more institutions as well as more places. In the 1960s a number of new universities were created, some out of what were previously colleges of advanced technology and some built from scratch (such as the 'campus' universities at Lancaster and York), and all of them receiving central government funding via the University Grants Committee (UGC). After this expansion, however, the then Labour government channelled future growth in higher education into a new form of institution, the polytechnics, established and run by LEAs (although with national funding), which concentrated on less elitist and more vocational provision, often delivered on a part-time basis. The only new university created after the mid-1960s therefore was the Open University, an entirely new venture which delivered its learning to part-time students all over the country via a distance learning model incorporating the use of television.

The polytechnics and the new universities contributed to a gradual growth in higher education provision throughout the 1970s and 1980s, although it remained the case that a higher proportion of those from middle-class families than lower-class families undertook undergraduate study. Towards the end of the century, therefore, there was another sustained attempt to expand and to broaden access to higher education. This involved removal of polytechnics from LEA control in 1988 and in 1992 their transfer to university status, all 30 of them changing their titles to become the 'new universities', and coming under the same national funding regime as the 'old universities': the Higher Education Funding Council (HEFC). All universities and higher education colleges (of which there were also by now a significant number) were also provided with financial incentives to accept more students by a shift of funding for teaching on to a per capita basis. In 1997 a second official report on higher education, the Dearing Report, recommended yet further expansion of provision to increase the proportion of young people going to university to one-third and to extend places to older adults and disadvantaged groups.

However, the cost of such expanded provision created an ever greater upward pressure on public funding, and so costs were contained by reducing the per capita funding paid to universities and by replacing the maintenance grants paid to students with loans (which would be repaid out of future earnings). Furthermore, after 1998 better-off students (or their parents) were required to pay a proportion of the cost of education through an annual fee; and in 2003 it was announced that all universities would be able to charge higher levels of fees (up to £3,000 per annum) after 2006, although these will only be paid retrospectively out of future earnings. Despite the introduction of student loans and fees, the Labour governments have remained committed to even further growth in higher education, setting a notional target of 50 per cent of the 18–21 age group having experience of higher education, and further encouraging the widening of access to disadvantaged groups and older adults as part of the more general promotion of what is now called 'lifelong learning'. There is an element of contradiction in these plans, however, and concern has been voiced by some commentators that loans and fees will in practice operate to exclude the very groups to whom policy makers wish to extend places.

This has raised a more general debate about who should pay for university education: to what extent is it an individual privilege leading to enhanced career opportunities in later life for which those who benefit should be expected to contribute to the cost, and to what extent is it a part of a public commitment to the creation of a better skilled and qualified society from which all benefit and therefore all should pay? To put it more sharply, doctors and lawyers, and even teachers, can expect to secure reasonable salaries later in life; but we all need well-qualified doctors, lawyers, teachers and other professionals. Who should therefore bear the cost of training them? This debate is further complicated by the claims by university staff and managers that the funding that they now receive for the teaching and research that they do, after years of gradual attrition, is no longer sufficient for them to maintain standards and meet further targets for expansion. And, despite some commitments to increased support for universities, in part from the new fees announced in 2003, expansion and quality are still competing for priority in the future development of higher education.

QUESTIONS: COMPREHENSION

- Why did comprehensive provision replace the post-war tripartite structure of secondary education; and why, despite this, do some grammar schools still remain?
- To what extent did the introduction of parental choice and LMS in 1988 achieve the flexibility and responsiveness in state education which government claimed it was seeking?
- Why has FE expanded so significantly in the last two decades or so?

QUESTION: REFLECTION

- What are advantages and disadvantages of the expansion of access to higher education?

Equality and selectivity in education

Since the Butler reforms of state education in 1944 at least there has been concern within policy circles about the extent to which educational provision should be governed by the principle of equality. If public education, free to all, is a public good, then should not all benefit equally from it? The answer to this question, however, raises a number of dilemmas which have significantly influenced education policy development over the last 50 years or so.

First there is the distinction between different degrees of equality, sometimes referred to as:

- equality of *opportunity*: should all have the same chances to succeed and reach their potential?
- equality of *outcome*: should all receive the same service and achieve the same result?

In practice both of these principles have informed policy development: the shift from tripartite to comprehensive secondary education was driven in particular by a belief that all secondary pupils should get the same curriculum and teaching; and yet the differentials in achievement at GCSE, A level and (especially) university education mean that those better able to benefit from provision are encouraged to do better out of it. Of course, it would be unlikely that all could be expected to achieve the same results in all circumstances, and therefore the increasing emphasis that there has been since the 1980s upon equality of opportunity suggests that, in practice at least, this is now recognised as a more critical underlying goal.

However, even a commitment to equality of opportunity raises other problems. If some pupils are achieving lower standards than their peers, is this because they have lower innate abilities or is it because the opportunities afforded to them have not in fact been equal to those available to others? Evidence that there are links between overall performance and social class, family background or attendance at particular schools suggests that this may, at least in part, be down to the opportunity factor. The issue of whether all pupils are receiving the right kind of support and encouragement in education was a major concern of the government reports of the 1960s, particularly the Plowden Report of 1967. One of the conclusions of this was that there was a need for 'positive discrimination' in the targeting of additional resources to particular pupils and schools. This was taken up by government with the creation of Educational Priority Areas (EPAs), where additional public resources were available to support the employment of more teachers and to promote work with parents (including pre-school parents) to encourage their children's education.

The EPAs were a relatively short-lived experiment in positive discrimination, but more recently the idea of targeted additional support has been revisited in the Education Action Zones (EAZs) established by the Labour government after 1997, although these do not exist in Scotland or Wales. Support for work with pre-school children has also now been provided on a targeted basis under the Sure Start programme and for school-age children under the Children's Fund. The government also now seeks to promote best practice in school education more generally by identifying 'beacon schools' which act as a model for less successful schools around them, and by identifying 'failing schools' which are the focus of specific state intervention to improve provision and standards, although this too has not been taken up in the devolved administrations.

There are some other important dimensions to the question of equal treatment in education, however. First there is the issue of gender. Since the sex discrimination and equal treatment legislation of the 1970s girls and boys have been provided with equal access to education, formally speaking at least, although before this it was not uncommon for a different curriculum to be offered to the different sexes, with (for instance) boys studying carpentry and girls home economics. Nevertheless formal gender equality does not necessarily lead to practical equality of treatment. For a start it is still quite common for some schools to offer only single sex education, with girls and boys therefore experiencing quite different institutions and teachers, a separation which supporters argue can be of benefit to both. Even within mixed schools, however, there is evidence of differential achievement, with boys doing better in science and technology and girls doing better in literature and arts; although more recently the evidence suggests a more general tendency for girls to outperform boys at all ages in their school careers, leading to (unresolved) questions about how best to provide equality of opportunity for both.

There is also evidence of differential performance of some black and ethnic minority children in UK schools, and this too has prompted policy debates about how best to address issues of equality of opportunity here. In 1985 there was a government committee report on the education of children from ethnic minority groups, known as the Swann Report. This argued that underachievement by non-white pupils was an issue for the education system and that this was linked to the more general disadvantage and discrimination experienced by non-white people in Britain. The report recommended that 'greater sensitivity' (DES, 1985, p.9) needed to be shown to the particular circumstances and needs of ethnic minority children, and that more attention should be paid more generally in education to the ethnically diverse society which Britain had become by the end of the twentieth century. At the beginning of the twenty-first century, however, debate about diversity has extended to some disagreement over the desirability of faith-based schools, which in effect provide specialist education for particular religious and ethnic groups and can lead to divisions between social groups being reflected within the school system.

Standards

Underlying much of the recent debate about the need to ensure equality of opportunity within the education system has been an increasing emphasis within policy delivery on the measurement and maintenance of education standards. The notion of a set of standards against which educational achievement can be objectively assessed has of course been a key feature of provision throughout most of the modern era. This is just what the tests and examinations that all pupils and students know so well are designed to ensure. In particular, the national public examinations at 16 and 18 (GCSEs and A levels) have for some time been established as the main goal, and measure, of educational achievement. This is true for pupils, but also now in England for schools, where the requirement to publish information about the levels of achievement of their pupils in these examinations can be used to compare performance and to construct 'league tables' which are published by the press and lead to competition between schools.

In 1988 national control over educational standards was extended by the introduction of the national curriculum and the standard attainment tests (SATs) at 7, 11, 14 and 16 (although in Wales testing at seven has been abandoned). Since 1997 the government has been overtly concerned with the levels of achievement in schools, in particular at primary level where there is now a requirement to provide literacy and numeracy hours on a daily basis to ensure that all pupils reach certain basic standards early in their school careers.

Concern with standards does not just apply to the outcomes of education, however; there is now a range of measures available designed to ensure that the process of providing education is properly managed and delivered. This is part of a more general concern within public service provision with 'quality assurance', and it is focused particularly upon the use of independent inspections of providers to ensure that established minimum standards are being met. For school education the inspections are carried out by OFSTED, who must visit all schools on a regular six-yearly cycle and produce a report on all aspects of educational provision, which is made publicly available to pupils, parents and the general public (on the OFSTED website). Quality assurance also extends to higher education, where a Quality Assurance Agency (QAA) arranges for assessment of teaching provision in different subjects, again on a rolling review process, although here the reviews themselves are carried out by academic peers, and in 2003 moved on to a broader institutional basis.

Whether quality assurance procedures really do lead to improvements in the setting and maintenance of standards in education is a controversial question. Many teachers and university lecturers are critical of the process of inspection which they claim is unnecessary and diverts large amounts of resources (predominantly their time) into a bureaucratic process which is not necessarily an accurate measure of performance. Nevertheless minimum standards and independent assessment are now core features of public policy delivery, and are strongly supported by government as a means of ensuring that service providers are accountable for the quality of the public services that they deliver, as we shall discuss in Chapter 18.

Ancillary services

Education policy is primarily concerned with the delivery of learning and teaching. Nevertheless, for some time is has been recognised that effective learning may depend not only upon teaching but upon other forms of support for attendance and performance at school. From the early days of formal school education it was recognised that healthy and well-fed pupils were more able to learn effectively. Schools were thus encouraged, and later required, to provide school meals at lunchtime for their pupils, and also milk at break times. The compulsory provision of milk was abandoned in the early 1970s. However, school meals remain (at least for those pupils choosing to take them); and, although pupils are charged a nominal cost, for those on social security benefits (specifically income support) meals are free.

LEAs have also provided a range of other ancillary services to support school attendance, including free transport for those living too far to walk to school and free or subsidised school clothing for parents on low incomes. Some have also offered small maintenance awards on a means-tested basis towards the living costs of pupils staying on at school after 16, and these are now to be extended to all pupils on a national basis. In addition LEAs must run an Educational Welfare Officer service to provide targeted support and assistance to children experiencing difficulties attending school, although this is also to some extent a 'policing' service to ensure that pupils who should be attending school on a compulsory basis are in fact doing so regularly.

At the beginning of the new century the concern of government has also focused more directly upon the problem of pupils who miss out on school attendance, and hence on education itself. The problems of truancy (pupils refusing to attend school) and school exclusion (the exclusion by schools of disruptive pupils) were one of the first priorities determined by government for the new Social Exclusion Unit (SEU) established in 1998. The aim of the unit was to reduce the levels of both over the following few years, with the objective of seeking to ensure that the equality of opportunity which the education system should be providing for all was not lost even by those most on the margins of it. This is another example of the importance of the current policy tendency to see education as an investment in human capital, which should be of benefit to all individuals in securing their future place in society.

QUESTIONS: COMPREHENSION

- How does the targeting of additional resources seek to overcome inequalities within the experience of education?
- In what ways can public inspection led to improved standards in education?

QUESTION: REFLECTION

- To what extent is education a public good rather than a private gain?

FURTHER READING

The collection of papers in Halsey et al. (1997) provides a good overview of many of the issues involved in the development of education policy. A more detailed history of post-war provision can be found in K. Jones (2002). Tomlinson (2001) is a good guide to the policy context within which education provision is developed, and Demaine (2001) is a useful source for information on recent policy developments. Government papers can be found on the national website at **www.dfes. gov.uk**, with the devolved administration websites providing similar services (see Chapter 15).

Health

SUMMARY OF KEY POINTS

- Health policy aims both to promote improved health and to treat illness; at times these may lead to different priorities for policy development.
- Measuring health needs is complex. Rates of mortality and morbidity are used for this. They show gradual improvements in time over health standards, but continuing inequalities between different social groups.
- Health promotion at both individual and social levels is now directly supported by government.
- The National Health Service (NHS) was established in 1948, by the Labour Minister of Health, Aneurin Bevan.
- The structure of the NHS has been reformed on a number of occasions, most recently to break it into a series of self-governing trusts in primary care and acute provision, with different structures now found in Scotland, Wales and Northern Ireland.
- Recent reviews of health funding have led to significant increases in planned expenditure on the NHS, linked to promises to improve service delivery and access.
- Although largely a free service the NHS does make charges for some services, notably prescriptions.
- Private health providers deliver services outside the NHS. Around 7 million people in the UK have private health insurance.
- Private finance and private contractors now work in partnership with the NHS in some areas of provision.

Health and illness

Our health is one of the most precious features of our lives as human beings. This applies at an individual level: we all want to enjoy good health. However, it also underpins our collective interests as a society since healthy citizens make for a more successful and prosperous social order. And viewed negatively, this message is even more emphatic: poor health is debilitating and costly. It is not surprising therefore that health has been a central concern of social policy in the UK, and across the world, throughout the last two centuries of modern development; and it remains at the beginning of the twenty-first century one of the core priorities for future policy development and public spending. Health policy is therefore at the centre of welfare planning; but at the heart of our concern with health policy is a fundamental dilemma which has also underpinned much of the debate about how to develop and deliver health policy. This can be summed up in the question, 'Should the focus of policy be health or illness?'

In part this is a definitional question. It is not necessarily clear what is meant by good health. For instance, should we all aspire to the standards of fitness of the professional sportsman or woman, or are overweight and inactive office workers in good health if they are not actually suffering from any obvious debilitating condition? And what do we mean by illness? Illness can range from the common cold to terminal cancer, and one is clearly more serious than the other. Furthermore, illness might be separated from disease, with the latter implying the medical diagnosis of a known infection or disability and the former the unspecified symptoms experienced by individuals who feel ill. For practical purposes this distinction is captured to some extent in the way in which absence from work for sickness is treated, with the first few days being recorded as the self-diagnosed symptoms of the individual, but longer periods requiring medical diagnosis and certification of a specific condition by a doctor. The medical diagnosis of particular conditions is of course a very complex and highly specified science, but the more general terminology of health and illness is far from clearly agreed or consistently used.

More significant perhaps are the very different models of health services, and indeed the different philosophies and practices underlying these, that flow from a concern with illness rather than health. In the UK we have a National Health Service (NHS), of which more shortly, but it has sometimes been dubbed by critics a national *illness* service, because by and large the development and delivery of policy has been focused upon the diagnosis and treatment of sickness, rather then the promotion of good health. The vast bulk of health service resources are expended on treating patients who are ill, with relatively little effort directed towards preventing healthy people from becoming ill in the first place. This is a balance which has been challenged by some of those working within, and outside, the NHS; and it has been subject to change over time, with the promotion of public health coming to occupy a more prominent place in health service planning in recent years. However, there is a more general consequence of the focus in practice upon treating illness rather then promoting health: it has meant that to a significant extent health provision has developed as a demand-led welfare service.

The demand-led focus of health care can be seen in the General Practitioner (GP) model that dominates primary health care. When we think that we may be ill we go to a doctor, who confirms that we are (or not), provides a diagnosis and (in most cases) prescribes some form of cure. In more serious cases, where the cure involves extensive medical intervention (an operation), the GP may refer us on to an acute service (usually a hospital), and in serious emergency cases we may go to hospital direct, generally to the accident and emergency (A&E or casualty) department. In all cases, however, it is the circumstances of the citizen which determine the service provided and drive the need for resources to meet these. When the NHS was first introduced in the UK it was assumed that access to health care for all would reduce the amount of sickness in society, and so demand on, and expenditure on, the service would gradually decline. Ironically, as we shall see, the reverse has been the case. Demand for health services has increased, leading to increased expenditure. In part this is because improved medical knowledge and techniques mean that we can treat more illnesses more effectively (though in some cases more expensively); but in part it is also to some extent the product of increasing expectations of good health and service provision amongst individual citizens. Whatever the balance here, there is no doubt that demand on the health service has driven up service provision; and yet demand still outstrips the ability of current providers to meet all needs so that, in practice, the provision of health services is in many cases a process of rationing, as graphically revealed in the concern over the lengths of waiting lists for medical treatment.

It would not be correct to characterise health service provision as entirely based upon attempts to ration services to meet consumer demands, however. Budget setting and service development require some element of planning and prioritising by service providers; and planning for health needs does occupy an important place in health policy development. The Department of Health (DoH) provides a general steer over the identification of health needs and the prioritisation of health service resources, and the health authorities and trusts administering services have a specific responsibility to identify and respond to the health needs in their areas (a responsibility which, as we shall see, has been becoming more extensive and intensive in recent years).

However, measurement of health needs within society is far from a simple matter, in part because of the definitional problems outlined above. In practice the most widely used measures are mortality rates: that is, the ages at which people die or the number of deaths per 1,000 population. Mortality data can provide a measure of life expectancy, which can be used on a comparative basis over time or across different sections of the population. In particular this is done through the use of Standardised Mortality Ratios (SMRs) which compare death rates within particular groups with a national average, controlled for variables such as age and sex, giving a measure of above or below the average. Of course mortality rates measure death, not health or illness. Therefore attempts have also been made to gather data on morbidity, the experience of illness. The problem here is what to count as illness and this varies: for instance, some measures use visits to health services, some are based on self-reporting and some use evidence of absence from work, although all have their problems.

In general the evidence from the mortality statistics is an encouraging one. Over the last century mortality rates declined and life expectancy rose: a person born in the 1900s could expect to live to 45 if male and 49 if female, but by the end of the century these ages had risen to 73 and 79 (Ham, 1999, p.185). This is not just a question of improved health services, of course: improved diets and better working and living conditions have probably had a greater influence. And one of the major problems involved in the measurement of changes in health and illness levels is the difficulty of establishing causal links between measured improvements and policy interventions made.

If the overall message on health and health needs is a positive one, there are nevertheless some significant limitations within this. In particular there is evidence that improved standards of health are not evenly distributed across the population, or, to put it another way, there are inequalities in health within the UK. The extent of inequalities in health were revealed in the Black Report in 1980, based on research carried out in the 1970s by an expert team including social policy researcher, Peter Townsend. A later report, called *The Health Divide*, confirmed these trends, but the then Conservative government refused to publish it. It was released, however, with a reprint of the Black Report, in a commercial publication led by Townsend (Townsend, Davidson and Whitehead, 1988); but throughout the 1980s official research into the issue was stopped and the proposals of the Black Report ignored. However, when the Labour government came to power in 1997 they commissioned an independent inquiry led by Acheson to revisit the research on health inequalities, which was published in 1998.

The Acheson Report (1998) revealed that, in some areas, inequalities in health had increased rather than declined towards the end of the last century, and argued that tackling these inequalities should be a major policy priority for health policy planning. The measurement of health inequalities is a complex issue both methodologically and conceptually, however, and the data presented to the Acheson inquiry was voluminous. Much of it was collected together and published by Gordon *et al.* (1999) at Bristol, and the evidence showing a continuing link between poor health and social class was incontrovertible, as revealed, for instance, in Table 4.1, taken from the evidence submitted to Acheson, although some overall improvement over time is also revealed here.

Table 4.1   Annual age-adjusted rate of years of potential life lost per 1,000 population for all causes of death for men aged 20–64, England and Wales

Social class	1970–72	1991–93
I	48.7	28
II	51.9	31.6
IIIN	65	45.7
IIIM	66	50.5
IV	75.6	52.8
V	103	93.3

Source: Adapted from Blane and Drever (1998), p.255.

Following the publication of the Acheson Report the government did reinstate the reduction of health inequalities as a major policy goal, although by the early years of the twenty-first century it had been overtaken in prominence by the commitment to improve health service delivery, as we shall see below.

The group of researchers at Bristol also engaged in other work in the 1990s to measure the gap in health standards between the ten Parliamentary constituencies in the UK with the worst and best health records, which they concluded was widening (Shaw *et al.*, 1999). This was evidence of geographical, or spatial, inequalities in health, which were linked to social class and other variations in the dispersion of poverty and deprivation; but may also be evidence of spatial variations in access to health service provision. It has been recognised for some time that there are geographical variations in the provision of health services, and in the 1970s a formula was devised, by the Resource Allocation Working Party (RAWP), to steer additional NHS provision into underprovided areas in England. This steering has been retained since, although the principles underlying the formula have changed and different measures have been adopted by the devolved administrations. The Labour governments have also taken further the targeting of additional resources on to areas of known health need with the creation in 1998 and 1999 of 26 Health Action Zones (HAZs) in England to develop a range of initiatives to tackle local health problems in deprived districts, through partnership working with other local agencies, notably local authorities.

Underlying the evidence of the link between social status and health is the problematic question of cause and effect, sometimes referred to as the 'artefact' problem: are poor people ill because they are poor, or poor because they are ill? This raises questions therefore about the appropriate policy response to health inequalities; and in the case of geographical targeting this is complicated further by the problem that many healthy people live in deprived areas and many unhealthy people live outside them. More generally, however, there persists the dilemma raised earlier about whether the focus of policy should be upon illness or upon health. The RAWP approach is in effect a response to the demand-led, illness model of health service development, and to some extent so too are the HAZs. However, there is a long tradition within health policy debate and practice about the more generic role to be played by policy-makers in tackling both inequalities and illness through the promotion of universal improvements in public health.

Policies for the promotion of public health can be traced back to the mid-nineteenth-century initiatives to tackle problems of poor sanitation and living conditions, and they have been continued since, both within the NHS (for example, by the use of vaccination programmes to prevent the spread of infectious diseases) and through other policy interventions in housing, education and social security policy. Improvements in public health can prevent illness and disease, and they can also help to reduce health inequalities by ensuring that minimum standards are applied to all. Such public health provision is formally included within both health service and local government responsibilities. It has also been taken further by development of health promotion work.

Health promotion aims to support the creation of a healthier society by tackling the potential causes of poor health. It was endorsed in a government

White Paper in 1992 entitled *The Health of the Nation*, which set targets for improvement in a number of areas (DoH, 1992); and more recently it has been taken further with new and more specific targets set by the White Paper, *Saving Lives: Our Healthier Nation* (DoH, 1999). There is something of a debate within health promotion circles about the extent to which policy action should focus upon the exhortation of individuals to pursue healthier lifestyles (changing diets, quitting smoking and taking more exercise), which to some extent characterised the approach underlying the 1992 paper; or the extent to which policy should aim to tackle the social factors behind poor health (inadequate housing, dangerous working conditions, and poverty). This is sometimes referred to as the 'social model' of public health and received more support in the 1998 document produced by the Labour government. Of course, in practice both individual and social factors can contribute to poor health and both can, and should, be the focus of health promotion activity.

The development of the National Health Service

Public policies to combat poor health can be traced back to the nineteenth century: for example, in 1848 a Public Health Act sought to improve public health by tackling water supplies and sewerage systems, and in the 1870s further legislation along similar lines followed. It was in the twentieth century when public health services began to develop more systematically, however, inspired in part by the revelation that many of the recruits for the army to fight in the Boer War were found to be unfit. In 1919 a Ministry of Health was established; and, when national insurance for sickness was developed after 1911, free access to GPs was provided for certain groups of workers. By the 1940s some 21 million, half the population, were covered by the scheme and two-thirds of GPs were taking part (Ham, 1999, p.7). In the nineteenth century institutional provision for sickness had been dominated by the Poor Law workhouses and infirmaries; but in 1929 these were transferred to local authorities to be developed into a local hospital service, alongside the private and voluntary hospitals that had also by then begun to be built, and the 'lunatic asylums' for the mentally ill which had been growing in number since the 1800s.

In the 1930s a number of reports from official bodies commented on the shortcomings in the varied pattern of provision which had emerged from these developments and recommended greater coordination of policy and planning, including the influential British Medical Association (BMA), the collective voice of GPs and hospital doctors. With the outbreak of war national planning emerged out of national need, with public and voluntary hospitals being combined in an Emergency Medical Service; and in 1942 Beveridge's influential report on social security argued that a comprehensive national service should be developed after the war to combat the evil of disease. In 1944 a White Paper contained proposals for a national health service; in 1946 legislation was passed, and in 1948 the NHS came into operation.

The introduction of the NHS was a seminal moment in the development of British social policy, enshrining as it did the universal principles of access to services for all, free at the point of use, and the financing of provision through general taxation. It is a model of universal service which has remained fundamentally unchallenged throughout over 50 years of policy development in the UK since, and it provided a example for public health services in many other countries across the world. The introduction of the NHS is often credited to the Labour minister, Aneurin Bevan, who steered it through Parliament; and there is no doubt that his vision and skilled political manoeuvring were critical in ensuring support, in particular from the medical profession who were concerned about the loss of professional autonomy that it might entail. However, there was in practice cross-party support for the NHS (the White Paper came from the wartime coalition government), and this has been retained over subsequent years.

As we saw above, the initial expectation was that the introduction of the NHS would lead to a reduction in general health needs; and indeed there was a concern that many who might need help would not in fact use it, leading to an advertising campaign to promote access to the new services. In practice, however, service use did not decline but increased, and in a report on NHS costs by the Guillebaud Committee in 1956 it was suggested that more funding was required to meet service plans. Spending on the NHS did rise in the latter half of the twentieth century, both in absolute terms and as a proportion of GDP; and in the new century, as we shall see, it is set to rise even more (see Figure 4.1).

The principles of the NHS have remained largely intact since its introduction in 1948, and the scope of the service has gradually increased. At the organisational level, however, there has been significant, and frequent, change. The original structure of the NHS separated provision into three parts: the executive councils (administering GPs, dentists, and such like), the hospital boards (managing hospitals) and the local authorities (responsible for environmental health, health visitors, ambulances and other personal services), each responsible

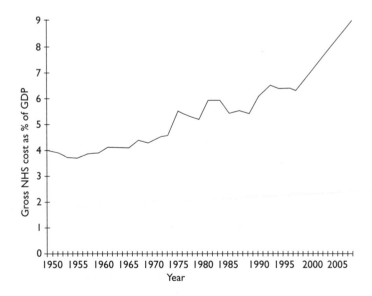

Figure 4.1   Cost of NHS as percentage of GDP
Sources: Ham, 1999 Figure 4.1, p.74; and HM Treasury.

directly to the government ministry. This tripartite structure lasted until 1974, when reform was introduced in an attempt to provide a more coordinated focus for planning and delivery. This led to the establishment of Regional Health Authorities, Area Health Authorities and District Management Teams with responsibility for all health services, except that GPs remained outside the area authorities under separate Family Practitioner Committees, and some environmental and personal services remained with local authorities.

This structure was more coordinated, though still diffuse; but it was also more cumbersome. And in 1982 further reorganisation was introduced in effect to remove the area authorities and promote District Health Authorities as the major administrative units, but with Family Practitioner Committees still separate and now responsible directly to the Department of Health and Social Security (DHSS), as it was then called. This structure applied to England only, however, with different changes made in Wales, Scotland and Northern Ireland; and these national differences have become more marked since.

The 1980s did not just see structural changes to the NHS. There was a concern amongst some analysts that the radical, anti-public welfare, policies of the Thatcher governments would lead to a complete dismantling of the national service; and some New Right protagonists, such as the Adam Smith Institute, were proposing replacing the universal public service with private insurance for health care. However, the Conservative government won the 1983 election claiming that the NHS was 'safe in our hands', and showed no inclination to move away in practice from the principles of a universal free service. Where change did take place was in the management of NHS services.

In public services generally the 1980s was a period of the increasing influence of what came to be called the 'New Public Management' (see Chapter 18), and in the NHS this new ethos of managerialism was strongly felt. This meant increasing efficiency and making the NHS more businesslike, through target setting and budget planning. It also meant, following the recommendations of a report in 1983 by Roy Griffiths (the managing director of Sainsbury's), the appointment of specialist managers throughout the service to take over from medical professionals as the key decision makers over service development and delivery. This was a significant practical change, for the professional autonomy that medical professionals (particularly doctors) had enjoyed before this had in practice extended to administrative control (or lack of it, critics argued) over NHS services. And now this control largely passed to non-medical managers, who, it was argued, could develop a more coordinated response to the different needs of patients.

The other change which the Thatcher governments promoted was more open support for private health care as an alternative to NHS provision. As we shall see, private health provision has always operated alongside the universal NHS, albeit only appealing to a small minority of patients. In the 1980s the support for choice through market competition as a means of improving the user accountability of services meant that it received formal endorsement, and patronage, by government ministers. Private markets could never provide choice or accountability for most NHS users of course; but in the late 1980s the government began to turn towards a different means of achieving this goal. An American academic, Enthoven (1985), had suggested that markets of a kind could be created within health services by encouraging service providers to compete with each other for patients, thereby driving up standards and accountability (in theory at least). In a White Paper entitled *Working for Patients*, published in 1989 by the DoH (now separate from social security), the new Secretary of State for Health, Kenneth Clarke, proposed the establishment of such a *quasi-market* within the NHS.

These changes were incorporated into the NHS and Community Care Act 1990, which made some similar changes to social services (see Chapter 6) and was part of a more general shift towards the marketisation of public services discussed in Chapter 9. Once again this led to a restructuring of the NHS, now to represent the distinction between the purchasers and the providers of services. The *purchasers* were the District Health Authorities and Family Health Services, managed by the Regional Health Authorities; although provision was also made for GP practices to opt out of these structures and become fundholders, receiving a budget (based on patient registrations) with which they could contract directly with providers. The *providers* were the NHS trusts, now quasi-independent bodies managing acute services (the hospitals) or providing ambulance services or community health. The idea was that contracts for specific treatments for individual patients would focus service delivery on to user needs; but in practice such an individualistic approach was quite unworkable and more generic 'service agreements' were reached between the two different wings of the service, which in some cases largely replicated existing practices and provisions.

In practice, too, the implementation of the internal market and the associated organisational changes was a gradual one, with NHS trusts and GP fundholders increasing more and more rapidly on a cumulative basis from 1991 to 1996. This led some critics to suggest that policy was in effect emerging from practice rather than establishing the basis for this, leading to uncertainties for both providers and users (see Ham, 1999, pp.39–45). There were other criticisms, too: in particular, the claim that the internal market in practice gave even more power to health service managers, and that, far from improving efficiency, much time (and money) was being taken up in the technical processing of budgets, contracts and agreements.

Some of the criticisms of the internal market reforms had come from the Labour Party whilst in opposition; and when they were returned to power in 1997 there was some expectation that the changes might be reversed. In practice, however, the Labour government embraced many of the features of the reforms, particularly at the organisational level, and no radical upheaval took place. However, the new government did make some significant changes, in particular the removal of the GP fundholder scheme. They then went on to make further major alterations to organisational structures, and to health policy planning more generally. Indeed by the 2001 election the NHS had become the major priority in political debate and public expenditure planning.

QUESTIONS: COMPREHENSION

- Why is the NHS sometimes referred to as a national *illness* service?
- Why do health inequalities persist despite the establishment of a universal health service?
- To what extent has the introduction of professional managers and the division between purchasers and providers resulted in improvements in health service delivery?

QUESTION: REFLECTION

- Are health inequalities a problem only for the NHS?

Shifting the balance of power

The 1997 election was not followed by any rapid reform of health policy therefore; and the government's commitment to remain within the public spending limits set by the previous administration for the first two years of office meant that few additional resources would be available to support any significant changes. Nevertheless in December 1997 a White Paper was published, called *The New NHS* (DoH, 1997). This outlined six principles behind the government's plans, including the setting of national standards, commitment to partnership working and rebuilding public confidence in the health service. It stated that there would be no return to the centralised bureaucracy of the past and no continuation of the divisive market systems of the 1990s, but rather, as in all other areas of social policy, a 'third way' based on partnership and performance.

As in other areas of social policy it was not at all obvious, initially at least, what this new 'Third Way' approach implied for the NHS. It did include the withdrawal of the GP fundholder scheme; but these were replaced with primary care groups (PCGs), which were effectively larger groups of GP practices serving a local population of up to around 250,000. The PCGs were responsible to their district health authorities, who became the key planning agencies determining the needs for health services in their district, distributing resources to PCGs and entering into agreements with the provider trusts. The idea was that this would lead to a strategic approach to the identification of needs and the planning of service provision, captured in a Health Improvement Programme (HImP) to be drawn up by each health authority in partnership with other relevant local interests.

These changes were intended to move health service provision towards a planning process focused more directly on user needs and national standards, delivered through strategic planning and partnership working, although the division between the purchasers and providers of services remained. The partnership working meant in particular that health authorities would need to work more closely with local authorities, especially in the area of social care planning and delivery, although this did not always work out straight away in practice, as the bed-blocking crises (discussed in Chapter 6) revealed. The strategic planning process was intended to result in health services moving towards a more primary care led approach to the identification of need and the provision of services. This was achieved in part by the permitting of some PCGs to move up to primary care trust (PCT) status, becoming independent of health authorities and offering the full range of services (including community nursing, dentistry and so on) short of acute hospital care, with devolved financial responsibility for NHS budget planning.

By 2002 there were over 160 PCTs and this new primary care focus received further impetus with the full implementation in April that year of *The NHS Plan* (DoH, 2000), which resulted in yet further restructuring of health service agencies. The plan was described by the government as shifting the balance of power away from central government and towards front-line service staff. In practice what it meant was the abolition of the 95 local health authorities and their replacement as the major planning and service delivery agencies with 315 PCTs, incorporating the (by then) 480 PCGs across England. The regional offices were also disbanded, with four regional officers working from within the DoH, and more general regional strategic planning devolved to 28 strategic health authorities collectively covering the whole of England.

Health is another area where policy powers have been devolved to the new administrations, however; and significantly different structural patterns are now developing within the health services in Scotland, Wales and Northern Ireland. In Scotland the NHS Trust boards have been absorbed into Health Boards. In Wales new Local Health Boards, coterminous with the 22 local authorities, have been established. And in Northern Ireland health services are administered alongside social services (elsewhere these are separate: see Chapter 6) by four joint boards and 15 joint trusts (Woods, 2002).

In all areas, however, there has been a significant shift towards a primary-care-led approach to health service delivery, with the new PCTs in England expected to be responsible for 75 per cent of the NHS budget, some £40 billion, by 2004 (compared to the old GP fundholders who controlled just 15 per cent). Alongside the organisational changes were other moves to reinforce service quality which did not depend on the professional self-regulation of the old NHS or the managerialism of the 1980s. These included the establishment of a National Institute for Clinical Excellence (NICE) and national service frameworks setting standards for service delivery, including the waiting times for operations; and the creation of a Commission for Health Improvement to monitor operational practice. In between the two *clinical governance*, the marrying of local trust accountability for service quality with clinical involvement in service development, would aim to ensure that quality services were delivered in practice. This also linked in with more general government concerns to promote evidence-based improvements in public services (the 'what counts is what works' approach) and to make local accountability for service delivery transparent (and competitive) through the publishing of performance against standards, so that (as in education) league tables of achievement could in effect be compiled.

Although the principle underlying these changes, in theory at least, was to transfer operational management and responsibility to service delivery agencies via the notion of clinical governance, in practice both policy goals and performance targets under Labour were set by central government. In the late 1990s, following the publication of the Acheson Report, there was an explicit policy focus upon health inequalities. However, in their 1997 manifesto Labour had made a high-profile pledge to reduce hospital waiting lists, and after 2000 the focus of policy planning began to centre more directly on service delivery targets, although this was less emphatic in the devolved administrations in Scotland and Wales. These targets included reducing waiting lists, and waiting times, although measuring these is a complex process and the achievements made were contentious. They also included specific commitments to reduce the death rate and prevalence of illness from heart disease, cancer and mental health, and to cut accidents by at least one-fifth, by 2010.

Service delivery improvements do not just involve reductions in serious illness, however: there are also more general issues of the relationships between NHS and service users. In the early 1990s the Major governments had developed the Patient's Charter as a means of establishing, and enforcing, standards of service access and response. This initiative was in practice continued by Labour, and extended to cover other innovative forms of service response, notably *NHS Direct*, a nurse-led telephone helpline and advice service. The Health Action Zones also provided a vehicle for the development of innovative and collaborative service development to identify and meet health needs in selected deprived areas. The HAZs were an example of a more 'bottom-up' approach to policy planning, and in their four years of operation they were relatively successful in developing a wide range of new service initiatives aimed at tackling local issues which had not always been addressed by more traditional agencies, although after 2003 these activities were 'mainstreamed' into PCT provision.

QUESTIONS: COMPREHENSION

■ Why have PCTs replaced health authorities as the major organisational focus of health service delivery in England?
■ What is 'clinical governance', and how is it intended to lead to improved quality in health service delivery?

QUESTION: REFLECTION

■ What are the advantages and disadvantages of a primary-care-led NHS?

Health service funding

Over the last two decades in particular, therefore, there have been significant, and ongoing, changes in the organisational structure of the health service in the UK. This has created upheaval and concern for many working within the NHS, and it may also have engendered some confusion amongst users and citizens more generally. Despite the organisational changes, however, the basic principle of a publicly funded service free at the point of delivery has remained intact, and indeed has been reaffirmed by politicians and policy makers of all complexions. For many citizens this constancy may in practice be more impor- tant than the organisational shifts; what matters to most people is whether the health service is there when they need it. However, the ability of the NHS to meet all potential health needs has always been limited in practice. As we said earlier, to some extent the delivery of health services is a process of rationing.

At the beginning of the twenty-first century this rationing process came into sharp focus in political and policy debate. In part this was a product of the gov- ernment's pledges to reduce waiting lists and improve service standards and accountability. What these commitments revealed was that targets could not readily by met, primarily because resources within the NHS were too stretched. Despite the gradual increases in NHS expenditure over the latter part of the twentieth century revealed in Figure 4.1, critics (and health service staff) began to argue that spending levels were too low. This issue was compounded by the two-year moratorium on public expenditure expansion adopted by Labour after 1997; and, in the Comprehensive Spending Review (CSR) that they undertook to plan for public spending over the ensuing three years, a clear commitment was made to increase NHS spending by £21 billion up to 2002, an annual increase of 4.7 per cent in real terms and the largest increase of any area of public spending.

This was a significant acceleration of support for the NHS and it contrasted sharply with the constrained approach to public spending which had dominated social policy planning in the 1980s and 1990s, with public spending on the NHS falling by 0.1 per cent in 1996–97 before Labour took office. It did not prevent the issue of health service delivery, or non-delivery, becoming the major issue in the 2001 general election, however, with the Prime Minister being famously harangued on camera by the irate partner of a heart patient outside a Birmingham hospital. Further commitments to expand expenditure were there- fore made after the election, with the opposition parties agreeing that more improvements were needed and more resources would have to be found.

As a result expansion of NHS expenditure was a key feature of the 2002 budget and the second CSR, with a commitment from government to increase spending by £40 billion over the following five years across the UK, with much of the expenditure going on the training and recruitment of more doctors, nurses and other professionals. This was a massive increase, as can be seen from Table 4.2. It will mean an annual increase in real terms of 7.4 per cent and will take the proportion of GDP spent on the health service from below to above average EU expenditure levels. And it is to be paid for, in part, by a 1 per cent increase in NI contributions from April 2003, the first major increase in direct taxation by the Labour government since 1997.

Table 4.2   NHS expenditure in the UK (2002/03 prices)

	1996–97	2001–02	2002–03	2003–04	2004–05	2005–06	2006–07	2007–08
Total expenditure (£ billion)	42	59	68	73	78	85	96	106
Percentage of GDP	6	7	7.7	8	8.3	8.7	9	9.4

Source: HM Treasury.

Whether these increases will meet both the increasing demands on and expectations of health service agencies is far from certain, however. Indeed, at the time they were announced in April 2002, Derek Wanless produced a report commissioned by the Treasury outlining the factors likely to impact on health service funding over the next 20 years, to 2022 (Wanless Report, 2002). The report identified a range of factors likely to affect the demand for resources for the NHS, including demographic changes and health needs, rising expectations of citizens and continuing advances in new technologies, and it argued that these should lead to very substantial further increases in funding of up to £154 billion (10–11 per cent of GDP) by 2022.

Important though public funding for health services is, however, it is not the only source of funding for the NHS. As we can see from Figure 4.2, a significant contribution still comes from NI contributions, although this is in effect a form of taxation and is off-set against income from general taxation. There are also investment receipts and income from charges.

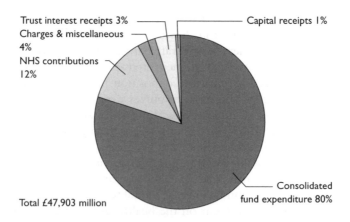

Trust interest receipts 3%
Charges & miscellaneous 4%
NHS contributions 12%
Capital receipts 1%
Consolidated fund expenditure 80%
Total £47,903 million

Figure 4.2   NHS sources of finance, 2000–01
Source: DoH (2002a), Figure 3.11.

Charges have always occupied something of a controversial role within the NHS, not surprisingly perhaps given that it was designed in principle as a free service. Charges were first introduced for prescribed medicines and some aspects of optical and dental provision as early as 1951, prompting the resignation from the Labour government of Bevan, the architect of the 1948 reforms. Since then the levels of prescription charges have increased, most notably in the 1980s; and charging for optical and dental care has been expanded, with the effect that the income from charges now comprises a significant, if minor, aspect of NHS funding. The increased scope and scale of charges has also led to the need to exempt those on low incomes and other groups, such as pensioners and children, from payment in order to ensure that cost of treatment does not deter them from seeking help. This has introduced an element of means-testing and targeting into the (supposedly) universal health service, increasing the complexity of administration in some areas; although, because of the exemptions, most NHS patients do not in fact pay the charges.

Private resources have been brought into the NHS in a number of other rather different ways in more recent times, too, through a range of measures to encourage private investment in some aspects of health care. In the 1980s hospitals were required to put catering, domestic and laundry services out to tender so that private contractors could take over these services if they met required criteria; and in a number of areas this led to a transfer of provision into private hands. More recently NHS trusts have been encouraged to seek out private investment in joint capital programmes under the private finance initiative (PFI). Shortly before the 2001 election the DoH announced a major programme of new hospital building to be financed in part by such joint PFI funding.

Despite these developments, however, the role of private funding within the NHS remains small. So, too, does the level of private spending and investment in health service provision outside the national service, at least when compared to some other advanced countries, notably the USA. Nevertheless private provision for health care does exist in the UK, and has retained a significant role despite the development of a universal free service. In total, private health spending accounts for around 15 per cent of health expenditure in the UK (Ham, 1999, p.74). Around 7 million people (1 in 8 of the population) have private health insurance; and this proportion has been growing significantly over the last two decades.

Private health care can be provided in separate private hospitals employing their own staff and medical professionals; however, it can also be provided within NHS trusts, with separate beds or sections set aside for paying customers. Private patients can pay for additional services, such as their own room and television, but they can also in effect pay for accelerated (and perhaps superior) treatment. It is this issue in particular which has caused some controversy in recent times, with private patients being in effect able to jump the waiting list queue, and private care being marketed as able to do just that. Of course, private medical treatment can be extremely expensive and the vast majority of people could never afford to pay the necessary fees and charges. This is a significant problem in countries, such as the USA, where there is no universal public service, and there a means-tested (Medicaid) system provides a safety-net service for the very poor. In general, therefore, private health care is provided through private insurance companies, with members paying a regular subscription which buys the care they need when they need it (which is how most health care in the USA is financed).

In the UK there are a number of private health insurance schemes, the most well known being that provided by the British United Provident Association (BUPA). The problem with much of this insurance provision, however, is that, in order to keep contributions down (and attract custom), the range of services provided is often limited, with the most extensive and expensive hospital treatment often not included. There is also an incentive for insurance providers to seek to attract only those least likely to make heavy demands on the scheme, so that the chronically sick and other groups in need are sometimes excluded (this is referred to by economists as 'cream-skimming'). In short, therefore, private health insurance does not in practice always deliver a comprehensive service, and in the UK even those with insurance also rely on the NHS.

Private health care is supported by the NHS in another sense too. This is because the doctors, nurses and other staff who treat private patients and work in private hospitals have by and large been trained and gained experience within the NHS. A private health care system in the UK which had to train and support all its professional staff could not survive with current rates of investment. However, since the concern over NHS waiting times became accentuated after 2001, there has been something of a reversal of relationships here, with NHS trusts sometimes buying places in private hospitals to secure urgent treatment for seriously ill patients who could not be found beds in NHS hospitals.

This was presented as a temporary measure by health ministers, but it presaged a new turn in relations between public and private health care in the country. The exploration of further collaboration between the public and private sectors was explicitly endorsed in the Wanless Report (2002, ch.7); and it is, of course, well established in the area of social care, as we discuss in Chapter 6. It is clear therefore that the 'Third Way' approach to policy planning pursued by the Labour government at the beginning of the new century does embrace recognition of the mixed economy of provision in the health field, as in other areas of social policy. The joint funding initiatives and the use of NHS funds to purchase private care mean that public and private investment is now to some extent within a joint planning framework; and if the spread of private health insurance continues the balance between the sectors could alter further still in the future.

Thus the development of the NHS is entering a new era in the early decades of the twenty-first century. The containment of public expenditure on health in the 1990s is now challenged by a new consensus on the need for expansion, even to meet existing and predicted demands and developments. Health services also have a high profile politically. The government has set targets and will be required to deliver on these; and so the new resources provided for the NHS will be expected to lead to service improvements, most obviously in waiting lists, but more generally across both primary and acute services.

QUESTIONS: COMPREHENSION

- Why is it argued that additional expenditure on the NHS will be needed over the next two decades, and what has been the government's response to this?
- How is private investment in the NHS intended to help the development and delivery of public health services?
- Why have waiting list targets become such an important feature of NHS policy planning?

QUESTION: REFLECTION

- To what extent is health service provision rationed? Could we, and should we, aim to remove such rationing?

FURTHER READING

The best general text on the history and development of health services in the UK is Ham (1999). Klein's (2001) book on the policy and politics of the NHS is a useful guide to the broader context of provision, and Baggott (2000) looks at the current public health dimension of these. Baggott's (2002) text contains extensive coverage of current provision and Wall and Owen (2002) provide a useful summary. Government documents can be found on the Departmental website at **www.doh.gov.uk**, with the devolved administration websites providing similar services here (see Chapter 15). Another useful website is the King's Fund **www.kingsfund.org.uk**.

Housing

5

SUMMARY OF KEY POINTS

- Housing policy aims to balance private housing markets against public housing needs.
- Fluctuations in the supply of and demand for housing have strongly influenced the development of housing policy, leading to major shifts in policy over the course of the last century.
- Housing provision is structured by the existence of *tenure* divisions. There are now four different sectors of provision: owner-occupation, public renting, private renting and renting from registered social landlords.
- Exploitation of private renting by landlords set the scene for the development of housing policy in the last century.
- At the end of the First World War government accepted responsibility for providing homes for all households requiring adequate housing.
- Owner-occupation began to increase once *mortgages* became available to help people to buy their own homes, becoming the major tenure in the latter half of the last century.
- Public rented housing expanded rapidly after the Second World War, but since then it has declined within individual tenants having the 'right to buy' their homes after 1980 and whole estates having the right to transfer out of the public sector after 1988.
- Rent levels in both private and public sectors have risen in recent decades, with poor tenants entitled to a means-tested subsidy through housing benefit. The cost of this has been rising significantly and is currently under review.
- The Labour government has embraced a 'mixed economy' approach to housing provision with support for both public and private provision.
- Certain categories of homeless people have a statutory right to public housing.
- Current housing policy initiatives are frequently focused upon districts or neighbourhoods experiencing acute housing (and social) problems.

Houses or homes?

Having a home is a basic human need; we all need somewhere to live. For those people within society without a home life is barely tolerable, and for a society (especially a modern welfare state) a continuing problem of homelessness is an indictment of the ability of that society to meet the welfare needs of all of its citizens. Yet homelessness remains a significant problem in affluent, welfare, Britain at the beginning of the twenty-first century, with hundreds of people sleeping rough on the streets of towns and cities every night because they do not have a home of their own to go to. In general terms the study of housing policy is the study of the ways in which this need for housing is met within society; and, in one important sense therefore, this is a study of policy failure in modern Britain (though the same is true of most other advanced industrial nations too).

We will return to look at some of the specific, and more recent, policies designed to respond to the problem of homelessness later. However, more general policy intervention to seek to control the availability of (and access to) housing has been a feature of social policy for over a century, and one which has occupied a critical, and fluctuating, role within public policy debate. Indeed, it is probably fair to say that over the last hundred years or so policy change has been more marked in the area of housing than in any of other major areas of social policy discussed in this book. This has led to critics sometimes suggesting that housing has been like a 'policy football', first kicked one way and then the next, although, if the analogy holds, it is a game in which there have been a few 'own goals' scored. Nevertheless housing policy has influenced the structure and operation of housing provision, and the role of public investment and public regulation have been central in this.

The provision of housing is not just the result of public policy action, however, for housing is not only about homes, it is also about markets. Houses are provided as commodities within a market, within which the principles of supply and demand operate to determine who owns houses, who buys them and how much they cost. Actually ownership of houses is a rather complex legal and economic issue. Technically, as lawyers will point out, ownership rights apply to land rather than buildings (though in practice, of course, the two are inseparable), and, more significantly, these rights may be held outright (freehold) or shared (leasehold). The existence of leases means that the (freehold) owner of a house can rent (lease) it out to someone else in return for payment. The effect of this, in simple terms, is to create two different sorts of housing provision, generally referred to as different housing *tenures*.

- Owner-occupied housing is where the house is bought for a capital sum from the builder or from a previous occupier.
- Rented housing is where the house is leased from an owner, who retains a legal interest in it and collects rent payments from the occupier.

Markets for housing have operated across both these different tenure divisions. Going back to the nineteenth century the rich aristocracy and new middle classes would live in houses that they owned, generally built for them in grand style by renowned architects. These houses were expensive to build, they were generally solid and well-proportioned, and many can still be seen today in the countryside and the posher parts of towns. For the vast majority of people, however, buying or building their own home was financially impossible, and so in practice most people lived in houses which they rented from someone else.

The massive population growths and shifts which accompanied the Industrial Revolution in the nineteenth century meant that those (few) people who did own the land in the new urban conglomerations could exploit this by building houses to rent to the new working classes. This private rented housing market grew rapidly in the latter part of the century; and, although it meant that houses were provided for the workers, it resulted in high levels of exploitation by the (rentier) landlords who provided them. Most of the housing that was built for rent was small, insanitary and of poor quality; and many poorer families did not rent a whole house, but rather had to manage in one or two rooms. Homes were not the same things as houses, and nineteenth-century rented houses were generally overcrowded.

At the beginning of the twentieth century, therefore, it was clear that the private market in rented housing had not provided adequate homes for all people, and much of the history of housing policy in the twentieth century is the story of how public policy sought to intervene to regulate the private market and to provide alternatives to it, as we shall discuss below. This led to a relative decline in the size of the private rented market and the growth of publicly owned houses to rent, thus dividing the rented housing sector in two. The other major development in housing provision in the twentieth century was the development of a new market in the building and sale of owner-occupied housing. This was made possible, as we shall see shortly, by the spread of mortgages, which allowed people to borrow the capital sum needed to buy a house; this meant that land owners could exploit their property by building houses for sale, rather than rent, thus ensuring a more rapid and more secure return on their capital investment.

Housing markets have therefore been structured by tenure divisions. But they have been driven, as are all markets, by the profit motive since those who own houses (or land) have sought to profit from their holdings; consequently they have not necessarily responded to housing needs. Social policy has sought to respond to such needs; but it has had to do so through intervening in, or providing an alternative to, that private market. Housing policy in practice therefore has been about the relationship between the operations of private markets and the meeting of public needs; and, as we shall see, this has been a relationship of fluctuating fortunes and priorities.

The outcome of this policy change has been a significant shift in the balance of provision across the different tenure types. As can be seen from Table 5.1, over the last century there was a decline in the role of private rented housing and a rise in the role of owner-occupied housing, with public rented housing experiencing a rise, and then fall, in prominence.

These variations in housing policy and practice have left a legacy of a changing balance between private markets and public provision. However, past changes in housing provision leave another kind of legacy to the present

Table 5.1   Changes in distribution of housing tenure in Britain, 1914–2000 (percentages)

	Owner-occupied	Public rented	Private rented	Social rented*
1914	10	0		90
1951	31	17		52
1971	49	31	15	1
1981	54	34	8	2
2000	68	16	10	6

* Social rented are Housing Association lets (see below) not separately recorded before 1971; other categories mean not all rows total 100.
Sources: Adapted from Office for National Statistics (2002), Table 4.1; and Malpass and Murie (1999), Table 1.1.

because, by and large, the houses that were built to rent or to sell over the past hundred years or so are still with us. Unlike most other commodities houses generally are built to last, and today's houses are those that have been left to us by yesterday's builders and owners; it is a cumulative legacy. A walk around any city or town will reveal the different types and ages of housing currently in use, and indirectly will tell us much about how and why it was developed when it was.

Much of current housing is actually quite old. Approximately 40 per cent was built before 1945 and 86 per cent before 1984 (Department of Transport, Local Government and the Regions, or DTLR, 2002). But this legacy of old housing is something of a mixed blessing. Some old houses are lavishly sized and proportioned and, especially where they have been renovated or modernised, provide some of the most desirable and expensive housing around. Some were built cheaply and were sparsely equipped, however, especially those initially built to rent, and since then have fallen into further disrepair; these now constitute some of the poorest quality housing on the market. As a result of this some older houses are unfit for human habitation under the 1989 Local Government and Housing Act (around 1.5 million, 7.5 per cent, in 1996), or are lacking a basic amenity such as a bathroom or indoor toilet (around 200,000, or 1 per cent, in 1996: DTLR, 2002). The quality of the housing stock is a significant issue for policy makers; and, as a result of some of the improvement initiatives discussed later, the numbers of poor quality homes have been declining in recent decades, although many remain across all sectors.

Whatever the quality of it, however, for most people their home is a house: 82 per cent of households live in houses (DTLR, 2002). But not all do; around 15 per cent live in flats and 2 per cent in bedsits or other shared accommodation. In some housing sectors these proportions are higher: in particular, large numbers of public rented homes are in blocks of flats, built mainly in the latter part of the twentieth century as a replacement for poor quality private rented houses. Some of these flats are themselves of poor quality and in need of repair, and some have even been demolished. But not all flats are low quality; indeed, in the early twenty-first century high-quality flats newly built in the centre of big cities such as London, Birmingham and Manchester have become an expensive and highly desirable form of housing.

As we saw at the beginning of this chapter, housing policy is concerned with the ways in which societies meet the needs for homes of their citizens (or do not). In general this is about balancing the supply of houses in the market with the demands for homes by households; and over the course of the past hundred years this balance has fluctuated between a broad surplus of houses over households and a broad surplus of households over houses, with consequent changes in pressures on policy development and delivery. Measuring both the supply of and the demand for houses is complicated, however; and so all calculations are to some extent necessarily crude approximations of the real relationships which citizens experience in their search for a home.

Supply

Supply of houses is affected by both the quantity and the quality of houses. In the early part of the last century there were large numbers of rented houses in Britain's urban centres, but many of them were of poor quality. Throughout most of the rest of the century most of these 'slums' have been demolished and replaced with other dwellings, and those that remain have been 'improved' to make them more habitable. At the end of the First World War the poor quality of much of this housing was a key policy issue in early development of public housing policy, captured by the slogan about the need to build new 'homes for heroes', for those returning from the war. At this time supply was mainly about *quality*, therefore. During the Second World War, however, all house building was stopped and as a result of enemy bombing 450,000 houses were destroyed and 3 million damaged. After the war therefore there was a shortage in the *quantity* of houses (and a shortage of building materials, too, at first), which led to the largest building programme ever undertaken in the country.

The relatively large numbers of houses built in the decades following the Second World War meant that towards the end of the last century there was calculated to be a crude surplus of houses across the country, although there was a geographical dimension to this apparent surplus, because not all of the empty houses were in places where people most needed them: for instance, there were empty houses in some of the declining industrial cities in Scotland and the North and yet shortages in the rapidly developing towns and villages of the South East. Economic changes in the latter part of the twentieth century meant that workers increasingly had to be mobile and move to areas where new jobs were being created. But houses do not move with the workers, with the result that shortages (and therefore markets) have become increasingly geographically differentiated, with the supply of housing becoming an acute problem in the South East of England.

Demand

At the beginning of the twenty-first century the overall surplus of houses has been challenged by changes in the nature of the demand for houses, due to demographic and cultural changes in the nature of household composition. In the new century people are living longer and thus there are more elderly households, often composed of a single elderly person; young people are also leaving their parents' home sooner and living as single persons or childless couples for longer; and more married couples are separating or divorcing, dividing what was one household into two. All of these, and other related changes such as immigration patterns, have increased the need for houses and so affected the overall balance between supply and demand, with around 3.8 million new households estimated to be looking for housing in 2021 compared with 1999 (DTLR, 2002). And they have also altered the nature of demands, with more small households looking for smaller houses and flats in particular areas, where employment prospects and local services are best.

These changes in demand and supply are the major factors influencing the housing market: for instance, they are driving up the prices of houses to buy or to rent in those areas where prospects are good and large numbers of people want to live (sometimes now referred to as 'hotspots'), and leading to low demand and empty houses in other areas (often those with other significant social and economic problems). They are also the issues that most concern policy makers as they seek to ensure that housing is available for those who need it, at prices that they can afford to pay. And it is the price, and the cost, of housing that is one of the most important concerns for both citizens and government.

QUESTIONS: COMPREHENSION

■ What have been the main changes in tenure division over the last hundred years?
■ To what extent did the existence of a surplus of houses at the end of the last century mean that housing problems had been solved?

QUESTION: REFLECTION

■ Should we be concerned about the growing domination of owner-occupation in the provision of housing?

Paying for housing

The cost of housing is determined by two factors: the initial cost of building and maintaining the property (sometimes referred to as 'bricks and mortar' costs) and the tenure costs of renting or purchasing the property from the legal owner. The cost of building a new house is significant and more than all those except the very rich could afford. Few people are able to have houses built for them therefore. Once it has been built, however, the cost of maintaining a house is relatively small, especially if it has been well built; and, as houses can last for a long time (hundreds of years in many cases), then these costs decline in relative significance over time. To put this another way, capital spending on house building can provide a long-term return on investment: for individuals the investment provides them with a home (potentially) for life, and for governments or private speculators the investment provides an asset that can be rented or sold to recoup building costs.

Rents

As most people cannot afford to build their own houses, it is the way in which the owners (governments, companies or private individuals) seek to recover their costs (or make a profit) that in practice determines what people will have to pay to get access to housing. Private and public landlords will want to recoup their capital investment (sometimes called the historic cost) and the cost of maintenance and repair through rent payments; but private landlords in particular also expect to make a profit from their position. Over time the size of this profit, and hence the size of the rent charged, is likely to be determined more by the market demand for housing than the cost of building or repair. In a market of short supply rents will go up; and this is just what happened at the beginning of the last century. For publicly owned and rented houses, mainly built by local authorities in the UK, the profit motive does not apply; however, as we shall see, there has been pressure at different times to raise rents in the public sector too beyond the historic cost of the houses to match (more or less) those in the private market.

One of the main problems with rising rents is the fear that many would-be tenants may not be able to afford to pay them. In the early part of the last century this led to attempts to control private rent levels through legal regulation, as we discuss below. It also led to government giving subsidies to public housing authorities either to reduce the historic cost of building houses (capital subsidies) or to reduce the costs of managing and maintaining them (revenue subsidies). These subsidies were critically important for the development of publicly rented housing by local authorities; and, particularly after the Second World War, they led to a gradual increase in overall public expenditure on housing. Towards the end of the twentieth century, however, rent controls and public subsidies towards the cost of providing houses were abandoned and replaced by means-tested support for poor tenants unable to meet the full market costs of their rents, through a social security payment called housing benefit.

Housing benefit is administered by local authorities, unlike most of the other social security benefits discussed in Chapter 2. This is partly because it was based upon the rent rebates initially developed by local authorities to subsidise the costs of rents in the houses that they rented to poor tenants. Rent rebates were a way of ensuring that all tenants could meet the costs of even relatively high rents, so that public landlords could set rent levels without recourse to concern over tenants' ability to pay. They were first introduced by some authorities in the 1940s, and their use expanded in the 1960s. In 1972 the provision of such means-tested subsidies was made a statutory requirement by the Housing Finance Act, at the same time as local authorities were required to raise all their rents to market levels. At this time rebates (or allowances) were also extended to poor tenants in the private sector, for the first time providing some element of subsidy to tenants (and landlords) here.

In 1982 the old system of rebates and allowances was replaced by a single housing benefit scheme, providing a full, 100 per cent, rent subsidy for those on income support and a contribution towards rent costs for those on low wages, tapering off as wages rose so that those with the highest rents and lowest wages received most. After 1982 central government also reduced the subsidies paid to local authorities for the costs of building and maintaining rented houses and prevented authorities from subsidising rents from the local rates or council tax. This resulted in an increase in rent levels in the sector as many authorities had been seeking to keep rents down through subsidies to their housing accounts. At the same time rent controls in the private rented sector were largely removed, leading to rent rises here too. The effect of these changes was to increase the cost of housing benefit, compounded by the increased numbers of people entitled to benefit anyway due to rises in unemployment and low wages.

By the mid-1990s the general subsidy to local authorities for the cost of maintaining rented housing had been removed altogether, apparently reducing public expenditure on housing; but the annual cost of housing benefit had risen to around £12 billion (Malpass and Murie, 1999, p.93). This was evidence of a continuing increase in public expenditure on housing, despite government claims at the time that expenditure should be reduced; but also of a massive shift in the nature of the expenditure from subsidising 'bricks and mortar' to subsidising poor tenants. The high cost of housing benefit, and the problems caused by subsidising poor tenants in this way, are now major issues for government policy makers, and the Labour government has instituted an (as yet unresolved) review of policy in the area. One of the consequences of such indirect subsidies, of course, is to fuel yet further increases in market rents, since poor tenants are shielded from their worst effects. Some attempt has been made to control this by imposing a ceiling on the level of rent for which housing benefit will be paid; but this has penalised some tenants without controlling rent rises, and has been criticised by independent researchers (see Kemp, Wilcox and Rhodes, 2002). Housing benefit thus remains the main way in which rent costs are subsidised through public housing policy at the beginning of the new century, although most commentators are in agreement that it is in desperate need of reform.

Mortgages

As we have seen, owner-occupied housing has gradually replaced rented housing as the majority tenure form over the course of the last century. In part this is because of the problems associated with rising rent levels and concern over the extent of public subsidies to tenants, but in part it is also because other changes in housing finance have made the purchase and sale of properties accessible to a wider range of the population. The main barrier to buying a house is the capital cost of purchase; this is the case with new houses being sold by builders and with older houses for which their current owners expect to receive a market price. Most people will never have enough money to pay such a capital sum. However, during the early part of the twentieth century a legal mechanism was developed to permit people to borrow such a large sum and repay it gradually over a long period of time.

This legal mechanism is the mortgage. In simple terms the mortgage is a loan of a capital sum which is repaid, with interest, over a period of (usually) 20 or 25 years. Normally such loans would be too risky for lenders (what happens if changing events mean that the borrower cannot repay?), but in the case of mortgages the house which is purchased is pledged as security for the loan so that, if the borrower does default, the lender can repossess the house and sell it to recoup the unpaid loan. For the lender therefore the risk is removed, provided of course that the loan is not for more than the market value of the house. For the borrower a sum large enough to buy a house can be borrowed and repaid over a long period, albeit with much added interest and dependent upon being able to keep up the monthly payments.

It was not just the existence of mortgages which promoted owner-occupation in the last century, however (indeed, the legal device is an old one); it was also the growth of new financial institutions who were willing and able to lend money to buyers on these terms. These were the *building societies*. They were initially set up as mutual investment and lending organisations which were 'owned' by the *borrowers*, who repaid their mortgages and interest, and the *investors*, who deposited sums of money in return for interest payments on them. For some time these building societies were rather conservative bodies, who would only lend on mortgages to buyers in secure and well-paid employment who were purchasing homes at reasonable prices in safe sections of the market: for instance, some operated 'red-lining' policies and refused to grant mortgages on properties in areas (often inner cities) marked by red lines drawn on local maps. However, in the 1980s, after some legislative restrictions on the granting and servicing of loans were removed by government, banks began to compete with building societies to grant mortgages, and building societies then became less restrictive (indeed later many converted into banks, dropping their mutual status) and in effect control over mortgage lending disappeared, so that most people who wanted to borrow to buy were able to do so.

The wider availability of mortgages therefore underpinned the massive growth in owner-occupation which was experienced in the twentieth century. This was further fuelled, however, by the granting of tax relief for the interest element of mortgage repayments. Mortgage interest tax relief meant that those earning enough to pay tax would have their tax bill reduced by the amount of mortgage interest they paid. It was a direct subsidy to owner-occupiers with mortgages, and one which benefited largely the better-off who were paying tax and borrowing large sums on mortgages. In the 1970s and 1980s, as house prices rose, the cost of tax relief also expanded, adding to the indirect subsidies going into housing, which were also rising in the rented sector due to housing benefit. In the 1990s, however, this policy was reversed, and the rate of subsidy was reduced by fixing, and then gradually reducing, the size of loan upon which relief could be claimed, so that at the beginning of the new century tax relief on mortgages had disappeared.

The expansion of owner-occupation and mortgage lending in fact led to a range of problems, which we will discuss below. In particular, however, it created a problem for borrowers who lost their jobs and moved on to social security benefit, after taking out a mortgage. In order to avoid such people becoming homeless, as lenders sold their house to recoup their loan, the social security scheme paid the interest payments of claimants on income support, in a comparable way to the payment of rents through housing benefit. This support was never extended, as housing benefit was, to those on low wages, however, creating an unemployment trap for some owners who would be better off unemployed with their mortgage interest covered by benefit than in low-paid work. Moreover, its availability to unemployed claimants was drastically reduced towards the end of the last century, with new claimants being expected to take out private insurance cover to meet the cost of mortgage repayments, or risk losing their home.

Building and selling

The changing costs and subsidies for house renting and purchase have had dramatic effects on the housing market and on housing policy. Rent control and competition from public housing and owner-occupation removed many of the financial incentives for private landlords, and so the building of new private houses to rent declined rapidly in the early decades of the last century. Conversely, as we shall shortly discuss, both public rented housing and owner-occupied housing began to expand in the period between the wars; since 1950, both have played the major role in new house building. As can be seen in Figure 5.1, house building generally rose in the two decades up to the 1970s and then began to decline; and after 1980 public house building by local authorities was reduced to almost nothing as the subsidies from central government were removed and councils were prevented from borrowing money to build.

In the last three decades of the last century, however, house prices began to increase significantly. In part this was a product of growing affluence and the greater availability of mortgages; but it was also a product of the growing popularity of owner-occupation and the consequent demand for house purchase. These price rises have not just been linked to the higher costs of newly built houses; indeed, by and large it has been the prices of existing houses which have risen most as more buyers have come into the market and existing owners have sought to 'trade up' by selling their existing house and moving to a better one.

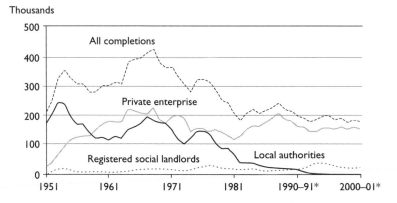

Figure 5.1   Housebuilding completions, UK
* From 1990–91, data are financial year.
Sources: Office for National Statistics (2002), Chart 10.03 (Department for Transport, Local Government and the Regions; National Assembly for Wales; Scottish Executive; Department for Social Development (Northern Ireland)).

In all markets the prices of commodities reflect supply and demand as well as production costs, and this is true of houses too. A house may be a home, but it is also a commodity and many owners have been able to exploit their position in the market to make a capital gain out of the sale of their house. In practice there is a limit to the extent to which public policy can control such market activity, although, in order to respond to the need which everyone has for a home, policy intervention has sought to control and regulate some aspects of housing market development.

QUESTIONS: COMPREHENSION

■ What are the advantages and disadvantages of housing benefit as a means of subsidising the costs of rented housing?
■ Why has tax relief towards the cost of repaying the loan used by owner-occupiers to purchase their home been gradually reduced over the last decade or so?

QUESTION: REFLECTION

■ To what extent should we expect citizens to bear the full cost of providing for their own housing needs?

Housing policy

The development of housing policy in the UK is largely a twentieth-century phenomenon. In the nineteenth century the *laissez-faire* approach dominated much official thinking, and legislative intervention was mainly concentrated on questions of sanitation and public health, which had some consequent effects on house building and public investment. As we shall see shortly, however, philanthropic provision of housing, based on need, began to play a significant and symbolic role at this time.

It was at the beginning of the last century, when the failure of the private rented market to provide adequate housing for all became more and more apparent, that modern public housing policy began to develop, and to have a significant effect of the structure of housing provision in the country. Part of the initiative for housing policy planning emerged as a consequence of the more general development of town planning controls as a means of shaping the environment in which people lived, such as the 1909 Housing and Town Planning Act. A more striking example of this new philosophy was the development of the Garden City movement, where whole new urban settlements were developed according to a planned vision of coordinated housing development. This had been pioneered by industrial philanthropists – such as Cadbury in Bournville and Rowntree in York – at the turn of the century, and it now led to the development of Letchworth in Hertfordshire in 1904 and Welwyn Garden City in 1920 (Malpass and Murie, 1999, p.34).

During the First World War, however, the cost and availability of existing housing became more pressing political issues, highlighted by rent strikes by working-class tenants in Glasgow. The first response to this was the introduction of controls over rent levels in the private rented sector in 1915. This was initially intended as a temporary measure but, in practice, once the controls has been introduced it was difficult to remove them without risking a massive inflation in rents and consequent problems for tenants unable to pay these. So rent control remained in force in some form or other throughout most of the rest of the century, and has been blamed by some commentators for leading to the decline of the sector revealed in Table 5.1, for without the incentive of high rent returns few landlords would want to invest in the development of private rented housing.

By the end of the First World War the political climate underpinning housing policy had begun to change significantly. In short, government now accepted that it had a responsibility to respond to the need for 'homes for heroes', and that this would mean public investment in the building of new houses to rent. The 1919 'Addison Act', popularly known by the name of the minister behind it, introduced central subsidies for local authorities to provide houses for rent; and, although this particular measure was later withdrawn, over the next two decades a range of subsidies was provided and many authorities, especially the larger metropolitan councils, began to build houses. These new houses were primarily aimed at working-class tenants, but they were also generally of good quality, especially when compared to those in the private rented market. This issue of quality became more prominent in the 1930s when local authority building was directed more at 'slum clearance' (that is, the replacement of dilapidated private rented houses with new public ones), a shift which also contributed further to the decline in the scale of the private rented sector.

Public sector house building between the wars added an average of 50,000 dwellings a year to the housing stock (Malpass and Murie, 1999, p.39). In the 1930s in particular, however, this was outstripped by the growth in private house building for sale, prompted by the availability of mortgages from the new building societies and averaging around 200,000 a year by this time. This changing balance meant that by the 1930s public house building was mainly directed at slum clearance for the poor with private owner-occupation meeting the needs of the majority for new houses.

In the Second World War, however, all house building stopped; and at the end of the war, with many houses now destroyed or damaged, there was an acute housing crisis. The end of the war also saw the election of a Labour government committed to the public provision of welfare services to meet all the basic needs of citizens, captured in Beveridge's famous five giants (see Chapter 1). For the new government, and for the housing minister, Bevan, in particular, this meant the building of new, and high quality, houses to rent by local authorities for all social groups. Initially virtually all building was concentrated in the public rented sector, with restrictions on private building for sale, in part because of the overall shortage of materials and labour. The consequence of this was that over the ensuing two decades almost 3 million local authority dwellings were built, twice the number in the same period before the war and a million more than were built in the private sector (Malpass and Murie, 1999, p.53).

This major shift in housing policy and practice resulted also in a significant increase in the relative size of the public rented sector which, as can be seen in Table 5.1, had reached almost one-third of overall provision by the end of the 1960s. During the early post-war years the quality of new public houses was also high, with national standards set for space and specification, sometimes called 'Parker Morris' standards after the chairman of the committee that recommended them. However, towards the end of the 1950s central government subsidies for council house building were cut, and authorities were encouraged to concentrate their activities once again on slum clearance. This change of direction was accentuated by the development of new low-cost building methods for the erection of blocks of flats (system building), with the result that much new public housing was in the form of blocks of flats in inner-city areas, replacing the private rented slums that had previously housed the residents there.

Some of these new flats were well designed and built, even winning architectural awards; but many were not. And, as they largely housed those who had been displaced from the slums, they did not add significantly to the overall stock of housing available, but rather shifted public sector housing once more into the role of providing housing largely for the poor. In fact some of the flats were so poorly constructed that they soon became slums themselves, and in the 1980s and 1990s were demolished by their local authority owners. More dramatically, a gas explosion which caused one side of a tower block to collapse at Ronan Point in London in 1968 revealed the fragility of this new development and signalled the end of public and political confidence in system-built mass public housing.

The changing role of public housing in the 1950s and 1960s was also linked to developments in the private housing sector, however. Once the Conservatives had taken over from Labour in the 1950s they removed the restrictions on private house building and, as can be seen from Figure 5.1, this had begun to outstrip public building by the beginning of the 1960s and has remained much more significant ever since. One of the reasons for Conservative support for private house building was their belief that housing policy should include explicit support for owner-occupation as a key element of housing provision, with mortgage interest tax relief providing an instrument to achieve this. In the 1960s and 1970s Labour also made clear their support for owner-occupation, thus cementing its central role in housing policy.

In the 1980s policy began to change once more, with the Thatcher governments seeking directly to shift the balance of provision, and principle, away from public ownership to private ownership of housing. In part this was achieved by cuts in central government support for local authority housing and restrictions on the powers of authorities to borrow money to build, or even repair, houses, and by the removal of restrictions upon the lending of money on mortgages. More prominently it was achieved by the introduction in 1980 of the council tenants' 'right to buy' their rented dwelling. As we shall see below, this led to around 2 million public rented houses moving into the owner-occupied sector and, as these tended to be the better and more desirable houses, to a decline in the quality and popularity of the remaining stock of council houses.

Critics of the right to buy argued that it was, in part at least, motivated by political considerations. The council tenants able to become owner-occupiers (at a discount) would be likely to vote for the government that delivered this to them, and many of their erstwhile local authority landlords were Labour controlled. More generally, however, it was in keeping with the pro-market and anti-state stance of the Conservative government, and was one of the more successful examples of their attempts to 'privatise' elements of public policy provision. This principle was taken further in the 1988 Housing Act which gave tenants the power to 'opt out' of local authority ownership *en masse*, if a majority was in favour of shifting their tenancies to a private sector landlord, or to one of the new non-profit registered social landlords (RSLs) discussed below.

As we shall, see these transfers led to a growth in the non-profit rented sector in the 1990s; and the sales of council houses contributed to the growing scale, and popularity, of the owner-occupied sector. The Conservative governments were also keen, however, to promote the private rented sector, which had been in continuous decline for most of the century. This was done by gradually removing the system of rent control and security of tenure for private tenants discussed below. After 1988 most private sector tenants were excluded from protection, leading to an escalation in rent levels, especially in popular inner-city areas (and, as revealed in Table 5.1, to a slight increase in the size of the private rented sector by the end of the century).

The other feature of the changes in housing policy in the 1980s and 1990s was the shift in public subsidies for housing from bricks and mortar to poor tenants, as exemplified in the rising costs of housing benefit outlined earlier. This shifting, and yet rising, cost was inherited by the Labour government which came to power in 1997, along with the changes in tenure balance which flowed from the reducing role of public rented housing. This changing balance had been a feature of housing policy over the whole of the previous century, however, with different governments at different times favouring (and so supporting and subsidising) different forms of housing provision. The Labour government has more openly embraced the notion of a mixed economy of welfare provision and taken a practical approach to policy planning which does not assume either private market or public sector domination of provision. It has also, of course, devolved much power over housing policy to Scotland, Wales and Northern Ireland, leading to growing divergence in policy developments here in the new century.

More generally government policy on housing has begun to move away from the past focus upon support for particular tenure division towards a focus upon overall levels of housing supply and demand. This includes responding to the need to promote new building to meet the projected shortage in the supply of houses in the South East and South Midlands by sponsoring new development sites here, and acting directly to tackle particular problems such as homelessness, repairs and improvements, and unpopular (hard to let) dwellings. This new policy emphasis was revealed in the words of the new housing minister, Hilary Armstrong, shortly after the election victory in 1998: 'I am agnostic about the ownership of housing – local authorities, or housing associations; public or private sector – and want to move away from the ideological baggage that comes with that issue. What is important is not, primarily, who delivers. It is what works that counts.' Despite this formal shift towards a more pragmatic approach, however, many of the difficult issues which have underlain recent housing policy development remain important in the new century, including in particular the rising costs of housing benefit. And, though tenure divisions may no longer be so important to government, they are still of critical importance to tenants and owners, and continue to structure the practical operation of housing policy.

Housing provision

Owner-occupation

Owner-occupation is the most popular and widespread form of tenure in the UK, and this dominant position has been growing in scale for over half a century. This is a pattern that has been repeated in most other advanced industrial countries, with most having over 50 per cent owner-occupation by the 1990s; although, in some countries – notably Germany, the Netherlands and Sweden – the proportion is lower, and is less than one-third in (wealthy) Switzerland (Doling, 1997, p.159). The dominance of owner-occupation is a significant trend, but it is not a universal one; and in part, therefore, its role reflects the particular economic and cultural traditions of different societies.

In the UK both economic and cultural pressures towards home ownership are strong. Once mortgages became widely available most people were in a position to borrow money to acquire not only a home but also a capital investment in an appreciating asset. Throughout most of the last quarter of the twentieth century these assets were appreciating rapidly with the rise in house prices generally far outstripping overall price inflation. Despite the problems for some to which we shall return shortly, the financial returns on investment in housing have been one of the great success stories of economic development, with some ('property developers') making a comfortable living simply out of the buying and selling of houses in a rising market. Those who could afford a mortgage would therefore have been well-advised to take one out, and that is just the advice that many who sought it were given. When the right to buy council houses was introduced in 1980 the attractiveness of such an investment was spread to public sector tenants too, and it is no surprise that over the next decade or so around two million took the opportunity to move into home ownership.

For many, therefore, the financial gains have been large, although of course in most cases the financial assets that their home represents can only be realised by leaving the housing market, which for the most part means via inheritance to family members on death. This financial climate has fuelled the cultural attractions of owner-occupation which, despite the assertion of some natural cultural lineage captured in the old adage that 'an Englishman's home is his castle' (obviously a rather male view), are primarily related to the relative undesirability of the other tenure forms. Private renting has never really escaped from its associations with the high rent/low quality slums of the nineteenth century; and, as we shall see, public housing has become increasingly seen as a residual provision for the poor who cannot afford to buy. Thus home ownership is best because renting is clearly second best.

Home ownership is not without its problems, however; indeed, many owners face serious difficulties in buying and maintaining their homes. For a start there are the costs of maintenance itself, since owning your home means that you must pay to keep it habitable, a responsibility which falls to landlords where houses are rented. For older and/or low quality homes this can mean a potentially significant expenditure; and for poorer owners this can be prohibitively expensive. Some of the worst quality houses in Britain are therefore owner-occupied homes owned by poor, and frequently older, people who cannot afford to maintain them.

For the most part, however, the problems associated with home ownership are linked to the cost of houses and, more particularly, the costs of the mortgages taken out to pay for them. Although access to mortgages is no longer restricted in the way that it was before the 1980s, the wider availability of borrowing means that some may overreach their capacity to repay a loan. Most mortgages are repaid over 20 or more years. Where circumstances change for the worse people may find that they cannot sustain such a commitment; and so repayments may get into arrears and ultimately lenders may repossess a house and sell it in order to recoup their loan. In the early 1990s the number of repossessions a year reached over 75,000 (Malpass and Murie, 1999, p.85); and, although levels have declined as economic circumstances have improved since then, there were still 3 per cent of owners in arrears with their mortgage payments in 1999 (Office for National Statistics, 2002).

The repossession of a house means that the lender gets their money back; but for the borrower it is generally the end of their aspirations for home ownership. Repossession only works for the lender, however, where the value of the house exceeds the outstanding loan. Generally speaking this is the case, because lenders are careful to get houses valued before the loan is agreed and only to lend a proportion of the total value. However, on occasions when house prices are rising especially rapidly, as was the case for instance in the late 1980s, lenders and borrowers may be less cautious with 100 per cent loans being agreed for houses at high prices. If the market then declines, as it did in the early 1990s, this may leave the owners with a house which is worth less than the money borrowed to buy it (referred to as 'negative equity'). Where the loan can still be repaid this may only be a temporary setback (if the market revives), but where it cannot it is a financial disaster, which can leave home owners both homeless and still heavily in debt with no means of escape. The cultural attractions of home ownership begin to wane in circumstances like this.

The ability of borrowers to repay their mortgages depends upon how much they have borrowed and how much they earn; and in a rising market people may be pressured into borrowing as much as they can to buy the best possible house. There is another variable affecting mortgage repayments, however, and that is the rate of interest charged by banks and building societies on loans. For most mortgages the lenders reserve the right to alter this rate as more general economic circumstances change. When they put it up mortgage costs rise, and when they put it down mortgage costs decline; and for those with relatively large mortgages even slight fluctuations of less than 1 per cent can add or detract significantly from monthly repayment rates. Rising mortgage rates can therefore affect the ability of home owners to repay their mortgage, and hence keep their home (again, as happened in the early 1990s). Indeed, so important has the effect of mortgage rates become as a control on the spending capacity (or not) of the majority of households who are now owner-occupiers that the government, through the Bank of England, uses the fixing of bank lending rates (which in effect determine mortgage rates) as a means of regulating the wider economy, increasing rates to curtail spending when inflation is rising and reducing them to encourage spending when demand is weak. It is telling evidence of the major role that owner-occupation now plays in British society, and in many other comparable nations, that the costs of home ownership are a major regulator of economic performance.

Public rented housing

The story of public rented housing in the UK is one of rise and fall. The rise began primarily after the First World War with the encouragement, through subsidy, of local authorities to build houses to rent; and developed most rapidly after the Second World War when public house building dominated the response to the housing shortage and more houses were built to rent than at any time before or since (see Figure 5.1). The houses that were built after the Second World War in particular were generally of good quality and for all social groups. On the outskirts of large cities and in the planned 'New Towns' they offered a new form of housing intended to appeal to all. And, although building costs were relatively high, rents were kept as low as possible by council landlords to ensure that as many as possible could afford to rent.

In the second half of the last century, at least up until the late 1980s, such was the popularity of public rented housing that local authorities had to ration access to tenancies. Generally this was done through the operation of *waiting lists* (in effect, putting all those seeking to rent in a queue). In many cases, however, the place in the queue was not just determined by time of application but also by some measure of housing need, with families and homeless people being accorded greater priority. In some cases this was done using a formula, usually a 'points system', with more points and a higher place on the list going to those in most need; but in some cases it was more discretionary and judgemental (see Merrett, 1979, ch.8), and there are accusations that in some cases this could lead to discrimination and unfair treatment (see Henderson and Karn, 1987, on treatment of ethnic minorities in Birmingham in the 1970s). With the decline in the popularity of much public housing in the 1980s and 1990s access became a more varied and complex matter, with much depending upon the levels of demand for different types of housing and some becoming so unpopular that they were 'hard to let' and were left empty. Furthermore, in the late 1970s certain homeless people were given a right of access to public rented housing, as we shall discuss in a little more detail shortly.

After the initial boom of the post-war period, however, local authority house building was channelled largely into slum clearance, leading to the development of the system-built high rise flats described earlier. The poor quality of much of this city centre rented housing was partly to blame for the decline in popularity of public rented housing towards the latter decades of the last century; and this was compounded by the fact that those who were allocated these new flats were generally those who had been occupying the poor quality private rented slums that they replaced. Inevitably this meant that large numbers were poorer tenants who could not afford to escape from the slums by buying a house of their own. This accentuated a link between public housing and social class which had existed at a more formal level throughout the century in the early requirement that public sector house building be geared to the needs of the working class. With the growing popularity of owner-occupation public rented housing was coming to be seen by many, not least those occupying it, as a second-class provision for those who could not afford to buy.

In 1980 the introduction of the 'right to buy' in effect cemented this secondary role. The legislation gave all tenants the right to purchase their home from the council with a guaranteed mortgage, and the right to a substantial discount based upon the length of their occupation within the sector. This was a significant incentive to buy, and many did (around two million by the end of the century). Of course, by and large it was the better-off tenants living in the better quality homes who bought their houses; and the effect of this was rapidly to accelerate the process by which the remaining public rented housing became a tenure of poor quality dwellings for poor people, a process referred to as *residualisation* (see Cole and Furbey, 1993). This was compounded further by the removal of government subsidies for local authorities to build and maintain rented houses which meant that no new dwellings came on to the rented market, and the condition of many of the existing ones deteriorated rather than improved.

The right to buy was the most significant policy change affecting council house tenants in the 1980s, but it was not the only one. The 1980 Housing Act also introduced a broader 'tenant's charter' which strengthened the legal rights of council tenants against their local authority landlords (for instance, restricting the grounds for eviction and giving tenants the right to alter their homes or exchange them with other tenants by mutual agreement). In 1988 the government went further and gave tenants the right to opt out of local authority control altogether and transfer their tenancy to a private landlord or an RSL. Such transfers required the support of a majority of the tenants to be affected; and in practice, and the early years in particular, they were not as popular with tenants as their protagonists had hoped. In certain special cases, where run-down public estates needed reinvestment and revitalisation, the transfer could be to a Housing Action Trust (HAT), with additional financial support; but even these were not very popular, and a number of proposed HATs were abandoned after ballots of tenants had shown insufficient support for them.

In the late 1990s, however, large scale transfers began to be initiated not by tenants but by their local authority landlords, who were aiming to pass over their responsibility for council house management to independent landlords, generally a tenant-controlled RSL. These began to expand more rapidly after 1997, in part because of the greater financial support and flexibility given to the new RSLs.

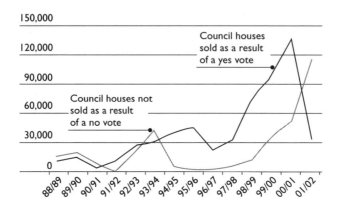

Figure 5.2   Council house transfers
Source: The Guardian, 8 May 2002.

As a result of this some major transfers began to take place with tenants in Glasgow (over 80,000) voting for a transfer, and by 2002 over 600,000 had been passed over by authorities across the country. However, as can be seen in Figure 5.2, the growing number of transfers was accompanied by a growing tenant resistance in some areas, with many tenant groups voting not to approve a change even where it had been developed and promoted by the council itself, most notably in Britain's largest housing authority, Birmingham, in 2002 when a majority of the over 86,000 tenants voted against the council's plans for transfer.

One of the fears of the Birmingham tenants was that their rents could go up once they had been transferred to an independent landlord, in part because they would no longer enjoy the protection of the political authority of a democratically elected council landlord. More generally, of course, rent levels have been one of the key issues of public housing policy throughout the last hundred years. Because local authorities are providing a public service rather than making a profit they have generally aimed to fix their rents according to housing costs rather than market forces. On occasions this has meant relatively high rents, but over time it has more generally meant that councils have been able to keep rents down. It did not mean that all tenants could afford all rents, however, and in the post-war decades many authorities developed rent rebate schemes to subsidise rents for poor tenants through the operation of a means-test.

In 1972 the Conservative government changed all this by introducing legislation which required local authorities to fix their rents at market levels, at the same time extending on a national basis the provision of means-tested rebates for poor tenants. Since then, and in particular during the 1980s, central government has pressured local authorities to raise rents and has cushioned the effect of higher costs through the expansion of rebates. One result of this has been the massive rise in the cost of housing benefit discussed earlier. Coupled with the increasing domination of public housing by poorer tenants, many of whom are entitled to housing benefit, however, another result has been to compound the problem of residualisation with a problem of subsidisation. Large numbers of council tenants do not pay the full costs of their (higher) local authority rents because of their receipt of housing benefit; and, as this is generally deducted from rent due rather than paid to tenants, the appearance (and the reality) of this is subsidy from the social security budget to the council house budget, via poor tenants. It is no surprise, therefore, that the government has now seen housing benefit as major target for policy review.

Registered social landlords

The provision of rented housing by non-profit independent organisations can be traced back to the nineteenth century and the activities of philanthropic agencies such as the Peabody Trust, established in 1862. Perhaps the most well known of these early philanthropic providers was Octavia Hill, who aimed in particular to provide housing for those most in need, and was herself a prominent member of the Charity Organisation Society (discussed in Chapter 1) which, as in other areas of policy, saw such provision as a – more desirable – alternative to the public provision of housing. To a significant extent, therefore, the development of public housing in the twentieth century saw a decline in the scale and profile of independent non-profit housing provision.

In the latter part of the last century, however, non-profit providers returned to play a newly developing role in the provision of rented housing. Now called *housing associations*, they began to grow again after the Housing Acts of 1961 and 1964, which made government loans available to associations for low-cost renting and created the Housing Corporation as a quango to provide a link between individual associations and government departments. In 1974 support for housing associations was expanded with new government subsidies to support them in building and renovating houses for rent, and a requirement to register with the Housing Corporation and meet certain organisational criteria to gain access to these. This led to a significant growth in the scale of activity by housing associations. As can be seen in Table 5.1, in the last two decades of the century they began to play a more and more prominent role within the broader housing market, and, as Figure 5.1 reveals, after 1990 they outstripped local authorities in the building of new housing.

In 1996 new legislation in effect rebranded associations as RSLs, although this term applies to a wider range of organisations than those approved under the 1974 Act, including in particular the new bodies set up by local authorities to administer rented dwellings transferred under the 1988 Housing Act. And, at the beginning of the twenty-first century, they represent a leading example of the Third Way, public/private partnership, approach to housing provision so widely championed by the Labour government.

Private rented housing

Whilst other forms of housing provision have grown in prominence over the last hundred years or so, private rented housing has witnessed a dramatic decline.

From comprising over 90 per cent of housing at the beginning of the last century it had declined at the end to under 10 per cent. This was not just a relative decline, either: the overall absolute numbers of private rented houses were reduced as many were demolished in slum clearance and others were sold to owner-occupiers, who promptly renovated them and raised their market value. For many, and in particular many private tenants, this was no bad thing. Private landlords had exploited their tenants, providing poor quality homes at high rent levels, and those who could afford to buy or to move to a council house were in most cases undoubtedly improving their housing conditions. It is perhaps for this reason that housing policy makers have generally done little to seek to reverse this decline.

Housing policy has not entirely ignored the private rented sector, however. Indeed there has been significant regulation of private renting through the controls imposed by the Rent Acts. Dating back to 1915 government has at various times sought to control the levels of rent charged by private landlords and to provide tenants with security of tenure by protecting them from arbitrary eviction. In the 1950s, when these controls were relaxed, there was an explosion in rent levels and tenant harassment, achieving public notoriety through the activities of one unscrupulous London landlord called Rachman. In the 1960s a more extensive scheme of regulation was introduced based on the fixing of 'fair rents' for tenants by appointed government officers.

Rent control was blamed by some critics, however, for removing any incentive for landlords to enter the private rented market; and in the 1980s government policy changed and rent controls were gradually removed to permit landlords to charge market rents and evict tenants, if they wished, at the end of a fixed (shorthold) period. This once again led to a rise in rents, although now poorer tenants were protected against this to some extent by housing benefit. There is also evidence that by the end of the last century it was leading to some reverse in the declining role of the sector. In particular there has been some growth in private letting at the upper end of the market for flats and apartments in popular inner-city locations targeted at young professional people and provided by new property companies. This creates something of a contrast with the more traditional end of the rented market, however, which largely comprises poorer and older tenants in low quality older housing, sometimes renting from an individual landlord who is little better off then they are.

Underlying this divided market is a continuing uncertainty about policy direction in the sector. One of the reasons for the overall decline in the private rented market has been the lack of subsidies from government for this form of housing, when compared to the other sectors. Some subsidy is now provided, indirectly, via housing benefit; but this is hardly a strategically planned intervention, and it is far from clear whether it is evidence of a government commitment to boost private renting through public support. In the absence of such a policy, and the resources to support it, it is unlikely that the slight reversal in the fortunes of the private rented sector will be the beginning of a major renaissance.

QUESTIONS: COMPREHENSION

- To what extent has public sector housing become a 'residual' provision for those unable to buy their own home, and how has the introduction of the 'right to buy' contributed to this development?
- What are registered social landlords, and can they provide a new Third Way for housing provision?
- To what extent has the decline in the private rented sector been reversed? How sustainable is this change?

QUESTION: REFLECTION

- What have been the advantages and the disadvantages of the shift in housing policy from 'bricks and mortar' to people?

Homelessness

Homelessness is at the sharp end of the housing policy scale. Where people are homeless it is because housing policy in a sense has failed. However, it is far from clear exactly what is meant by homelessness and, as a result, how housing policy should respond to this. Homelessness can mean literally having no place to sleep tonight: sometimes referred to as rooflessness or, more recently, rough sleeping, where it is closely linked to poverty and social exclusion. Large numbers of people do sleep rough in Britain's urban areas, and since 1998 the government has made this problem a priority target for its new Social Exclusion Unit, with the result that it is claimed that the numbers of these homeless persons has begun to decline.

However, people may be homeless even though they do have a bed for the night, if that bed is insecure or inadequate. This applies to people threatened with eviction, people living with family or friends in overcrowded housing, people living in uninhabitable or dilapidated houses, or people threatened with domestic conflict or violence. We may regard many people in such circumstances as homeless, but there has generally been no direct policy response to such problems and no legal right for such people to gain access to a home. Until 1977 such homeless people were simply placed on a council house waiting list, albeit perhaps towards the top because of their desperate need. In that year, however, legislation was passed to place a statutory duty on local authorities to provide housing for certain categories of homeless persons. The categories were restricted, because of a concern that otherwise authorities would not be able to meet their duty, and so only families with children who had not made themselves deliberately homeless were entitled to require authorities to house them, with other people having a right to receive advice and assistance only.

The homeless persons legislation was a significant policy change, nevertheless; and in 1988 it was consolidated into the general duties of local authorities in the provision of public housing. However, the existence of a legal right did not automatically mean that houses would be available for all homeless people. In some urban areas, most notably in London, there are frequently more homeless people than empty council houses; and in these circumstances authorities have been forced to house people temporarily in 'bed and breakfast' accommodation (generally cheap and crowded rooms in down-market hotels).

Furthermore, although the right to housing for homeless people has been in existence for over 20 years, the numbers of homeless people applying for such housing continues to rise. In England in 2000 over 250,000 made an application to their local authority as homeless and over 111,000 were accepted as having a legal right to be housed, an increase of around 5,000 on the previous year (Office for National Statistics, 2002). In some areas therefore homeless people constitute a significant proportion of those gaining access to public rented housing, further contributing to the residualisation of the sector and its unpopularity with tenants more generally.

Policy development

Housing policy in England is formally the responsibility of the Office of the Deputy Prime Minister (ODPM) since a separate Department of Transport was created in 2002 and significant powers were devolved to the separate sub-nations. In large part this is because much of housing policy relates to the development and management of public rented housing through local authorities. In practice, therefore, much of the daily administration of housing policy is in the hands of local, rather than central, government, although this is not the case in Northern Ireland where a single authority (the Northern Ireland Housing Executive) has for some time been managing public housing in the province. The separation has led to some conflicts between central and local government over housing policy, most notably in 1972 when some Labour-controlled authorities refused to implement government policy to raise council rents, especially in Clay Cross in Derbyshire where the councillors were eventually removed from office. In the new century, however, disputes between central and local government are of less significance, and in many areas local authorities are seeking to divest themselves of responsibility for the ownership and management of housing.

It is evident now therefore that, as in many other areas of policy, housing provision is in fact a mixed economy of private and public provision with state policy playing a role in regulating and subsidising different forms of provision in different ways at different times, as revealed in the quotation from housing minister, Armstrong, above. The effect of this, of course, is that housing policy and practice is not just determined by government, but also by other major providers such as housing corporations and RSLs providing new rented properties, and the banks and building societies providing (and controlling) mortgages in the owner-occupied sector.

The ability of government to plan and develop policy across these different agencies, and the different sectors in which they operate, is perhaps the major challenge now facing housing policy makers; and, if the unchecked and yet unwelcome growth of housing benefit over recent decades is anything to go by, then it is a challenge to which they have still to rise. Indeed, rather than tackling such broad and strategic policy planning, the trend within housing policy in recent years has been rather to direct attention towards smaller and more targeted interventions to combat particularly acute problems in generally limited geographical areas.

This can be seen most clearly in the growth of neighbourhood-based housing action, where policy intervention is targeted at areas of known deprivation of which poor housing is only one dimension. These problem estates, as they were called when first identified as a priority for the Social Exclusion Unit in 1998, have become targets for investment of new resources and new ideas to revamp infrastructure, including public (and sometimes private) housing in the area, alongside other initiatives to develop community cohesion and social inclusion (SEU, 2001). It is perhaps encouraging that in such neighbourhood renewal activity, housing problems are being addressed within a policy framework that embraces the broader social and community context of local needs. However, this broader approach is being implemented on a micro focus, and there is some concern that such targeted activity is too narrowly directed to neighbourhood action. This means that the new integrated approach to policy planning is restricted to a small number of local areas where problems are most acute, and that a more generic approach to the social and economic context of housing is no longer receiving the prominence that it did throughout much of the previous hundred years of policy development.

QUESTIONS: COMPREHENSION

- Why have the measures introduced to give homeless people a right to public housing not solved the problem of homelessness?
- What are the advantages and disadvantages of the focusing of policy action on to deprived neighbourhoods?

QUESTION: REFLECTION

- To what extent do you think that it is market forces rather than government policy that determine housing provision in the UK?

FURTHER READING

Malpass and Murie (1999) is the main text covering the history and structure of housing provision, although it is to be succeeded shortly by an even broader text, Mullins and Murie (2003). The best book on the history of housing in the UK is Burnett (1985), although it is a little dated. An up-to-date introduction to housing policy is provided by Balchin and Rhodes (2002), and Lund (1996) provides a broader summary overview. Government papers for England can be viewed on **www.odpm.gov.uk** with similar provision on the websites of the devolved administrations (see Chapter 15); local government publications can be viewed at **www.lga.gov.uk**.

Social Services

6

SUMMARY OF KEY POINTS

- The personal social services include social care and social work carried out through local authority Social Services Departments (SSDs) and other statutory, private and voluntary agencies.
- Social services provide for the particular needs of vulnerable adults and children, within fixed budgets administered by SSDs.
- The early development of social services was dominated by voluntary provision, and only in the welfare reforms of the 1940s was statutory responsibility passed to local authority Children's and Health and Welfare Departments.
- In 1971 services for all groups were consolidated into generic SSDs. However, since the 1990s there has been a return to more specialised provision for children's and adult services.
- High-profile media reporting of child abuse and death has sometimes created pressure on social workers and SSDs, although in practice agencies have to deal with large numbers of children at risk.
- Work with child offenders has fluctuated between *welfare* and *justice* approaches, and both continue to influence current provision.
- There has been a significant shift in adult services from residential to community care. All SSDs now are required to produce community care plans outlining service provision in their area.
- Community care is a mixed economy of provision with private and voluntary agencies providing services under contractual agreements with SSDs.
- Domiciliary services support care in the home. Charges are now made for many of these services with rebates for those unable to pay.
- Some SSDs have appointed welfare rights workers to help poor clients to improve their incomes through the take-up of social security benefits.

The personal social services

The personal social services are a complex and diverse area of social policy provision. This is in part a product of the range of different services that are provided to different client groups; but it is also in part a product of the various terms that are used to describe these activities, which are sometimes confusingly used in different ways by different commentators. As a result of this there is probably no single, correct, usage of words here; but for the purposes of clarity we will distinguish the major terms and the different activities that they are generally used to refer to, and use these terms consistently in this way throughout the book. The main distinction is between three core terms:

1. *Social care.* This is the provision of individual support and attendance to vulnerable, sick or disabled people who are unable to provide fully for themselves. The support is provided by other members of society, sometimes on an unpaid basis (generally by family members), sometimes on a paid basis by social care workers; paid workers may provide care at a person's home or in a residential establishment. Social care is, of course, provided to children, but in this context the term is generally used to refer to the provision of support to adults. The scale of such care provided, informally, by family members is a significant part of overall welfare provision, as we discuss in Chapter 11.

2. *Social work.* This is the professional activity carried out by social workers employed by local authorities, health service agencies or voluntary organisations, and usually having a formal professional qualification (currently a Diploma in Social Work). Social workers act on behalf of their employers to identify those adults or children who might be in need of individual support or protection as a result of their social or family circumstances, and, where possible, aim to provide this support or, more generally, to assist their clients in securing support from other agencies. For their adult clients social workers generally work in this 'enabling' role, as we shall discuss below. In their work with children in need social workers more often aim to protect children at risk, perhaps by removing them from their family home.

3. *Social services.* This is the generic term used to refer to the provision of both social care and social work, and in particular the provision of this by public agencies to all those who might need such services within a defined area. For the most part this is provided in the UK by departments or sections of local authorities, although in Northern Ireland it is administered jointly with health services by joint boards and trusts. All local authorities are required to provide such personal social services (PSS) and in general do so through a Social Services Department (SSD), in Scotland called Social Work Departments. Social services includes social care and social work; but the term also generally encompasses a wider range of services provided for local people on an individual or community basis, including community work, welfare rights advice and even financial support, as we shall discuss briefly later. Social services may also be provided by other agencies, such as health service bodies or voluntary sector organisations.

One of the central features of all these different dimensions of social services is their focus upon the particular needs of individuals. This is something of a contrast to the other major policy areas such as education, which is concerned with the provision of learning, or social security, which is concerned with the provision of financial benefits. The provisions made by social services cover a wide range of individual needs, and in effect are driven by these individual needs rather than a predetermined service framework. For this reason they are sometimes referred to as 'human services'. Baldock (2003) refers to them as a 'residual service', which is available to those who cannot be helped by more specific providers. Those individuals supported by social services are still therefore sometimes referred to as *clients*, but the supplicant nature of this term is now challenged by critics who argue that those receiving social services should be referred to as users, or even citizens (an issue we return to in Chapter 18, and see Beresford, 2000).

The conception of social services as a response to individual needs suggests that this is largely a demand-led area of social policy; and to a significant extent this is true. The operation of social work and the provision of social care are based upon processes of identifying the needs of individuals (or families) and providing services in response to these. Organisationally speaking social services respond to individual needs. Where needs are growing therefore, we would expect service provision to expand; and a broad review of recent patterns of public spending on local authority social services suggests that this is indeed the case. Figure 6.1 shows that expenditure on personal social services has been expanding consistently over the last decade or so. In 1999–2000 gross expenditure was around £12 billion, an increase of 11 per cent over the previous year.

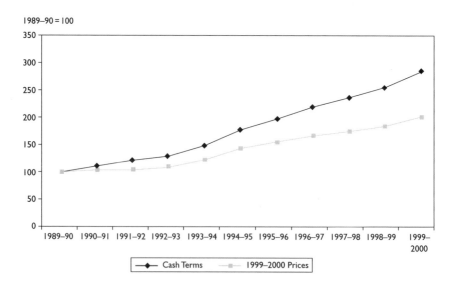

Figure 6.1   Local authority gross expenditure on social services
in England from 1989–90 to 1999–2000
Source: DoH (2002b), Chart 5.

This pattern of increasing expenditure can be found in other areas of social policy, of course, as we discuss in Chapter 17; and public expenditure increases have taken place under Conservative governments ostensibly aiming to contain spending, as well as Labour governments committed to expanding services. In part this is a product of increasing demand, reflecting expanding needs. At the same time, however, public spending is subject to national budgetary planning and controls, and these controls mean that the demand-led nature of social services does not quite work out in practice as a direct response to changing demands.

Public spending on social work and social care is, by and large, managed by local authority SSDs. The money available to SSDs is determined by the grants which come from central government, together with local council tax and fees and charges made for certain services (see Chapter 17), and these in effect constitute a fixed budget from within which the support for local citizens must be provided. For social services managers, therefore – and, indeed, for social workers themselves – the practice of delivering social services involves the prioritisation of needs within fixed and limited cash resources, rather than any open response to individual demands. This was revealed graphically in a court case involving Gloucester County Council SSD in 1995, where the council sought to withdraw services from certain user groups on financial grounds. The court held that such indiscriminate budgetary control was unlawful, but ruled that local authorities could 'take resources into account both in the assessment of need and the provision of services' (Thompson and Dobson, 1995, p.20).

Determining the allocation of expenditure across those in need of social services support is no easy task. In practice the different individuals in need of support have very different social circumstances, and in effect all cases must be treated on an individual case basis, leading to the 'casework' tradition in social work discussed below. Nevertheless there are some broad categories of need which are likely to be specific to certain kinds of groups of clients or users. The pattern of expenditure across these different groups is illustrated in Figure 6.2,

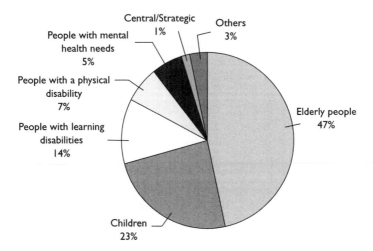

Figure 6.2   Client group as a share of gross expenditure
Source: DoH (2002b), Chart 1.

which reveals that it is elderly people who take up almost half of social services expenditure, with children accounting for almost one-quarter. There is a clear life-cycle pattern to the individual needs to which social services respond therefore.

It is local authority SSDs which manage these budgetary priorities and dilemmas. Policies on the provision of social work and social care are determined by national government of course; and formal responsibility for these services lies within the Department of Health (DoH). The DoH provides advice and guidance to the local authorities who deliver social services and publishes aggregate information about patterns and trends although, as result of devolution, these are now provided separately for Scotland, Wales and Northern Ireland. But it is local government which is responsible for operational delivery and budget management; and it is local authority SSDs which employ most social workers.

Not all social services are delivered by local authority SSDs, however; social workers can also be found in other public service agencies. There are social workers within the health service working with patients who have social as well as health problems; and, as we shall see, the boundaries between social services and the health service have become increasingly blurred in recent years. There also social workers in education: for instance, the education welfare officers who work with truants and problem pupils, and the youth service workers who engage in community work with teenagers. Many of these workers will have formal social work qualifications.

Like other areas of social policy, social services is also a mixed economy of care. In addition to public service provision there is also a wide range of private and voluntary sector social services providers, and in social care the overwhelming bulk of individual care and support is provided informally. Child protection work, now a major feature of SSD provision, originated in the work of voluntary sector agencies such as Barnardo's and the National Society for the Prevention of Cruelty to Children (NSPCC), which were founded in the nineteenth century and are still operating today. The provision of residential care has always been in part delivered in privately run residential homes and in voluntary sector, or non-profit, homes. These have grown significantly in scale and scope over the last two decades, as we shall discuss below, as too have the private and non-profit providers of domiciliary care for people living in their own homes but in need of support as part of a package of 'community care'.

This broader picture of the mixed economy of personal social services underlines the fact that the qualified social workers working within local authority SSDs are only a small part of social services provision. Such qualified workers represent under 20 per cent of all those employed within personal social services, with residential, day-care and domiciliary workers making up the vast majority. Many of these social care staff do not have formal qualifications, although some do, and increasing numbers are undergoing professional training at National Vocational Qualification levels. For the 'professional' social workers, however – and for their clients – qualifications are of critical importance. Standards of professional qualification were set in the latter part of the twentieth century by the Central Council for Education and Training in Social Work (CCETSW). However, this has now been replaced in England by the

General Social Care Council (GSCC), and from 2003 onwards all social workers here will be required to achieve graduate status in their qualification. The specialist nature of social work and its rapidly changing policy environment also means that even qualified workers need further training at certain times, and there is a range of 'post-qualifying' awards linked to specialist practice within different aspects of social services.

The development of social services

Modern social service provision can be traced back to the ideals and innovations of private philanthropists in the Victorian era. This included the work of the so-called 'childsavers' (Platt, 1969), such as Thomas Barnardo who influenced the establishment of voluntary sector agencies such as Barnardo's and the NSPCC, to protect children from cruelty at home and to prevent them from falling into delinquency outside it. More generally the work of the Charity Organisation Society (COS) in providing a mixture of assistance and moral guidance to people in need provided a legacy which underpinned the development of more formal, individually-based, social work in the twentieth century. The COS established the first School of Sociology to provide formal training for social workers in 1902. This later merged with the social policy department at the LSE (see Chapter 1); similar provision also developed at other universities, such as Birmingham.

Public provision for individual need in the nineteenth century largely took the form of the Poor Law. As we discussed in Chapter 2, the Poor Law was primarily designed as a response to destitution, and a pretty harsh response at that. However, many people were destitute because of illness, disability or vulnerability and in practice the Poor Law Guardians were expected to provide for these too, in effect providing public support for vulnerable adults and children. The review of the Poor Law by the Royal Commission of 1905 resulted in a disagreement about the future development of social security and social work policy between the philanthropic model of the COS and the (Fabian) public service approach championed by the Webbs (see Chapter 1). For social work and social services this remained a largely unresolved division throughout most of the first half of the twentieth century. Although there was some limited expansion of public provision for children and adults outside the scope of the increasingly disparaged Poor Law, philanthropic and private provision remained of central importance for many.

It was only after the Second World War and during the period of the rapid development of state welfare services under the 1945 Labour government that public social services provision really developed on a comprehensive basis. In part this was a product of the political and policy commitments to state welfare of the post-war era. In part, however, it was a response to a media outcry over an individual tragedy which exposed the failure of society to protect its most vulnerable members. The tragedy was the death in 1945 of a child, Dennis O'Neill, murdered by his foster parent in Shropshire, which prompted the establishment of an independent inquiry, the Monckton Report (Kirton, 1999, p.379). The report argued that future such tragedies could only be prevented by the recruitment of social workers trained to identify and prevent child abuse, and in 1946 a government report, the Curtis Report, recommended that public agencies should be created to employ such workers.

On a number of occasions since, similar high-profile private tragedies have exposed the vulnerability of both children and adults within modern society, and have resulted in public debate about the proper role of public social service provision, leading in some cases to policy reform. It is an unfortunate irony that social services generally only reach the public eye when their ability to identify and prevent harm have failed so dramatically; and unfortunate, too, that the policy changes which often follow such cases end up being driven by short-term political pressure rather than longer-term policy planning.

In the late 1940s, however, longer-term policy planning was very much the pattern of the times; and in the Children Act of 1948 major development of public social service provision followed the deliberations of the Curtis Report. The Act led to the establishment of children's departments within all local authorities, within which social workers would be employed as public service workers with the specific task of identifying and protecting children at risk of cruelty or abuse. In the same year local authorities were also required to establish health and welfare departments to provide residential and domiciliary care for the needs of vulnerable adults, when the Poor Law basis for such provision was finally abolished in the National Assistance Act.

These local authority departments provided the basis for the development of social work as a professional public service over the following decades. In 1968 the work of these departments was reviewed by the Seebohm Committee, who recommended that they should be merged to form a single point for the development and delivery of personal social services (referred to as a *fifth* social service, after education, health, housing and social security). Implicit in the Seebohm vision was the idea of a holistic service for all individuals in need delivered by generic social service professionals who could identify and respond to all aspects of individual need. These changes were realised in 1971, when all the separate departments were amalgamated into SSDs. Three years later local government restructuring also resulted in a smaller number of larger local authorities with a wider range of powers and responsibilities, enhancing the scale and scope of the new SSDs. At around the same time the professional qualification for social workers was also reformed to create a single generic training for all.

The big new SSDs of the 1970s offered the prospect of large scale, generic provision for individual human needs. However, there was something of a contradiction in this broad-based approach to personal social services, and towards the end of the twentieth century there was a significant retreat away from the holistic model towards smaller scale and more specialist services. In part this was achieved through geographical restructuring, with a number of the larger SSDs in the 1980s devolving service delivery to neighbourhood offices within which workers would service those living within a particular local area (sometimes referred to as 'patch' working). One of the ideas behind this was that local workers would be able to integrate services more closely into the needs, and structures, of local communities. This was given something of a formal endorsement by the Barclay Report of 1982, which argued that social workers should concentrate on enabling local communities to provide mutual support along-side public services, although this was within the context of a view that additional public resources to meet growing social needs would probably not be forthcoming.

The move away from generic social services became more formalised in the early 1990s, however, following the reforms initiated under the Conservative governments of Thatcher and Major. In 1989 the Children Act introduced tighter controls over the procedures for the protection of children and in 1990 the National Health Service and Community Care Act made sweeping changes to the provision of support for vulnerable adults. We shall return to discuss both in more detail shortly. In general, however, their effect was to increase specialisation within social services, through a separation between adults' and childrens' services similar to that found in the immediate post-war era. These changes have largely been retained by the Labour government. However, in the early twenty-first century social service provision has been influenced by the new commitments to 'joined-up' government and partnership planning (see Chapter 18), and in particular joint planning of services across the health and social care divide is now a formal requirement on both parties, with the aim of providing a more coherent service for users moving between the two agencies. In Northern Ireland this has already been achieved in the joint management of health and social services.

Over the past two decades the provision of social services has also been affected by the more general managerial changes that have been introduced to improve efficiency, effectiveness and service accountability across all public services (see Chapter 18). Local authorities are now required to specify the nature of service provision for adults in their local area in published 'community care plans' and to enter into contracts and service level agreements with other service providers for the delivery of these. Many departments also produce children's service plans on a similar basis. Quality standards for service provision are also set by government and service providers are subject to regular inspection, by the Social Services Inspectorate (SSI), to ensure that these are being maintained.

The intention behind these moves towards greater specialisation, specification and service accountability has been to improve the services offered to local people by personal social service providers. However, within these moves too there have been some contradictory pressures, and outcomes. Greater specialisation has targeted the activity of social workers, and SSDs, on to those needs and activities specified in the statutory standards and service plans. The effect of this has been a narrowing of the range of services provided and the loss of some of the more generic preventative work with communities and user groups, which social services in the past might have provided. Community work in particular has been reduced in scale as a result of these trends, with social workers being pressed into a more individualistic casework approach to social needs, although it is just such broader interventions which may be more effective in the longer term in addressing the more general problems of deprivation and social exclusion which lay behind many individual social needs.

Children's services

The prevention of harm to children, and the care and protection of children who cannot be adequately provided for within their family, has always been a core focus of social services. It consumes almost one-quarter of public expenditure on social services and a much higher proportion of the time of qualified social workers. It is also the area which receives most public attention, and concern. The death of Dennis O'Neill was a key factor in leading to establishment of the local authority children's departments of the post-war era. In 1973 the death of seven-year-old Maria Colwell, after being returned from foster care to her mother and stepfather without the SSD contesting the application, sparked a renewed concern with the delivery of public services to protect children. Since then there have been a number of further tragedies brought to the public eye, more recently that of Victoria Climbié, murdered by the relatives caring for her despite the fact that she had been visited by social workers who had not acted on evidence of potential abuse.

Unfortunately such personal tragedies are hardly a recent phenomenon; and it was in response to just such similar events that the NSPCC was established in the late nineteenth century (it continues to operate today). Furthermore, the grounds for social services intervention in such cases are far from clear cut. In 1987 social workers in Cleveland intervened to take into public care a number of children who were thought to be at risk of sexual abuse by their parents, based upon evidence from physical examinations by clinicians. There was widespread publicity of the affair and public criticism of the professionals involved for overreaction and heavy-handedness; this was reinforced in the official inquiry which followed. The conclusion that many might draw – and many social workers in particular – is that social services are 'damned if they do act' and 'damned if they do not'. In all such cases it easy to be wise about the risks involved after the event; but social workers are required to make judgements before problems arise, and to do so in thousands of cases every year.

The Children Act of 1989 sought to clarify the responsibilities of SSDs and social workers for the prevention of harm and abuse of children (a similar act was introduced in Scotland in 1995). It reaffirmed the notion that the welfare of the child should in all cases be the paramount concern, but that parental responsibility should be maximised and families involved as much as possible in the care of children, with courts also playing a greater role in decision-making in critical cases. Legislative provisions cannot identify when children are at risk of harm, however; and inevitably the operationalisation of services to protect children remains a matter of professional judgement. As with the creation of the children's departments in 1948, therefore, policy provision has focused upon the process, rather than the content, of child care provision. Local authorities are now required to maintain child protection registers of all children 'at risk' in their area. In recent years the numbers on these registers have been declining, from over 32,000 in the mid-1990s to 26,800 in 2001 in England, of which 52 per cent were boys and 48 per cent girls (DoH, 2002b).

Most children at risk remain with their families, with social workers supporting and monitoring the care that their parents provide. However, where there is a fear of genuine harm workers have the power to take children 'into care', and potentially therefore away from home. In these circumstances formal parental responsibility is transferred to the SSD, or other agency, and the children are 'looked after' by them. In 2000 over 58,000 children were being looked after by local authorities in England, a gradual increase on the numbers in the mid-1990s. In practice two-thirds of these children are being cared for in foster homes: that is, living with families who are paid and supervised by local authorities to provide care for such children. Around 10 per cent are in residential homes or schools, and 11 per cent are still living with their own parents under the supervision of the local authority (DoH, 2002b).

About 5 per cent of looked-after children are placed with families for adoption. Adoption involves the formal transfer of parental rights and responsibilities to 'new' parents, severing the legal tie to the natural parents. At one time adoption was quite widely used in the UK to provide an alternative family for unwanted and abandoned children, and such adoptions were popular with would-be parents unable to have children of their own. Over the latter part of the twentieth century, however, such adoptions (generally of young babies) have declined dramatically as birth control and abortion have reduced the numbers of unwanted births, and the stigma surrounding single parenthood has lessened. In the mid-1970s there were over 20,000 adoptions a year; now there around 5,000, and the majority of these are of older children who have been taken into the care of local authorities because they were at risk in their natural families.

Another concern of social services are those children who come into contact with the public authorities because of criminal offending behaviour. Children under the age of 10 (8 in Scotland) are presumed not to be responsible under criminal law for their actions. Beyond this age children can, and do, commit crimes, however; but until they reach the age of 18 they are dealt with under separate procedures and through separate courts. How to respond to the problems, and needs, of child offenders has been a matter of significant policy debate, and disagreement, in the UK, and has resulted in different policies and procedures being developed by the devolved administrations, most notably in Scotland. In the 1960s a *welfare* approach was promoted, under which child offenders would generally be cared for by local authorities as part of their social work functions. But in the 1980s there was a shift towards a greater emphasis upon a *justice* model under which punishment and deterrence were felt to be more appropriate. In reality both principles continue to inform policy and practice, and social workers are now involved in working with other professionals to tackle the problem of youth crime and to seek to ensure that young offenders are supported in addressing the problems which have led to their offending behaviour (see Pitts, 1999; Muncie, Hughes and McLaughlin, 2002).

It is in part because of their role with young offenders within the juvenile justice process that social workers have sometimes been characterised as carrying out a 'policing' function over problematic or unacceptable behaviour within families. This role has even been dubbed that of the 'soft cops', and it has been extended to include also their interventions into families to protect children at risk. A French critical theorist called his book on the historical development of this activity *The Policing of Families* (Donzelot, 1980). For the children at risk such a policing role is of critical importance, as its well publicised failures in the cases of Maria Colwell and others have revealed. However, from the perspective of the parents under suspicion such surveillance may be rather less welcome, especially in those cases where the risk of harm is less clear cut, or even strongly contested.

The casework approach which underlay much child protection work in the early years of the children's departments after the Second World War relied heavily upon social psychological evidence of appropriate parenting. In particular this included the work of Bowlby (1963) which purported to show that those children who did not benefit from the full time care of their mothers would be more likely to experience problems in later life (the problem of 'maternal deprivation'). As feminist critics in particular have since pointed out, this could provide a licence for social workers to intrude into the lives of ordinary families and make judgements about the appropriateness of parenting arrangements, in particular where mothers were in paid employment and not always able to provide individual care for their children 24 hours a day. In one of the earliest of feminist critiques, Wilson (1977, p.87) quotes a comment on such casework in a textbook from 1953:

> The progress Mrs M had made was obvious. She had gone a long way towards femininity; she showed a new interest in the home, in sewing and cooking. While … she seemed pleased about her achievements, she made angry remarks to the [social] worker, suggesting that she wanted to make her into a 'humdrum housewife'.

In practice the work of Bowlby has been widely discredited by more recent research on child rearing, and social work interventions are less intrusive, and generally less judgemental, than that experienced by Mrs M; not the least reason for this is the large caseloads of children at risk that social workers now carry, which leave them little time for significant individual casework. More recently, research has revealed a more positive reaction to the child and family support services provided by social services agencies, although structural and organisational constraints continue to provide some hindrance to effective practice in all cases (McDonald and Williamson, 2002).

However, a significant policing role still does remain with social services in their responsibility for the provision of *child-minding* services within their local area. The temporary care of children by another family, usually whilst the legal parents are out at work, is a longstanding practice and takes a number of forms in modern Britain. Much of such care is informally provided by families or neighbours, and is largely unregulated. However, commercial provision is also offered, often by mothers themselves who are seeking to increase household income by caring for one or two additional children during the day. Such commercial provision is monitored and approved by SSDs, who maintain registers of approved child minders and conduct regular inspections of their premises and practices.

Adult services

The public provision of services to vulnerable adults can be traced back in their modern form to the establishment of the local authority health and welfare departments which formally took over this responsibility from the Poor Law in 1948. In practice the adults benefiting from these services vary tremendously, and to a significant extent their needs are unique and individual. Nevertheless major groups of the users of such services can be identified, and service provision has largely been developed to meet the kinds of needs experienced by these groups. The main groups, in terms of public spending specifically, can be seen in Figure 6.2, which reveals that by far the largest group are the elderly. This presents a rather misleading picture, however. Elderly people do not need help because they are old, and most elderly people do not need any individual help at all. But amongst those over pension age are many who may experience difficulties because of chronic sickness, disability or frailty; and in effect all such users over that age are lumped together for accounting and statistical purposes. They may also be perceived, and treated, by the social workers and care workers who work with them primarily as elderly people, and there is no doubt some implicit element of *ageism* underlying service provision here (see Chapter 16).

Provision for vulnerable adults under the Poor Law was dominated by the institutional approach which underlay nineteenth-century public service philosophy, symbolised by the workhouse. By the middle of the twentieth century workhouses had disappeared, but many vulnerable adults (including significant numbers of older people) were still being looked after in residential establishments, many run by local authorities. In 1962 the publication of *The Last Refuge* by Townsend exposed the poor conditions and uncaring nature of some of this residential provision and fuelled a shift within social services policy debate and policy planning towards the provision of support for vulnerable people to live in their own homes and be cared for within the community, which is generally now referred to as *community care*.

The relative merits of residential and community care – and the most appropriate forms in which each should be provided – continue to dominate social service provision for adults. The issues extend across all user groups; for instance, in the last three decades of the twentieth century there was a massive shift of provision for those with mental health needs from psychiatric hospitals (many of which closed down) to community-based settings. They also extend across the range of different service providers: residential homes are run by private and voluntary agencies (indeed, the majority have always been outside the public sector) and such agencies also provide services to support community care, as we shall discuss shortly. Within the public sector the issues also extend across the organisational divide between social and health services, or more specifically SSDs and the NHS, for a significant amount of residential care is provided for chronically sick adults in hospitals, and it is in part in order to move chronically sick patients out of hospitals that community care has been so strongly promoted in recent times.

The changing balance of residential and community care for adults is thus a complex, and to some extent a contradictory, story which has resulted in some dramatic changes in the scale and scope of public and private or voluntary services. In the 1980s the pressure to reduce residential care in hospitals and other public institutions was met by a major expansion of private and voluntary provision for residential care. In practice, however, this care was financed by public funds because those running such institutions were able to receive means-tested social security benefits for those residents (in practice a large number) entitled to them under social security regulations. The result of this was a massive growth in the number of residential places in these institutions, and a massive growth in the social security budget to support this.

For the Conservative governments of the time, which had pledged to reduce public expenditure on social security, this was a serious embarrassment. In 1989 they published a White Paper outlining a different approach towards the public funding of care for vulnerable adults, and in 1990 this was enacted in the NHS and Community Care Act, which finally came into force in 1993. The 1993 changes were not just aimed at tackling the growth in the social security budget to support private residential care, however; they were also part of a more general reform of public services in the early 1990s to introduce an element of market discipline into service planning (sometimes referred to as quasi-markets: see Chapter 9). What is more, they were intended to promote community care as the preferred option for social service provision for vulnerable adults (Means and Smith, 2003).

The 1993 reforms transferred responsibility for what was now generically referred to as *community care* to local authority SSDs, transferring with this some of the money which would otherwise have been paid out in social security benefits. SSDs were expected to work closely with local NHS agencies (hospital trusts and the then health authorities) to develop a comprehensive local service for adults, which could be specified in 'service level agreements' between the different agencies. Whether such effective collaboration has taken place in all circumstances is questionable, however, as the 'bed-blocking' scandals of the early years of the twenty-first century revealed. *Bed-blocking* is the problem caused when beds in hospitals cannot be allocated to new patients on waiting lists because they are occupied by chronically sick adults who could be provided for in other residential or community settings, but for whom no such provision is available. It is a telling example of the difficulties experienced in planning for community care across such different agencies and different budget streams, and has led to pressure within some DoH quarters for all adult services to be moved directly under NHS control.

The quasi-market dimension of community care is revealed by the new role expected of social workers acting on behalf of vulnerable adult clients. Social workers, now referred to as 'care managers', act in an enabling capacity to assess the needs for care that individuals have and then to assist them in securing the most appropriate package of care to meet these. In part this is a casework support task; but in part it is also a financial broker role, for in 'purchasing' the care services which the client needs the care manager is also managing (and rationing) the (fixed) budget for these services held by the SSD. And, as we saw in the Gloucester case referred to earlier, in taking such decisions social service workers must take into account the financial constraints imposed by such budgets.

The packages of care that social workers design for their clients may include residential or community-based care, and they may involve the use of publicly provided services or those provided locally by private or voluntary sector organisations. Care management takes place now within a mixed economy of care, and the extent of public support provided to people depends in part upon their ability to pay for the provision within their package, with public support for residential care and other community-based services being subject to means-tests which target resources on to those with limited private savings or investments. This is a complex pattern, which means that packages of care will indeed vary from individual to individual. In principle this means that service provision is oriented towards individual needs rather than generic provision to particular client groups. However, it also means that different individuals with broadly similar needs will be treated differently depending upon their financial circumstances, the judgement of their care manager, and the local area in which they live.

Local authority SSDs are required to provide an overview of local services via the publication of an annual community care plan outlining the services available from different providers and the policies to be adopted by the authority in utilising these. Community care planning therefore requires that authorities contract with private and voluntary sector providers for the provision of those services which local users are likely to need. This contract relationship has significantly altered relations between the state and the private and voluntary sectors in the social services field, and it has led in practice to a considerable increase in the number of independent (non-state) providers receiving state funding under contracts to deliver services to local people. For instance, of the approximately 250,000 publicly supported residents in residential and nursing care homes in England in 2001, 210,000 were in independently run homes (DoH, 2002b).

It is not just residential care which is provided under such new community care provision, however. Indeed the underlying policy thrust behind the 1990s reforms, as with previous trends over the latter part of the last century, was to promote care in the community rather than residential care. For the most part this means in practice care within the home of the client, or in the home of a family member who is caring for them, since most community care is provided informally by family members (see Chapter 11). Family care for vulnerable adults frequently requires additional support and assistance, however; and here SSDs, and their contracting independent partners, continue to have a significant provider role.

Carers at home cannot always provide support for 24 hours a day every day of the week. Additional facilities are needed therefore to provide *day care*, so that those needing care can get out of the house during the day, or *respite care*, to provide longer periods of alternative support to relieve both carers and those being cared for. More generally *domiciliary care* services can be provided to support vulnerable adults living at home, whether or not they are being informally cared for by relatives. Domiciliary care includes services such as home helps (to assist with housework) and 'meals on wheels' (regular hot meals delivered to the door); and, like other services, these are provided by public, private and independent agencies. Local authorities can also provide other forms of support for vulnerable adults living at home, for instance aids and adaptations to their homes; indeed, under the Chronically Sick and Disabled Persons Act of 1970 they are required to provide such support, although what *is* required is a matter for the local authority to judge.

Domiciliary and other services to support community care can be provided free of charge by local authorities; but in practice it is more common these days for them to be subject to fees or charges. In fact central government encourages such charging by assuming a certain income from charges in the financial provision for community care that is distributed to authorities. Charges do not always cover the full costs of providing the services, however, and patterns of charging vary from authority to authority. Furthermore poor clients are unlikely to be able to afford to pay, and in most cases authorities offer rebates or exemptions to those on low incomes. Charging thus further complicates the pattern of provision for community care, with different individuals experiencing different forms of support in different local areas. It also introduces a further element of means-testing into the adult social services. In effect there is now something of a contrast between health care services, which are largely provided free at the point of use, and social care services, which involve means-testing; and this makes the joint planning of health and social services, now required by government, much more difficult to achieve, and to justify.

Some of these issues were considered in 1998 by a Royal Commission on Long Term Care (Sutherland Commission), which reported in 1999. The Commission made a distinction between the living costs and the care costs of those needing long-term care, and argued that care costs should be provided free and living costs subject to means-testing. The government did not accept this recommendation, however, and has indicated its intention to continue to use charging, together with means-testing, for all care, primarily for financial reasons (although the devolved administration in Scotland has decided to provide for care needs without charge). Once again it is clear that financial, and political, considerations are determining the nature of provision of adult social services, despite the rhetoric of individual needs assessment that now supposedly underlies community care policy. The relationship between care and cash is one that runs throughout social services, however.

QUESTIONS: COMPREHENSION

- What is the difference between the *welfare* and *justice* approaches to service provision for children with criminal offending behaviour?
- What are the advantages and disadvantages of the 'casework' approach to social work practice?
- What is 'care management', and how does it seek to improve the provision of services to vulnerable adults?
- How has contracting altered the relationships between statutory and non-statutory agencies in the provision of community care?

QUESTION: REFLECTION

- To what extent should citizens be expected to provide for their own future needs for long-term care?

Cash and care

There is a link between cash and care in all public services; someone has to pay for the care provided, usually either the recipient of services or the taxpayer (see Chapter 17). However, in the personal social services this relationship is complicated by a number of further factors. As we have seen, social services are delivered by a mixed economy of providers, and in many cases users are having to pay fees or charges to providers; in effect they are buying their care for cash. This is likely to be a problem for those users who cannot afford to pay such charges, however; and it is for this reason that means-testing is used to exempt poor users from such payments.

Means-tests introduce selectivity into social service provision, however; and there are some, including the Sutherland Commission, who have argued that this is an undesirable feature of such needs-based services. Furthermore, large numbers of social service clients are in practice poor, and therefore in need of the selective support that means-tests provide. This raises the *practical* question of whether selectivity through means-testing is an efficient means of controlling public expenditure when so many users fall below the means-test limits, but also the question of *principle* as to whether targeting in this way will not reinforce the sense of stigma and dependency that may lie at the heart of many of the problems of vulnerability amongst adults and neglect or abuse of children. Selective social services may come to be seen as services for the poor and, as some commentators have suggested, that may lead to them becoming poor services too.

The cash and care issue is further complicated, however, by another dimension, which is the power which local authority SSDs have to provide cash (or equivalent) support for some clients. As we have seen, support can be provided for chronically sick and disabled people under the 1970 Act. Local authorities also have the power, under the Children Act 1989, to provide cash support for families whose children are at risk, a provision which dates back to 1963; and since 1997 they have also had the power to make payments directly to adult service users in lieu of direct provision. In practice few of these powers have been widely used by local authorities, although for those who do benefit the payments can be a significant form of support. Further, of course, all such payments are inevitably subject to cash limits imposed by annual expenditure plans, and they make the balancing of provision between cash and care a particularly acute dilemma for SSDs, and for their clients.

More generally, however, the advantages to be gained by increasing the incomes of poor social services clients has prompted the development of further, quite dramatic, extension of service provision by local authorities (and some voluntary sector agencies) over the last three decades or so. This is the employment by local authorities, usually as part of SSDs, of *welfare rights* workers to work with poor clients to seek to maximise their incomes, in particular through encouraging and assisting them to claim all the social security benefits to which they might be entitled.

As we discuss in Chapter 2, there is evidence that significant numbers of people do not take up all of the benefits to which they might be entitled, and this is especially the case with means-tested benefits. Providing people who might be entitled to benefits with advice and assistance could help to address this problem, and improving the financial circumstances of local people may strengthen their ability to meet their individual and family needs. For this reason Manchester City Council SSD appointed a welfare rights officer to work with poor clients in 1972, and in the years that followed a number of other authorities, especially those serving large urban areas, followed suit. By the 1980s this welfare rights work had become an established feature of social services (see Fimister, 1986), and by the 1990s it had grown to become a major element in local strategic planning to combat poverty more broadly (see Alcock, 1997, ch.15).

In the twenty-first century welfare rights activity extends beyond the clients of social services, and those providing such advice and assistance operate from within a wide range of public and voluntary sector agencies. However, many local authority employed welfare rights officers are still based in SSDs, and work predominantly to increase the incomes of social work clients. In some cases this has taken on a further complex dimension of the changing cash and care relationship. One of the areas of benefits where levels of take-up are particularly low, and can be increased with welfare rights support, is that of disability benefits. Securing such benefits for social services users can increase their income, and mean that they are more able to pay the charges for services that the local authority are providing for them. Improved take-up of these benefits can therefore mean more cash for the SSD in return for the care which is provided to those users who are entitled to the social security benefits, which are aimed at meeting the costs associated with the needs these services address.

The relationship between cash and care in social services is therefore an extremely complex one, extending across the divides between central and local government and between different departments of government concerned with different aspects of individual and social needs. Pressures for more joined-up government at the beginning of the new century may require some of these divisions to be addressed, and behind this lie some important questions of principle about the most appropriate balance between providing people with cash, so that they can buy the services they need, or with care, so that guaranteed standards of services can be assured.

QUESTION: COMPREHENSION

- Why did local authority welfare rights provision largely develop within SSDs?

QUESTION: REFLECTION

- What are the advantages and disadvantages of providing *cash* rather than *care* to social service users?

FURTHER READING

A good general introduction to social service policy is provided by Parrott (2002), with more extensive coverage found in Denney (1998). A good guide to the history of social work is provided by Adams (1996). The best book on adult services policy is probably Means and Smith (2003) and on working with children Colton, Sanders and Williams (2001). Government papers on social services can be found at **www.doh.gov.uk** with similar provision on the websites of the devolved administrations (see Chapter 15).

Employment

SUMMARY OF KEY POINTS

- Employment policy was not one of the major public programmes developed in the welfare reforms of the 1940s, but since then policy intervention in employment has become more widespread.
- Employment policy is now merged with social security policy in the Department for Work and Pensions (DWP).
- Employment policy has fluctuated between *supply-side* and *demand-side* approaches to the promotion of employment.
- Labour markets have altered dramatically over the past half century, moving from *Fordism* to *post-Fordism*.
- Women's participation in paid employment has been increasing gradually since the 1950s.
- From the 1970s on more interventionist policies to promote employment have been pursued by government, with the current Labour government making 'welfare to work' a key policy priority and introducing the *New Deal* for the unemployed.
- EU policy has been significant in expanding employment rights in the UK.
- Employment protection has grown in scale, including health and safety protection, control over working conditions and protection against discrimination at work.
- Employment regulation also covers collective labour regulations and the rights, and limits, of trade union action.

A UK employment policy?

When Beveridge listed the 'five giants' of social evil which he hoped would provide the foci for the public welfare policies of the post-war era in 1942 *idleness* was included as one of these. Like many policy makers and politicians Beveridge had been concerned by the social and individual costs of the large numbers of unemployed workers in Britain in the economic depression of the 1920s and 1930s, and he saw the waste of experience and potential that this represented as one of the main targets for social policy action (Beveridge, 1944). As we shall see, the evil of idleness did largely disappear in the decades following the social and economic reforms of the 1940s. However, this was not the product of any direct commitment to the development and implementation of a specific policy for employment or the commitment of public spending to support such a policy, as happened in response to the other evils discussed in the other chapters in Part I; rather it was the product of more general economic growth, supported on occasions by Keynesian-style stimulation of demand (see Chapter 13).

The study of social policy has therefore sometimes overlooked employment as a focus of policy intervention, and concentrated instead upon the major areas of social expenditure in social security, health, education, housing and social services. However, this spending-driven approach ignores the importance of employment to the pursuit of welfare and wellbeing in society, and the wide range of policy implements which have in fact been employed by governments to promote and regulate it. It is also something of a contrast to the way in which employment policy is viewed in many other developed nations, especially in continental Europe. In the other EU countries employment has often been a central concern of policy planners, in particular through the development of relatively strict regulatory frameworks to ensure that employment relations do support, rather than undermine, the welfare of working citizens. This has also been a major area of EU regulation, as we shall discuss shortly.

The inattention to employment policy within social policy analysis is probably largely a historical feature of the subject today, however. Most policy analysts, and more importantly most politicians, now recognise the important role that policy intervention can play in the employment area; and there are now identifiable elements of policy development with a clear focus on employment relations within society: although, as we shall discuss later, they have largely conceived employment and employment policy as concerned with the work of men rather than women. In general these policy measures now cover two broad areas:

   the promotion and support of paid employment
   the regulation of individual and collective employment conditions.

The centrality of employment policy within public planning is particularly evident under the Labour governments of the early twenty-first century. Support for employment through policy intervention is one of Labour's highest-profile policy commitments, which finds expression most overtly in the catchphrase used to describe a number of distinct but interrelated policy initiatives, *welfare to work.*

The important role that employment policy now plays in social policy practice can also be seen in the organisational changes aimed a creating a departmental and civil service structure which can give effect to new commitments to policy development and implementation. In the 1990s the old Department of Employment was merged with the Department of Education to create a Department for Education and Employment (DfEE), the intention being (in part at least) to link education and training to the needs and demands of the labour market. In 2001, however, this department was broken up and responsibility for employment policy was merged with social security in a newly created Department for Work and Pensions (DWP).

The central role of welfare to work in policy planning is clearly evident in these changes, and it has also been translated into direct policy delivery with the creation in 2002 of a new agency to administer both employment support and social security benefits for all citizens of working age, *Jobcentre Plus.* Jobcentre Plus replaces the Benefits Agency for working age claimants (see Chapter 2). It also replaces the old Jobcentres run before 2002 by the Employment Service, the quasi-autonomous administrative agency of the DfEE. As we shall see, Jobcentres in fact have a long history dating back almost one hundred years, although their role has changed in many ways over this time; and, as with other areas of employment policy practice, current structures and procedures are really a development and adaptation of past practices rather than any wholly new departure in policy planning.

Policy context

As with other areas of welfare, employment policy has been influenced by the wider policy context within which it has been introduced and developed. This is a complex and changing context, but within it the influence of broader political and ideological perspectives can be identified. In particular we can contrast the influence of two counter-posed strands of thought and practice:

1. *Laissez-faire* – this approach draws on nineteenth-century liberalism and the neo-liberalism of the New Right in the late twentieth century (see Chapter 12). It is based upon the assumption that any interference by government policy makers in the workings of the free market is likely to lead to imbalance and inefficiency in the market, and hence to economic and social problems (*laissez-faire* in French means 'leave alone'). This applies to the labour market as much as any other market, and hence neo-liberals have argued in recent times that governments should not interfere in the regulation of employment conditions or in the creation or support of employment opportunities. Such thinking underlay some of the rhetoric of the Thatcher administrations of the 1980s, although it did not in practice mean that they withdrew entirely from either regulating or supporting employment.
2. *Regulation* – this approach draws on labourism and social democracy and is associated much more closely with the politics and the concerns of the working classes. Labourist policy makers are more politically committed to government intervention to protect workers and support employment. Social

democratic thinking more generally is also underpinned by the belief that governments can, and must, act to regulate social relations (including employment relations) and to promote virtuous economic development within capitalist economies. Labour governments in particular therefore have frequently openly championed workers' rights and the pursuit of 'full employment'; this is certainly true of the Blair administrations of the early twenty-first century.

The history of employment policy is something of battle between these two opposing conceptions of the role of public policy, although of course the reality of policy practice has remained somewhere in between the extremes of *laissez-faire* and full employment.

Despite the rhetorical support which the *laissez-faire* approach enjoyed from most governments in the nineteenth century, policy intervention in labour market relations can be traced back to the early decades of the century with the introduction of the Factories Acts and other statutes restricting by law the hours of work of some employees and controlling the employment of women and children in some industries (Fraser, 2003, ch.1). At the beginning of the twentieth century intervention was taken much further by the Liberal governments of 1906–14 who also championed a number of other significant developments in public welfare policy (Fraser, 2003, ch.7; Thane, 1996, ch.3). In 1909 more measures of employment protection were introduced, including the setting of minimum wages in some industries and the establishment of 'labour exchanges'. The latter were public bodies providing information and advice about employment opportunities to unemployed workers. They were the first significant step towards policy intervention to promote employment and have remained a major feature of policy practice since, becoming in 2002 the new Jobcentres Plus.

The early twentieth century was also, however, the period of the early growth and influence of the trade union movement. Trade unions were independent organizations of workers, generally based on specific trades or industries, whose aim was to promote and protect the conditions of their members through collective action, or the threat of it. The movement was instrumental in the establishment of the Labour Party, which it was hoped would pursue workers' rights through political and legal reform; but its primary concern was to press employers to enter into collective agreements to guarantee basic rights, and improved wages, for their workers. The trade unions therefore provided an avenue for employment protection outside the public policy instruments of the state; and this alternative means of policy development has been instrumental in creating a pressure on even Labour governments to consider carefully how much job protection should be a matter for government and how much it should be left to private bargaining. They have also created pressure for additional policy intervention to control the activities of trade unions themselves, as we shall discuss towards the end of this chapter.

In the 1920s and 1930s economic depression led to high levels of unemployment in the UK. There were also major conflicts between employers and trade unions, with Britain's only general strike being called in 1926. However, government intervention in employment policy remained relatively limited and was concentrated mainly upon using social security administration to ensure that those claiming unemployment benefits (now referred to as 'the dole') were 'genuinely seeking paid work' (Deacon, 1976). This was in contrast to developments elsewhere, notably the 'New Deal' policies in the USA, where high levels of public expenditure were used to create work opportunities for some of the unemployed.

However, the legacy of the hardships of idleness in the 1930s did influence political thinking during and after the Second World War. Wartime production needs soon reduced the scale of the dole queues; and policy makers began to talk directly about the responsibility of peacetime governments, too, in actively promoting full employment. Beveridge's (1942) report on social security policy reform was predicated on the explicit assumption that benefit support for the unemployed would be linked to government commitments to ensure that full employment meant that jobs were available for all those (men) able to work. And at the same time Keynes's (1936) economic advice to government was that full employment would ensure demand for goods and services and hence promote economic growth, and therefore should be supported by government through increased public expenditure if necessary. In 1944 the ideas of Beveridge and Keynes received official support in a White Paper on Employment Policy, outlining commitments to pursue high and stable levels of employment after the war.

In the three decades immediately following the war these commitments were largely met and the level of unemployment generally remained under 500,000, or 2–3 per cent of the working population. In large part this was due to consistent economic growth across the industrial world in the 1950s and early 1960s; and the demand for labour which flowed from this even led to Britain seeking to recruit additional workers through the encouragement of immigration from its ex-colonial Commonwealth partners. However, in the mid-1970s there was again economic recession and unemployment levels began to rise to over a million; the ability of Keynesian economic policies to restore full employment was openly questioned by the supporters of monetarism, as we discuss in Chapter 13.

With the election of the Conservatives under Thatcher in 1979 Keynesian economics was formally and finally abandoned, and with it the commitment of government to seek to maintain full employment through public investment. The Thatcher administrations were strongly influenced by the neo-liberal view that governments should not intervene in labour markets to stimulate demand for employment; during a period of massive economic upheaval unemployment levels rose rapidly and dramatically to over 3 million, or more than 10 per cent of the workforce (see Figure 7.1).

The 1980s and 1990s saw a shift away from the post-war economic policies which had helped to support full employment. However, they did not result in any abandonment of employment policy. Indeed, important changes were made by the Conservatives to individual and collective employment regulations; and policies to promote training and work experience which had been introduced in the 1970s were much expanded, as we shall see below. More significantly the changes did mark something of a shift in the broad focus of employment

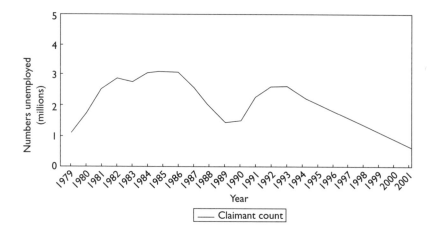

Figure 7.1   Unemployment in the UK, 1979–2001 (percentage)
Source: Adapted from *Social Trends and Labour Market Trends*,
Office of National Statistics (2002).

policy from a concern with control over the *demand* for labour to concern over control over its *supply*.

1. *Demand-side* policies for employment are concerned with the provision of employment opportunities within the labour market and the belief that these can be expanded (or contracted) by government investment in labour-intensive production either in the public or private sectors (in short, the provision of jobs for the workers).
2. *Supply-side* policies for employment are concerned with equipping potential workers for the labour market through public investment in the provision of skills training and job experience programmes for the unemployed, in the expectation that well-equipped workers will be able to secure a place in the labour market (in short, the provision of workers for the jobs).

It is debatable, of course, whether either demand- or supply-side approaches to the promotion of employment can be effective on their own, and governments concerned to create and support paid employment need to pay attention to both sides of the labour market contract. However, the balance of emphasis between the two has changed over time and shifted significantly towards the supply-side approach in the 1980s and 1990s. The welfare to work, which we discuss in more detail below, policies of the Labour governments have continued the trend to some extent, although improved economic growth at the beginning of the twenty-first century helped considerably in leading to the major reduction in unemployment recorded in Figure 7.1, and it has also permitted the government to begin to talk again about policy commitments for the promotion of full employment.

In the latter part of the twentieth century, however, the policy context within the UK was influenced not just by the policies and practices of government here but also by the policy prescriptions and directions of the EU. As we discuss in Chapter 14, Britain's membership of the EU has meant that the country must subscribe to certain policy directives emanating from Brussels. In practice Britain has sometimes been a rather reluctant partner to the social and economic policy agendas of the EU, and in the early 1990s under the Major government Britain secured the right to 'opt out' of the agreed provisions for the regulation of workers' rights across the EU in the Maastricht Treaty, as discussed in Chapter 14. However, the Labour government has since reversed this provision and agreed to abide by this and future EU provisions for employment and other social rights.

Employment regulation has always been a central feature of EU economic and social policy planning. This is in large part a product of the underlying commitment within the EU to secure open and fair economic competition across all member states, and it means that the EU has sought to introduce a 'level playing field' in which the rights and protections offered to workers are similar across all countries. This is intended to combat the problem of 'social dumping' under which those nations offering the worst pay and conditions to workers can seek to attract capital investment away from those requiring higher (and therefore more expensive) forms of employee protection (James, 1998). EU regulation of employment relations covers a number of areas including health and safety standards, maximum hours of work, equal treatment of men and women, and the right to work (and receive social security protection) in any member state. Many of these rights are now collected together in a 'Community Charter of the Fundamental Rights of Workers', sometimes referred to as the *Social Charter*. The Charter ensures a measure of equal competition for employers and employees; but it also provides the framework a common employment policy across the Union. And, despite initial reluctance, this framework has significantly influenced the policy context within the UK; most of the key elements of the Charter are now embedded features of employment policy practice within the country, from which future governments would be unlikely to be able, or willing, to retreat.

QUESTIONS: COMPREHENSION

■ What is the difference between demand-side and supply-side approaches to the promotion of employment?
■ Why has the EU taken such a leading role in the enforcement of workers' rights within member nations?

QUESTION: REFLECTION

■ Would it be more accurate to say that UK employment policy is really an *un*employment policy?

Economic context

The ability of governments to commit themselves to policy interventions to secure full employment has depended, as we have seen, on the broader economic climate within which these policies are required to operate. Changes in the economic context affect all social policies; but in the case of employment policy the relationship is a direct one for levels of employment, and the pay and conditions of workers are directly affected by changes in economic performance and production processes. The development of economic policy in the UK is discussed in Chapter 13, and we do not have the space here to engage in any thorough review of the ways in which labour markets have changed as a result of this changing economic context. However, it is worth outlining briefly some key elements and the implications which they have had for the development of employment policy within the UK.

To some extent these changes are a product of the shift from *Fordist* to *post-Fordist* modes of production (see Chapter 13). Under Fordist mass production, economic activity is dominated by the mass production of consumer goods which requires large numbers of manufacturing workers (and their managers) working on specific tasks in big factories, as pioneered by the Ford motor company in the USA. Workers thus acquire core skills early and remain in relatively secure jobs throughout their working lives. In the latter part of the twentieth century this production and employment pattern began to disappear. Manufacturing processes became more automated (machines do the tasks previously performed by workers) and more labour-intensive production was transferred overseas to developing nations with lower wage levels. Employment in Britain and other (former) industrial nations became concentrated instead in service work – banking, insurance, tourism, catering and leisure – and in the design and development of new (computer-based) technologies. Here working conditions required more flexibility in working hours and contractual commitments (more jobs are part time or temporary) and technological change meant that skills had to be updated or relearnt at different times throughout the life course.

These changes have been described as post-Fordism because they result in a significant shift away from employment in manufacturing. Over the last century employment in manufacturing (and agriculture) has declined, whilst employment in office-based activity has grown (see Figure 7.2).

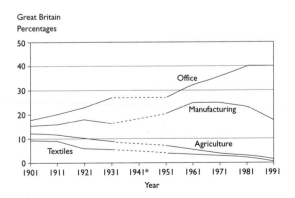

Figure 7.2   Workforce by selected industry
Source: Social Trends, Office of National Statistics, 2002.

* There was no census in 1941.

Employment patterns have been altered by these labour market changes, leading in general to less secure employment for many and to increased unemployment for some, as we saw in Figure 7.1. These changes have affected all workers; but, as mentioned above, early post-war employment policies were directed mainly at men rather than women, which raises the issue of gender differences, and discrimination, within the labour market.

The full employment policies of the post-war era were really only intended to apply to men, under a model of family life within which the man was the employed 'breadwinner' and the woman was the unpaid home carer. Of course, this never represented reality for many men and women, and large numbers of women (both single and married) were in paid employment and their families were reliant upon their wages for essential financial support (Crompton, 1999). However, alongside more general changes in family structure in the latter part of the twentieth century (a decline in the birth rate and increases in divorce and lone parent families) there has been a significant increase in the proportion of women within the labour market, rising from below 30 per cent in the 1950s to over 45 per cent in the 1990s, with over 70 per cent of working age women now economically active (see Callender, 1996).

Women's patterns of employment are generally speaking very different from those of men (see Abbott and Wallace, 1997, ch.8). For a start, average wages are lower, women earn between 70 and 80 per cent of men's wages depending on whether weekly or hourly rates are compared. Women also work in different areas of the labour market (for instance, in food and drink manufacture, in catering, and in health and social services); and they tend to occupy lower status jobs as secretaries, teachers and nurses rather than managers, school heads or doctors. Within a segregated labour market, therefore, female employees tend to be found in the more disadvantaged areas, and this has consequences for their career development and security. Nevertheless most women do now engage in paid work, and the post-Fordist labour market is one in which women as well as men expect to enter employment.

However, the high levels of unemployment which have affected all industrial nations since the last two decades of the twentieth century have meant that not all who want (or need) to work have been able to do so. Higher unemployment is one of the main consequences of restructuring which accompanied the collapse of Fordism; but in practice it is only a part of the broader changes in patterns of economic activity and inactivity. Those who are counted as unemployed are those either claiming unemployment benefits or looking for work: that is, those seeking to be active in the labour market. There are other people of working age who are not active in the labour market and, amongst men in particular, the numbers of these have been growing.

The economically inactive include those at home caring for children or dependent adults (both women and men), those in education and training (now large numbers, especially amongst younger adults), those who have 'retired' from employment early, and those unable to work because of sickness or disability. Of course, many of these people might wish to be employed if appropriate labour market opportunities existed, and for this reason some commentators have referred to some of these inactive workers as the 'hidden unemployed' (Beatty *et al.*, 2002). The evidence is that the numbers of such economically inactive men, in particular, have been growing significantly in recent years (Alcock *et al.*, 2003). This reveals that in the labour markets of the early twenty-first century patterns of both employment and unemployment are more complex than the traditional models of manufacturing work and male breadwinners might at one time have suggested. These high levels of unemployment and inactivity have also prompted governments to take a more interventionist approach towards the support that is provided to facilitate labour market participation.

Promoting employment

Throughout most of the last century policy measures were in force to provide encouragement and support for those seeking to gain (or regain) entry to the labour market. Support came from the labour exchanges or jobcentres, and encouragement from the expectation that those seeking social security support from the state should make themselves available for work. The requirement to be available for work can be seen as a threat as well as an encouragement, however. There has been much dispute over whether it means that unemployed workers must take any job that is offered to them and what the consequences should be if they do not. In practice the conditions that are attached to receipt of unemployment benefits to encourage claimants to seek employment have varied over time, and have often been at their most draconian at times when labour market demand is weak and levels of unemployment high. This is particularly true of the 'genuinely seeking work' test which was applied in the 1930s and the conditions attached to the renamed Jobseekers' Allowance in the 1990s, which required claimants to enter into an agreement to take positive steps to search for work. And for those who do refuse a reasonable offer of work, or leave past employment without good cause, temporary reductions in social security support are imposed.

This general encouragement and support through the social security system has not provided much by way of direct assistance to people finding it difficult to gain paid employment, however. Indeed it has operated more as a general underpinning to the market basis of employment than as a form of intervention in that market on behalf of those experiencing difficulties with it. In the last quarter of the twentieth century, at a time when the economic restructuring discussed above was beginning to make significant changes to past patterns of employment and unemployment, this situation began to change as more specific programmes were introduced to provide training and work experience for unemployed workers, targeted in particular at those groups finding it most difficult to secure entry to the changing labour market.

The declining role of traditional manufacturing employment which began to take effect in the early 1970s resulted also in the collapse of the skills training which had accompanied such work, notably the apprenticeship system under which employers would provide on-the-job training for young workers to equip them with the practical skills that they would need for their future working lives. With the need for such lifetime skills disappearing and with some of the employers who had provided them going out of business, the apprentice-ship model disappeared too, making entry into the labour market for those leaving school with limited academic qualifications much more difficult. It was these young unemployed workers who were one of the target groups for the new programmes introduced by the new agency established by government in the 1970s, the Manpower Services Commission (MSC).

The MSC was an important policy innovation, for a number of reasons. It began a series of employment support activities which have grown in scale and intensity since. It was also an early example of a quango (quasi-autonomous non-governmental organisation), supported by public funds but managed by an independent board on which representatives of employers and employees were joined by civil servants and politicians. In the 1980s the MSC was replaced by locally managed Training and Enterprise Councils (TECs), and these in turn were superseded in 2001 by the Learning and Skills Council which had a broader responsibility for all further education provision (see Chapter 3). Such independent agencies have now become a key element in the delivery of many public services, including the Jobcentres Plus which now carry responsibility for some of the employment support activities first developed in the MSC.

The most significant of the early employment support programmes was the Youth Opportunities Programme (YOP). This provided training and work experience for 16–19 year olds and in many ways was a direct substitute for pub-lic support for the old private apprenticeships. However, because YOP place-ments were publicly funded and temporary they did not automatically guarantee the young trainees access to paid employment, and at the end of the experience many were little better off in labour market terms than they had been before. This has become an intrinsic feature of many similar subsequent employment support schemes, which seek to equip workers for employment in a market where jobs may still be scarce. In simple terms employment support is not employ-ment. Indeed, it may even be that the work experience provided in such place-ments can reduce the number of opportunities available in the labour market as employers seek to take on (publicly subsidised) trainees rather than paid workers (a problem referred to a job displacement).

Nevertheless such programmes have become more widespread and more established over the last quarter century or so. YOPs were replaced by a broader Youth Training Scheme (YTS) in the 1980s, which became the Modern Apprenticeship in the 1990s (a clear reference back to the old apprentice train-ing model). The other main group targeted in such programmes were the long-term unemployed, those out of work for six months (or a year) or more, whose numbers also began to grow in the 1970s and after. The MSC ran a Community Programme to provide a range of work placements for these people. And in the 1980s this was replaced by Employment Training (ET), which relied more heav-ily on provision through private employers, although here problems of job dis-placement were more acute.

When the Labour government came to power in 1997 it did so with a clear manifesto commitment to replace much of the past employment support pro-vision with a *New Deal* for the unemployed, in which training and work expe-rience would be aligned with a renewed commitment to help key groups amongst the unemployed gain entry to the labour market. Indeed the New Deal was the only element of Labour's social policy reforms to receive additional public support in 1997 for, although the government had committed itself to remaining within the past Conservative administration's spending limits for the first two years of office, it levied a 'windfall' tax on the profits of the new private utilities to provide over £3.6 billion to fund the new programmes.

The government has developed several different New Deal programmes targeted at different groups amongst the unemployed:

- young people: 18–24 year olds
- long-term unemployed: over 25s claiming benefits for over 2 years
- lone parents: with children over 5, and over 3 months on benefit
- partners of the unemployed: where partners have been on benefit for over 6 months
- disabled people: on incapacity benefit or other disability benefit
- 50 plus: over 50s and their partners on benefits for over 6 months.

The programmes vary in principle and in practice. That for young people is by far the largest, consuming over 70 per cent of the resources (£2.5 billion) between 1997 and 2002. It offers young people out of work the choice of subsidised employment, voluntary work, environmental task force work or full-time education and training, and all must choose one of these. In the now famous words, there is no 'fifth option' of remaining on benefits. The young people are helped to find the most appropriate option by a Personal Adviser allocated to them within the Employment Service (now Jobcentre Plus) as part of a 'gateway' period of assessment and guidance. For the long-term unemployed the programme is also compulsory, with all four options available from April 2001. For the other groups, however, it is the access to the Personal Adviser which is the main source of support, with an optional training grant available in some cases.

The early results from the New Deal, especially the flagship programme for young people, were quite dramatic, with a fall in the number of 18–24 year olds unemployed for over six months from 169,500 in 1997 to under 52,00 in 2000 (Finn, 2001). However, this was at a time when unemployment levels were falling more generally (see Figure 7.1), and it is unlikely that all of this change can be attributed to the New Deal itself. In a review of the detailed evaluations of the New Deal commissioned by the government and others, Millar (2000) commented that one of the most positive outcomes had been the support and guidance provided by the Personal Advisers. This is important because it suggests that the general policies of encouraging, or enforcing, employment which have dominated employment support may not be sufficiently sensitive to the different circumstances of those who find themselves outside the labour market, and that individually tailored advice and support may be more valuable. However, it remains to be seen whether such an individual service can be developed and sustained as a central feature of future employment policy planning.

The New Deal is only one element in the broader strategic approach to employment policy taken by the Labour government, publicised more generally as the commitment to promote the move from *welfare to work*. The training and work experience of the New Deal has also been accompanied by other policy initiatives designed to support those in paid employment, sometimes referred to as making work pay, which include the following:

1. *Statutory minimum wages*, introduced in 1999 for all employees, initially fixed at £3.60 an hour and later raised to £4.20 in 2002. This was the first time that a national wage floor had been introduced in the UK, although it has been common in other industrial countries.
2. *Working families tax credit* was a replacement for the previous family credit, a benefit which acted as a subsidy to low wages for parents of young children. The tax credit was introduced in 1999; it could be paid to the employee and provided support across a wider range of the low-income scale. There were also credits for disabled workers, and they were extended to all low-wage employees in 2003.
3. *Family friendly employment* was the extension of rights for maternity and paternity leave, and the introduction of tax credits for the costs of children and child care into the general tax system.

Implicit in the welfare to work strategy, however, is the belief that entry into paid employment is the major (perhaps the only) route out of poverty and dependency, and that, providing that economic growth can be supported and sustained, employment opportunities should be there for those who are equipped to take them. These are contentious assumptions. In a situation of economic downturn employment opportunities may not be so plentiful, and in these circumstances an employment policy which focuses exclusively on a supply-side approach may not be sufficient to ensure employment for all; indeed, there is evidence that this has been the case for some time in those parts of the country where economic growth has not been so marked, such as the former coalfield and manufacturing areas of the North and Midlands of England, South Wales and Central Scotland. And if employment opportunities are not available, then work cannot be a route out of poverty and welfare for all.

This raises some more general questions about the broader policy goals which underlie employment support. To some extent the New Deal programmes of the Labour government have been modelled on the welfare reforms introduced in the USA as part of a similar strategic commitment to reducing social security dependency. Here compulsory participation in publicly funded work placements is more widespread, in some states even applying to the lone mothers of young children; and it is to some extent based upon a moral belief in the value of paid employment. Such compulsory employment participation is sometimes referred to as *work first* or *workfare*.

This approach can be contrasted with the employment programmes developed in some continental European countries, where the support provided for those outside the labour market includes a wider range of forms of social activity including voluntary work and caring responsibilities; entry into paid employment is not treated as the only viable option. These programmes are sometimes referred to as *social activation* and they are based upon a very different understanding of role of employment support in post-Fordist economies (see Lodemel and Trickey, 2001). The UK government's welfare to work strategies include elements of both workfare and social activation, although it is far from clear that the different principles underlying these two approaches can in fact operate side by side within the same schemes. Nevertheless, what is clear is that the broader promotion of employment opportunities is now a central feature of policy planning in the UK.

QUESTIONS: COMPREHENSION

- Discuss the implications of post-Fordist labour markets for employment policy planning.
- What is 'job displacement' and why is it a potential problem within supply-side policies to promote employment?
- What are the key elements of Labour's *welfare to work* strategy, and how have these altered past employment policy practice?
- What are the differences in principle and in practice between *workfare* and *social activation?*

QUESTION: REFLECTION

- Should we aim to encourage all adults of working age to enter paid employment?

Employment protection

Much of the recent discussion of employment policy in the UK has focused upon the development of provisions for employment support. However, measures to promote employment protection have in practice had a longer history and cover a wider range of policy interventions and legal safeguards. As mentioned above, employment protection can be traced back to the Factories Acts of the early nineteenth century. These controlled hours and conditions of work for some employees in certain industries. These forms of protection were extended in the early twentieth century (for instance, in the Trade Boards Act of 1909). They were followed by the establishment of minimum wage levels for some industries, enforced by Wages Councils, although these were later abolished in the 1980s.

The twentieth century also saw the development of extensive provision for health and safety at work. This included the setting of safeguards and standards for various workplaces (such as fire precautions and safety guards on machines) enforced by public officials in what became the Health and Safety Executive. It also extended to compensation for injuries sustained at work or specified diseases contracted as a result of exposure to certain workplace risks.

In the 1960s and 1970s a wider range of rights for individual workers were introduced in order to secure some minimum standards beyond those which individual workers could negotiate within their own employment contracts. These new employment rights covered compensation for losing employment through unfair dismissal or redundancy, rights to information about terms and conditions of employment, paid leave for sickness and maternity and rights to equal pay and equal treatment between men and women. The equal treatment provisions were also extended as a result of legislation to outlaw discrimination on the grounds of gender and race, which included discrimination in the work-place; and in 1995 this was extended further to cover discrimination on the basis of disability too.

These individual employment rights have also been the subject of EU policy provision, flowing from the concern of the Commission of the EU to combat 'social dumping' by ensuring equal employment protection across member states. Measures concerning health and safety, equal pay, and maximum weekly working time have all been incorporated into British legislation to comply with EU directives. In 1989 the then member states adopted the Social Charter to guarantee a range of employment protection for all workers; and after 1997 this was incorporated into British law too.

As discussed earlier, however, there has always been some dispute over the extent to which statutory employment protection should underpin (or under-mine) the bargaining over contractual relations which takes place between employers and trade unions, acting on behalf of individual workers. In practice this is less of an issue than it was on occasions in the last century, with most trade unions now regarding statutory protections as a floor from which they can seek to negotiate even greater levels of protection for their members. However, the activities of trade unions within employment relations have led to a separate set of policy initiatives and legislative measures to seek to control union activity and seek a balance between collective action and individual employment rights. Industrial relations legislation, as this is generally called, has at times been con-troversial, with unions claiming that (particularly Conservative) governments have used this to prevent them from acting in support of their members. Nevertheless such provision is now an established element of the more general regulation of employment protection covering such issues as the right to join (or not join) a union, the procedures to be followed by trade unions before instructing their members to take industrial action, and the extent to which dif-ferent forms of action are a legitimate means of pursuing a grievance or dispute within any particular industry or employment site.

Employment protection has always occupied something of a secondary sta-tus within debate about, and study of, employment policy, and this continues today with a number of texts focusing primarily upon employment promotion (Baldock *et al.*, 1999; Page and Silburn, 1999). Nevertheless policies to ensure minimum standards of job security, working conditions and remuneration are an essential counterpart to provisions aimed at promoting paid employment, especially from a supply-side approach. It is only if the jobs do offer sufficient security, protection and reward that potential workers can be justifiably coerced into taking them on. Thus employment policy does require government to intervene in the regulation of the labour market, alongside any measures to promote increased participation within it.

QUESTION: COMPREHENSION

■ In what ways have statutory employment measures sought to protect the interests of workers?

QUESTION: REFLECTION

■ Some critics have argued that employment regulation interferes with the natural operation of labour markets and the collective bargaining between workers and employers, and so operates to inhibit rather than support employment growth. To what extent do you agree with this view?

FURTHER READING

There is no single comprehensive text on employment policy in Britain. Philpott's (1997) collection includes papers on unemployment and policy responses. A Deacon (2002) reviews the theoretical arguments behind recent policies for employment promotion; and Lodemel and Trickey (2001) provide examples of policy developments in a range of different advanced industrial countries. The best guide to employment protection is produced by the Trades Union Congress (TUC, 2000). Government papers can be found on the departmental website at **www.dwp.gov.uk**. A useful website for employment issues is the Institute for Employment Studies: **www.employment-studies.co.uk**, and the TUC website is a good source of information about workers' issues and workers' rights: see **www.tuc.org.uk**.

Part II

Structure

The State

SUMMARY OF KEY POINTS

- State provision of welfare is an essential element of social policy, for only the state has the power and the legitimacy to act on behalf of all citizens.
- The provision of welfare through the state has operated both to support economic growth and to protect citizens from some of the social problems caused by economic markets.
- The welfare reforms of the 1940s have sometimes been argued as leading to the establishment of the 'Keynes/Beveridge welfare state' in Britain.
- Expenditure on state welfare grew gradually both in absolute and relative terms throughout the last century, and in particular after the 1940s reforms.
- The British state is made up of an executive (the Cabinet), a legislature (Parliament) and a judiciary (the courts). However, much control over policy is in practice held by civil servants working in government departments.
- Policy making in the UK is partly devolved to the different national administrations and to local government.
- As well as acting as a *provider* of services the state also *subsidises* and *regulates* other providers, and acts as a major *employer*.
- The continued expansion of state welfare has been questioned by ever increasing demands for services and by problems in securing popular support for tax revenues to pay for expansion of public services.

The 'welfare state'

The main focus of study and debate in social policy has been the 'welfare state'. As we discussed in Chapter 1, the Fabian pioneers of social policy in the early twentieth century were concerned first and foremost with developing academic research and political argument that would put pressure on the government in the UK to use the power of the state to introduce welfare reforms to respond to the social problems which they had identified. Their expectation was that if evidence could be produced to demonstrate that the capitalist economy was operating in ways which were leading to hardship or deprivation, it would be the duty of the state to intervene to alleviate or prevent this hardship. Their intention was that this intervention should take the form of services provided directly by the state, using resources collected from citizens in the form of taxation.

Quite how far the state should go in providing such services, of course, has always been a matter of debate and disagreement, both within social policy and beyond. However, after the introduction of public provision for education and social security in the early decades of the last century, the debate about state welfare has become very much one about *how much* state provision there should be, as opposed to *whether* there should be any. And as the textbooks on the history of the welfare state explain (Thane, 1996; Page and Silburn, 1999), throughout the first half of the century state welfare provision began gradually to expand.

The growth of state welfare provision in Britain was not a product only of the persuasive moral and academic arguments of the Fabian policy reformers: academic and moral argument does not necessarily bring about political change. Nevertheless, the hardship about which the Fabians argued was real enough and, for those who were its victims, it created a source of active social and economic conflict. Britain's capitalist economy thus produced conflict between the poor working class and the rich and powerful; and this was a conflict that produced social movements, not just the theories and statistics of the academics.

The early part of the twentieth century saw the rapid development of such movements, in particular the trade union movement, designed to protect the interests of workers against their capitalist employers, and the Labour Party, supported by the unions to pursue the collective demands of workers through the winning of political power within the electoral system. In the 1920s and 1930s the trade unions engaged in conflict with capital over hardship and deprivation at work; and the Labour Party achieved political power – for periods at least – in central and local government. In these ways the deprivation produced by capitalism created conditions of conflict and struggle from which intervention by the state became an achievable political goal. With Labour governments, in particular, the Fabian policy reformers had a base within the British political system at which to direct their arguments on the need for welfare reform.

However, the causes of the growth in state intervention for welfare in Britain do not lie only in the successful struggle of the working class and its Fabian middle-class allies, for welfare reform has always had a double-edged impact within capitalist economies. Improved state education, for example, provides employers with a better trained and more able workforce; and, as the development of machinery and the introduction of new technologies have made the process of production ever more complex, this has permitted industry to operate more efficiently. Improved housing and health conditions for workers have also improved their overall efficiency, and so have helped the development of the economy. Even social security benefits, although financed in part by contributions from employers, have helped to maintain the unemployed as a labour force in waiting to be rejected or re-employed as economic forces dictate.

The development of the welfare state, therefore, is not only the product of the attempt to remedy the failings of a capitalist economy but also of the recognition of new ways in which this economy might be maintained and developed. On the one hand, therefore, social policy challenges the operations of capitalist economics, and yet on the other it helps these economies to develop and function more effectively. This dual character was identified by Gough in his seminal text on the political economy of welfare (1979); and more recently international analysis of the development of welfare provision across capitalist economies has revealed the continuing importance of state welfare provision to the economic performance of these countries (Pierson, 1998; Goodin *et al.*, 1999). The provision of public welfare is now an intrinsic feature of all advanced industrial economies.

In the period immediately following the Second World War these pressures for welfare reform, both from within capital and within the working class, appeared all to come together in Britain:

1. A Labour government was elected, after a landslide victory, with manifesto commitments to reform capitalism through state intervention.
2. Fabian academics and their allies occupied influential positions within the state: notably Beveridge, author of the report on social security reform, and Keynes, a senior economic adviser to the wartime government.
3. British capitalism had experienced significant government intervention as part of the war effort, and it needed rapidly to adjust to the changing demands of peacetime production within a restructured world economy.

It is for these reasons that commentators argued that during this post-war period there was a *consensus* in Britain over the desirability of welfare reform between capital and labour, and between their 'representatives' within the major political parties, and that this consensus created a unique opportunity for the rapid development of the welfare state (Addison, 1975).

The Labour government reforms of the 1940s are widely credited as providing the basis for the establishment of the welfare state in Britain, informed by the social policy prescriptions of Beveridge and the economic policy plans of Keynes (see Chapter 13). For this reason it is sometimes referred to as the *Keynes/Beveridge* Welfare State. The post-war reforms encompassed a wide range of social and economic changes aimed at eliminating Beveridge's five evils (see Chapter 1); but three features in particular established a new role for the state within the British capitalist economy:

- the development of public social services
- the nationalisation of major industries
- the commitment to full employment.

The development of *public social services* included the NHS, state education and the National Insurance scheme. These were financed out of taxes and contributions from citizens and they recruited employees into state-run organisations to provide services to all who needed them, generally on a universal basis with free access. These state welfare services could be seen as almost 'socialist' in their aims and structures; and there were some on the left (and the right) who hoped (or feared) that they would be a first step towards a more far-reaching socialist restructuring of Britain's capitalist economy. As we shall see, however, Britain's welfare state, even in this immediate post-war period of expansion, was never socialist either in aim or in achievement; as in the earlier part of the century, state provision for health, education and social security operated as much to support the broader capitalist economy as to challenge it. It was also not comprehensive, and private and voluntary provision of many services remained alongside the new state services (sometimes even in competition with them).

The *nationalisation* programme of the post-war Labour government also established a new role for the state within British society. Major industries such as coal and steel were taken into public ownership; they were run by state-appointed managers, and their workers became state employees. The same happened to the main infrastructural services such as gas, electricity and public transport. Again, these nationalisation measures could appear to be elements of a strategy for the 'socialisation' of the entire capitalist economy. Certainly they significantly restructured British capitalism by introducing a large state sector no longer under the control of private ownership and the profit motive, and this led some commentators to argue that Britain had therefore been transformed from a capitalist economy into a *mixed economy* (Crosland, 1956). However, even the nationalisation of major industries left the vast majority of British capital in private hands, and there was never any intention of carrying through a state take-over of all private firms. Furthermore, the nationalised industries had to trade and contract with private capitalist enterprises and, although they were supported and sometimes subsidised by the state, they were required to operate in the marketplace with profit and loss accounts like private companies. Indeed, the guaranteed operation of such major state industries and services after the 1940s provided both a stable physical and economic environment for private industry and a secure market for many private products. In the welfare field, for instance, the National Health Service provided a major boost to the development of private drug companies.

The commitment to *full employment* was in part based on a reaction to the high levels of unemployment experienced in Britain during the economic depression of the 1930s, as we saw in Chapter 7. State intervention to promote employment fitted well with the wider role for economic policy recommended by Keynes. It was Keynes' belief that governments could, and should, use their role as employers and investors to encourage growth within market economies, as we discuss in Chapter 13; and one of the major triggers for such intervention was the commitment to maintain unemployment below an agreed minimum level.

Therefore, although the post-war welfare state transformed the capitalist economy in Britain, it did not replace it. The political consensus in favour of welfare reform through the state was as much a matter of compromise as a meeting of minds; it was predicated upon the assumption that state welfare reforms would support, and not prejudice, wider economic growth. What is more, as we saw in Part I, the development of state welfare did not entirely displace private provision for health and education, and the voluntary and informal sectors of welfare provision continued to operate despite the 1940s reforms. In welfare, as in manufacturing, post-war Britain became a mixed economy in which state provision was only a part of the overall picture.

This was a picture, nonetheless, in which it seemed that state welfare provision was able to grow ever more rapidly to meet more and more social needs as British society became generally more and more affluent in the years following the war; expanding welfare could even be seen as part of an inevitable process of development within a capitalist economy. This can be seen most clearly in the growing size of the state welfare sector both in expenditure terms and as a proportion of economic activity in the country. As Table 8.1 reveals, welfare expenditure had grown dramatically from around 2.6 per cent of GDP in 1900 to about ten times that by the end of the century.

Table 8.1   Expenditure on welfare (education, health and social security), 1900–95

	1900	1921	1941	1951	1961	1971	1981	1991	1995
Expenditure (£billion, 1996 prices)	3.6	8.8	12.7	28	43.7	75.1	112	147	169.8
Expenditure as percentage of GDP	2.6	6.4	5.6	11.2	13.2	17.3	22.2	22.6	24

Source: Adapted from Tables 2A.1 and 2A.2, Glennerster and Hills (1998), pp.25–6.

As a result of this growth in state welfare services significant social improvements have been achieved: for example, educational standards have risen, mortality and morbidity rates have declined, housing problems have been reduced, and basic living standards have been increased. However, as we shall discuss in more detail in Chapter 13, such growth was far from inevitable; it was the product of international economic trends and national government policies, both of which could change. And when these did change, particularly in the 1970s, the future of an ever-expanding welfare state began to come into question, and the role of public provision became subject to a much more critical scrutiny.

What is the state?

We probably all have some idea to what we are referring when we talk about the state and state involvement in welfare provision in a country such as Britain; but in fact the various institutions and individuals which comprise the state in an advanced capitalist country together make up quite a complex constitutional picture. Furthermore, the various parts of the state are subject to rules and political conventions that sometimes define fairly closely the powers and responsibilities that they are able to exercise. We do not have room here to examine the complex constitutional processes of the British state, which has now been made more complex by devolution within it; but a brief overview of the main constituent parts, and the different functions that each fulfils in the implementation of economic and social policy, will provide us with some background understanding to both its scale and scope.

Many people perhaps assume that the state is the same thing as the government; and it is obviously the case that in a democracy such as the UK the government has overall power over, and responsibility for, the activities of the state, through the electoral mandate which it secures from the population. However, technically speaking, the government is merely the collective views of the majority of Members of Parliament (MPs) in the House of Commons. Parliament also includes the House of Lords. This can, and sometimes has, disagreed with the views of MPs; and it is now being reformed by the government in the Commons to remove the role of hereditary peers and introduce a second chamber made up of a mixture of elected citizens and individuals appointed by government on the basis of their experience or social situation. All laws enacted by Parliament must be agreed by both Houses, and subsequently must be ratified by the Queen as the constitutional monarch, although in practice this is a formality as the monarch is a figurehead and plays no active part in the legislative process.

However, because of the system of political parties which contest elections in Britain, the government is in practice made up of the senior MPs from the majority party. These meet regularly as a *cabinet* under the leadership of the Prime Minister to plan future policies and the legislation required to implement them. Most policy decisions are thus made in the cabinet, and later approved by the majority of MPs in Parliament at Westminster. Policies are then implemented by state employees (civil servants) based in the different departments of the state, with each department being under the overall control of a Secretary of State, who is a member of the cabinet.

In theory, then, policy is decided by the cabinet in *Westminster*, and is implemented by the civil servants in the departments based (mainly) in *Whitehall*. This Westminster–Whitehall division symbolises the split between the democratic (policy-making) aspect of the state, and the bureaucratic (policy implementation) aspect of it, although, as books that concentrate in more detail on the policy-making and policy-implementation process reveal, this division is far from a watertight one in practice: many MPs play little part in policy making and some civil servants have much power and influence over it (see Bochel and Bochel, 2003).

Political scientists also often attach importance to the distinction that is made between the policy-making, or legislative, process, and the enforcement of the rights granted by this through the courts under the control of the *judiciary*. Where there is a dispute over the implementation of policies in particular cases, or even over the powers of government to make policy, everyone has the right to go to court for a judicial ruling (although, given the cost of using the law, this is a right that in practice may only be open to those with significant financial resources or to those poor enough to qualify for state support through legal aid). The judges in court are bound to follow the rules laid down by Parliament and by previous legal rulings, through precedent; but in exercising judgement under these rules they are quite independent of the government, and of the civil service, and they sometimes make decisions that government ministers or civil servants do not like. Like Westminster and Whitehall, however, the judiciary is part of a centralised state power within Britain. The policies that are developed and the rules that are enforced here are produced on behalf of, and are provided for, the whole of the population.

However, these central state institutions are not the only features of state power involved in the provision of welfare services in the country. State welfare is now developed and delivered within the devolved administrations operating at subnational level within the UK, and there is a significant range of policy delivered by local government (see Chapter 15). UK social policy is also affected by supranational developments within the EU, and beyond (see Chapter 14). In practice, these aspects are as important in determining the shape of the welfare state in the UK as are the main arms of central government in London.

The devolved context of state policy making in Britain is a peculiar product of the constitution of the country as a 'United Kingdom' of formerly separate nations. Britain thus comprises in effect the four *subnations* of England, Scotland, Wales and Northern Ireland. These countries have always had some degree of legal and policy-making autonomy: for instance, Scotland has always had a separate legal system from that operating in the rest of the UK. However, significant areas of policy-making practice were devolved to separate administrations in these countries by constitutional changes introduced at the end of the last century, and since then these differences have become more accentuated. Scotland now has a separate elected Parliament with the power to legislate in a number of key policy areas, and this has led to some major differences in policy development north of the border, such as the abolition of fees for university students and the provision of free care services for frail older people. The Northern Ireland Assembly also has legislative powers in certain areas, and in Wales the National Assembly has secondary legislative responsibility in areas devolved by Westminster; and in both cases policy divergence has taken place here too. There is also significant devolution of administrative support for policy implementation with separate civil service structures supporting the different policy regimes in each of the three countries replacing the central control exercised by Whitehall (see Chapter 15 below, and Adams and Robinson, 2002).

Within England policy making still takes place in the Parliament at Westminster; there is no separate English legislative body. However, as we discuss in Chapter 15, some element of devolution has taken place within England to the broader *regional* areas within the country, such as the North West or the West Midlands. Regional Development Agencies have been set up to lead on aspects of economic and social policy development in their areas; and separate government offices have been established in each region. The role of *local* government has been of critical importance in the development of welfare in Britain. Local authorities (or local councils) became subject to democratic election towards the end of the nineteenth century, and since then have played a major role in promoting state provision for education, health, housing and other social services. Indeed, in many ways the creation of the welfare state in the 1940s was really a period of the centralisation and standardisation within Whitehall of the welfare services developed, albeit unevenly, by local government in the first half of the century.

Public policy making also operates at a *supranational* level in Britain as a result of the country's membership since 1973 of the EU. As we discuss in Chapter 14, the EU now provides an ever more influential international context for policy development in Europe; and, more immediately, policies and rules determined by the Commission and other EU bodies in Brussels now have a direct impact in all member states, including Britain. In fact Britain has sometimes been a rather reluctant partner in the development of EU policy initiatives: for instance, the country did not join the new single currency (the Euro) when it was first established. However, membership of the EU requires all nations to adopt and implement the policy decisions taken by the partner nations, and this has had a cumulative effect in altering British social policy to fit in with broader European practices.

QUESTIONS: COMPREHENSION

- To what extent is there central state control over policy making in the UK?
- What is the relationship between the civil servants (in *Whitehall*) and the politicians (in *Westminster*) in determining the development of state social policy?
- Why is the British welfare state sometimes referred to as the Keynes/Beveridge Welfare State?

The functions of the state

Provision

Most discussion of state welfare is focused upon social services which are provided for people by the institutions or agencies of the state; in other words, where the function of the state is as the provider of services. State provision in Britain includes, for example, the NHS, the state education system and the social security benefits schemes. In all of these the state employs workers (doctors, nurses and teachers) based in publicly owned and operated institutions (hospitals and schools) to provide services to all citizens who are in need of, or are entitled to, them. To do this the state uses public money collected by government, largely in the form of taxes, to purchase buildings and equipment and to pay workers; and the plans for spending this money have to be justified and agreed through the political process either nationally or locally. These spending plans are therefore a central – and potentially therefore a controversial – feature of government policy development.

Clearly such comprehensive provision of services is the most obvious, and arguably the most extensive, function of the state in welfare provision, but it is far from the only one. In addition to being a provider of welfare the state also fulfils other functions that have an equally direct and important impact on the development and implementation of welfare policy within the country.

Subsidisation

As well as using public money to provide welfare through public agencies, the state also provides public money to subsidise welfare services which are provided on a private, voluntary or informal basis. The role of state subsidies has always been important in the development of non-state welfare, including both direct subsidies (for example, state support for voluntary agencies such as the Women's Royal Voluntary Service, the WRVS, or the Citizens Advice Bureaux, or CABs); and indirect subsidies (for example, exemption from taxation for voluntary agencies or for income spent on purchasing private services). Indirect subsidies have been of particular importance in the development of both private and voluntary welfare services in Britain, as we shall see in Chapters 9 and 10.

Regulation

Public subsidies can shape and direct the development of private and voluntary welfare provision. However, this provision can also be controlled more directly by legal regulation through the state. The state also functions therefore as a regulator of welfare, through the law; indeed, this is perhaps the oldest aspect of state policy intervention. Legal rules set the limits within which private markets have developed and voluntary organisations have operated and, of course, regulation also determines the structure of state-provided welfare. As we discussed above, the courts and the judiciary are an important aspect of the use of state power. Through the enactment and enforcement of rules and procedures the state can control a wide range of welfare provision, even though it is not owned or funded by any public body. Thus private pensions and private health insurance, for instance, are closely regulated through statute law; and voluntary bodies are subject to a range of legal controls such as those on the definition and extent of charitable purposes.

Employment

Finally, in its role in the provision of services, and in its roles in subsidising and regulating these, the state is also acting as an employer of those working in state institutions such as the courts or government departments. Indeed, the state, through both central and local government, is by far the largest employer in Britain. And, of course, for those working for the state their welfare as employees – and any broader occupational protections, such as sick pay or pensions, which they enjoy – are determined by the state as an employer and the policies that it adopts towards its workforce.

As an employer, the state in fact has a rather inconsistent record in Britain. Some state employees (for instance, senior civil servants) enjoy some of the best working conditions and most extensive occupational benefits of any employees in the country at large. However, there are others (for instance, cleaners or porters in schools or hospitals) who are on part-time contracts and levels of pay that leave them needing to claim social security benefits to top up their weekly incomes in order to meet their families' needs. And at times of high employment and economic growth the poor conditions in some areas of public employment can make it difficult to recruit and retain public sector workers, with shortages of teachers and nurses being experienced in the early years of the new century.

The role of the state as employer is not one that is usually directly addressed in policy planning by government or by civil servants; this is also true to some extent of the relationship between this function and that of the state as a regulator or subsidiser. Social policy commentators might argue that it ought to be the case that these various aspects of state welfare should be seen as complementary and therefore should receive greater coordination; but they must also recognise that this is not consistently understood by those responsible for these different functions. Thus analysis of the role of the state in the provision of welfare involves analysis of the separate development of these different functions and of the sometimes contradictory relationship between them, as well as assessment of the overall extent (and the limitations) of the state's welfare role.

The limits of the state

During the period of the gradual, and incremental, growth of state welfare provision in Britain, in particular in the decades following the Second World War, it seemed to most commentators – and certainly to those acting as protagonists for the growth of state welfare – that there were no limits beyond which state welfare might not extend. There seemed to exist a widely shared assumption that the greater identification of social needs would create the case for improved state services and that the continuing growth of economic production would provide the resources that could be harnessed, through taxation, to pay for these. Thus, although there might be questions about the speed or emphasis of the development of state provision, there could be no doubt about its overall desirability, or viability.

In the last quarter of the last century, however, this assumption about the limitless role for the state began to come into question in Britain (and, indeed, in all other welfare capitalist countries). Questions about the limits of the welfare state arose primarily as a result of two developments that may appear to be contradictory but, in practice, are inextricably interrelated.

First, despite the successes of state welfare in meeting welfare needs and reducing social problems, social policy research has continued to provide evidence of further needs and problems that could, or should, be the focus of additional state provision. Some of these problems might be argued to be the result of the failure of state welfare services to meet existing targets: for instance, Abel-Smith and Townsend's (1965) 'rediscovery of poverty' which identified over a million people, mainly pensioners, living below state assistance benefit levels in the early 1960s. Others, however, are the product of the more general social and technological progress that has gradually overtaken past provision: for instance, expanding demand for higher education in universities, or for heart transplants or chemotherapy treatment in the NHS. Whatever the reasons, however, there is no shortage of evidence of the continued existence, and continuing growth, of needs which current state welfare provision does not meet.

Second, alongside the evidence of growing needs, there was the acceptance in the last quarter of the twentieth century, by both Labour and Conservative governments, that state expenditure on welfare could not simply be expanded indefinitely to meet increased demand. The economic recession of the 1970s and early 1980s forced first Labour and then the Conservatives to restrict, and in places to cut, state welfare expenditure. For Labour this was predominantly in order to reduce the economic 'burden' of public spending, although for the Conservatives, especially in the Thatcherite years of the 1980s, cuts in public provision were also aimed at promoting expanded take-up of private market welfare services.

In fact, despite the cuts, public welfare expenditure continued to grow during these periods, as we saw in Table 8.1; and this was something of a contradictory outcome for the more outspoken critics of state welfare in the Thatcher governments of the 1980s. Nevertheless, the controls introduced over state expenditure were real, and they did have an effect in restricting some of the planned expansions of spending. By the 1990s both the government and opposition parties seemed to have reached a consensus that it was not possible, or desirable, to continue to raise taxation levels significantly in order to finance further expansion of the welfare state; and Labour's election victory in 1997 was based on a commitment not to seek rises in (especially income) tax and to remain within the previous Conservative spending limits for two years.

The incremental growth of state welfare is thus no longer regarded as an inevitable development; and this is true not only in Britain but also in other similar nations (Bonoli, George and Taylor-Gooby, 2000). The political consensus, or the political compromise, of the 1990s has focused attention rather on the question of how to balance the desire to meet growing welfare needs against the desire to control growing public expenditure. It is the need to address this balance that lies at the heart of the Labour government's promotion of the 'Third Way' for social policy at the beginning of the new century. The Third Way is based on a recognition that neither the state nor the market can meet all welfare needs and that in practice policy development and delivery will be based on a mix of different forms of provision. The key aim of policy planning, therefore, is to harness evidence about the effectiveness of different forms of provision to determine how to plan for, and support, the optimum mix in any particular area at any particular time; and within this is an explicit acceptance that there are limits to the extent to which state provision can be supported, in part because of the costs this imposes on taxpayers (for instance, in pensions or hospital building).

However, it is not only cost which sets limits to the extent of state welfare. In particular, as the provider of welfare services, there are limits on the ability of the state to recognise and to meet all social needs; and these limits apply, if less obviously, to the state's subsidising and regulatory roles too. State provision of welfare requires the departments of central or local government to identify social needs and then to provide services that meet them. However, this is neither a non-controversial nor a one-way process.

Critics have argued that state welfare often fails to identify the welfare needs of many people: for instance, it is often (rightly) accused of failing to address the needs of many of Britain's ethnic minority communities. Even where needs are identified, state welfare also sometimes provides services that do not adequately satisfy those needs (for instance, the tower blocks of council flats have often created as many housing problems as they have solved). Although such failings sometimes mean that needs go unmet, they may also lead, indirectly at least, to the development by people of alternative, non-state, forms of welfare service to fill the gaps left by inadequate state services: for instance, through the establishment of community-based, self-help groups in black community areas, or through the development of housing cooperatives to build, or to renovate, houses for rent. However, although such alternative provision may complement state welfare, it may also create pressure for state provision to be expanded to meet these additional or new needs; and so in some cases non-state activity can led to an extension of the limits of public provision.

Even where they are successfully meeting a range of social needs, however, state welfare services can also acquire complex, and remote, bureaucratic structures that can alienate or exclude some potential service users (an issue to which we will return in more general terms in Chapter 18). In an influential book published in 1981, Hadley and Hatch argued that there was in fact an inevitable contradiction here between the development of state bureaucracies and their ability to meet real social need; and that alternative forms of provision should therefore actually be welcomed and supported both by policy analysts and by citizens. Of course, as we discuss in Chapters 9, 10 and 11, alternative forms of welfare provision, through the informal, voluntary and private sectors, have in any case continued to co-exist, and to grow, alongside state welfare; recognition of their role in welfare was not a new discovery in 1981. And also, as we shall see, these other sectors of provision are not without their own problems and shortcomings. However, recognition that there must be limits to the ability of state provision to identify and meet all needs, or to anticipate and support or regulate the development of all community or private alternatives to state services, is significant in pointing to the limitations in the role of the state that arise from organisational and cultural factors, as well as simply from economic ones; and it is now widely accepted by politicians and policy makers. There are not just limits to the *maximum* role of the state, however: there are limits to its *minimum* role too.

In any complex society a state structure will be needed to organise, to support and to regulate the activities of citizens; and this applies to the provision of welfare as much as it does, for instance, to the control of crime. Although voluntary agencies or private companies may develop services for groups of people, only the state has the legitimacy and the power, politically and legally, to act on behalf of *all* citizens. Where regulation of the activities of non-state providers is required, for instance to guarantee minimum standards in private education or health care, only the state has the power to provide this. Where financial support is sought, as it often is, to help the development or maintenance of private or voluntary social provision, only the state can call on public resources to provide this. Where private, voluntary or informal providers cannot, or will not, operate to provide for social needs, only the state can be required to step in.

Despite the beliefs, or the hopes, of some right-wing theorists who would like to see a return to a society in which all citizens are able to provide for themselves (for instance, Murray, 1984), no advanced society has been able to remove or to replace entirely state welfare provision. Even where state provision is restricted to the role of a 'safety net', to catch those who slip between the gaps in private and voluntary provision, it is still there to prevent citizens falling through, and perhaps starving or freezing to death. Of course, in practice the safety net may not always work, but that has not been used as an argument for removing it: indeed, it is more likely to be used to argue for strengthening it. Despite the growing cost of public welfare and the impact of economic retrenchment, state welfare remains both necessary and popular; and in Britain (and in other advanced capitalist economies) democratic political structures will ensure that support for state welfare provision will exercise a powerful influence over politicians and policy makers of all complexions (Esping-Andersen, 1996, ch.9).

As we discussed at the beginning of this chapter, therefore, the debate about the role of the state in welfare services in Britain, and indeed in other advanced industrial societies, is a debate about the *extent* of state welfare, not about the overall *need* for it. Welfare provision in modern capitalist societies requires the state to play a range of roles in the provision and control of social services. Of course, such state provision and control of welfare have their limits, both minimum and maximum; but the extent of those limits is the result of political processes, not some iron laws of market freedom or socialist development. The role of the state thus varies in different countries, and it changes over time, but in some form or other it is always there.

QUESTIONS: COMPREHENSION

- To what extent has the burden of taxation set a limit on the scale of state welfare provision?
- Why is argued that it is only the state that can legitimately claim to provide services for all citizens?

QUESTION: REFLECTION

- Could a welfare state ever hope to provide comprehensive social services for all citizens?

FURTHER READING

A good introduction to the academic study of the role of the state is provided by Schwartzmantel (1994). Johnson (1999) puts the state and other sectors of welfare in comparative perspective. Timmins (2001) provides the best, and most interesting, account of the development of the welfare state in Britain. For a broader introduction to political processes and issues it is worth looking at one of the introductory political science texts, such as Coxall and Robins (1998). Recent and current information from the government can be accessed at **www.ukonline.gov.uk**.

The Market

SUMMARY OF KEY POINTS

■ Markets, or commercial provision of welfare, exist in all countries, but the balance between the state and the market (the *welfare mix*) varies significantly across different countries.

■ The proponents of free markets argue that they constitute a natural social order and that state intervention will inevitably distort this by reducing choice and introducing inefficient monopoly providers.

■ Critics of free markets argue that state intervention is needed to support and control market activity, to ensure that those who cannot afford market prices are not excluded, and to meet those needs which markets cannot address.

■ Private market provision exists alongside public services in all areas of welfare in Britain, including those such as health and education where public provision is free for all.

■ In the 1980s a policy of 'privatisation' encouraged the development of a wider range of market-based welfare, although basic state services were largely retained.

■ Quasi-markets are an attempt to use market principles of choice and competition to shape state welfare practice. They were introduced in a number of British public services in the 1990s.

■ Quasi-markets can impose hidden costs (transaction costs) on public service providers through the need to manage purchaser and provider relations.

The commercial sector

The provision of social services through the welfare state is often discussed by commentators as public provision of welfare, and this is contrasted with *private* provision arranged by individuals, families or organisations outside the state. This distinction between public and private welfare is a bit misleading, however, because much private provision is public in the sense that it is in the public domain and available to any would-be purchaser. Private health care, for instance, is publicly available, and indeed is advertised as such on television. The public–private distinction might, therefore, be better used to distinguish between individual and family-provided services and those provided collectively to a range of people either through the state or by other agencies. We will return in Chapter 11 to examine this 'private' dimension in more detail; but such a distinction is not one widely used in social policy literature.

More commonly, social policy analysis makes a distinction between state and non-state services. This too can be misleading, however, if non-state is taken to mean exclusively profit-based, private market provision for, as we shall see in Chapter 10, not all non-state welfare provision is profit-based. There is in fact a vast range of non-profit organisations engaged in all kinds of welfare activity, and operating according to quite different aims and principles from both the state and the market sectors. We need to distinguish in addition, therefore, between these non-profit (voluntary) organisations and those operating for profit on a commercial basis. It is perhaps this commercial aspect that does serve best to distinguish these organisations from both the state and the voluntary sector (and from the private, informal, sector too).

Commercial organisations operate with budgets and balance sheets. They levy charges for services and use these charges to employ workers and invest in equipment to provide future services. They also generally seek to make a profit out of the difference between their charges and the cost of providing the services. For most commercial organisations it is the expectation of profit that is the motivating factor for the establishment and development of them by their owners or shareholders, who will benefit from the profit, although on some occasions charges may not exceed costs and no profit, in practice, is made. In fact there are many small (and not-so-small) commercial organisations which do not set out to make a profit. These include small residential homes, whose owners merely wish to recover their operating costs, as well as some major institutions, such as building societies providing mortgages to house buyers, which are mutually owned by their investors and borrowers and do not pass on profits to shareholders.

Nevertheless, even where they are not profit-seeking, commercial organisations such as these can still be distinguished from both state and voluntary sector agencies by their financial structure, in particular by the charges they make for services, and the location of their operations within a competitive market. We might, therefore, most accurately call these organisations the *commercial* sector but, in practice, social policy commentators commonly refer to them as the *market*, especially when the market is being contrasted with the *state*.

Market-based activity of course extends much beyond welfare services. Most goods and services in Britain are exchanged through markets, and the labour market provides the main means of employment and subsistence for the majority of the population, either directly or indirectly. It was the development of a market basis for production and distribution in the seventeenth and eighteenth centuries that established the basis for the development of capitalism in Britain, and for the creation of modern society in the nineteenth and twentieth centuries. And it is into this capitalist market economy that state welfare has been developed in the twentieth century, as we discussed in Chapter 8. Despite the development of state welfare, we all of us rely heavily on markets for a large part of our daily individual and social needs; and, as we shall see in Chapter 13, the economic development of markets, and the ability of states to control or manipulate them, are crucial factors in structuring the broader context in which social policy planning takes place.

Welfare state provision has thus influenced, and in some cases has altered, markets; but it has not displaced them. It is for this reason that commentators refer to all modern economies with developed state welfare provision as *welfare capitalism*: a compromise, or collaboration, between the state and the market. Of course, the nature of this compromise – the relationship between state and market – varies significantly between different welfare capitalist countries (see Alcock and Craig, 2001). In social democratic countries, such as Sweden, much welfare support is provided by the state and the state takes an active role in controlling and regulating many aspects of commercial markets. By contrast, in the liberal USA many welfare services, such as health care, are provided on a private market basis and the state plays a much more residual role. In Japan occupational and private services are the 'front line' of welfare provision, and it is through the labour market that most social protection is delivered.

Furthermore, the relationship, or the balance, between state and market in any one country is not fixed, and it can change over time. In Britain in the 1980s, for example, the role of commercial market provision was expanded significantly at the expense of state provision as a direct result of government policy, in some cases by requiring state services to be put out to private tender by commercial providers. In the former socialist countries of Eastern Europe rapid changes have been taking place since the collapse of their communist regimes to replace previous state monopoly provision with private markets for a wide range of goods and services. Indeed, the changes in the balance between state and market are an intrinsic feature of the development of welfare provision in all countries, and are a major focus of the study of social policy.

The case for markets

Proponents of market-based welfare have often claimed that the operation of markets to provide services is preferable to the use of state power. Indeed, some have argued that state intervention is not compatible with the successful operation of markets and that, where it is pursued, it results in 'perverse incentives' which disrupt the natural flow of market development, by encouraging people to rely passively on state support rather than seeking to provide for themselves through entry into market relations. These arguments received particular prominence in social policy debate in Britain in the 1980s, associated with the rise of the New Right (see Chapter 12 below and Barry, 1987; King, 1987); but they are not new arguments. In fact they are based on long-standing liberal theories of the workings of markets, which go back to the work of Adam Smith in the eighteenth century.

In his book, *The Wealth of Nations*, Smith (1776) argued that in theory markets created a natural equilibrium within the social order, because individuals exercising free choice over the purchase of goods and services would create a demand for those services which they wanted. This demand would be expressed in terms of the price that they would be prepared to pay for the service, and the price would then attract suppliers to provide such a service in order to profit from the price charged. The profit motive would not lead prices to rise unduly, however, because high prices would attract large numbers of suppliers, who would then be in competition and would thus be required to reduce prices to reflect more closely the costs of production and the demand for the product. Therefore, in a situation of perfect equilibrium, all needs would be met by suppliers and all prices would reflect the legitimate costs of production.

Since the exchange of goods and services (buying and selling through the market) arises naturally in any social order, supporters of markets claim that they constitute a 'natural' social order, and also that they are self-regulating, with new demands leading to new supply and inefficient providers being weeded out by their unacceptably high prices. Smith referred to this as the 'invisible hand' of the market mechanism; and its cause has been taken up in modern welfare capitalist countries such as Britain by new neo-liberals, such as Hayek (1944) and Friedman (1962).

As a result of this, therefore, pro-market theorists also argue that attempts by governments to intervene in, or control, markets will be doomed to failure. Government support for inefficient producers will distort the price mechanism; state provision of services will create potential monopoly producers not subject to the influence of purchasers' choices; and state regulation of providers or purchasers will prevent their free choice of the most optimal forms of service provision. Hayek argued in the 1940s (Hayek, 1944), at the height of political support for state intervention in the capitalist economy in Britain, that such intervention would be ineffective and self-defeating. In the 1960s, as Keynesian interventions in the economy began to come under question, the same theme was taken up by the American economist, Milton Friedman (1962).

Hayek, Friedman and others argued that the fundamental weakness of state intervention is the problem that no agents of the state, such as government ministers or senior civil servants, could have sufficient knowledge of the needs, wants and circumstances of the individuals living in a complex modern society to be able to judge when, or where, to intervene in the market, or what sort of goods or services to provide. The result is that interventions distort, rather than support, markets, and that state services become paternalistic and bureaucratic monopolies. This, they argued, was the cause of the economic crises experienced by welfare capitalist countries in the 1970s and 1980s, and also of the hostility found in these countries towards some of the unpopular features of state welfare provision, such as unresponsive local authority landlords and long hospital waiting lists. The solution to these problems, they argued, was a return to free market provision through the removal of state intervention and the break-up of state monopoly services. However, in theory there are problems in relying on markets to deliver welfare provision in modern societies, as we shall discuss shortly; and in practice the operation of market provision has always relied heavily on the support of the state.

The market and the state

Indeed, even the most ardent supporters of the free-market provision of goods and services recognise that the state does have some role to play in supporting markets. In order for markets to function freely there must be laws concerning property ownership and contract rights, and these need to be enforced independently through the state. There must also be a policing function provided by the state, to detect and prevent abuses of the law, and there must be provision for defence of society against the threat to the markets of one country imposed by the imperialistic designs of external enemies. Even the liberals thus concede the need for state law, a police force, and national defence.

It is clear, however, that other state functions are also necessary in any modern economy: for instance, the provision of air traffic control and the development of motorways and trunk roads. Obviously for such functions it is quite possible for providers or governments to have a full understanding of people's needs, and of the importance of a centrally planned response to these. Furthermore, as we suggested in Chapter 8, there are many other state activities and services which operate in effect to *support*, rather than to *undermine*, the operation of a modern market economy:

1. State provision (for instance, of education and health care) meets the long-term strategic demands for an adequately equipped labour force that individual employers alone could not efficiently replicate.
2. State regulation ensures maintenance of minimum standards that private individuals could not be expected to monitor (for instance, in housing or pension provision) and ensures that competition takes place according to criteria of efficiency and price rather than basic quality.
3. State protection (for instance, for the unemployed or chronically sick) ensures that individuals do not suffer unduly where the market fails or is unable to reach all.

Furthermore, the limitations and contradictions of market provision in complex modern welfare capitalist countries mean that state interventions are needed to prevent potential social problems and to protect all citizens:

1. There is the ever-present danger of monopolies or cartels developing that would subvert the natural self-regulation of the market operation (for instance, in the supply of gas and water or in the production of specialist drugs).
2. In many areas where markets do operate consumers are clearly unable to make informed choices about how best their needs might be met: for

instance, consumer ignorance of medical needs and practices or of higher education standards mean that real free choice cannot in practice mean the freedom to choose anything on offer.

3. Most importantly of all in our unequal society, free choice in the market will be constrained by consumer immobility and consumer poverty; so, for instance, for most children the state will have to ensure provision of a local school, and for certain categories of people free or subsidised access to essential services will have to be guaranteed.

Perhaps the best example, however, of a case where state provision, organised according to altruistic rather than profit-oriented principles, was argued to be superior in social and economic terms to market-based provision is Titmuss's comparative study of blood donation, *The Gift Relationship* (Titmuss, 1970 and 1997). In this he argued that the state-organised system of blood donation in Britain, which relies upon free donation of blood, is both safer and more effective than the market-based systems of countries such as the USA and Japan, which pay donors for their blood. This is because the financial incentive provides an inappropriate inducement where the primary concern, as here, is with the quality and consistency of the supply of blood across a range of blood groups, some of which are in scarcer supply than others. Thus Titmuss found that the blood banks in countries where donors were paid were much more likely to obtain and to distribute contaminated blood, and to experience problems in securing donors in some areas.

It seems clear, therefore, that the free, and unregulated, market to which Hayek and Friedman aspire does not exist in practice in modern capitalist states, and what is more could not effectively be 'revitalised' within them. Nevertheless, market provision of many goods and services continues to be of major importance in these societies. There are of course two sides to this coin; just as markets in practice need the state, so in many ways does the state need markets.

From the purchase of clothing to provision of housing there is no doubt that individuals expect to have a large measure of choice over their lifestyle, and are prepared to 'shop around' in the market to secure this. In many welfare services the retention, or introduction, of elements of commercially-based provision in the market has enhanced both consumer choice and consumer responsiveness (for example, in the marketisation of optical services in the 1980s). Market provision also provides an attractive supplement to basic state protection for many people in certain areas of welfare: for instance, private and occupational pension protection, or private rooms and additional 'hotel' benefits during hospital stays.

In these more general terms, therefore, the case for regulated market provision alongside state welfare is now widely accepted within welfare capitalist societies, and has been embraced by the former state socialist regimes of Eastern Europe. However, the pure markets espoused by the neo-liberals do not exist, and never have. Market freedom has always in practice needed to be balanced by state regulation, and state subsidy and protection, in order to guarantee effective policy development and delivery.

QUESTIONS: COMPREHENSION

- To what extent does the pressure of commercialism mean that all private sector providers must seek to make a profit?
- What are the relative merits of state and market provision as explored in Titmuss's study of blood donation?

QUESTION: REFLECTION

- Could free markets ever meet the welfare needs of all citizens?

Forms of commercial welfare

Within a complex welfare mix, such as that in modern Britain, the commercial development of welfare takes a variety of forms, some of which in practice overlap, in part at least, with aspects of state provision or with provision in the voluntary or informal sectors. At the time of the creation of the modern welfare state in Britain in the 1940s, however, commercial provision was consciously retained alongside public services, even in the areas of major universal provision, such as education and health:

1. In education private schools (misleadingly called public schools) which charge pupils for attendance have continued to operate on a fee-paying basis, and have continued to attract pupils.
2. In the health service doctors have been permitted to retain fee-paying patients who pay for special treatment in NHS hospitals (in so-called *pay beds*) following a much-publicised compromise between the government minister (Bevan) and the British Medical Association (BMA) when the NHS was first established.

What is more, in the 1950s, after the establishment of state welfare, commercial provision – as an alternative, or a supplement, to state provision – actually began to grow. As we saw in Chapter 5, at this time private house building rapidly began to outstrip the building of public rented housing. At the same time occupational pensions providing additional pension protection for workers also began to grow, and by the mid-1960s over 12 million workers were members of such private schemes.

In the 1980s this growth was accelerated as the Thatcher governments of the time adopted a policy of openly encouraging commercial provision as a substitute for state provision, sometimes described as a policy of *privatisation* (Johnson, 1990). The largest privatisation measures of the 1980s were the highly publicised break-up and sale of the major utilities (gas, electricity and water) that had initially been developed by local, not central, government, as we discuss in Chapter 15. State industries, such as British Steel, were also sold to private shareholders, although here what really occurred was a *re*privatisation as these had first been set up by state takeover of old private companies. In the welfare field privatisation in the 1980s took a number of forms, including the replacement of state provision, the removal of state subsidies, and the withdrawal of state regulation:

1. The sale of *council houses* to tenants, and later the wholesale transfer of estates to private landlords, was a significant, and high-profile, example of the transfer of provision from the state to the market sectors, although many estate transfers in practice went to housing associations in the voluntary sector.
2. Private provision in health was directly encouraged, and began to grow. Between 1979 and 1989 the proportion of the population covered by private *health insurance* grew from 5 per cent to 9 per cent, and over 50 new private hospitals were opened.
3. Similar changes occurred in education; between 1979 and 1991 the number of children in *private education* increased from 5.8 per cent to 7.4 per cent.
4. The introduction of sick pay and maternity pay transferred *social security* protection from the Department of Social Security to private employers.
5. The use of charges increased, in particular *prescription charges* for drugs purchased as part of medical treatment under the NHS (these went up from 20p in 1979 to over £3 in 1990).
6. The public regulation of services, such as *public transport*, was largely withdrawn, with these being thrown open to competition between various commercial providers.

Important and far-reaching though these provisions were, however, they did not amount to anything like a full-scale privatisation of welfare services and, although this had been called for by some commentators from the New Right, it is not at all certain that the government of the 1980s considered it either feasible or desirable. For instance, although private education and health care grew, they remained very much a minority provision alongside the comprehensive state provision in these fields; and by the 1990s it had become clear that what had happened in practice in Britain in the 1980s had been not so much a replacement of the state with the market but rather a change in the welfare mix, in which state welfare was retained and market provision was more widely, and more variously, developed.

At the beginning of the new century this mix of market and state provision has been openly embraced by the Labour government and captured in its promotion of the Third Way in welfare policy planning. What we have therefore is a range of private welfare services co-existing alongside, or operating in partnership with, state welfare provision:

1. Direct purchase of services is available (for example, in the provision of houses or spectacles).
2. Insurance-based protection operates in the fields of pension protection and health care.
3. Occupationally-based provision is widespread, with many workers getting additional benefits, such as sickness pay, pension cover and private health care, from their employers on top of their cash wage.

4. Charges have been introduced to cover the costs of much provision previously provided free within the state sector (for example, charges for personal social services such as home care).
5. Private providers are delivering publicly funded services, such as residential care, under contracts with government or state agencies.
6. Private companies are operating in partnership with government to invest in capital projects for developments such as new hospital buildings.

Of course, not all of these forms of provision are profit-making: indeed, occupational pensions and home care charges are not motivated at all by the goal of profit maximisation. In fact, many features of market-based provision cannot even exist on a break-even basis and effectively only continue to operate with the support of major subsidies from the state. Many private and occupational pensions rely upon the indirect subsidies provided by the tax relief available on contributions; and direct means-tested subsidies are provided to support poorer users who cannot pay the full cost of commercial prices or charges (for instance, through housing benefit or free NHS prescriptions).

Nevertheless, the market basis for provision of welfare services is now widely and securely established alongside the state, and voluntary, sectors in Britain, as it is in all other welfare capitalist countries. Further than this, however, attempts have been made in recent years to integrate some of the key features of market principles within the delivery of state services themselves. In Britain over the last decade or so this has taken the form of the widespread development of *quasi-markets* within the state welfare sector.

Quasi-markets

The extension of quasi-markets within welfare provision in Britain is a relatively recent phenomenon. Most of the legislative changes were introduced at the end of the 1980s, but the provisions themselves largely came into force during the 1990s (Bartlett, Roberts and Le Grand, 1998). However, the idea behind them is really quite an old one and is based on an attempt to combine in one form the advantages of both market and state provision of welfare:

1. The advantages of markets are that they gear the allocation of resources towards consumer needs and consumer preferences and that, in operating on a cash basis, they maximise cost effectiveness through price sensitivity. Compared to this, state provision is paternalistic, because consumers' needs cannot all be accurately identified and accommodated, and decisions are taken by professional providers; state provision is also potentially expensive because, since services are provided free of charge, neither providers nor consumers have any incentive to reduce costs.
2. The disadvantages of markets, as we have just discussed, are that they cannot afford to meet all needs and that they require consumers to have knowledge and power to be able to exercise realistic choices between competing service providers. By contrast, state provision can guarantee that no one will be excluded from access to provision and that minimum service

standards will be provided even where consumers are unable themselves to monitor these.

Quasi-markets are based in state services and funding is guaranteed by the state, with access to services generally being free so no one is excluded on grounds of poverty. However, a division is introduced between the *purchaser* (or consumer) and the *provider*, so that purchasers can choose from which provider they will select a service, and providers are forced to gear their service provision to meet these consumer preferences. One example of this, although it has not been widely utilised in Britain, is the education *voucher*, which provides pupils (or their parents) with a voucher equivalent to the cost of schooling that can then be 'cashed in' at any school of their choosing. In higher education the part or full provision of student fees plus access to guaranteed loans operates something like a voucher scheme for adults, permitting suitably qualified applicants wishing to go to university to choose a place on a course.

As we saw in Chapter 3, since the implementation of the Education Reform Act of 1988, local management of schools has meant that these now can accept any pupils that they choose to, giving children and their parents some freedom of choice between schools (Bartlett, 1993). This choice has also been facilitated, in theory at least, by the requirement for schools to publish regularly information about their achievements and the school 'league tables' that are constructed from this. Local management is not a fully fledged voucher scheme, however, as schools can also refuse pupils and local authorities are still required to secure local places for all children.

As well as the education reforms of the late 1980s, quasi-markets have also been introduced into health and social services, as discussed in Chapters 4 and 6. Here the market operates through the split between purchasers and providers. For instance, in health care hospitals and other major service providers, such as ambulance services, have become organisationally and financially independent trusts, whose income depends upon the services they provide; and the primary care trusts representing doctors and other community-based patient services contract to purchase these services on behalf of the service users in their area. In the community care field the purchasers are the care managers who negotiate packages of care on behalf of their clients from a range of service providers, which could include private market or voluntary sector agencies operating under contracts with the state.

Unlike the working of quasi-markets in education, health and social service provision remains under the control of the welfare professionals who are acting on behalf of their clients, in part because of the difficulty which individual citizens would be likely to face in making difficult decisions about the choice of medical treatments or care packages. Nevertheless the principles of market allocation within state services now co-exist here; and, as Le Grand and Bartlett (1993, p.10) argued, similar trends could be identified in other areas such as housing and social security provision too. They identified three features of these quasi-markets as:

> non-profit organisations competing for public contracts, sometimes in competition with for-profit organisations; consumer purchasing power either centralised

in a single purchasing agency or allocated to users in the form of vouchers rather than cash; and, in some cases, the consumers represented in the market by agents instead of operating by themselves.

As we discuss in Chapter 17, there are some problems involved in paying for welfare services in this way. The danger is that such mechanisms can operate to introduce the distorted incentives of the private profit principle into public service delivery. However, quasi-markets also introduce some more pragmatic problems into state services because of the commercial procedures that they inevitably require.

Managing budgets, for instance, requires a fair degree of accounting, and now also computing, skills. Doctors, social workers and other welfare professionals often do not have these skills and might understandably be reluctant to develop them. However, budget management is now a central feature of much policy delivery within welfare services, and where budgets are not managed well then service provision – and hence service users – will be likely to suffer. Furthermore, such budgeting exercises take time, and, as all accountants (at least) know, time costs money. When welfare professionals are engaged in accountancy, they are not engaged in service provision; and in this way the operation of quasi-markets has introduced significant extra administrative costs into welfare systems, many of which may be unknowingly disguised in unplanned and even unidentified service cuts. In practice, therefore, quasi-markets require additional resources and additional skills that state welfare services may not have been used to providing. It may be that efficiency savings generated by market allocations can create the scope for these to be met within existing service provision; but, where they are not, quasi-markets could prove to have been an expensive means of importing price sensitivity into state services.

Problems with markets

The neo-liberal claim that a free market economy will provide for efficiency and consumer sovereignty through self-regulation, even if it were attractive in theory, cannot realistically be applied to the welfare provision of modern welfare capitalist countries. Markets in such countries are too complex for individual consumers to negotiate and they are inextricably intertwined with state, and voluntary sector, provision. So, although neo-liberal theorists have pleaded for a return to a pure market economy, no government has in practice sought to pursue such a radical path.

Thus markets exist in welfare, as in the economy generally, alongside state and voluntary provision, as government support for public/private partnerships and a mixed economy of welfare providers now openly recognises. In this context they frequently provide advantages in service development and delivery that could perhaps not be achieved in any other manner. Where consumers have resources and knowledge, their ability to choose – and the incentive for providers to improve services in order to secure that choice – provides a powerful motor for innovation and improvement. In the case of housing provision, for instance, it is this consumer sovereignty that has made owner-occupation so much more attractive to people than public renting.

In a mixed economy of welfare, markets have their advantages. However, they also have their problems. Even where they do not actually make a profit, the commercial operators within markets are inevitably driven primarily by financial considerations rather than service priorities since, through the charges that they make for services, they must ensure that they continue to retain the viability to operate. This means that all commercial operators are forced to levy charges that at least meet their costs. However, in the unequal social order in which these charges operate, some consumers will be better able to meet them than others. Wealthy people are able to purchase a wide range of services through the market that arguably they do not need, such as colour televisions and mobile telephones in private hospital rooms. More importantly from the point of view of social policy, poor people faced with charges are therefore unable to pay for services that they desperately need.

In an unequal society a pure market system will inevitably fail to meet the service demands of poor people in need. Indeed, it is just such market failure that motivated the Fabian reformers, and the trade union and political representatives of the poor working classes, to press for state welfare services to be introduced in the early part of the twentieth century. Unlike the drive for profit, which distributes market-based provision to those most able to pay, state services or state support can be allocated according to need. Thus state provision can ensure that poor people are not excluded from protection, either through direct non-market provision to them or through the subsidisation of poor purchasers within markets. Even where they do operate to provide welfare, therefore, markets have to be supplemented by state provision.

However, markets do not only fail individual poor people; they also fail to meet certain welfare needs which may often be associated with poverty more generally. Because commercial operators must seek to ensure financial profitability, or at least viability, there are likely to be certain services areas that they will not be willing to enter at all.

This is largely true, for instance, of protection for unemployment. Unemployed people are outside the labour market and they, and their dependants, need financial support. Commercial provision of this support would only be likely if charges could be levied on employed people, on an insurance basis, to cover the costs of their potential unemployment. However, many employed people may be unwilling to pay charges to meet the support needs of the unemployed, especially if they themselves are unlikely to be threatened with unemployment. A scheme collecting charges only from those who did fear unemployment might not be sufficiently buoyant to meet the needs of all those unemployed, especially in periods of economic recession. For example, in the early 1990s the government sought to encourage private protection for the repayment of mortgage debts for those becoming unemployed by removing some of the state protection for this. However, few private insurance providers were willing to develop insurance protection for those most at risk of unemployment and such schemes as were developed offered only very limited and short-term financial protection. Commercial provision for protection for the unemployed has thus not developed in Britain or in other welfare capitalist countries; and, although a variety of different schemes providing support for unemployment exist, they are all organised (and partly financed) by the state, on behalf of society as a whole.

Whatever the extravagant claims of its protagonists, therefore, the fact remains that market provision cannot meet all the needs of all the people all of the time. It is for this reason that voluntary organisations and state welfare services have developed in all modern market economies, even though their development has to some extent operated to supplement, rather than to displace, market-based services. Successful policy development in the future will need to ensure that markets continue or develop where they can genuinely provide a responsiveness and sensitivity which monopolistic state services could not do; and that they are replaced, or supplemented, where they threaten to exclude necessary services or needy consumers. This is what the Third Way, between the state and the market, now places as the central principle of policy planning; but it is only in the detail of policy practice that the most effective balance between the two can actually be arrived at.

QUESTIONS: COMPREHENSION

- To what extent did the privatisation reforms of the 1980s replace state welfare with private provision?
- In what ways do quasi-markets aim to import market principles into state welfare services?
- Why is it argued that there are natural limits to the scope of markets in meeting welfare needs?

QUESTION: REFLECTION

- Have quasi-markets succeeded in reforming public welfare in Britain?

FURTHER READING

There are no books on the subject of private welfare in Britain itself at present, but one is in preparation by May and Brunsdon (2004) that should provide a good coverage of the major issues. Johnson's (1995) collection provides a comparative analysis of international trends. Drakeford (1999) provides a good guide to the recent policy developments around privatisation, and Bartlett, Roberts and Le Grand (1998) is a critical discussion of the implementation of quasi-markets.

The Voluntary Sector

SUMMARY OF KEY POINTS

- The scale of voluntary activity in welfare is often underestimated. In 2002 UK charity income was around £15.6 billion and had grown significantly over the previous decade.
- The voluntary sector is broad and diverse. It is difficult to find a description of the sector that would include all types of organisation.
- The voluntary sector overlaps with the other sectors and in particular has a complex and changing relationship with the state.
- All voluntary organisations require funding and many have complex packages of funding from a range of different sources.
- Voluntary organisations vary in aims and structure; they are thus uneven in their distribution and sometimes narrow in their focus. They cannot provide a comprehensive approach to service provision.
- Some commentators have differentiated between the voluntary sector and the community sector, which is comprised of smaller and more informal organisations.
- 'Umbrella' agencies play an important role in supporting and representing voluntary organisations and the sector more generally.
- Public support for the voluntary sector from central and local government has continued despite the development of state welfare services.
- Current government policy includes active promotion of partnership working between the state and voluntary organisations, including the development of a formal *compact* to govern relations.
- The future of voluntary action is likely to continue to include a range of different forms of activity and different relations with the state.

The scope of voluntary activity

The focus of debate and policy development on the relative roles of the state and the market in the provision of welfare services has meant that the size and the scope of the voluntary organisation in the development and delivery of welfare has sometimes not been fully appreciated in the study of social policy. These are significant omissions since the voluntary sector in the UK, and in other welfare capitalist countries, has played a key role in policy practice, often in the very areas that state and market provision is least effective. As we shall see, the complex and varied nature of voluntary activity makes it very difficult to arrive at any accurate assessment of the scale and scope of the sector. Nevertheless focusing just on recognised UK charities, the total gross income of the sector in 2001 was around £15.6 billion, a growth of 32 per cent over ten years, and their total assets were worth £74.4 billion. Furthermore these organisations employed over half a million workers, around 2 per cent of the UK workforce (National Council for Voluntary Organisations, 2002). In one sense at least, therefore, the voluntary sector is large, and growing.

In historical terms, too, the role of the voluntary sector is of central importance in the development of welfare provision. In practice the collective provision of both self-protection and altruistic service to others preceded both the state and the market; and, as we shall discuss below, both state and market forms of welfare have built on structures and practices developed by voluntary organisation and activity. Indeed, although the development of state welfare provision, in particular the 'comprehensive' provisions of the post-war welfare state, did take over some of the structures and functions of previous voluntary sector provision, voluntary organisations have continued to operate alongside the new statutory services of the welfare state (Finlayson, 1994; Davis Smith, Rochester and Hedley, 1995). What is more, in the latter part of the last century voluntary action was growing in scale and the scope of the sector was becoming ever wider and more varied (Harris and Rochester, 2001).

The voluntary sector thus plays an important role in the development and delivery of welfare services but the complexity and diversity of this role make it difficult to pin down. Voluntary sector organisations vary in size and shape, from neighbourhood parent and toddler groups to international aid organisations such as Oxfam; they were once famously described by Kendall and Knapp (1995) as 'a loose and baggy monster'. It is almost impossible to generalise about their structure or their activities, or to come up with a definition or description that will fit all cases. However, problems of definition should not detract from recognition of the centrality of an understanding of the voluntary sector for social policy; and in general terms we can provide some definitional parameters to shape our study of the sector, even if only negatively by specifying what is not encompassed within it.

Voluntary sector organisations are *not* part of the state provision of services, either at central or local level. They are *not* constituted by statutory legislation, although their activities are of course affected by legislation. They are *not* directly accountable to elected state representatives either nationally or locally; their employees, where they exist, are *not* officers of government or local authority departments. Voluntary organisations are thus in one sense *private* bodies but they are *not* part of the private market or commercial provision of welfare, primarily because they do not operate with profit and loss accounts. Commercial organisations seek to make a profit out of their activities, or at a minimum to cover their costs, and thus have to charge for the provision of services (at least in most cases). Voluntary organisations are *not* motivated by the pursuit of profit and in most cases will seek to avoid charging for services.

As they are not part of the state, voluntary organisations are sometimes referred to as the *non-government sector*. Because they are not generally established by state legislation, they are sometimes referred to as the *non-statutory sector*. In the USA, in particular, their distinction from commercial organisations has led to them being referred to as the *non-profit sector*. It was also in the USA that the more neutral, but nevertheless still essentially negative, notion of the *third sector* developed (after the first, or state, and second, or market, sectors). And this is now adopted more generally: for instance, in the title of the major international research body focusing on the sector, the International Society for Third-Sector Research (ISTR).

This intermediary role between the public, market and family sectors of provision, and between the formal and informal, public and private, and profit and non-profit features of provision, can be presented in diagrammatic form to reveal how this notion of the 'third sector' distinguishes it from other aspects of welfare provision. In this model third sector organisations can be seen to be formal, non-profit, private agencies existing in between the state, the market and the family (see Figure 10.1).

This non-state, non-market nature of the sector can also, more positively, be stressed by referring to this as the *independent sector*. The focus on independence emphasises the value of operating outside the constraints of public accountability or the profit motive; it is a term that has become more widely used in recent years, in particular by some voluntary organisations to refer to themselves. However, in practice the term is not widely used, perhaps because of its continued association with some private sector provision, such as the term 'independent schools' being used to describe private education.

The relationships between the voluntary sector and the other forms of welfare provision are critical to an understanding of the distinctive features

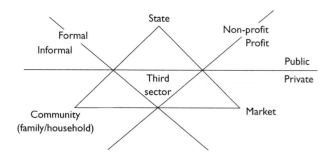

Figure 10.1   The intermediary role of the voluntary sector

of voluntary action. However, in practice the relationships are far from clear cut and the boundaries between the different sectors are porous or overlapping. In the 1980s Billis reviewed the relationship between voluntary organisations and the other 'worlds' of government bureaucracy, business bureaucracy and the personal sphere, and represented these relationships as a series of circles which intersect in various places, demonstrating the overlap between the different sectors (see Figure 10.2).

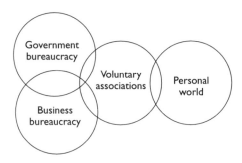

Figure 10.2   The overlapping boundaries of the voluntary sector
Source: Billis (1989), p.20.

As Billis pointed out, these overlapping boundaries provide challenges to the organisation and development of those voluntary sector bodies which are, or might be, situated within these boundary areas: for instance, those on the boundary with business will be under pressure to operate according to commercial criteria and those on the boundary with government will probably be restricted by public policy and statutory control. Thus, although the voluntary sector is distinct from the statutory, commercial and personal sectors, it is not entirely separate from, or independent of, them.

Furthermore, both for individual voluntary organisations and for the sector as a whole, these boundaries are neither fixed nor immutable. They may change as individual voluntary organisations change and develop, or decline. They may also change as the policies and priorities of the other sectors change. This is particularly true of government and relations with the state, of course. As we shall discuss below, the history of the development of voluntary action is to some extent a history of its changing relationship with the state, both through links developed in particular policy areas and through the general regulation and support provided by state agencies, such as the Voluntary Service Unit (VSU) in the Home Office.

The location within the voluntary sector amidst a complex of relations between the state, the commercial market and the individual has more generally been discussed by social theorists as the sphere of *civil society*. Civil society is a more generic notion than voluntary action and organisation, and has been identified by many authors as encompassing more generally that set of relations within society not governed by either statutory control or market forces. Deakin (2001) reviews the development of the concept and its different usages and understandings. As he points out, it involves a conception of social action within which some of the core features of voluntary action can be located, and from which theoretical understanding of the role of voluntary action can perhaps be developed. Others have argued that the extent and depth of voluntary action within civil society is itself a measure of the strength and sustainability of any social order, that these organisations are a form of *social capital* (an expression of our collective investment in social relations), and that this can even be measured to provide some indication of the health, or otherwise, of any particular society (Putnam, 1993 and 2000).

Whatever the importance of this broader context, however, the focus of this chapter is upon voluntary organisations and their narrower role in the provision of welfare within society. And, however they are defined or located, voluntary organisations are *organisations*. Even the neighbourhood parent and toddler group requires organisation. There have to be meetings, which require notification and premises. There has to be a membership list, to know who to invite to the meetings. This will require a secretary and perhaps a chair and other officers. All this requires organisation and results in body which is something much more than the informal support and services that are provided, without any organisational structure, by families and neighbours (see Chapter 11). These organisational aspects of voluntary activity are important in determining its development (and sustainability), in shaping the way in which it operates to deliver services and in structuring its relationships with other sectors, such as the state and the market. These issues have in recent years become a more significant focus of academic debate and research (see Billis and Harris, 1996).

Voluntary organisations

Due to the wide variety of organisations operating within the voluntary sector, it is not easy to specify exactly what we mean when we talk about a voluntary organisation. For a start, the term *voluntary* can be misleading. The unpaid time, freely given, of volunteers is in one sense the essence of voluntary activity. It is virtually the sole resource of many, in particular local community-based organisations; and, if it could be costed in financial terms, or in comparison with full-time paid employment, it would probably outweigh the paid employment and financial assets referred to earlier (Hedley and Davis Smith, 1992). However, not all volunteering takes place *within* the voluntary sector: for example, statutory welfare agencies such as social services departments and probation services make quite extensive use of volunteers to supplement the statutory services that they provide through the use of public money. And, more importantly, many organisations in the voluntary sector in practice have public funding and employ paid workers (sometimes well-paid ones).

Any organisation operating at more than a neighbourhood level is going to find it difficult to survive as an organisation by relying solely on volunteers. Volunteers, no matter how well meaning, can only give up so much of their time since they are also likely to have jobs or family commitments. What is more, volunteers, no matter how capable, are likely to have limited skills; but large organisations require secretaries, and accountants and managers. Where these organisations are providing complicated services, specialist skills or training for staff may be required. If some specialist tasks can be carried out by paid workers on a full-time or a part-time basis, the organisation may be better able to meet its service goals, and may be able to make better use of its volunteer labour.

Large international or national voluntary organisations, such as Oxfam or the NSPCC, employ a wide range of paid staff both to run the organisation itself and to provide services to users. They have a salary structure and career structure, and provide training and development for their workers. However, many smaller local organisations also employ paid workers. For example, most Citizens Advice Bureaux (CABs) have at least one paid, and trained, manager and advice worker, as well as relying heavily on the commitment of volunteer advisers. Many of these paid workers have made a career out of their work in the voluntary sector, and many have an ideological or political commitment to working in organisations that are not part of the state and also do not seek to make a profit. However, some workers have also moved from, or between, the statutory, commercial and voluntary sectors in pursuit of a career; they are able to bring knowledge and experience of the strengths and weaknesses of each sector to their work in the others.

Of course the employment of paid workers means that organisations need to have the financial resources at their disposal to pay workers. To do this voluntary organisations require more than just the efforts of volunteers. Those organisations with paid workers may be distinguished from those without because of their need to secure regular funding to support their work; but in fact even organisations relying entirely on voluntary efforts usually require some financial resources to pay for equipment and materials, which these days may mean a telephone, a computer and a photocopier, and to pay for premises in which to work or to meet. Thus the funding which voluntary organisations can secure may be a central feature in determining their shape and structure, as well as their ability to deliver the services which they are aiming to provide.

Funding the voluntary sector

In principle the first source of funding for voluntary organisations is *giving*, or charitable donation. Just as some people may be willing to give their time to a particular local or national group, others may be willing, and able, to give money. Charitable giving has been the financial mainstay of many major voluntary organisations in Britain and elsewhere for over a century. The nineteenth-century pioneers of voluntary social service agencies relied largely upon such charitable sources, coordinated by the Charity Organisation Society (COS) (Humphries, 1995; Lewis, 1995); and over the last century the scale of charitable donation expanded significantly.

Although private altruism is the essence of charitable giving, not all donors are individuals; and not all donations are entirely altruistic. Private corporations also donate large sums to voluntary organisations, in part as a genuine support to their activities; but in part also, in some cases, to improve the profile or reputation of the corporate donor, or even to establish or promote their commercial business activity. Such charitable giving, both individual and corporate, is also now frequently coordinated and directed; for instance, the Charities Aid

Foundation (CAF) acts to provide advice and support to both donors and voluntary organisations looking for support. Charitable support may itself also be channelled through separate organisations established to disburse funding for voluntary action. These include in particular the charitable trusts and foundations established by wealthy individuals or corporations to manage their support (such as Nuffield or Rowntree) as well as some local trusts and 'community chests' established with a mix of funding, sometimes coming in part from public sources.

The status of charities, however, is a particular – and a particularly important – one within British social policy because recognised charities enjoy significant tax concessions, which act as a form of indirect public subsidy to them. For instance, some donations to charities from earned income are exempt from income tax and charities using premises do not have to pay local property taxes. However, determination of charitable status has traditionally depended upon an obscure legal statute of 1601 that limited charitable status to organisations performing specific services for specific groups of beneficiaries (Brenton, 1985, pp.96–100, 248–9). In 2002 the government announced plans to update this archaic law with a broader definition of charity as public benefit and to create a new regulatory body to replace the current Charity Commission in the granting and monitoring of charitable status. But establishing a more modern basis has not so far proved easy, especially because it is likely to mean that some existing charities will lose their status. In addition to the obscurity of the rules themselves, the process of applying for, and securing, charitable status has been a complex and costly one. Thus many smaller voluntary organisations have not bothered going through with it, although they do rely heavily (or entirely) on charitable funding; consequently they may have lost out on some sources of charitable funding and the tax advantages associated with it, and also have not appeared in analysis and measurement of charitable funding.

Charitable giving for altruistic purposes to provide services for others can be distinuished from making payments into voluntary organisations that are intended rather as a form of *self-protection*. Collective self-protection through pooled donations was also a form of voluntary organisation that developed significantly in Britain in the nineteenth century (for instance, in order to provide income protection for workers in times of sickness or temporary unemployment). Unlike insurance protection on the private market, this protection involved a joint commitment to collective self-protection for specific groups of workers and their families, into which contributions would be made in the expectation of future support at times of need. The *friendly societies*, as these organisations came to be known, were an important feature of the early development of social security protection outside the state. Their model of mutual self-protection was later copied and incorporated into the national insurance scheme proposed by Beveridge, however (see Chapter 2), and after this they largely disappeared from the scene.

Nevertheless, new forms of mutual voluntary action have developed in recent times. These include *credit unions*, where groups of people establish membership organisations into which they contribute regular payments and from which they can then borrow lump sums at low rates of interest (Thomas and Balloch,

1994). They also include those where no direct cash funding is provided but rather goods and services are exchanged between people who are unable (or unwilling) to buy what they need on the private market. These are generally referred to as *local exchange and trading schemes* (LETSs), and they frequently operate under a set of arrangements governing exchanges to which members agree on joining the scheme, perhaps even developing their own (non-cash) currency to ensure equity in exchanges (C. Williams, 1996).

Charity and mutual support are key features of voluntary action and core elements in the funding of many voluntary organisations. However, they are not the most important sources of funding for many; instead, public support through the state is. The state may fund voluntary sector organisations in a number of different ways and for a number of different reasons. Exemption from payment of taxes is a form of state support for charities; however, money is also given directly to organisations to help them provide services or employ workers. For instance, CABs are supported by national government grants through their umbrella organisation, the National Association of Citizens Advice Bureaux (NACAB). National funding is also provided to other established charities, such as the WRVS. Much state funding for voluntary organisations is provided and regulated through the VSU in the Home Office, and this has become more important under the initiatives developed over the last 20 years or so by both the Conservative and Labour governments, which we discuss later. Other programmes of funding from central government have also been important in providing support for voluntary organisations, in particular the programmes aimed at regenerating local social and economic activity through projects which may be run, in part at least, by voluntary organisations, such as the Urban Programme of the 1970s and 1980s, the Single Regeneration Budget (SRB) in the 1990s and the New Deal for Communities (NDC) in the new century.

It is not just central government which funds voluntary action, however; local authorities also provide public financial support for many other voluntary organisations operating within their area, such as play schemes or tenants' associations. Local authority funding has, in the past, often been provided in the form of grants to voluntary groups but, as we shall discuss shortly, it now also takes the form of a more formal contract for the delivery of services. However, public support, from local government in particular, does not always take the form of cash payments. Assistance may also be provided in kind (for instance, through free use of council premises, such as schools, or free access to council equipment or mailing facilities), or through the provision of paid workers to support voluntary groups (for instance, community social workers who may help to set up and to manage community-based activities).

State funding is thus a crucial feature of the resource base and organisational structure of many voluntary organisations in the UK; and this pattern is common throughout other similar welfare capitalist nations, as Kramer (1990, p.3), concluded: 'In fact, there is no country today where there is a substantial voluntary sector, that is not dependent on governmental support to a greater or lesser degree.' This is also widely understood by voluntary agencies and by other funding agencies. Thus, one of the key priorities of many voluntary organisations including both local neighbourhood groups and major national charities, is to campaign to secure state support for their activities or for activities or services that their members want. Voluntary organisations thus actively seek state support. Furthermore, charitable funding for voluntary organisations – for example, that provided by some of the major charitable trusts – is often provided on a temporary or pilot basis, on the assumption that, once operating, the organisation will be able to secure more permanent funding from the state.

Important though public funding is, however, it is not the largest source of funding for the voluntary sector, at least according to the review of the major charities conducted by the NCVO (2002). The largest single source, perhaps surprisingly, is earned income and returns on investments. Although they are not commercial organisations many voluntary bodies do charge for some of the services that they provide. They may also have assets such as properties or capital funds invested in financial institutions. In addition to this some organisations engage in (quasi-)commercial activity to provide income, which can then be used to pay staff and provide services (for instance, through running small high street shops selling second-hand or specially produced merchandise).

The great attraction of earned income, of course, is that to some extent voluntary organisations have more control over these sources than they do the donations or grants of others. Control over resources, or lack of it, is a more general problem for many organisations, however; and this is particularly true where, as is often the case, funding in practice comes from a number of different sources. Mixed funding streams mean that there is no need to rely on one funding agency; but they also mean that there may be a need to maintain different procedures and deliver different outputs to satisfy different funders. What is more, the balance of these sources may well change over time, so that what the organisation does, and what it is, are forced to shift as demands change and new funding sources come on-stream. As some studies of the mixed funding of organisations have shown, managing a package of funding can itself be a core issue for the sustainability and development of voluntary action (Alcock *et al.*, 1999).

QUESTIONS: COMPREHENSION

- What did Kendall and Knapp mean by their description of the voluntary sector as 'a loose and baggy monster'?
- To what extent could the voluntary sector be described as the 'independent sector'?
- What are the advantages and disadvantages for voluntary organisations of public, private and charitable funding?

The structure of the sector

The voluntary sector is a vast and varied collection of organisations composed of different groups of people pursuing different aims at different levels of society: 'a loose and baggy monster'. Indeed, the variety is so great that it is almost as difficult to identify any structure within the sector as it is to arrive at a consistent definition of it. As we have seen, funding for the sector, although it may not have helped to define groups, does provide one structural dimension to it; funding may be provided for altruistic reasons or with the expectation that the providers of funding will receive some service in return. This provides a basis for distinction, based on structural goals and procedures, between protective, representative, campaigning and service organisations:

1. *Protective* organisations have been set up by their members for mutual self-protection or benefit. These include the nineteenth-century friendly societies and the twentieth-century credit unions, and also more ad hoc self-help groups such as those providing support for drug or alcohol users and mental health patients. The organisation of these protective associations is focused internally on maintaining their effective operation. The motivation for participation is self-interest.
2. *Representative* organisations promote or represent the self-interest of members but do this through external activity, in particular promoting their needs and campaigning for improved services from other sources. These include small lone parent groups such as Gingerbread; but they would also include some of the largest, and most powerful, voluntary sector organisations, such as the trade unions.
3. *Campaigning* organisations do not act specifically on behalf of their members but campaign more generally on issues that affect large numbers of people throughout society. These organisations are motivated primarily by altruism rather than representation, although in some cases it may be an altruism with a clear political message. They include the Child Poverty Action Group (CPAG), campaigning for poor children in Britain, and Greenpeace or Friends of the Earth, campaigning for world-wide environmental change.
4. *Service* organisations are also generally motivated by altruism, in particular the charitable motive of giving in order to help others. Many of the largest and most successful voluntary sector groups continue to be those whose aim is to provide services to others in need. These include international agencies such as Oxfam and national organisations such as the WRVS and the NSPCC, as well as others that may also have a religious dimension, such as Christian Aid or the Salvation Army. They also include the many small and diverse neighbourhood activities designed to help local people in need.

As with funding differences, of course, these structural features do not constitute watertight boundaries between organisations. Some campaigning organisations may include a mixture of representative and altruistic activities, and they may also provide services to members or to others. This is true, for instance, of the CPAG, which has branches representing local poor people but which campaigns primarily at national government level, and also provides advice and advocacy services both to its own members and to non-members who use its handbooks and its Citizens' Rights Office. Nevertheless, the boundaries do provide us with something of a guide to the different structures of voluntary organisations, and these differences can be supplemented by comparing the levels at which different organisations operate. As we have seen, some voluntary sector organisations work at an international level while others operate at a national level, although in the UK they may have separate organisations for England, Scotland, Wales or Northern Ireland.

National and international organisations are by definition large in size; but many (indeed most) voluntary organisations are not. If we were to look in any town, city or other local authority area we would almost certainly find not only the local branches of some larger national organisations but also a wide range of smaller, locally-based, voluntary organisations, such as tenants' associations, luncheon clubs or associations of people with disabilities, which are measured by researchers such as Putnam (1993) as evidence of the extent of social capital in the area. Sometimes a distinction is made between the more formal (and implicitly larger) organisations of the voluntary sector and these smaller community-based groups to suggest that there are in effect two different sectors – the voluntary sector and the community sector – with different characteristics and roles.

In part this distinction is based upon recognition of the community as separate sphere within society more generally, and this is to some extent a controversial view. Much has been written about communities and a community base for social activity (Frankenburg, 1966; Willmott, 1984; Mayo, 1994), and more recently the idea of such a community base has even been championed as the only realistic location for collective action to provide for social support and social services (Etzioni, 1995 and 2000). Community relations are not easy to define, however, or to distinguish from other aspects of social relations. For instance, distinctions have been drawn between traditional and modern communities, as set out below:

1. *Traditional* communities are generally seen as being determined geographically (for example, by the local village or neighbourhood). Here local organisations may represent many aspects of the lives of local people.
2. *Modern* communities are a product of the declining importance of geographical boundaries as mobility and communication increase, and of the growing diversity of modern life. Thus modern community-based organisations represent different aspects of our lives, such as the lone parents or disabled persons group, and may even be based on cultural or political ties, such as the music collective or the wildlife protection group.

Thus community-based voluntary activity takes a wide variety of forms in different community settings at different times, as research into such activity has revealed in the UK and elsewhere (Chanan, 1992). In such a context the boundaries between community activity and voluntary activity are far from clear cut, and therefore the idea that these are separate sectors is a difficult one to sustain. Rather it may be that the community dimension is one aspect of the broader structural diversity within the sector and perhaps we could consider all of these together to produce a diagrammatic approach outlining the various dimensions and classifications of voluntary organisation (see Figure 10.3).

	Level			
Structure	*Community*	*Local*	*National*	*International*
Protective	LETS	Credit union	Friendly society	World Health Organisation
Representative	Music collective	Gingerbread	Trade union	International Labour Office
Campaigning	New bypass opposition	Local transport campaign	CPAG	Greenpeace
Service	Lone parent group	CAB	WRVS	Oxfam

Figure 10.3   The dimensions of voluntary organisation

Thus far we have been discussing individual voluntary organisations; but organisations do not exist or operate in isolation; indeed, many work within networks or broader groups. For instance, all CABs are members of a National Association (NACAB); and other organisations have local groups which are members of a national coordinating structure, such as Age Concern. National federations of voluntary organisations are in fact quite common; but there may also be local federations to which several organisations belong (for example, many cities and towns have local federations of tenants' associations representing all the associations from estates across the area).

Local federations are not only based on particular types of organisation, however. Most local areas also have more general umbrella organisations representing a wide range of (indeed, potentially all) voluntary local groups, usually known as the local Council for Voluntary Services (CVS) or some similar title. Such umbrella federations also operate now on a regional basis, reflecting the increasing importance of regional support for policy development and service delivery and providing a voice for the sector within the new regional development agencies. More important still are the national agencies which provide support services for the sector as a whole and often play an influential role in major national policy planning. The leading national body is the NCVO, which has separate agencies operating in Scotland, Wales and Northern Ireland. There is also the Community Development Foundation (CDF), which represents smaller community-based organisations. Umbrella federations exist on an international basis too: for example, the European Anti-Poverty Network (EAPN) which represents various locally-based organisations campaigning against poverty within the EU.

The history of voluntary activity

Voluntary sector organisations representing people and delivering services preceded the development of both state and market provision of welfare in Britain and in other welfare capitalist countries, yet they have also survived the development of these newer sectors and have continued to accommodate and adapt their activities alongside them. Thus even the major protagonists of state welfare have recognised the significant and continuing role played by the voluntary sector. In the early part of the twentieth century, for instance, the Webbs (strong supporters of state welfare) talked about the continued importance of a voluntary sector operating alongside state welfare provision. They contrasted two ways in which such a partnership might operate, although they made it clear that they preferred the second model:

■ the 'parallel bars' approach, where the state and the voluntary sector each provided separately for different social needs.
■ the 'extension ladder' approach, where voluntary activity was developed as a supplement to the basic state services that were guaranteed for all.

Beveridge, too, became an advocate for the voluntary sector, when he wrote in 1948 that state provision should not stifle the initiative and enterprise of citizens for voluntary action (Beveridge, 1948).

As we have seen, the state welfare services that developed in the first half of the twentieth century drew heavily on voluntary sector models and voluntary sector organisations: for instance, on the friendly societies for social insurance and on the COS for social work. The establishment of the 'welfare state' following the Second World War in the 1940s saw the replacement of the friendly societies and the COS with state welfare agencies for major social needs, including social security and social work. However, comprehensive state welfare provision in the 1940s did not signify the end of voluntary sector activity. New local organisations, such as the CABs established earlier in 1939, continued to flourish and some important new national organisations, such as the Marriage Guidance Council and the Samaritans, were set up.

Indeed, once state welfare had been established in the latter half of the twentieth century, this in fact operated to provide a new and different impetus for voluntary organisation. This included groups campaigning against the state to challenge or extend state provision, such as the CPAG, as well as those working in partnership with the state to develop and deliver new forms of public service, such as Age Concern.

By the 1970s, therefore, rather than state welfare displacing the voluntary sector, state support was being used extensively to foster its expansion and further development. It was in this context that an independent committee was set up by the Rowntree Memorial Trust, headed by Lord Wolfenden, to review the future role and function of the sector in the UK (see Brenton, 1985, pp.48–53). The main conclusions of the committee were that the voluntary sector would have an important role to play in the future development of welfare services and, consequently, that this role should be the subject of strategic planning by government and would require the support of public funds (Wolfenden, 1977). In 1980 the government introduced a Local Voluntary Action programme within the VSU to provide support for innovative action and evaluation at a local level (Rochester, 2001).

In the 1980s, however, the commitment of the Thatcher governments to reduce public expenditure and to 'roll back' the boundaries of state welfare provided a broader, if in one sense indirect, incentive for the expansion of voluntary sector activity. In general the reduction or withdrawal of public services provided pressure on voluntary organisations to expand or extend their service provision to continue to meet expressed needs. More specifically other dimensions of government, notably local authorities in areas where these were controlled by Labour councillors keen to protect welfare provision, began to work directly with voluntary organisations as a means of supporting and funding local action to provide welfare services that might be under threat from government cuts (most notably in London by the Greater London Council, or GLC).

Central government was not keen on the support that some local authorities were providing for local action, however, especially where this was pushing up public expenditure at the local level. As we shall discuss in Chapter 15, this led them to introduce strict controls on local authority spending, and, as in the case of the GLC, to abolish some local authorities altogether. Later in the 1980s therefore local authority grants to voluntary organisations began to decline in some areas. But by the beginning of the 1990s another shift in national policy was providing the framework for a new set of relations between the state and the voluntary sector, and a new expansion in public funding for voluntary action.

This new expansion was the product of the community care policies introduced by the government in the health and social services reforms discussed in Chapters 4 and 6. Community care meant a change in the role of public service agencies, particularly local authority SSDs, from the providers of services to the purchasers, or enablers, of packages of support, which might include elements delivered by voluntary agencies to the clients placed with them, under agreed arrangements which would channel public funds to support these. As enablers, therefore, local authorities and other agencies are expected to work in partnership with providers in the private and voluntary sectors, and in practice this is expressed through the establishment of legally binding contracts to deliver agreed packages of care.

This new contractual basis marked a significant departure from the previous grant regimes under which many voluntary organisations had been supported by local and central government; and it has sometimes been referred to as a move to a 'contract culture'. Such a culture was welcomed by some organisations for whom it provided a clearer recognition of the services that they were being expected to provide and it gave them a right to consistent and relatively secure funding for these in return. However, a number of commentators have pointed to the problems which may flow for some organisations from moving into a contract culture (Russell and Scott, 1997), and have argued that this could even undermine some of the core principles and values of the voluntary sector (Billis and Glennerster, 1998). Certainly contracting is a model that may not be appropriate for all, and in particular may exclude many small or community-based organisations, who, according to Kramer (1990, p.9), 'may be unable or unwilling to compete for contracts because they cannot meet the requirements for greater specificity, accountability and compliance with regulations'.

The moves towards contracting were not the only policy changes affecting voluntary organisations in the 1990s. In 1994 the Prime Minister, John Major, gave his personal support to a new programme to promote volunteering more generally through support for a national and local infrastructure to encourage voluntary activity, called the 'Make a Difference' initiative (see Davis Smith, 2001). At around the same time the NCVO commissioned a major inquiry into the future of the voluntary sector in England (Deakin, 1996), and a similar review was commissioned in Scotland (Kemp, 1997). Both commented on the growing strength and depth of voluntary action and the critical role that the sector was by then playing in policy development and delivery, and argued that relations between the sector and the state should be conducted on a more formal basis (perhaps through some formal agreement or concordat).

Following their move into government in 1997 Labour acted quickly to take forward and develop a number of the initiatives to promote voluntary action and improved relations which had been developing earlier in the decade. Blair himself made a number of statements supporting civil society and community spirit, arguing that the role of voluntary action should be raised in profile within policy planning; and this was followed by the establishment of a new Active Community Unit (ACU) within the Home Office to promote and develop voluntary organisations. In 2002 the government conducted a cross-cutting review of the sector (HM Treasury, 2002) and followed this with a renewed commitment to government support to develop the capacity of the sector and improve relations with government, described by the Home Secretary as a 'change in culture' and including a 20 per cent increase in funding to the ACU (£188 million over three years) and an additional £125 million 'future builders' fund to assist voluntary organisations in developing public service work.

It is also clear that the government's new Third Way for policy development involves a renewed commitment to collaboration between the public and 'third' sectors. In particular this was expressed through the promotion of partnership working between the state, the private and the voluntary sectors in policy delivery, which was rolled out across a number of policy dimensions (see Chapter 18, and Glendinning, Powell and Rummery, 2002). The need for the formalisation of these relationships, recommended by the Deakin Commission, was also taken up through the development of a national *compact* to govern relations across the sector (Home Office, 1998); and this was later followed by the development of local compacts in many local authorities (Craig *et al.*, 2002).

Local partnership working was also widely promoted and supported through the various area-based regeneration programmes supported by the government after 1998. The action zones and NDC programmes all prioritised partnership working across the public and voluntary sectors and promoted participation by community groups in new approaches to policy planning (see Chapter 18). By the beginning of the new century, therefore, the scale and scope of voluntary activity was broader than it had been at any time in the previous hundred years; and the contribution that the voluntary sector could make to policy planning and delivery was recognised at the centre of government policy making and replicated in a wide range of new programmes and policy initiatives.

■ To what extent can we differentiate between the voluntary and community sectors in terms of the aims and structures of different organisations?

■ Compare and contrast the 'parallel bars' and 'extension ladder' approaches to state support for voluntary activity.

■ To what extent have the introduction of contracting and partnership working with the state affected the independence of voluntary organisations?

■ Can voluntary organisation ever be entirely independent of the state?

The future of voluntary action

The future development of the voluntary sector in the early twenty-first century therefore looks to be a promising one. Voluntary action is widely valued and supported, both within government and outside. The questions to be faced therefore are perhaps not so much whether the voluntary sector has a role in policy planning and delivery, but rather what that role should be, and in particular how the sector should relate to other sectors. There are a number of different forms which such relationships could take:

1. *Alternative.* Voluntary organisations could aim to be an alternative to the state and the market. This is what some purists might argue that they ought to be. Such a role can be an important one, especially in some areas where both the state and the market have failed to meet social needs. This has arguably been an important factor in the growth of many of the voluntary organisations based in ethnic minority communities in Britain. These communities have frequently experienced discrimination in, or exclusion from, state and market services, as we shall discuss in Chapter 16, and have developed independent, ethnically-based, organisations to provide some of the services that otherwise they would lack.

2. *Complementary.* Voluntary activities may also be complementary to other service provision, as in the 'extension ladder' model championed by the Webbs. Voluntary organisations thus complement the basic services provided, in particular, through the state: for example, play schemes catering for children outside school hours or in the holidays complement collective education and child care provision for working parents.

3. *Partnership.* Rather than complementing state provision, voluntary activity may work in partnership with the state. For decades the NSPCC has worked in partnership with social services departments in providing for children at risk, with NSPCC officers sometimes working alongside state social workers in particular cases. Partnership working between the public, private and voluntary sectors is now openly promoted by government and is a key feature of many new programmes and initiatives.

4. *Contractual.* The development of community care planning and other quasi-market policy delivery has led to a rapid growth in the use of voluntary organisations to deliver public services for particular clients or client groups. These agreements generally take on a contractual form; and contractual working has become a more widespread feature of the operation of a wide range of voluntary organisations as they enter into a range of service agreements with local authorities and other statutory agencies.
5. *Advocacy.* Finally there are some organisations that will not wish to be seen as partners with the state, because they wish to adopt a campaigning, or an advocacy, role towards it. Challenging the state, or the market, either collectively or on behalf of individuals pursuing their rights is an activity where independent organisations have a crucial function to perform, as the national Consumers' Association or the local rights and advice centre testify.

Of course, some organisations may have different relations with the state and the market at different times, or in different circumstances. For example, advocacy organisations may also be seeking contractual funding for their work, and in cases like this the dilemmas inherent in these different relations can readily come to the fore: for instance, should funding agencies be able to specify what sort of individual cases a rights and advice agency can take on?

As well as their changing relationships with other bodies, many voluntary organisations also face other dilemmas concerning their internal structure and forms of operation as they face up to their future development. For a start, there are the problems of developing and managing their own organisational structures. These include the maintenance of infrastructural, or core, support arrangements (premises, equipment, accounts and personnel management), the identification and implementation of monitoring and quality assurance procedures, the discharging of their responsibilities as employers, and the tendering and managing of contracts and other forms of funding agreements. Support is provided for many of these things by the umbrella agencies supporting voluntary organisations, such as the NCVO and the local CVS; but these organisations themselves need to be recognised and supported for the roles that they play in ensuring that the sector as a whole can function effectively.

It is also important to remember that, although it is sometimes referred to and even promoted as one entity, the voluntary sector is in practice both diverse and complex. The great strengths of the voluntary sector – its variety and spontaneity – are also to some extent its greatest weaknesses. Voluntary sector organisations have largely developed on an ad hoc basis, as activists and innovators have turned their ideas into collective action. The distribution of such activists, however, is both uneven and unplanned. There may be an excellent community play scheme or independent advice centre in a local area; but it is equally likely that there may not be. The NSPCC provides an important additional service to protect children in need; but there are other needy groups for whom no such charitable body exists. Furthermore, some organisations receive much more popular support, and charitable donations, than others (for example, the national association for the blind has always been more popular than similar organisations for those with hearing disabilities). Voluntary sector activity is thus not comprehensive, or even equitable; it is partial, patchy and sometimes unreliable, and against the good initiatives must be contrasted the major gaps.

Exclusion and discrimination can also be problems within organisations as well as across the sector; and here, arguably, is an even more serious dilemma. Not all voluntary organisations are outward looking. Some can be quite narrowly focused and dominated by a few powerful individuals and their individual interests. Because voluntary activity relies, in essence, on voluntary participation this can often mean that many are excluded either passively (because they do not take part) or actively (because they are told that they are not wanted). And this exclusion, too, can be structured by race, gender, class or other social divisions. Indeed, it may be argued that most voluntary organisations exclude some potential activists, or potential beneficiaries, through social divisions of one kind or another.

Nevertheless the voluntary sector has been strongly supported by both academics and policy makers (see Hadley and Hatch, 1981), and at the beginning of the twenty-first century it occupies a central role in political dialogue and policy planning. This central role is borne out too by international comparison. In countries such as the USA, with more limited state welfare provision, the non-profit sector, as it is often called there, is large both in scale and scope. By contrast, in many European countries with well-developed welfare states, the sector nevertheless has crucial roles to play. In the Netherlands, for instance, although welfare services such as education and health are largely funded by the state, they were developed and initially administered by independent bodies based around the 'pillars' of religious affiliation and membership of organisations linked to the Catholic or Protestant churches. Religious organisations, especially those based in the Catholic Church, are also important in providing services in the Mediterranean countries such as Italy and Spain. Indeed international research studies on the sector have revealed its variety, and underlined its importance, across all welfare capitalist countries (Salamon and Anheier, 1996; Anheier, Carlson and Kendall, 2001).

The voluntary sector is varied, flexible, innovative, non-bureaucratic, accessible and, perhaps most significantly, cheap; but it is also unpredictable, unstable, incomplete and sometimes oppressive and exclusionary. It has developed largely on an unplanned basis. Social policy planning must recognise this, and also recognise the limitations inherent in it. In the future, greater recognition of the role and structure of the sector will undoubtedly lead to its closer incorporation into social and economic planning. This may act to minimise some of the problems of inconsistency and non-comprehensiveness; but at the same time planners must recognise that complete control over voluntary activity never could – or should – be achieved. Voluntary sector organisations will always seek out, and challenge, the gaps and contradictions in state and market welfare provision; this capacity for innovation cannot be suppressed.

QUESTION: COMPREHENSION

■ Discuss the problems for voluntary action that result from the uneven nature of voluntary provision and the tendency for some organisations to focus only on a narrow range of services or user groups.

QUESTION: REFLECTION

■ The great and enduring strength of the voluntary sector is its diversity. To what extent do you agree with this view?

FURTHER READING

The best introduction to the voluntary sector remains Kendall and Knapp (1996), and a comprehensive collection of papers discussing contemporary issues is provided by Harris and Rochester (2001). Deakin (2001) discusses the broader conceptual concept of civil society as a space for voluntary action. Detailed information on the shape of the sector in England can be found in the NCVO *Almanac* (2002), which is updated every two years. Two useful websites are those of the NCVO, **www.ncvo-vol.org.uk** and CAF, **www.cafonline.org.uk**.

Informal
Welfare

SUMMARY OF KEY POINTS

- Informal welfare is family, friends and neighbours providing a range of services through unorganised helping networks.
- The continuing existence of informal care and support is assumed by the other sectors of providers in the planning of welfare provision.
- Informal care is not organised or regulated and in practice is based on individual dedication and goodwill or reciprocal commitment.
- Informal care is sometimes referred to as 'community care', yet is it not clear that caring communities exist in the ways anticipated by some policy makers.
- The form and structure of informal welfare is affected by changes and developments in the other sectors.
- Support for child care, especially of very young children, is limited despite commitments to 'family friendly' policy planning.
- The availability of family members to provide informal care has been affected by broader demographic and social changes within society.
- The needs of carers may not be the same as those they care for.
- Social security benefits are available for those unable to enter paid employment because of caring responsibilities.
- Support for the personal and care costs of adults needing long-term care is provided through means-tested support in England and Wales, with care needs met for all in Scotland.

The importance of informal provision

Analysis of the structure of social policy provision focuses our attention on the different ways in which welfare services are provided and the different mix of providers within any particular social context, as we have seen in the other chapters in this part of the book. However, despite this broadened focus, it remains the case that debate about the different sectors of welfare still pays relatively little attention to what is, in volume terms at least, the major provider of social services: the informal sector (although, as Means and Smith, 2003, have pointed out, there is now recognition that the informal sector has played the 'dominant' – if often 'invisible' – role in all welfare regimes).

The unorganised and unrecorded activities of family, friends and neighbours in caring for and supporting each other has always been the underlying social fabric upon which all other welfare activity is based. That such care and support will be provided is something that we take for granted as academics and policy makers and, more importantly perhaps, that we take for granted as members of society too. It is of course understandable that we should take such support for granted; and in practice it is desirable – indeed, even essential – that we should be able to do so. There is an implied reciprocity and mutual interdependence in all interpersonal relationships that could never fully be planned, predicted or neatly pigeon-holed. However, taking such support for granted should not prevent us from recognising its importance in broader social policy terms, or from analysing, and acting upon, its interrelations with other forms of support in other sectors.

It is precisely because informal support has always been there in the past and, we trust, always will be in the future, that we must seek to understand its scope and its problems, and to make sure that what we take for granted, we do not also ignore or exploit. In practice the state welfare services that were developed over the last century in Britain largely took for granted, or more positively were predicated upon, the support and care provided informally by families and communities. In other words, certain responsibilities have been assumed to exist within particular restricted groups: for example, education policy assumes that parents will be available to support children outside the school day and school year; health policy assumes that both minor acute conditions and chronic sickness or disability can be provided for informally at home; and social security assumes that some family members will pool resources and support one another.

Without the informal services provided at home and in the neighbourhood, state services, and private or voluntary services, would not be able to operate in the way that they do (or, indeed, in many cases would not be able to operate at all). Informal provision is thus crucially important. It is also massive. Because it is not organised or recorded, it would be impossible to measure the size of the informal sector, although, as we shall see later, some attempts have been made to count the numbers involved in giving and receiving some aspects of informal care. However, the fact that we cannot measure informal welfare activity does not mean that it does not have any costs. As K Wright (1987) pointed out in a study of the economics of informal care for the elderly, in broader economic terms informal care is in fact very costly. It is costly immediately in terms of the time provided by carers and supporters; and it is costly indirectly to these people in terms of the lost earnings and opportunities that this caring work imposes on them, which is sometimes referred to as *opportunity costs* (Joshi, 1988).

Recognition of the costs involved in the informal provision of services is an important part of social policy analysis of them. It also suggests important policy responses. In some cases these costs could, and perhaps should, be covered by others, or at least subsidised. For instance, this could be done through the provision of income in the form of social security benefits for informal carers, and this does, to some extent, take place. Informal service providers could also be supported and assisted in their tasks by a range of other means and measures, and we shall discuss these shortly.

Where such support is provided, however, informal provision is clearly going to overlap with support from the state, or from the private sector where these means are purchased on the market. As we discussed in the case of the voluntary sector, the informal sector too overlaps with the others and, where this overlap exists, the distinction between informal provision and organised services in the state, private or voluntary sectors becomes blurred. The relationship with the voluntary sector, in particular, can be a complex one: for instance, when does a baby-sitting circle cease to be neighbourly support and become a voluntary organisation? There are problems, therefore, in defining precisely what we mean by the informal sector; and, even if these definitional problems cannot be entirely resolved, they must be addressed.

The problem of definition

In fact it is the question of overlap that is perhaps the most important difficulty faced in seeking to define what we mean by the informal sector. As we discussed in Chapter 9, public provision is often contrasted with private provision within social policy debate. Although private provision is sometimes taken to mean commercially provided welfare in the market, it can also include informal services provided privately at home. Private provision thus includes the informal sector, although it is not conterminous with it.

However, there is a danger in perceiving informal provision simply as private welfare. The public–private dichotomy can be a misleading one, especially where it is used to suggest that somehow private provision is not a matter of public concern or that it cannot, or should not, be the subject of public policy. Feminist critics, for example, have pointed to attempts to reduce family relations to such a private (or personal) sphere and have argued strongly that such relationships are not in reality separate from broader socio-economic structures. As they have often put it, 'the personal is also political'. And, as Ungerson (1987) signified in the title of her book on informal care, *Policy is Personal* too. Just as it is unhelpful to define commercial services as private, so it is inaccurate to perceive the informal sector as a separate private sphere.

A more significant feature of the informal sector, for definitional purposes at least, is its unorganised (or, more accurately, *non*-organised) nature. State bureaucracies and business companies organise the services they offer to their clients, or customers. Indeed, it is just this organisation, and the bureaucracy which accompanies it, that has often been a feature of the criticisms that have sometimes been levelled at these sectors. Voluntary organisations aim to avoid these structural constraints; but, even where they are controlled and managed by their own users, these bodies are nevertheless organisations. In contrast, the provision of care and support on an informal basis is not organised, either by an external agency or by those providing the service themselves. There are no rules or regulations governing what is done or how it is done. There is no enforceable contract or even a formal goodwill agreement: there is only the willingness to care and the expectation to benefit.

This is not to say, however, that services provided informally are not both reliable and predictable. Indeed they are usually both, and often more so than those supposedly provided under strict legal rules and statutory obligations. The willingness to care and the expectation of support are the two sides of the reciprocal nature of most informal services; in practice this reciprocity ensures that we do care for others because we know that others will care for us, even if this may be a different 'other' at a relatively distant time. *Reciprocity* is thus at the heart of informal care and support; and reciprocal relations between individuals are not generally amenable to formal organisation or control, for then the obligation moves from the individual to the structural level. Of course, as with all definitions in this area, the distinction is a blurred one; support provided by a neighbour may, for example, be incorporated into a package of care by a social worker, thus including it within a form of state service. However, insofar as the commitment to provide the support moves from an individual offer to a structural obligation, the service moves from the informal to the state, or perhaps the voluntary, sector.

The non-organised provision of informal care and support is usually based within families or communities: thus the informal sector might be identified with the relationships within families and communities. As a definitional base, however, this too provides us with some difficulties. For a start, the definition and structure of family relations is constantly changing. Despite appeals in some quarters and at some times for a return to 'traditional' family values, family relations have always been in a state of flux. Relationships change: people marry earlier (or now later, or not at all), have fewer children, or separate and divorce; and definitions change: those whom we might have included within our (extended) family in the past may now be regarded rather differently as distant relatives, from whom support would not be expected. If the informal sector is based on families, then what exactly does this mean?

Much the same problems arise with the notion of community. As we saw in Chapter 10, types of community differ significantly. Although commentators and policy makers often refer to 'the community' and talk – usually in complimentary terms – about things such as community schools or community policing, quite different things are often meant, and understood, by these references to community structure. As we discussed in Chapter 6, recent policies to encourage the 'community care' of people with mental or physical health problems are based, at least in theory, on the assumption that there are community structures existing in modern British society that will automatically provide a supportive and caring environment to cater for the needs of such people.

Some commentators, such as Etzioni (1995 and 2000), have even argued that the community provides the natural base for the emergence of welfare services more generally.

However, it is in fact doubtful whether such close-knit and caring communities have ever been widespread within British society; certainly they do not exist in this simple form now. There are community activities and organisations in which people may, or may not, be involved or to which they may feel allegiance; but these are constantly changing structures from which allegiances may be withdrawn or transferred. Furthermore, as we have seen, modern communities are political and cultural, as well as geographical and social; and many such community structures are quite ill-equipped – and indeed unwilling – to be a base for informal social services. In practice, therefore, it is usually the individual family, friends and neighbours of those in need who provide services rather than any broader community group. Family, friends and neighbours can sometimes constitute what one American commentator called 'helping networks' (Johnson, 1987, p.64), and these networks may provide a range of support and care services; but they do not do so on behalf of any given community structure.

Families in particular, of course, provide care and support, at least for those within the close family group (whether that is a lone parent or a three-generation household). Friends we choose, and presumably they choose us. They may expect to give, and receive, support; as the old saying goes, 'a friend in need is a friend indeed'. Neighbours we probably do not choose; but they are likely to know us and to know of our needs for care and support. Friends and neighbours can undertake a wide range of informal services, including shopping, cooking, gardening, providing transport or even just keeping a watchful eye (surveillance), albeit only in a minority of cases: for instance, Rossiter and Wicks (1982) calculated that around 8 per cent of elderly people received regular support of this kind from neighbours.

Drawing on evidence from research into informal care, Johnson (1987, p.90) lists five categories of social service regularly provided on an informal basis:

- personal care – washing, dressing, feeding, etc.
- domestic care – cooking and cleaning
- auxiliary care – gardening and odd jobs
- social support – visiting and companionship
- surveillance – keeping an eye on vulnerable people.

Family members may provide services in all these categories, but friends or neighbours are more likely to provide those in the last two or three only. Thus, here we have a classification of the types of activity involved in informal social services and some idea of who might be involved in providing these. As far as a definition of the informal sector goes, this may be as good as we can get: it is family, friends and neighbours providing a range of individual services through unorganised helping networks.

The development of informal care

The informal provision of care and support preceded the development of modern social policy planning, and to some extent it has since then remained outside the formal service planning process. The point about informal welfare provision is that it is not planned or organised like other sectors. However, informal activity is affected by the changes and developments within the formal welfare sectors; indeed, such developments have been crucially important in changing the context within which voluntary activity takes place, and the expectations that both service providers and recipients have of it.

Many voluntary sector organisations have grown out of informal activity. These include the baby-sitting circle that becomes the local mother and toddler group, or the squatters' group, that becomes a campaign against homelessness. The boundaries between the voluntary and informal sectors remain constantly blurred and, in particular, changes in the size and scope of voluntary sector activity are likely to relieve, or to accentuate, pressure on informal service providers to take on caring or supporting roles. Furthermore, these changes occur both over time and across different places.

The development of commercial welfare services has also affected the informal sector. The wider range of services available commercially can displace informal care. Those with resources have always been able to buy the personal care that they need (for example, through the employment of nannies and nurses); and with growing affluence this commercial replacement of informal care is utilised by a broader range of the population, albeit still largely by a better-off minority. Commercial services can also, however, support informal activity. Adaptations to homes, such as a stair lift, and personal aids, such as an electric wheelchair, can make the provision of informal care much less onerous. Commercial care plans or health insurance policies can provide financial support if, or when, a need for informal care arises. Again, these services are likely to be more widely used by the better-off; nevertheless, their impact on the size, and shape, of the informal sector is extensive.

Most importantly of all, however, the development of state welfare services has affected the informal sector in a wide manner of ways; and changes within state welfare services have continued to alter the relationship between the two. To a large extent much of the early development of the welfare state was predicated upon an attempt to remove the burden of informal care and support for all welfare needs from the individual and replace this with collectively organised services provided by all, and for the benefit of all. The state health and education services have taken responsibility for much of the provision of these services away from the family who, perforce, would have provided more of them before. The development of state social work services has resulted in the provision of more and better quality public residential care for children and adults in need of extensive support, of day care and drop-in services for those with more limited needs, and of counselling and advice for those uncertain of how to secure the assistance they need.

During the post-war period the establishment of state welfare in Britain saw a major extension of public social services, which were intended, in part at least, to ensure that collective provision should replace the informal demands made on family, friends and neighbours in the past. However, since then the pendulum of policy planning has to some extent swung away from state provision and back towards an explicit expectation of, and reliance upon, informal sector care. Within two decades of the establishment of post-war state services, criticisms began to emerge of the discomfort, insensitivity and even brutality of state institutional care (for example, Townsend's classic 1962 study of homes for older people). These criticisms of the undesirability of 'total institutions' have now become widespread (Jones and Fowles, 1984); and children's homes or older persons' homes are still sometimes viewed negatively with a mixture of fear and pity.

Perhaps the most negative images of state collective care, however, have been reserved for mental hospitals. Here a state service is seen in popular culture primarily as a threatening place, to be avoided almost at all costs. Such negative imagery has resulted in a shift away from such residential care in social policy planning. In Italy, in the 1970s, this shift was a stark one; all large mental hospitals were closed down and their patients transferred to community-based care schemes. Policy change did not moved so rapidly in Britain; but it has moved in the same direction, in particular following the community care policy changes of the 1990s, as discussed in Chapter 6. Such community care can avoid the insensitivity, and the stigma, of state residential provision; it can also be more flexible and adaptable to the particular needs of different people, although it can also still require the support of organised services within the home.

However, the shift towards community care is not just a product of political and policy rejection of the value of public residential provision: it is also the result of financial pressure on state services provision and a narrower economic assessment of the (apparent) costs of these different models and sectors of care. Public residential care is expensive to provide and large amounts of public money are needed to purchase and maintain institutions and pay workers within them. Community-based care provided informally by family, friends and neighbours has much less of an impact on the public purse, especially where, as has often been the case in Britain, the state services to support such care have themselves been restricted by lack of resources. Of course, as we have already pointed out, informal care in the community is costly in other ways; in particular it imposes costs on those individuals who do the caring work. However, this does not register in the economic or political calculations of the resourcing of community care; and thus the shift back to the informal sector has been assumed to create much-needed savings in state welfare provision. These savings have been experienced as an increased pressure on the informal sector, resulting directly from developments within the state sector.

QUESTIONS: COMPREHENSION

- What are the 'opportunity costs' of informal care, and to what extent would it be desirable to try and quantify these?
- To what extent has the expansion of public and private care services reduced the demand on the informal sector?

QUESTION: REFLECTION

- Can communities care?

Supporting informal care

Although the welfare services provided informally vary widely in form and scope, the most significant feature of the sector, especially from a social policy perspective, is the role played by the informal provision of individual care in the home. Caring services can encompass a range of activities; in particular they include the personal and domestic tasks outlined above. These forms of care are provided by adults (usually parents, and especially mothers) for their young children; but they are also provided by adults (and occasionally by children) for other adults, in particular those who through illness or disability are unable to care adequately for themselves.

Care for children is not often discussed in social policy debates, largely because it is taken for granted that parents can, and do, provide such care. In practice, however, it is generally mothers, rather than fathers, who provide the majority of the care for young children and who, in particular, forgo paid employment in order to do this. As we have pointed out, the long-term consequences of this can be significant for mothers in terms of their lost opportunities for receipt of wages and for career experience and enhancement. When children are older and can go to school this relieves to some extent the burden of care at home, but the limitations of the school day and school year mean that it is still sometimes extremely difficult for mothers to combine child care with full-time employment.

Due to these pressures on family-based care for children, the provision of collective child care, particularly before school age, has become a more significant issue for social policy. Local authorities do provide some nursery places even for very young children; however, these are often in very limited supply and are frequently allocated primarily to children deemed to be in special need because of a troubled home environment. Private collective child care is also available, and increasingly is provided by large employers for the young children of their employees. Private and occupational provision generally has to be purchased by parents, however, and the cost of such care can be quite high. This is now recognised by government, and parents on low wages paying for the costs of private child care can recover some of these costs through means-tested child care tax credits.

Private child care can also be purchased on an individual basis and this form of provision is in practice much more common. From the full-time live-in nanny to the neighbour who is paid to look after the children for a few mornings a week, private child care provision supplements the informal provision of care through families and overlaps with it, as many private arrangements are extremely informal. Of course, such private child care arrangements are not new; they have always been a central feature of the family-based informal care of children, although one often overlooked and inadequately supported. Tax credits can provide some support for such private care now, but only where payment is made under formal agreements to approved carers; and the need to support child care (and parents) through 'family friendly' policy planning is now more widely recognised by government albeit sometimes only at a rhetorical level.

More generally, however, and perhaps unfortunately, policy planning for child care in the informal sector has traditionally concentrated largely not on the complex working arrangements that many families do successfully make for the care of their children, but rather on the failure of some families to provide care adequately and the consequent need for state intervention through social work to ensure that the harm done to children in such cases in minimised, as discussed in Chapter 6.

While the majority of informal care is that provided for young children, a significant, and growing, proportion of informal sector activity concerns care for vulnerable adults. In practice, such care is largely provided by close family members, especially spouses and adult children, and usually this is done without any formal support from either the state or the other sectors of welfare. Evidence from the General Household Survey (GHS) suggests that around 6 million people are involved in providing some form of care to vulnerable adults, with 1.4 million doing this on a more or less full time basis (over 20 hours a week: see Twigg, 1999, p.252).

It is feminist commentators, in particular, who have elevated the issue (and the problems) of informal care for adults on to the policy agenda. As they have pointed out, it is often women who provide such care and experience many of the problems related to it (Finch and Groves, 1983; Ungerson, 1987). Parker (1990, p.93) makes the point that there is a significant, yet hidden, burden being carried disproportionately by women here: 'Generally, female carers have been shown to be more likely to give up their jobs, lose more money and to experience more stress than are male carers.' However, it would be wrong to assume that all informal care in the home is carried out by women; indeed, according to the GHS figures, whilst 17 per cent of women provide such care, 13 per cent of men do (Twigg, 1999, p.252).

The contradictions that underlie this burden were brought out sharply in the title of Finch and Groves' (1983) edited collection in informal care, *A Labour of Love*. For women especially, the fusion of labour and love is manifest in the double meaning of the word care. Care can mean caring *about* someone and it can also mean caring *for* them. The provision of much informal care is predicated on the assumption that, because we care about someone, we can also therefore be expected to care for them in times of need. This is an assumption that may be strongly held, most significantly by those in need of care, and those who feel obliged to care for them. Here the presumed, and yet unplanned, reciprocity of the informal sector can begin to take on a coercive, and even an oppressive, form. The costs of caring for a vulnerable or dependent adult can be great, both immediately and indirectly over the longer term (Joshi, 1992). It can also, unlike child care, frequently be a long (and ultimately depressing) ordeal, ending only with the death of the recipient of the care. Yet the provision of such care is widespread and is vitally important at both an individual and a broader social level. It is also an area of provision that is growing rapidly, and is likely to grow further in the future, with larger numbers of older people and people with disabilities surviving within the population.

However, while the demand for informal care is growing, the 'helping networks', in particular the families, that provide it are changing in ways that seem likely to reduce their capacity to continue to do so in the future. There has been a continuing decline in the number of younger single people able to provide informal care, in particular the single daughters of older parents; and at the same time there has been a reduction in the size of families with the result that there are fewer children to provide a future pool of potential carers. Changes in family stability have also further reduced the potential source of carers here, with increased numbers of divorces meaning that previously experienced family obligations are now frequently severed. However, perhaps most significant is the continuing growth of women's (especially married women's) participation in the labour market. Of course, some married women do give up paid employment in order to provide informal care; but this is a hard financial, as well as emotional, decision which more are having to face, and which more may decide to refuse to make. These refusals may, of course, lead to a growth in the market provision of such care (perhaps even in organisations employing women as paid carers), but such a shift away from the informal towards the market sector is both uncertain and fraught with difficulties, especially for those too poor to purchase such services.

A shift from informal to market-based caring services may not, of course, necessarily be a bad thing for those requiring such care. The inclusion of 'community care' in recent policy planning seems to have been informed by an almost unquestionable belief in the desirability of informal, individual, care as against collectively provided services, founded largely on the criticisms of the worst of state residential provision. Yet, as research has shown (Qureshi and Walker, 1989), much depends here upon the dedication and commitment of the carer, and upon the support services available to supplement their informal provision, both of which can vary dramatically.

Support for community care has also focused almost exclusively upon the advantages of community care from the point of view of the recipients of it, the *cared for*, and has ignored the problems experienced by *carers* within the informal sector. Yet, as Twigg (1989) argued, appreciation of carers' circumstances and carers' needs may lead to a rather different emphasis within policy planning. For instance, carers may be perceived as *resources* for service provision, or they may be perceived as *co-workers* with those in other sectors, or they may be perceived as *co-clients* with the person they are caring for. These different perceptions lead to different ways of supporting carers, all of which have been variously pursued (sometimes simultaneously).

One of the most important problems facing carers is the source (and the adequacy) of their income, especially where they are excluded from paid employment as result of their caring work. Since 1975 there has been a social security benefit specifically designed to provide an income for carers, the Invalid Care Allowance (ICA). However, the value of this benefit is very low, so those without any other source of income are still left depending upon income support; and it does not extend to those caring for elderly people. Even this low level of benefit was not provided for married and cohabiting female carers prior to 1986, because of the assumption that they could be provided for by their male partners. The discriminatory perspective that informed this assumption reveals much about past (and perhaps still present) policy assumptions about the structure and workings of the informal sector which have been taken up by feminist writers.

Caring work is thus frequently associated with financial dependency upon inadequate social security benefits, with all the long-term costs of lack of saving and investment associated with this added to the immediate pressures of caring work on a low income. As Glendinning (1992) pointed out, however, such work is also associated with *interdependency* between the carer and the cared for. This is true at the formal level as entitlement to ICA is predicated upon receipt of Disability Living Allowance by the recipient of the care, a problem that significantly reduces take-up levels of both benefits because of the complexities involved in claiming them. It is also, and more significantly perhaps, true at the informal level. Where care is provided within family relationships, this may well involve a pooling of resources within the household; thus all sources of income, however inadequate, are likely to be used to support all family members. As a result of this the caring relationship can come to dominate the financial arrangements of the whole household (and, of course, their financial prospects for the future too).

Financial support for the provision of long-term care to vulnerable adults was reviewed by a Royal Commission established by the Labour government. The Sutherland Commission (1999) recommended a separation between the costs of providing personal care, which should be met by the state for all, and more general living and housing costs, which should be met by individuals, perhaps with some means-tested support. These recommendations were not endorsed by the government, who instead opted for a continuation of existing policies which use means-testing to ensure that state-supported care services are targeted on those that cannot afford to pay for these on the private market. However, in Scotland the devolved administration decided to follow Sutherland and institute state-funded personal care for all meeting defined categories of need.

In England, therefore, support for vulnerable adults and their carers is thus largely provided through the adult services branches of local authority SSDs, as we discussed in Chapter 6. Such support generally depends upon the packages of care negotiated by social workers (care managers), and may include the provision of domiciliary services (home helps and 'meals on wheels') to assist both cared for and carers at home. The recent embracement of 'community care' in the planning and development of services for vulnerable adults has at least placed the provision of support such as this at the centre of policy practice. At the beginning of the twenty-first century, therefore, the relationship between the informal sector and the services provided by public and private agencies is a recognised element of policy planning; and informal welfare is more closely embedded in the welfare mix than was the case for much of the last century.

QUESTIONS: COMPREHENSION

- What is meant by 'family friendly' policy planning, and to what extent can it reduce the demand on informal care of young children?
- To what extent have the needs of *carers* been overlooked in policy planning in the informal sector?
- To what extent does policy planning now seek to regulate the provision of informal care?

QUESTION: REFLECTION

- Should we be expected to care *for* those we care *about*?

FURTHER READING

Two early texts which put the policy on informal care into a broader perspective and developed a feminist critique of past policy development were Finch and Groves (1983) and Ungerson (1987). Up-to-date commentary on policy on 'community care' can be found in Means and Smith (2003). Twigg and Atkin (1994) look at the position of carers within the welfare mix. A useful website is **www.carers.gov.uk**.

Part

III

Context

Ideologies
of Welfare

SUMMARY OF KEY POINTS

- Ideologies structure our views of the world. They are *critical* and *prescriptive*, leading to disagreement and debate about what should be done. Those influencing social policy are called 'ideologies of welfare'.
- Ideologies of welfare have often been located along a continuum from *left* (pro-state) to *right* (pro-market) positions, although not all can be contained within such a simplistic framework.
- Neo-liberalism argues that state provision of welfare is incompatible with free market economic growth and leads to a 'dependency culture', although few supporters advocate complete withdrawal of state welfare support.
- Supporters of the Middle Way were part of the *Butskellite* 'consensus' on welfare which emerged in the mid-twentieth century. They support collective welfare provision in partnership with market-based economic growth.
- Social democrats believe that capitalist societies can (and should) be reformed to meet the welfare needs of all citizens. Social democracy is sometimes distinguished from democratic socialism, which advocates the ultimate replacement of all capitalist relations.
- Marxists argue that state welfare provision within capitalism is inherently unstable and will lead to failure and conflict, although socialist alternatives have not proved viable in practice.
- New social movements challenge the left/right orthodoxy of welfare ideologies by pointing to other social divisions and socio-economic issues which underpin welfare policy and practice.
- Postmodernists argue that single ideological frameworks cannot provide an effective basis for analysis of complex societies, and that ideological analysis should concentrate upon how such frameworks are constructed and influence policy development.

Ideology

The concept of ideology is one of the most important in social science. However, it is also one of the most contested, and one of the most misused and misunderstood. For instance, ideology is sometimes taken to mean the adoption of a false or inaccurate perception of the real world; this is then contrasted with the correct perspective which is supposedly provided by scientific inquiry. This is not the sense in which ideology is normally understood in social policy debate; and it is not the sense in which it is used in this book. We use ideology more broadly as a concept that refers to the systems of beliefs within which *all* individuals perceive *all* social phenomena. In this usage no one system of beliefs is more correct, or more privileged, than any other.

In this sense, therefore, all of us have ideologies; they are our own systems of beliefs that shape and structure the way we see the world, and make judgements about it. And, of course, each individual's ideological perspective is different and unique. We do not all agree with one another about everything. Indeed, it our disagreements and differences that make debate and development both desirable and possible. If we were all the same it would not only be a dull world: in terms of social development, it would be a dead one. Thus individual ideologies differ, and they are a source of debate and conflict. Individual ideologies are also both *critical* and *prescriptive*: we know what is wrong with what we see, and we know what should be done about it. As a result of this they are therefore *partial* and *value laden*; we do not know or understand everything but we do know what we like and do not like.

Ideological perspectives therefore condition the way in which all of us perceive the world in which we live, and they do so in a way that leaves all of us with a more or less restricted and biased perspective on it. If this seems to be a rather depressing starting point, it should not be judged so. No one can know everything or be right about everything; but that does not mean that we do not know anything or that our views are always only a product of our own personal values. Our individual ideological perspectives are limited and biased, and they are unique; but they are not isolated. As individuals we are also part of broader social structures from which we receive the support we need to survive, and through which we give support to others. Our individual systems of belief are also part of broader ideological perspectives from which we draw the ideas and values which we use to form judgements, and to which we may contribute ideas and values of our own.

Individual ideologies are constructed within wider ideological perspectives in which views are shared and debated, and within which shared views are held and disseminated. Such broader ideological perspectives may be held by relatively small social groups and may focus specifically upon particular issues (for example, the neighbourhood campaign group who all wish to preserve the character of their area and oppose new development plans). However, they may also be much wider in both scale and scope, enlisting adherence or support from the majority of people throughout the country (or even across countries) and addressing a range of social issues from a particular perspective. Such broader ideological perspectives influence the way individual ideological views are formed and developed, and through this influence on those individuals, or groups, who are in positions of power they are able to shape the world in which we live. Indeed it is *because* ideologies shape the social world that we debate so passionately about them, and within them. The power of ideology cannot be overestimated in social science; and, as we shall see, in social policy ideologies of welfare have shaped and structured all perceptions of welfare policy and the development of all policy planning.

It is important to recognise here, however, that ideological perspectives not only determine which policies we propose to develop or support but also influence how we view, and judge, policy developments that have already taken place. Take, for example, the introduction of the right of all tenants to buy their council houses by the Conservative government in 1980. For many commentators with a right-wing political perspective, including some members of the government, this was seen as a victory for the rights of individual freedom and self-determination over the paternalistic control of state welfare bureaucrats. For some other Conservative politicians, and for some social policy commentators, it was seen as a necessary development within housing policy to accommodate more rationally the 'mixed economy' of welfare and the overlap, or partnership, between state and private sector provision. For some on the political left, however, the sale of council houses was a dissipation of public assets and a betrayal of one of the major planks of the welfare state.

No one of these ideological judgements is any more right or wrong than any of the others, although they are all perspectives on the same policy development. They are merely different ideological judgements from different ideological standpoints, although there are some views (such as racism) which many people may find offensive; and, of course, they do not exhaust the different ideological views that might be held. However, they are not just the product of idiosyncratic individual attitudes: they are quite widely shared ideological views and are based within broader perspectives on welfare policy from within which similar judgements would probably be made about other policy initiatives. In other words, they are part of broader ideologies of welfare.

At this broader social level, however, the size and scope of ideological perspectives will vary dramatically. A perspective shared by the majority of people in a country will be rather more important than one shared by a small group of friends and neighbours. In their discussion of ideologies of welfare, George and Wilding (1994) discussed this point and argued that *major* ideological perspectives must possess certain characteristics in order to be regarded as of particular social importance. They outline four such characteristics:

- *coherence* – ideological perspectives must have an internal logic and theoretical consistency
- *pervasiveness* – ideological perspectives must be current and relevant, as old perspectives may have lost their social base
- *extensiveness* – ideological perspectives must be widely shared within, or across, societies
- *intensiveness* – ideological perspectives must command the support, and commitment, of those who share them; they must really be believed.

Therefore an ideological perspective is a shared view, or set of views, with a clear social impact. Of course not all ideological perspectives focus on, or even address, social policy issues; indeed, most do not. We are not concerned here, however, with all ideologies, but only with those that do address welfare issues and focus on description, and judgement, of policy development, and prescription for future policy reform. These we can call *ideologies of welfare*.

Ideology and theory

If ideologies of welfare are widely shared and coherent perspectives on policy and reform, this raises the question of what, if any, is the distinction between such ideological perspectives and theoretical analysis and debate of welfare issues. What about theories of welfare? In practice (and in theory!) the distinction between ideology and theory is not a clear or watertight one, and neither is it uncontested. Sometimes the two concepts are used more or less interchangeably: one person's theory is another person's ideology. However, it is probably fair to say that some broad differences in usage and understanding do exist, even though these would not be universally accepted.

A theoretical perspective may exist within a broader, and looser, ideological perspective. However, theoretical discourse is likely to be less partial and less value laden than ideology, and to be more comprehensive and logical. A theoretical perspective has more than an individual coherence: it has a systematic logical structure that is allied to a descriptive, rather than a prescriptive, approach to policy issues; it is generally presented in academic terms, for a largely academic audience. Theorists are not generally seeking to popularise or to persuade, but rather to describe and to convince; and they aim to convince only those who share their academic interests and can follow their academic arguments.

Theories of welfare are therefore produced by, and for, a relatively narrow group of academics and their students. In contrast, although ideologies of welfare are more partial, political and prescriptive, they are also more popular. While few people would claim any knowledge of, or support for, a theoretical approach to welfare, many would no doubt hold, and debate, ideological perspectives on welfare (or at least on welfare issues). Thus, although we are not all academics or theorists, we do all have, and share, ideologies of welfare. Or, to put it another way, we may not know about – or even understand – the welfare pluralist case against unaccountable state monopoly providers, but we do know that we want independent advice about the refusal of our claim for a social security payment.

Theories of welfare are therefore narrower and more academic than ideological perspectives; it is for this reason that we focus here on the broader category of ideology. Both theory and ideology, however, are also linked to *politics*. As we discussed in Chapter 1, social policy is a prescriptive subject: it focuses on the development and implementation of political changes. Inevitably, and in most cases avowedly, therefore, it seeks to intervene in, and influence, political debate. Ideologies of welfare are linked to the politics of welfare, and different political allegiances and practices are based in different ideological perspectives.

Commentators have frequently attempted to compare ideologies of welfare according to their location within a continuum of political preferences. George and Wilding did this in 1976 in their first book on ideology and social welfare. In their later text, George and Wilding (1994, p.9) produce a table summarising a total of ten separate analyses of ideologies of welfare. These various analyses identify a range of different numbers of perspectives and also sometimes give these perspectives different names. In practice, however, many analysts place the different perspectives that they identify at different points within a continuum moving from the political left to the political right, in particular in terms of their support for (or opposition to) the role of the state in welfare provision.

Thus on the *left* are socialists or Marxists, who believe that the state should play a major, or exclusive, role in the provision of social policy; on the *right* are anti-collectivists or liberals, who believe that individuals should be free to provide (or not) for whatever needs they wish. In between are the Fabians, the social democrats, the reluctant collectivists and others. Of course, not all ideologies of welfare can be so readily classified along such a left to right political continuum, as we shall see later. Nevertheless, the link between ideology and politics in social policy, and the central role played in both of debate about the relative roles of the state and the market, means that political differences here are also likely to represent ideological differences, and vice versa.

However, although ideology and politics may be linked, they are not the same thing. Ideology is concerned with ideas, ideals and principles; politics is concerned with pragmatism and results. Thus debate and study of the politics of welfare focuses not primarily upon differing perspectives and approaches, still less on the differing explanations that are the concern of theory, but rather upon events and achievements. Thus both Deakin's (1994) book, *The Politics of Welfare*, and Sullivan's (1992) book, *The Politics of Social Policy*, examined the changes in British welfare policy from the Second World War to the 1990s, pointing out how the changes in policy were the result of changes in the power and influence of different political perspectives; and more recently Pierson (1998) has developed this at an international level. In other words, the differences in view are contrasted in terms of their impact on the development and implementation of policy.

During the first two decades following the war, however, the appearance of political consensus over the future direction of policy development, characterised by the notion of *Butskellism*, suggested that such political differences had been superseded. Commentators argued that this also implied that ideological differences had disappeared (in particular, the differences between left and right over the role of the state) and that future political conflict would be 'a fight without ideologies' (Lipset, 1963, p.408). This *end of ideology* thesis proved to be a little premature, or oversimplistic, however, for ideological disagreements did remain and, in particular after the early 1970s, they were represented again in political debate and conflict over the future direction of reform, with a significant divide opening up between the Conservative right and the Labour left over the appropriate future direction for policy development.

At the beginning of the twenty-first century theoretical debates and political disagreements remain at the centre of discussion about the way the social policy should be developed, and these are underpinned by ideologies of welfare that provide very different understandings of the ways in which welfare and wellbeing should be identified and addressed within modern society. As we shall see, these different ideologies of welfare also extend beyond the more traditional left to right continuum of support (or not) for state welfare to embrace ideological perspectives that emphasise other divisions and disagreements, and even suggest that traditional ideologies can no longer provide viable explanatory frameworks in the complex (post)modern world that we now occupy.

QUESTION: REFLECTION

■ Are all ideologies of welfare equally plausible and acceptable?

Neo-liberalism

As we discussed in Chapter 1, the pro-market, anti-state ideological perspective of the New Right developed widespread support in Britain in the 1970s and 1980s, and also in some other countries such as the USA. This new-found political influence became associated with the Thatcherite Conservative governments of the 1980s and, together with the rapid growth in the numbers of commentators contributing their ideas to the government at that time, it made the New Right *new*. However, in practice these ideas, and the broader perspective from within which they are drawn, are not all that new and indeed are largely an attempt to adapt classical nineteenth-century *laissez-faire* liberalism to late twentieth-century circumstances. The New Right are thus also known as *neo-liberals* or *market liberals*.

Many of the recent neo-liberal theorists of social policy draw directly, and explicitly, upon the writings of Hayek, who had been consistently developing the case for market liberalism throughout the period of the establishment and growth of the post-war welfare state (Hayek, 1944, 1960 and 1982). Hayek's argument was that there was a fundamental contradiction between the operation of markets and the intervention of the state, and that state intervention would inevitably lead to market dysfunction. He also argued that state intervention involved an unwarranted interference with the freedom of individuals to organise their own affairs and, therefore, that intervention was only justified if its aim was to protect individual freedom (for example, the use of the criminal law to protect private property).

Hayek's preference for market over state was also shared by the other main source of New Right theory and ideology, the American writer Milton Friedman (1962). Friedman too argued that, left to their own devices, markets would naturally protect individuals because consumer sovereignty would ensure that producers adapted their services to meet consumer needs; but that, if the state intervened to seek to meet needs directly, this would distort the working of the market and lead to an economic collapse, in which both state and individuals would suffer.

Throughout the post-war period the ideas of Hayek and Friedman were propounded in Britain by a right-wing 'think tank', the Institute of Economic Affairs (IEA), but theirs was very much a minority voice against the welfare 'consensus' of the time. In the 1970s, however, the onset of inflation and rising unemployment and the collapse in the world economy appeared to demonstrate that the predictions of market distortion and dysfunction through state intervention were correct; and the IEA found a new confidence in, and a new audience for, their proposals for rolling back the boundaries of state welfare and restoring the free market. Other voices also then joined with the IEA in the chorus of anti-state criticism. In 1974 the Centre for Policy Studies (CPS), another think tank, was formed by Margaret Thatcher (later Conservative Prime Minister) and Keith Joseph (one of her close political allies); and in 1979 an independent right-wing policy centre, the Adam Smith Institute (ASI), was also formed. Together these new organisations, and their new-found political allies, gave neo-liberal thinking a powerful push towards the centre stage of ideological debate.

The main plank of neo-liberal thinking on welfare is its opposition to extensive state intervention to provide public services; in effect, opposition to the very idea of a 'welfare state'. The welfare state is undesirable, neo-liberals argue, on economic, ideological and political grounds, and also, because it is undesirable in theory, it is unworkable in practice.

In *economic* terms they argue that the welfare state is undesirable because it involves interference with the free working of market. This leads to a failure of markets to develop properly, because state monopolies dominate many areas of provision (for example, rented housing). More pertinently perhaps, however, it also leads to a crippling drain on private market wealth (and therefore investment) because of the ever-growing fiscal demands of public expenditure to meet the costs of expanding state welfare services. State intervention thus leads to economic recession as, it was claimed, was realised in Britain and elsewhere in the 1970s; and economic growth is only restored by cutting public expenditure and reducing the role, and scope, of the state as, it was alleged, was successfully achieved in the 1980s. What is more, it follows from this, therefore, that future economic growth can only continue to be sustained if welfare is further and further contained.

The *ideological* objections of neo-liberals to state welfare centre around their concern over the supposed problems of *perverse incentives* and the *dependency culture*. By providing welfare services for all through the state, it is argued, individuals are effectively discouraged from providing these for themselves or for their families. Indeed, people are not only discouraged, they are effectively trapped into wholesale reliance upon the support of others (the dependency culture). This is most clearly revealed in the 'problem' of perverse incentives, an idea associated in particular with the work of the American theorist, Charles Murray (1984, and see A Deacon, 2002). Murray focuses primarily upon the operation of social security protection which, he argues, by providing everyone with a guaranteed basic standard of living, makes it attractive for some people to opt for this rather than seeking to provide for themselves through paid employment. This is particularly the case with means-tested benefits, where entitlement is related to individual income levels, so that increases in income merely lead to loss of benefits. This has long been recognised in the problem of the *poverty trap* (Deacon and Bradshaw, 1983, ch.8). Murray's argument gives it a different ideological slant, focusing on the moral perversity of state dependency and its effect in driving people out of the labour market. The British Conservative MP, Rhodes Boyson (1971, p.7), put it rather more pejoratively when he argued that the welfare state 'saps the collective moral fibre of our people as a nation'.

The *political* undesirability of the welfare state for neo-liberalism is best exemplified through an examination of what they refer to as *public choice theory*. This too has its roots in US scholarship, especially in the writing of a group of theorists called the 'Virginia School' (Buchanan, 1986). Public choice theory involves the application of microeconomic calculation to party political behaviour (in itself a rather dubious exercise); and in particular it involves the analysis of politics from the assumption that all political actors are motivated only by self-interest. Despite the dubious assumptions, however, the argument is an important and a persuasive one. The main point is that within established welfare states all social groups will inevitably press for state support for their needs to be met, and that this pressure is likely to be supported by state welfare bureaucrats for whom expanded welfare services mean an expanded power base, and also by politicians who can make themselves electorally popular by promising to legislate to meet more and more welfare needs. Thus no one in the political process has any interest in controlling the expansionary tendencies of state welfare, with the result that it acquires the momentum of a runaway train (with, it is argued, ultimately much the same disastrous consequences for all on board).

State welfare is thus seen by neo-liberals to be economically distorting, ideologically perverse and politically uncontrollable. It is also, they claim, in any event hopelessly *impractical*. State provision of welfare services assumes that politicians and bureaucrats within the state machinery can be trusted with the provision of welfare services to all. Even if they could be trusted ideologically and politically (and of course New Right protagonists do not believe that they could be), how could they be trusted in practice to know what sort of welfare services different people want or need? In a large and diverse society, they argue, it is simply not possible to know how to meet all social needs. The result of this is, at *best*, that people act themselves to tailor or extend state services through private adaptations; and, at *worst*, that standardised services are provided which meet the real needs of no one (for instance, the council houses all painted alternately with red and green doors).

Nevertheless, although neo-liberals argue that state welfare is neither desirable nor practical, they are not necessarily prepared to countenance its complete disappearance. Even Hayek envisaged some role for state welfare, primarily as a selective and residual provision for those unable to provide for themselves on the private market, although Friedman's position was rather different (see George and Page, 1995). Most of the more recent neo-liberal theorists have also argued that such a 'safety net' state welfare sector will in reality still be needed (and therefore, presumably, still be desirable). Despite the anti-state rhetoric, neo-liberalism thus remains within the bounds of the mixed economy of welfare, which is found in practice in all modern welfare capitalist countries.

The New Right might shift the boundary between the state and the market sectors of welfare; but they would retain both.

During the Thatcherite Conservative governments of the 1980s, this limitation of neo-liberal welfare ideology to a shifting of the boundaries of welfare – rather than a revolutionary challenge to the state – was demonstrated in practice by the process of political change. Despite some of the recommendations of right-wing think tanks, such as the IEA and the ASI, for the removal of the NHS or the state education system, the Prime Minister and her closest followers had to wrestle with those within the Conservative Party – as well as those outside – who wanted to retain these universal state services. In the end reform was restricted to the restructuring of the management and operation of welfare services and to the more direct encouragement of separate private provision alongside these. Of course, in a sense this merely reveals in practice our previous point about the importance of the difference between ideological perspectives and real political practices. However, it also reveals that, even within the UK government of the 1980s, there were other ideological perspectives at play.

QUESTIONS: COMPREHENSION

- Why do neo-liberals argue that state welfare undermines economic growth?
- What is 'public choice theory' and what are its implications for the politics of welfare policy?

The Middle Way

The term 'Middle Way' is taken from the title of a book on social and economic policy written in 1938 by the Conservative politician (and later in the 1950s, Prime Minister), Harold Macmillan. It is used by George and Wilding (1994) to refer to a perspective which to some extent spans the political divide between the Conservative, Liberal and Labour parties, and which they referred to in their earlier analysis of ideologies of welfare as *reluctant collectivism* (George and Wilding, 1976). Other Conservative supporters of the Middle Way include the prominent post-war architect of the reform of state education, R A B Butler, and more recently Gilmour (1978). All of them were supporters of the positive role of state welfare within advanced capitalist economies, and this of course distanced them significantly from the neo-liberals of the New Right.

However, the Middle Way is more than just the ideology of the centrist wing of the Conservative Party. Through the views of Butler, in particular, it is associated with the supposed cross-party consensus on the role of state welfare that dominated politics in the period immediately following the Second World War, and is captured in the term *Butskellism* (see Chapter 1). It is thus the ideological perspective that informed Beveridge and Keynes in their recommendations for social and economic reforms that formed the basis of post-war policy development. Both Keynes and Beveridge were Liberals, and this perspective has also therefore been referred to as *liberal collectivism*.

The common theme which unites both left and right adherents to the Middle Way, therefore, is their commitment to the collective provision of social services and the planning of economic development, through the use of the power and legitimacy of the state. They do not believe that the free market alone can be relied upon to protect all citizens. However, as the phrase 'reluctant collectivists' implies, Middle Way supporters are concerned about the principles of collectivism espoused by socialist perspectives to the left. In particular, they justify the role of collective provision because of the practical benefits that it provides for a market economy, not because of the alternative to this that it might represent. In other words, reluctant collectivists stress the advantages of partnership between state and market rather than the opposition between them that those to the right and left foresee.

This partnership between state and market is based upon the practical benefits that state intervention can provide for the development and growth of a capitalist economy. Keynes envisaged state intervention as a means of ensuring growth and profitability in a market economy and his commitment was to state intervention, rather than merely state planning, as we shall see in Chapter 13. It is also a partnership that is based upon the obligations that the government in a market economy carries to ensure the social protection of all citizens. Thus, where the market cannot provide, the state must (perhaps reluctantly) be moved in. This is predicated upon a holistic vision of social structure and social obligations, captured in the phrase *One Nation*, which was the title adopted by a backbench group of Conservative Middle Way MPs in the 1950s. However, it is not a vision based on only one model of social protection. Middle Way support for a political partnership between the market and the state was also expected to be replicated within welfare provision; as Beveridge himself envisaged, the presumption was that a mixed economy of welfare agencies would continue to operate in which the state would rarely be a monopoly provider.

The Middle Way is thus an ideological perspective forged out of pragmatism rather than principle. Social needs are recognised and acknowledged to be a public responsibility; but so, too, is private investment and economic growth. Middle Way theorists, such as Keynes, argued that both were inextricably interlinked. Economic growth is needed in order to ensure that social needs can continue to be met; but economic growth will not be achieved in a society where social problems and social divisions are permitted to continue unchecked.

It might be argued that (albeit with mixed success) such a pragmatic perspective has dominated policy development in post-war Britain, although it certainly came under threat from the New Right during the Thatcherite governments of the 1980s. A similar picture can also be found in many other European welfare capitalist countries over the same period. In Germany, France, Belgium, the Netherlands and Italy, for example, welfare state protections have been supported, and introduced, within capitalist market economies and have contributed to continuing growth within these economies too. For example, within Germany the Christian Democratic party has allied support for state welfare and capitalist development to employment-based welfare and support for 'traditional' family structures, and has enjoyed significant political support, often encouraged by an electoral system that produces more frequent coalition governments.

At the beginning of the twenty-first century in both Germany and Britain, however, Conservative and Christian Democrat governments have given way to social democratic parties, under Schröder and Blair, which have also made an appeal to a centre ground, state and market, approach to welfare policy, which they have referred to as the *Third Way* (in Germany, *Die Neue Mitte*, or the new middle). There is much debate over the extent to which this new Third Way is an attempt to capture the old Middle Way ground of the liberal collectivists, or even the New Right (see Driver and Martell, 1998; Powell, 1999); although both Blair and Schröder would probably describe their approach as 'centre-left' and argue that in reality it is an attempt to forge a *new* partnership between the state and the market, or at least to adapt earlier social democratic ideology to the changed social and economic climate of the new century.

QUESTIONS: COMPREHENSION

- Why are Middle Way supporters sometimes referred to as 'reluctant collectivists'?
- To what extent is the Middle Way a pragmatic compromise between the state and the market rather than a principled alternative to both?

Social democracy

Social democracy is the main ideological perspective to the left of the Middle Way. In Britain it has traditionally been associated with the Fabian tradition on the left of the Labour Party, although it was centre-left Labour members (to the right in party terms) who left Labour in the early 1980s to set up a separate Social Democratic Party (which subsequently merged with the Liberals); and Blair's 'New Labour' party of 1990s was based on an attempt to adapt social democratic principles to twenty-first century social issues. In many continental European countries, parties going explicitly under the title of Social Democrats have frequently constituted the main political opposition to the Christian Democrats and have often been in government themselves, such as in Germany under Schröder.

There has sometimes been debate, however, about the extent to which the social democratic perspective can (or should) be separated from *democratic socialism*, the term used by George and Wilding in 1994. For instance, they can be distinguished on the grounds that democratic socialism implies a commitment to radical socialist change, albeit achieved by democratic means, whereas social democracy implies support for existing democratic structures but the use of these to pursue policies that are more interventionist and socially responsible. However, such a distinction is not consistently borne out in practice; and, even if there might be potential theoretical disagreement between the two perspectives over *ends*, there is substantial ideological and political consensus across them over *means*.

The common ground that social democrats and democratic socialists share here is the pursuit of social justice through the gradual reform of the – predominantly capitalist – market economy. As the early Fabians openly claimed, all social democrats are gradualists rather than revolutionaries; and, although they frequently identify major social problems within capitalist economies, they are committed to using the existing structures of power to seek a resolution, or amelioration, of these problems within immediate social circumstances. For social democrats, reform is very much a case of bread today rather than jam tomorrow.

The social democrat belief in the pursuit of social justice within a capitalist economy, however, is based both on practical politics and moral principles. The *practical politics* is the use of working-class power, both through the industrial muscle of the trades union movement and through the electoral success of the Labour Party (formed by the trade unions), to force the capitalist holders of wealth and control to concede to a redistribution of these privileges, under the implicit threat of otherwise more revolutionary or disruptive social change. Social democracy in Britain, therefore, has traditionally sought a political home in the Labour Party. The *moral principles* are those of fraternity (and more recently sorority) and solidarity; in other words, the desirability of mutual support. These principles have also sometimes been linked to Christian values of care and concern for one's fellow man, or woman. Many leading social democrats, such as Tawney (and now Blair), have been Christians, although of course many have not.

Perhaps the earliest theoretical exposition of the major themes of social democracy can be found in Tawney's (1931) discussion of the *strategy of equality*, in which he argued that social justice could, and should, be pursued within a capitalist economy through the introduction of state welfare services and redistributive tax and benefit policies. Fifteen years later the post-war welfare state reforms could be seen as an attempt by the left-wing Labour government of the period, under the leadership of Attlee, to engage directly in such a strategy. Subsequent criticisms of the achievements of state welfare, in particular in securing greater equality in access to services, have cast doubt upon the viability of such a strategy (Le Grand, 1982). However, during the early post-war years, Fabian politicians and academics such as Crosland (1956) and Titmuss (1958) argued that, despite remaining inequalities, the welfare state had resulted in an irreversible transfer of power and resources to the lower classes and had therefore fundamentally altered the character of the social and economic structure of society.

Despite the later criticisms – and the anti-state reforms of the 1980s – there can be little doubt that Crosland and Titmuss were, in part at least, correct in their assessment of the impact of the welfare state. The introduction of state provision for health, education and social security did effectively displace much private market provision in these areas, and of course this is why the New Right later opposed such measures. The universal welfare state is often claimed by social democrats as the embodiment of their ideological support for the pursuit of social justice, and they contrast this with the grudging support for more limited state welfare advanced by the Middle Way.

In twentieth-century Britain it is arguable that Social Democratic ideology only achieved any real political influence during the brief period of Labour Party government from 1945 to 1951, although even then by no means all members of the Labour government could be called social democrats. However, in some other European countries, notably in Scandinavia, social democratic governments were in power for the major part of the latter half of the century, and here the gradual transformation of capitalism and the pursuit of a strategy of equality through universal state welfare have been more consistently attempted and achieved (Baldwin, 1990; Kautto *et al.*, 2001).

Scandinavian social democrat theorists such as Esping-Andersen (1985) and Korpi (1983) have argued openly for the pursuit of a 'democratic road' to socialism through the transformatory politics of state welfare. In countries such as Sweden and Denmark universal state provision has led to more extensive welfare protection and to greater social equality than in other welfare capitalist countries, such as Britain. Electoral support for social democracy in Scandinavia suggests that such an ideological perspective can in practice be popular and, although more right-of-centre governments have enjoyed short periods of office in both Sweden and Denmark in more recent years, there has been no significant departure from the social democratic approach to welfare policy there.

Another Scandinavian theorist, Therborn (see, for example, Therborn and Roebroek, 1986), has argued further that, once achieved, the welfare state becomes an irreversible feature of any modern democratic society, both because it is functional for the economy and because the protection that it provides will guarantee its electoral popularity (or rather the popularity of those parties that claim to protect it). This may suggest that the democratic road to social reform is more than just an ideological vision: it is a social fact. For instance, research in Britain in the 1980s and 1990s demonstrated that popular support for state welfare services remained high even during periods of right-wing Conservative government (Taylor-Gooby, 1991, ch.5), and it was a significant factor in the second Labour election victory in 2001.

Towards the end of the last century the popularity and desirability of the social democratic approach to welfare began to be questioned, at least within the Labour Party in the UK. In part this was a product of the electoral successes of the New Right Conservative governments of the 1980s and early 1990s and the need for Labour to mount a credible opposition to these; but in part it was a product of a more fundamental review of the central role that state welfare (and the 'welfare state') had traditionally played within social democracy.

These questions were raised by some Fabian critics in the 1980s (Plant, 1988). However, they became more prominent in the early 1990s when, after the 1992 election defeat, the then Labour leader, John Smith, established a *Commission on Social Justice*, chaired by Gordon Borrie, to review past approaches to social policy make proposals for future development. The report of the Commission (Borrie, 1994) distinguished three different approaches to policy development:

- the *deregulators*, in effect the neo-liberals, who favoured private markets over public provision

- the *levellers*, who were the supporters of old-style social democratic justice through redistribution and tax financed public services
- the *investors*, who linked social justice to support for, and investment in, economic growth within a market economy.

It was clear that the Commission favoured the third of these; and, although it never achieved any formal status (in part because before it was completed Smith had died and been replaced as Labour leader by Tony Blair), this 'investor' approach became central to the 'Third Way' rhetoric which was championed by Blair's 'New Labour' governments after the 1997 election. Blair himself wrote a Fabian pamphlet extolling the virtues of the Third Way (Blair, 1998). In this he drew on the work of the academic, Tony Giddens (1998), who had also used the concept and had argued that such a 'new' approach was necessary to adapt policy development to the changed social and economic climate of the 1990s and the new century.

Many of the policy statements of the new Labour administrations referred explicitly or implicitly to the need for a new approach within social democracy, between the state and the market and emphasising individual and community responsibility as well as public support (see Powell, 1999 and 2003). Labour also drew on similar policy approaches which were being promoted elsewhere, including Schröder's 'new middle' in Germany and, in particular, the 'New Democrats' under Clinton in the USA (see Jordan, 1998). At the beginning the new century, therefore, social democratic politics in Europe and North America had moved to embrace a new, and more explicit, compromise between state support and capitalist market economy. However, this was not without its critics on the left, including within the Labour Party, who argued that the Third Way involved an abandonment of the principle of state welfare and hence of social democracy itself (Sullivan, 2003). Not all former social democratic thinkers have embraced this new shift therefore; and, for those further to the left, it is perhaps additional evidence of the fact that social democracy inevitably requires an undesirable level of compromise with capitalist market principles.

QUESTIONS: COMPREHENSION

- What is the difference between social democracy and democratic socialism?
- To what extent is the 'Third Way' approach of the Labour government a continuation of traditional social democratic ideology?

Marxism

Opposition to the inequities of the market and to the ineffectiveness of the welfare state in challenging or combating these has for some time come from the far left of the political perspective, and has been voiced by critics who sometimes trace this opposition back to the theoretical analysis of capitalist economies developed in the nineteenth century by Karl Marx (Marx, 1970). Marx's claim was that capitalism was an inherently oppressive economic structure in which the working class were exploited by the capitalist class through the labour market. The conflict to which this oppression gave rise would lead eventually to the overturning of capitalist power and its replacement with a socialist state in which all the people would own all the means of production, and all social needs could therefore be met. Marxists are thus also usually *socialists*. However, some also make a distinction between socialism and *communism*, which is a situation reached after state socialism when all production is in the hands of the people and the need for central state control has 'withered away'.

Socialism, or communism, is argued by Marxists to be the logical, and desirable, alternative to the failures of both capitalist markets and state welfare. However, their visions of socialist society are generally rather utopian, and generally contain no clear view of the route to be taken to achieve such equilibrium and harmony, except for the claim that revolutionary, rather than gradual, social change would be necessary, involving the overthrow of existing democratic governments (which in effect support capital) and the seizure of power by the representatives of the working class.

This is not a political programme that has ever attracted much effective support in Britain or in any other Western European country; thus its political potential here has been pretty limited. However, socialist revolution, inspired by Marx, did take place in Russia at the beginning of the twentieth century. Throughout most of the last century state socialism, under Communist Party rule, was practised in the USSR (as it became) and, after the Second World War, was extended to the countries of Eastern Europe too.

Despite some of the advances and achievements of state socialism in these countries, the collapse of the Eastern European and Soviet communist regimes at the end of the 1980s, and the exposure of continuing inequalities and hardships within them, cast a deep shadow over the aspirations of the supporters of Marxism. It seemed to many that in the only countries in which revolutionary socialism had been attempted as a solution to the problems of capitalism, it had failed. Some supporters of Marxism have of course pointed to the continuation of communist rule in a few other countries, such as China and Cuba (although here, too, traditional state communism has been much diluted). Others have suggested that perhaps state socialism was not proper socialism in any case, and that without international change to replace capitalism on a global scale it was bound to fail.

Despite such expressions of continued revolutionary optimism, the collapse of Eastern bloc socialism has severely undermined the appeal and the influence of Marxist perspectives on welfare, because it has appeared to give a lie to their prescriptions for a revolutionary utopia. In contrast to such prescriptive visions, however, much Marxist debate and scholarship has in fact been directed not so much at making out the case for socialist revolution as at pointing out the failings and limitations of capitalism in meeting the needs of all citizens. Marx himself, of course, was primarily known for his critical analysis of capitalism, including analysis of early examples of welfare reform such as the factory legislation of the mid-nineteenth century, rather than for his ideas on the future of socialism. Many Marxist critics have continued this tradition into the analysis of welfare capitalism, although ultimately their message is a negative one.

In the 1970s Gough and Ginsburg produced cogent critiques of the British welfare state from within a Marxist perspective. Ginsburg (1979) argued that institutions of welfare operated within British society to control and suppress people as well as to provide for them: for instance, arguing that the social security scheme in practice stigmatised benefit claimants and forced them into low-waged employment. Gough's (1979) more extended analysis took this further, pointing out the *dual* character of the welfare state, which – although it was in part a product of the success of working-class struggle, as the democratic socialists claimed – was also an adaptation of capitalism to meet changed economic and social circumstances. He argued, for example, that state education and health services operated in practice to prepare workers for skilled employment and to keep them healthy for work.

The strength of the Marxist critique of welfare within capitalism is its ability to demonstrate the contradictory nature of social policy as providing at one and the same time both social *protection* and social *control*. Some commentators, such as O'Connor (1973), have referred to these contradictory goals as the *accumulation* and *legitimation* functions of welfare. Through its support for the continued operation of the market, welfare permits capital to continue to accumulate; and yet, through its provision of social protection, it also legitimates capitalist power by providing protection for all its citizens. However, in times of crisis – for example, during the recession of the 1970s and 1980s – these two functions can come into conflict; continued support for accumulation requires cutbacks in the costs of legitimation. Indeed, cuts in welfare spending were introduced in Britain, and in most other welfare capitalist countries, during this period. The welfare state within capitalism is thus not only contradictory, it is also inherently unstable.

This Marxist critique of the development and operation of welfare within capitalist societies is considerably more plausible, and influential, than the appeal to support for a communist revolution; and, as a critique of capitalist welfare, the Marxist perspective has survived despite the collapse of the socialist regimes to which it might have been seen to have allegiance. However, the continuing changes in production processes, class structures and political activity in modern capitalist countries make the legacy of Marx, on which some commentators have claimed to draw, an ever more distant one.

Many such commentators, who continue to point to the contradictory and unstable nature of social and economic policies in welfare capitalist countries, no longer refer to themselves as Marxists, and some have begun to suggest that the perspective must now be called *post-Marxism* or *neo-Marxism*. This, they argue, is because the social and economic changes that have divided the workforce and produced a large group of unemployed and marginal workers have rendered the role of the working class in the transformation of capitalism obsolete; as a result of this, they suggest that revolutionary change will therefore take a different form in the future. In particular, it will no longer involve taking the means of production into the hands of the workers but rather will be based upon a post-industrial economy in which work and production are no longer at the centre of material life (Gorz, 1982).

The development of post-Marxism and the reform of former Marxists demonstrates that, despite its links to the past, this perspective, too, is constantly changing and adapting as new ideas develop and as social circumstances change. Marxism may have lost the concrete appeal of Soviet communism to oppose the inequities of capitalism, and it may have had to adapt to the restructuring of labour markets and class allegiances, but its ability to link a critique of the failings of welfare to the development of the structural forces of the capitalist economy retains a powerful ideological appeal. Thus, to the left of the social democrats, Marxist critics of welfare can still be found (Jones and Novak, 1999).

QUESTIONS: COMPREHENSION

- Why do Marxists argue that welfare capitalism is inherently unstable?
- To what extent has the collapse of Eastern bloc communism undermined the Marxist critique of welfare capitalism?

New social movements

One of the consequences of the declining size and influence of the traditional working class in modern societies and the growing fragmentation of labour market relations with more flexible (part-time and temporary) employment has been a growing recognition of the existence, and importance, of other social divisions as bases for conflict and political change in society, and of political and ideological issues other than exploitation within the labour market as a focus for critical comment and action. These include, for instance, gender differences and feminist politics, racial conflict and anti-racism, disability awareness and action, environmentalism and Green politics and the anti-nuclear movement. Of course, social divisions, such as gender and race, are not new sources of ideological and political conflict, even if widespread recognition of their importance has only relatively recently developed within social policy (F Williams, 1989). However, the recognition of this wider range of differences and divisions has challenged the dominance of those ideological perspectives which have sought to contain debate, and policy development, on a left/right continuum within which state welfare and redistribution of resources are seen as either the causes or the solutions of all social problems.

In part these changes are the product of political activity rather than ideological debate. New social movements grew up within many welfare capitalist countries in the latter part of the twentieth century, aiming to push new issues and different forms of discrimination and disadvantage on to the policy agenda (for example, the 'women's movement', anti-racist campaigners, and the Green Party and other environmental activists). Of course all of these different movements were quite distinct, pursuing particular political issues through different forms of organisation and political practice; however, their very difference and disparity distinguished them from the more traditional labour market and state welfare politics of the old right and left, and so they were sometimes collectively referred to as *new social movements* (F Williams, 1989), although in practice some were rather 'newer' than others and many are not new at all, except perhaps in the eyes of some commentators. And there have even been some attempts to bring together these different movements into a more coherent political force: for instance, through the so-called *Rainbow Alliance* in the USA in the 1980s and 1990s, which suggested the coming together of different colours (or political perspectives) across the spectrum.

Nevertheless, there are serious political and ideological problems involved in trying to lump together the very different movements and perspectives of feminism, anti-racism, Greenism, and others. Where some of these address social divisions, the divisions they focus on are very different (and sometimes mutually conflicting), as the disagreements over the allegiances of black women, for example, have demonstrated. What is more, not all movements focus on social divisions: for example, Green and anti-nuclear politics are responding to very different social and economic forces. There is thus no real common ground across the new social movements, even though some radicals might wish that there were.

These new social movements are discussed together here, therefore, not out of a misguided belief in their common features, but because the pressures of time and space do not permit adequate discussion of them all separately, although clearly some are more important than others, with feminism in particular having had a far-reaching impact on the study and practice of social policy (see Lewis, 2003). George and Wilding's 1994 text on ideologies of welfare makes something of a compromise in containing extended discussion of feminism and Greenism; and F Williams's (1989) social policy text focuses on feminist and anti-racist critiques of welfare. We will return to discuss the problem of the failure of past social policy development to recognise the important social divisions of gender and race in Chapter 16. These are clearly three of the more influential perspectives, though they are not the only important ones, and a number of other divisions which also impact significantly on social policy development and delivery are discussed in Payne (2000).

Environmental politics presents – potentially at least – an even more fundamental critique of social welfare, for Green ideologists argue that current welfare protection is based upon the continuation of forms of economic growth that are unsustainable in the world in the longer term because of their environmental destructiveness. However, this environmental argument is a complex one. For a start, both commentators and Green activists themselves often make a distinction between different perspectives within environmental politics. In particular, a distinction is made between the reformists (the *light* Greens), who argue for change within existing economic structures, and the revolutionaries (the *dark* Greens), who argue that only a fundamental transformation of socio-economic planning can guarantee a long-term future for welfare. Despite these differences, however, the focus of Green politics upon sustainable economic policy in order to support viable social policy is now an influential perspective within social policy debate (Huby, 1998; Cahill, 2001).

QUESTION: COMPREHENSION

■ To what extent is a 'rainbow coalition' of new social movements an achievable political or ideological goal?

Postmodernism

The challenge to the traditional left/right ideological debate over state welfare does not come only from new political activity, however. At the theoretical level too there have been critiques of the ideological frameworks outlined earlier from those who have argued that they are no longer adequate to provide an understanding of the changing world in which we are now living, or a model for how policies should be developed within that, and that previous analyses based upon class conflict within capitalist labour markets must also embrace other forms of difference and disadvantage. Actually, of course, some of these critiques are not all that new, either; and the theoretical challenge that they pose is not only based upon the premise that it is changing social circumstances that have invalidated other ideological approaches. Underlying much discussion here are more fundamental questions about how our knowledge, and our ideologies, are constructed and whether it is at all possible to produce ideological frameworks which can provide a comprehensive guide to social structure and social policy in complex modern societies: to use their terminology, these critiques reject the notion of such 'metanarratives' (Lyotard, 1984).

However, much of the writing on social policy from within such a perspective has been relatively recent and has been based in part upon a critique of previous ideological frameworks; it has also frequently linked its theoretical criticism to a broader temporal shift from modernity (the modern, welfare capitalist world of class conflict) to *postmodernism*. Much has been written about postmodernism both as a social condition (has the world changed so that old relations and conflicts have been replaced by new ones?) and as a theoretical approach (should we reject all past attempts to theorise about social relations?). Some have welcomed the alternative and radical perspective which it provides for social policy debate (Leonard, 1997), although others are more sceptical and argue that much of postmodernist writing is a distortion or abandonment of key policy issues (Taylor-Gooby, 1994). The debate is a complex one, however, and much of the theoretical literature is rather dense and jargon ridden.

In addition, many of the core tenets of postmodern thinking seem to be based on a negative critique of what has gone before rather than a coherent framework for future development. Fitzpatrick (2003) provides a summary of the role of postmodernist thinking within social policy in which he points out that postmodernists generally reject universalism, do not believe in absolute truth or essentialist explanations, and celebrate difference and identity. Rather than seeking to identify shared social problems and promote universal policy responses to these, therefore, postmodernist approaches to social policy emphasise relativity, diversity and particularity. They also focus on the way in which different (and diverse) understandings (and experiences) are constructed by people through discourse, and this applies to social theorists as well as ordinary individuals.

This draws on the theoretical work of Foucault and his analysis of how punishment and sexuality were constructed (and changed) by the professionals and experts who controlled prisons and medicine in the nineteenth and twentieth centuries (Foucault, 1977 and 1979). It is sometimes referred to as 'constructivism' or 'discourse analysis'. Postmodernist thinkers drawing on Foucault (also sometimes called 'post-structuralists') argue that no one construction can be correct or agreed, and that those which have dominated policy development have done so only because of the powerful positions occupied by their protagonists. Hence the role of ideological analysis is to expose such discourses, and the power which lies behind them, to critical review.

O'Brien and Penna (1998) undertake a broad overview of the rise of postmodernist theorising within the development of welfare theory more generally. Lewis, Gewirtz and Clarke (2000) provide some examples of the ways in which such postmodernist thinking impacts upon different aspects of social policy analysis, including a chapter (by Watson) on the influence of Foucault. In the final chapter of that book Williams outlines how this can lead to 'a new politics of welfare' which 'extends beyond the redistribution of goods ... [and] centres upon claims for the realisation of personhood and well-being, for cultural respect, autonomy and dignity' (2000, p.339).

Many social policy analysts would no doubt agree with the importance of the issues of respect and autonomy which Williams identifies in this chapter, and with some of the implications of this for social policy practice that she discusses, without necessarily sharing the more general postmodernist rejection of all past welfare theorising and policy practice. Indeed it is not at all clear, as Fitzpatrick (2003) points out, what the policy implications of much postmodernist analysis is. As we said, postmodernists are stronger on critique and exposure than they are on explanation and prescription, and so coming to a conclusion about how such an approach has influenced the development of welfare in practice is not an easy task; although, of course, true postmodernists would probably point out that this is exactly their point: there can be *no* objective analysis of social circumstances and *no* agreed policy response to these.

Nevertheless, this radical rejection of the certainties of past welfare ideologies has provided a far-reaching and (to some) refreshing critical edge to policy debate over the last decade or so, and it has helped to extend the debate about the politics and ideology of welfare beyond a relatively narrow focus on class conflict and public policy practice. However, welfare policy and practice are not just shaped by ideologies and discourses and the power of those who hold them: they are also influenced by the material resources available to people and to policy makers, and it is to this material context that we now turn.

QUESTIONS: COMPREHENSION

■ What are 'metanarratives' and why do postmodernists argue that they cannot provide an effective basis for understanding the ideological basis of welfare?
■ To what extent can postmodernism provide us with an ideological basis for future welfare policy planning?

FURTHER READING

George and Wilding (1994) is still the most comprehensive guide to the major ideologies of welfare. The chapters in Part II of Alcock, Erskine and May (2003) include short summaries of most of the major perspectives by expert authors; and Ellison and Pierson (2003) contains some chapters focusing upon different theoretical and ideological perspectives on welfare, including new social movements. Fitzpatrick (2001) offers an accessible coverage of a range of a range of key concepts and perspectives; and Williams (1989), although now rather dated, is still the best treatment of the impact of feminism and anti-racism on traditional perspectives on social policy.

Economic Development

13

SUMMARY OF KEY POINTS

- Economic and social policy are closely interrelated with changes in one resulting in changes in the other.
- The need to promote economic growth now lies at the heart of all economic policy planning.
- Capitalism is based on market exchanges of goods and services and on employment of workers in the labour market. However, modern economies also include non-market provision of some services and state intervention within markets.
- The *laissez-faire* approach of classical economics led to hardship and periods of recession in the late nineteenth and early twentieth centuries.
- Keynesian economic planning was based on government intervention to stimulate economic growth at times of low demand and was linked to social policy commitments to promote full employment.
- In the 1970s Britain's relatively weak international trading position led to problems of inflation and unemployment which could not be controlled by Keynesian economic management.
- Monetarists argue that reductions public expenditure may be necessary to control the supply of money and so reduce inflation within the economy.
- In the 1980s rising unemployment and a deficit trading balance led to a shift from monetarism to supply-side economics with tax cuts and deregulation aimed at stimulating economic growth.
- High levels of borrowing in the early 1990s followed by rises in the interest rates charged on loans led to another recession in the British economy.
- At the beginning of the new century all advanced economies have had to adapt to the need to compete within a global economic context. This has led the Labour government to make control over inflation and the creation of a stable climate for economic growth the core features of economic, and social, policy planning.

The economic context

The study of social policy in Britain has traditionally focused on the development and structure of welfare services. More recently, however, concern has widened to include analysis of issues such as the ideologies and theories that have shaped the welfare policies and the political context in which these have developed, as we saw in Chapter 12. However, welfare policies are not just the product of a particular political or ideological context; they are also affected by the economic forces that govern the development of the society within which they are located. Indeed, because they determine the resources that are available to meet all individual and social needs, it is arguable that economic forces are the *most* important factor influencing both the size and scope of all social policy.

At a simple level at least, this is certainly true. Welfare services cost money to deliver and, therefore, the economic circumstances of individuals and groups can dictate who pays for welfare and how much they pay (a question to which we shall return in more detail in Chapter 17). At a more complex level, however, social policy development is also closely dependent upon the economic structure of a society and upon the economic growth within it. Changes in such economic structure or economic growth can have a direct impact upon social policy. For instance, a decline in economic growth and changes in economic structure in Britain in the 1970s and 1980s resulted in significant shifts in social policy development and, in particular, in major cutbacks in many welfare services, whilst at the beginning of the new century a period of more stable economic growth led to major increases in spending on public services such as health and education.

However, it is not just the case that economic changes affect the development of social policy. In modern welfare capitalist societies social policies affect economic forces too. For instance, as we have seen, social security policies can maintain a reserve labour force during periods of low employment which is then ready to be re-employed when circumstances improve, and they can even operate to encourage employment through the subsidisation of wages for low-paid employees. Policies for education and training can equip, or re-equip, the workforce with the skills that they need to develop and implement new productive processes. In effect, in modern societies social and economic policies are inextricably intertwined, with changes in one area inevitably leading to changes in the other.

An understanding of social policy thus requires an understanding of the economic policy context in which social policies develop and of the relationship between economic and social policy. The study of economic policy is a vast and complex field, however, with its own theories, concepts and literature. To understand economic policy fully, therefore, we would first need to come to grips with the basic theories and concepts of economics, an enterprise that is well beyond the scope of this introductory book. Nevertheless we will look briefly at some of the major trends in economic policy that have influenced the study of social policy in Britain, and elsewhere, over the recent past, and discuss the implications of these for the development of social policy.

The early Fabian proponents of social policy in Britain at the beginning of the twentieth century argued that social policy was needed in order to counteract some of the undesirable consequences of economic development. In particular, they argued that the capitalist economic system, which was dominant in Britain, had resulted in the creation of significant social problems, most importantly high levels of poverty, and that social policy intervention was required by government in order to restructure socio-economic conditions in ways that would eliminate or prevent these problems (for example, in order to redistribute resources from wealthy capitalists to poor workers, or would-be workers).

As we have seen, therefore, the social policies that have been developed in Britain have been constructed within a capitalist economy, in order to mitigate some of the effects of the operation of capitalist economic forces. The consequences of such changes, however, have been to transform that capitalist economy, in particular through an enhanced role for the collective actions of the state in exercising some control and organisation over both production and distribution. In effect the crude (and cruel) capitalist forces, which were criticised by Fabians, have been supplemented, and in part replaced, by public provision and public ownership. This has led politicians and commentators to argue that Britain no longer has a capitalist economy but rather has a mixed economy, in which private capital plays only a partial role (albeit in practice a dominating one). Whether we conceive of Britain as a capitalist or a mixed economy, however, our understanding of the economic context that this economy provides for the development of social policy requires an examination of the basic structures of capitalist economic systems and the processes by which these have developed, and have been changed and adapted.

Capitalism

We can trace the growth of capitalism back over at least 200 years of British history, although, in practice, its roots extend back much further than that as the earlier feudal system was gradually transformed into an economic system based upon monetary exchange and the market mechanism. Writing over 200 years ago Adam Smith was one of the earliest, and most well-known, economic proponents of capitalism (Smith, 1776). His argument was that the market mechanism was the proper way in which society should be ordered because it ensured that goods and services would be produced and distributed in the most efficient and effective manner. In simple terms this was because of the impartial operation of the laws of supply and demand. Goods and services would be produced and sold on the market, and consumers would go to the market to purchase what they needed or desired. Because consumers would only purchase what they wanted at a price that they could afford, only those producers who were supplying such needs would be able to sell their products. Inefficient, or undesirable, production would thus be driven out of business and the market would produce a stable balance between the forces of supply and demand.

This is a persuasive model, in theory. However, economists quickly discovered that in practice such a comfortable balance was difficult to achieve as production processes changed and consumers' purchasing power fluctuated.

Even its theoretical explanation of capitalist development was questioned in the nineteenth century by Karl Marx, who produced a far-reaching and highly influential critique of the basic structure of the capitalist economy (Marx, 1970).

Marx's argument was that the basic structure of the capitalist economy was not the market mechanism of supply and demand but the wage–labour arrangement for the production of goods and services. This arrangement was founded upon the structural exploitation of the worker, who was paid less by the capitalist than the exchange (or market) value of the goods he or she produced, with the surplus value (or profit) being pocketed by the capitalist or reinvested through accumulation in further capitalist production, which would produce yet further profit. Therefore the capitalist, however morally righteous he or she might be, was inevitably motivated by the pursuit of profit for further production, with the result that the productive forces of capitalism were driven forward through the exploitation of the working class.

This process of the development of productive forces resulted in a growth in the range and scope of the production of goods and services; but it also, Marx suggested, led to an inevitable (and structural) conflict between the worker and the capitalist, or more generally between the representatives of the working class and the representatives of the capitalist class. Capitalists would pursue higher profits and workers would pursue higher wages; conflict between the two would be endemic. This conflict could lead to adjustments to profits or to wages as struggles were won or lost, or compromises reached; but the cause of conflict would always remain. Capitalism was not therefore, according to Marx, a stable economic order, but rather a fundamentally unstable one; and eventually, he predicted, it would collapse and be replaced by a more stable order: socialism.

However, in over 200 years of capitalist economic development in Britain there has been no fundamental collapse, or replacement, of capitalism with socialism. Indeed, where socialist economic systems have been introduced in Eastern Europe and the former Soviet states, these have now collapsed and capitalist market economies have been reintroduced. Thus, although Marx's explanation of the driving force behind capitalist development (and of the inevitable conflicts that this produces) may have been a convincing one, his conclusions about its fundamental instability seem to have proved to be unfounded.

Perhaps the reason why the conflicts generated by capitalist development have not led to its demise is because they have led instead to its transformation. Working-class demands for higher wages (and later for legal regulation and social protection of conditions of work) have, in part at least, been successful in securing changes in the private market economic order of capitalism. As we have already discussed, the development of social policy and welfare services have displaced private markets largely, or entirely, in the provision of some important goods and services: hence the reference to a mixed economy. Another phrase which is used to describe this mixture of private production and public welfare is *welfare capitalism*, and more recently still commentators have begun to refer to such societies as *social market economies*.

This does not mean that the exploitation, and resulting conflict, which Marx argued characterised capitalist society, has been removed; clearly exploitation and conflict both remain, as low wages and industrial disputes continue to demonstrate. However, the exploitation and the conflicts are more fractured and more complex than a basic head-on battle between the capitalists and the working class:

1. Exploitation is fractured: some workers earn good wages and work in good conditions, and also many workers produce no direct profit for their employer; not all exploitation at work is wage-based, as those engaged in unpaid caring work often experience.
2. Conflicts are complex: workers may be in conflict with each other (for instance, over a decision to close one plant to secure jobs at another) or with the state (teachers' and nurses' disputes over changing work practices); conflicts may be based on consumers' interests (tenants' campaigns against local authority landlords) or even general economic policy issues (fuel tax protests in the early 2000s).

However, British capitalism has also changed in other ways. In the early part of the twentieth century British economic policy was largely a matter of national development, even though this national development relied in practice on the exploitation of a large empire. Now, however, economic development in Britain is significantly affected by international forces within a global capital economy, in which production processes are owned or controlled by world-wide corporations and goods and services are produced and marketed on an international level, as we shall discuss shortly. This international context has been further accentuated by Britain's membership of the European Union. As we shall discuss in more detail in Chapter 14, the EU operates a single market for production and distribution throughout its member states, with a single currency operating in most countries, so that economic policy planning increasingly takes place at a supranational level.

The British capitalist economy is no longer, therefore, based on the simple process of capitalist ownership and workers' exploitation described by Marx, or on the simple market of supply and demand advanced by Adam Smith. It is no longer exclusively *capitalist* and it is no longer only *British*. However, it is still in large part a market economy, and one in which capitalist investment by major private corporations is a significant determinant of economic growth. Furthermore, economic growth remains a crucial factor in securing improvements in standards for both capitalists and workers and in providing the resources for the social policy developments that seek to mitigate the market's harshest effects. All major economic commentators, and certainly all important political actors, are now agreed that it is the prospects for economic growth within Britain's complex and fractured economy which are the major focus of economic policy concern, and thus, indirectly, they are the major concern of social policy too. The need to secure growth has become at least as important as the question of what to do with the fruits of it.

Classical economics

Policy based on classical economics drew on the relatively simple model of the capitalist market economy outlined by early economists such as Adam Smith. Classical economists believed that economic growth was the product of the free operation of market forces within society. Freedom did not imply anarchy, of course; there was a role for the state within society to provide a secure context in which the market could operate. Thus the government had a responsibility to protect property through law and contract, and to provide security through policing and national defence. Beyond this, however, the laws of supply and demand would determine investment, production and distribution, and therefore also prices and wages. Efficient producers of desirable products would survive and others would have to adapt or disappear; this was a process in which government could not, and should not, interfere.

This was referred to at the time as the *laissez-faire* approach (leave alone). In the late twentieth century the neo-liberal economists of the New Right called for a return to the policies of *laissez-faire*, claiming that the interventionist measures pursued earlier in the century (discussed below) had failed to secure growth. Neo-liberal economists such as Hayek (1944) and Friedman (1962) argued for a return to the classical economic policies of the (supposedly) free market, through the removal of government controls over investment, credit and employment relations, with the claim that this would restore the equilibrium of the market forces of supply and demand, and reproduce the capitalist economic growth that Britain had enjoyed in the nineteenth century.

It is debatable, as we shall see, how far the classical prescriptions for economic policy of the neo-liberals were taken up in practice by government in the late twentieth century, for there were many prominent economists and politicians who doubted both the desirability and the feasibility of a return to free market forces in the complex economy which Britain had by that time become. However, their assumption that the free markets of the nineteenth century had, in any event, produced sustained and non-problematic economic growth was almost certainly flawed.

In nineteenth-century Britain capitalist production certainly grew in scope and scale but at a heavy cost in terms of low wages, poor conditions and frequently high levels of unemployment for the majority of the population. At the end of that century, when the British economy was arguably at its most powerful, the early social policy researchers, Booth (1889) and Rowntree (1901), found high levels of acute poverty even in London, the capital city of the British Empire. In fact much of British economic growth, in particular towards the end of the nineteenth century, was based upon exploitation of the materials and markets that the empire provided. Despite this, however, growth had not continued uninterrupted; for example, in the 1870s the economy had experienced a major slump, leading to high levels of unemployment and threats of social unrest.

The poverty and social unrest that Britain's capitalist economy had produced in the nineteenth century were part of the pressure for social policy reform articulated by the Fabians, and orchestrated by the labour movement, in the early twentieth century. At the beginning of the century the Boer War and First World War revealed the need for the state to move in to guarantee that the working-class recruits to the army were fit and healthy and to ensure that the production processes were geared up to meet national military needs. This resulted in some abandonment of the strict principles of *laissez-faire* and the involvement of the state in social and economic planning. After the First World War, in the 1920s and 1930s, the country again experienced a period of deep economic depression, which by now was a world-wide phenomenon. Poverty and unemployment again rose dramatically, as Rowntree discovered in a repeat of his 1901 study of York (Rowntree, 1941). In the face of declining economic performance, therefore, the new social policies had failed to protect a large proportion of the population from deprivation and suffering.

The depression of the 1930s was seen by many social policy reformers as powerful evidence of the failure of the capitalist economy to provide adequately for the whole of the population. Beveridge's (1942) proposals for social security reform, which followed the depression, were intended to ensure that never again would economic change result in such social hardship. The depression was also seen by some economists as evidence of the failure of the *laissez-faire* approach to secure sustainable economic growth. Pressure for a change towards a more interventionist economic policy therefore began to develop. This was given greater impetus by the experience of 'total war' during the Second World War, during which government control over production and distribution throughout the economy in Britain and over relations with allied trading partners was essential to the success of the war effort.

Keynesianism

The welfare state reforms of the post-war period, associated in particular with the recommendations of Beveridge in his 1942 report, were the social policy response to the deprivations of the depression. At the same time as this change in the direction of social policy, however, the post-war period also saw a change in the direction of economic policy in Britain, associated with the economic policy recommendations of Beveridge's colleague, Keynes; indeed, the economic and social reforms of the period have sometimes been referred to as the establishment of the Keynes/Beveridge Welfare State (Cutler, Williams and Williams, 1986).

Keynes was an economic adviser to the wartime government and, although he died in 1946, his ideas dominated government economic policy in the two decades following the war. His recommendations had been formulated during the depression of the 1930s (Keynes, 1936) and were based upon a belief that government could, and should, intervene in economic markets, in particular to ensure that full employment was maintained. That full employment was a goal of both economic and social policy was a matter on which Keynes and Beveridge were firmly in agreement. Full employment was essential to Beveridge's recommendations for social security and family support, even though this was restricted to men's labour market participation. It was also the cornerstone of Keynes's prescriptions for future economic growth. Full male employment therefore became the main social and economic policy priority of the immediate post-war period.

Full employment was to be achieved, according to Keynes, by ensuring that growth was sustained in manufacturing production; and, as the depression had demonstrated, this could not be guaranteed by the free market alone. Classical economists had assumed that in a market economy supply would necessarily encourage demand: people would see goods and would want to buy them. In a depression, of course, many people could see goods that they wanted, but they were unable to afford to buy them. However, if they could be given the resources to buy the goods, they would do so, thus stimulating further production of these goods. This would lead to increased resources for those employed in the production of the goods, who themselves could then buy more goods, so stimulating yet more production elsewhere. In other words, Keynes argued that increased *demand* could stimulate *supply* and thus lead to economic growth.

This virtuous circle of increased demand leading to increased production is called by Keynesian economists the *multiplier effect*. The investment of an additional fixed sum of money into the economy will lead to further production, further spending and further investment that cumulatively will be of much greater value than the initial sum invested. Economists even claim that the growth potential of any particular investment can be calculated from the workings of this multiplier effect, thus giving economic planners a clear idea of how much to invest to secure any particular level of improved growth. Not surprisingly, advice along these lines would be likely to be warmly welcomed by governments, especially those promising to improve economic and social circumstances in the short term.

Keynes also argued that the means of securing such additional investment was in the hands of the government which, in times of reduced demand and supply, could afford to borrow money in order to increase government spending on public works and services, in the secure knowledge that the multiplier effect of this would be to stimulate economic growth from which the borrowed money could later be recouped and repaid. Such a period is called a *deflationary gap*, and at such times governments should increase spending or cut taxes to invest in economic growth. When full employment is achieved, however, continued growth in demand could lead to inflation (if more goods cannot be produced, prices go up: a problem to which we shall return shortly). This is called an *inflationary gap*, and at such times, Keynesians argue, governments should cut spending or increase taxes to reduce demand.

Through the application of Keynesian economic principles, therefore, it appeared that governments could control and manage economic growth through public spending and investment in the economy. This provided a great boost to the interventionist social and economic tendencies of the post-war Butskellite governments and, of course, a great boost to the profession of economists. Economic advisers were now much valued by government for the guidance they could provide on how to manipulate the economy. Mathematically constructed economic models could be used to simulate the performance of national economies and the effects of different economic policy measures could be estimated in advance. The Treasury began to use such a model to calculate the effects of government spending in Britain. This economic modelling is called *econometrics*. It is a complex, and to the non-mathematically minded, daunting 'science'; but in Britain, and in other post-war advanced economies, it became more important than the political ideologies of different parties in determining major economic policy decisions, further increasing the already overpowering influence of the Treasury on policy planning.

Throughout the 1950s and 1960s British governments of both political parties pursued Keynesian approaches to economic management of the economy, mirroring the political consensus that seemed also to exist in social policy over the central role of the welfare state. Indeed, state welfare spending and

Keynesian economics went hand in hand, with the one naturally supporting the other. Their success seemed to confirm the view that capitalism could be transformed from within through economic and social policy reform, with politicians such as Crosland (1956) claiming that capitalism had been replaced by a new 'classless society' in which all could benefit. In 1959 the Conservative Prime Minister, Harold Macmillan, entered the election campaign claiming that the British people had 'never had it so good'.

Certainly during the first two decades after the war Keynesian economic policies did appear to be successful. Britain was experiencing one of its longest periods of sustained economic growth, wages levels were rising in value and employment levels were so high that immigrants were encouraged to come from the old imperial colonies to fill gaps in the labour market. However, in practice, the government's management of the economy fluctuated from deflationary gaps to inflationary gaps, characterised by what commentators called *stop/go* policies on spending and taxation. No attempt was made to control the rises in incomes and prices that resulted from the increased industrial power which full employment gave to organised workers in manufacturing industry.

Furthermore, in spite of the consensus on welfare, there were also problems within the mutual interdependence of social and economic policy planning. In social policy terms it was argued by critics such as Titmuss (1956) and Townsend (Abel-Smith and Townsend, 1965) that, despite improved incomes and public services, not everyone was benefiting equally from the protection of the welfare state, and indeed some were still living in poverty. Economists talked about this as the trade-off between *efficiency* and *equity*, an issue which we shall discuss in Chapter 17. Efficiency could be achieved by economic growth if all were better-off, so that no one's gain meant somebody else's loss. However, equity required ensuring that all needs for protection were met and this might require some redistribution of resources to those who were poor, with consequent losses for the better-off. Keynesianism appeared to assume that greater efficiency would also lead to more equity but, as continuing inequalities revealed, this might not necessarily be the case.

QUESTIONS: COMPREHENSION

- To what extent is the exploitation of the working class, identified by Marx, still at the heart of economic conflict?
- What is *laissez-faire* and why did critics argue that it failed to provide an effective basis for economic policy in the nineteenth and early twentieth centuries?
- What is the 'multiplier effect', and how did Keynesians argue it could be used to manage economic development in post-war Britain?

QUESTION: REFLECTION

- Is it possible to study social policy without some understanding of the economic context within which policy is developed?

The collapse of Keynesianism

During the euphoria of the long post-war boom, however, these contradictions within the Keynesian approach appeared to be minor issues when compared to the overall success of sustained economic growth in Britain. However, there were other problems with this sustained growth. By this time Britain's economy was already part of a broader world capitalist economic order; and throughout this global economy economic growth was universally high. Indeed, by international standards, the growth rate within the British economy was fairly slow. Furthermore, throughout the 1950s and 1960s Britain was excluded from the new international economic bloc in Western Europe, the European Economic Community (EEC, now the EU), which the country was not able to join until 1973. The mutual benefits that the early members of the EEC were able to secure for each other were, therefore, not automatically shared with Britain.

The international context of post-war economic policy, however, extended beyond the EEC and the general growth in international trade. Economic planning was also now undertaken at an international level by the advanced industrial nations, in particular through the organisation of the International Monetary Fund (IMF), a kind of collective international bank. In 1944 the IMF had established an agreement under which all member countries would guarantee to maintain the exchange rate value of their currencies at a particular level in relation to the US dollar, called the *Bretton Woods* agreement. Confident of their powerful economic position in the world, the British government fixed the pound at a relatively high level within the Bretton Woods scheme and thus was committed to maintaining this level, despite Britain's relatively slow rate of economic growth in the international arena.

The high value of the pound internationally meant that British exports were relatively expensive for foreign buyers. It also conversely meant that imported goods were relatively cheap in Britain. These two factors together did not act positively to boost British manufacturing performance. In the mid-1960s, when the world economic boom was itself beginning to slow down, this poor performance began to be revealed in new economic problems in Britain.

The most obvious problem to flow from decreased exports and increased imports is a reduction in the *balance of payments*: that is, the overall surplus, or deficit, shown in Britain's trading with other nations within the world economy. A deficit in the balance of payments can be sustained for a short period as obviously not every trader can make a profit all the time. However, a sustained reduction in the balance is evidence of poor economic performance and thus a decline in the relative international economic standing of a nation's economy. This would be likely to reduce international confidence in such an economy and make it more difficult for the government to maintain the high level of the currency within the exchange rate agreement. In the mid-1960s this applied to Britain and was revealed in international pressure on the value of the pound.

However, balance of payments reductions do not just lead to difficulties at an international level: they are manifested in economic problems at home too. Lower exports and higher imports can lead to a decline in manufacturing activity and this can lead to the creation and growth of unemployment. They can also lead to inflation, as British manufacturers seek to off-set the loss of foreign sales by increased prices for goods sold at home. *Inflation* is a complex economic problem, and a much disputed one. In simple terms it means that the prices of goods and services, as measured by a national aggregation of the prices of a sample of major items (called the *Retail Price Index*, or RPI), is rising faster than the production of them. This rise in prices leads to workers demanding higher wages to pay for the more expensive goods and services. However, if wage rises are conceded, these result in yet further price increases to meet the higher wages, leading to a spiral of rising prices and wages. Once such an inflationary spiral has taken hold, the government is brought under pressure to print more money to meet the demand for higher prices and wages. This additional money (unlike the public spending investment foreseen by Keynes) does not contribute to increased demand and supply but rather is soaked up in meeting the higher prices of existing goods, simply adding to the amount of money circulating in the economy without any increase in production or economic growth.

Such inflation, with rises in prices and wages running ahead of economic growth, had not been foreseen as a significant problem by the early Keynesian economists, who assumed that full employment and economic growth would ensure an equilibrium between prices and wages because increases in wages would inevitably flow from improved economic activity. Thus Keynesian economic policy focused upon using state intervention in the economy in order to secure full employment rather than to control inflation. However, in the mid-1960s Britain's balance of payments problems and declining international confidence were threatening this single-minded focus on the need for demand-led growth to boost manufacturing employment.

Britain's problems were serious enough at this time to encourage the Labour government to seek international financial aid from the IMF. However, the IMF were only prepared to provide this on condition that Britain devalued the pound within the Bretton Woods exchange rate agreement, in recognition of the fact that the British economic performance could no longer justify sustaining it at the previous high level. Following IMF pressure, therefore, the government agreed to this; but they hoped that the devaluation would help restore a positive balance of payments in the country by in effect reducing the cost of British exports abroad and raising the price of foreign imports in Britain, thus stimulating home production.

There was some evidence that this did temporarily improve Britain's international performance in the 1960s. Unfortunately it was a relatively minor step taken at a time when international economic forces were in any event reducing demand, and thus production, on a global scale. What is more, if such a devaluation had not succeeded in boosting economic growth in Britain, it could have run the risk instead of adding to economic problems. If cheaper exports had not increased the volume of sales, manufacturers might have been tempted to put up prices at home to recoup their losses. This, together with increased prices for imports, could have put pressure on workers to demand higher wages to meet these higher prices, resulting yet again in an inflationary spiral.

There is in essence, therefore, an inevitable danger that attempts to stimulate demand in a stagnant or declining economic situation will result in rising inflation rather than improved economic growth. In Britain by the early 1970s this is just what was beginning to happen, as unemployment and inflation were both rising, and as on a world-wide scale the long post-war boom began to come to an end. Changes in economic policy thus began to take place as a result of this. The Conservative government of 1970–4 removed the pound from the fixed exchange rate (Bretton Woods) agreement and allowed it to 'float' on the international currency market. This meant that the government was no longer committed to retaining it at a particular level; but it also meant that loss of international confidence in Britain could lead to a decline in the value of the currency that the government would no longer be able to resist.

However, Britain's international position was expected to be strengthened at this time by the decision to join the EEC in 1973, when the original six members finally agreed to an extension of the community. It was hoped that this would boost Britain's trade with its partner members, although of course it also opened up British markets more directly to penetration from Europe.

In the early 1970s the government also made the first direct moves to control prices and incomes in order to reduce inflation, moving the focus of economic policy away from concentration solely on the creation and maintenance of full employment. However, the statutory controls on prices and incomes introduced by the Conservative government were not popular – especially with the trade unions – and they led to significant industrial unrest, including a miners' strike that reduced British industry to working a three-day week as a result of power shortages. At the same time economic growth failed to pick up, with the result that the government decided once again to try to stimulate demand through Keynesian-style measures including tax cuts and an increase in public and private borrowing (sometimes referred to, after the Chancellor of the time, as the 'Barber boom').

Even if such reflation had been a judicious policy response to Britain's growing economic problems, it was in effect too little too late; and it was probably born more of political desperation than clear economic planning. Reflation did not prevent the growth in unemployment, which by now had passed the one million mark; and it also contributed to rapidly rising inflation, which by 1975 had reached over 26 per cent a year (in other words, at the end of the year prices were 26 per cent higher than they had been at the beginning of it). As if this were not enough, Britain's problems were further compounded – as indeed were those of all other industrial economies – by the massive increase in the price of oil introduced by the Organisation of Petroleum Exporting Countries (OPEC) in 1973. Oil was by the 1970s the world's major fuel for economic production, and between 1972 and 1974 its price rose fourfold.

The oil price rise was a symbolic moment in the ending of the international economic boom that had followed the Second World War. In Britain, where problems were worse than in some other countries, it pushed the economy rapidly into recession (or, as the economists of the time called it, *stagflation*: high inflation in a stagnant economy). In the face of this, Keynesian demand management appeared to be impotent and the debate began for a shift in the focus of economic policy.

Monetarism

Throughout the period of the post-war boom the social and economic policies of the Keynes/Beveridge welfare state had appeared to be successful in securing both economic growth and social protection in Britain; and the picture was the same in most other welfare capitalist countries. In this period welfare spending grew in cash terms but it also grew significantly as a proportion of gross domestic product (GDP). GDP and GNP (gross national product) are general measures of the activity of a national economy. They are an attempt to count together all goods and services produced *in* the country (GDP) or, in the case of GNP, including also those produced *abroad*. In a growing economy, therefore, GDP and GNP would be increasing each year.

In such an economy a growth in public expenditure may not be problematic: as the economy grows so we can afford better public services, and the taxes used to pay for these can be afforded relatively easily out of the improved profits and wages that growth brings. Nevertheless, a growth in the *proportion* of public expenditure suggests a change in the balance of activity within the country, with more resources are going into welfare services than into industrial development. This again may not be a problem, especially in a growing economy. For example, much of the growth in public expenditure in the 1960s and early 1970s was the result of the growing numbers of public employees in welfare services, where employment increased by about one-third. This helped to maintain high employment levels, as well as stimulating demand through the purchasing power that these workers brought into the economy more generally.

In a declining economy, however, growth in public expenditure is more problematic. Growing levels of expenditure still have to be financed out of increased taxation and now this will compete with private investment or private consumption within a restricted overall economic climate. This may make taxes, and thus spending, less popular; but, more seriously in economic terms, it may also compound economic recession by reducing investment in industrial production and curtailing consumer spending, and thus the demand for goods.

It is just such problems that new critics of Keynesian economic management began to suggest were the source of Britain's declining economic performance in the mid-1970s. Right-wing critics such as Bacon and Eltis (1976), in their book, *Britain's Economic Problem: Too Few Producers*, argued that growing public expenditure was crowding out private investment in the economy. The reduced size and scope of private manufacturing ('too few producers') thus led to economic decline, which was compounded if, at such a time, public expenditure and public employment continued to grow as a proportion of GDP.

Growing public expenditure can, of course, be financed by increased taxation (although as we have suggested this might at such times become unpopular), or it can be financed by government borrowing. Governments can borrow against the expectation of future growth or future tax revenue. The level of this borrowing is traditionally referred to as the *Public Sector Borrowing Requirement* (PSBR). Keynesian economic management assumed that government borrowing would be needed in order to finance demand-led economic stimulation, with the borrowing being repaid, or at least reduced, once economic growth increased performance and thus raised the revenue from taxation. In the early 1970s the PSBR was rising as a proportion of GDP. However, economic growth did not now follow; and the new critics of Keynesianism pointed out that, instead of solving economic problems, the rising PSBR was contributing to them, because the growing amount of money available in the economy that resulted from it merely added to the pressures on inflation.

The conclusion that these critics were drawn to was that, at times of recession, it was not possible to stimulate economic growth through demand management, fuelled by public expenditure; and further that, if this were attempted, it would result only in growing inflation, which would make matters worse. To counteract Britain's accelerating economic decline, therefore, an alternative approach was required. This meant abandoning the policy commitment to full employment, which in any event had failed in practice, and seeking instead to control inflation in order to stabilise the economic climate and provide more security and encouragement for private investment, from which it was assumed growth would follow. Controlling inflation meant controlling the money supply and a move from Keynesianism to *monetarism* as the central plank of economic policy planning.

Monetarism was the economic policy favoured by the New Right critics of Keynesian economics, such as Friedman (1962). The 'failure' of Keynesianism appeared to confirm their views on the incompatibility of expensive welfare and an interventionist state within a market economy. In monetarism they saw the strategic means to reduce state expenditure and intervention and restore private market growth. The *narrow* goal of monetarism, therefore, was the control of inflation. This was to be achieved by restricting the supply of money within the economy, so counteracting the tendency for prices and wages to rise. The main factor leading to an increased money supply in the 1970s, it was argued, was government borrowing, as expressed in the PSBR. Thus the PSBR had to be reduced and, in order to do this, public spending would have to be cut. The *broader* goal of monetarism, however, especially for the New Right, was the general reduction of state expenditure, especially welfare expenditure, that otherwise seemed set to rise inexorably as yet more needs and demands for social protection were pressed on government.

A shift to monetarism in economic policy was not, therefore, merely a reaction to the limitations of Keynesianism in times of recession: it was a wholesale rejection of the Keynes/Beveridge welfare state partnership of social spending and demand-led economic growth. Thus the results of such a change in economic policy also had serious implications for the future development of social policy.

Of course the Labour government of the late 1970s, although it was faced with the most serious recession in the British economy since the 1930s, was not the natural political ally of New Right monetarism, and was reluctant to accept readily the anti-welfare message that monetarist economist critics espoused. Labour's first commitment, therefore, was to seek to control price and wage inflation by more direct means. Legislating against such increases had proved politically disastrous for the Conservative government in the early 1970s and so, through its partnership with the trade unions, Labour sought to secure voluntary wage restraint. The agreement on restraint was contained in a *social contract* between the government and the trade unions, in which, in return for reduced wage demands by the unions, the government would introduce employment protection legislation and other social measures.

In fact this social contract approach to wage and price restraint was not a new phenomenon outside Britain. In a number of European countries, especially in Sweden and some of the other Scandinavian countries, such *corporatist* economic planning between government, trade unions *and* representatives of industry had been a feature of economic policy throughout much of the post-war period. In some of these countries this centralised bargaining had resulted in greater wage and price restraint in times of growth and recession, although usually also in a context of greater wage equality and improved welfare services. It had also secured both greater public protection and lower rates of inflation. The corporatist approach is sometimes credited, therefore, with having prevented countries such as Sweden from experiencing the worst effects of international recession in the 1970s and 1980s; and certainly throughout that period levels of both inflation and unemployment remained much lower in Sweden than in Britain, although some problems began to develop there too in the 1990s.

In Britain in the 1970s, however, the corporatist remedy was both economically too late and politically too weak. Here PSBR and balance of payments problems were so great in the mid-1970s that the government had to turn once again to the IMF for assistance, and once again the assistance granted by the IMF was tied to required policy changes. In particular, they wanted the British government to implement monetarist controls over the escalating money supply and, consequently, to reduce public expenditure. Perhaps reluctantly, therefore, the Labour government of the 1970s was converted to monetarism, as Prime Minister James Callaghan explained to the Party Conference in 1976: 'We used to think that you could just spend your way out of a recession and increase employment by cutting taxes and boosting government spending. I tell you in all candour, that option no longer exists' (Callaghan, 1987, p.426).

In fact the Labour government of the 1970s did not wholeheartedly embrace monetarism. It did not reduce the overall extent of public spending but rather prevented its further projected expansion, mainly by cutbacks in a few areas (such as housing and education) balanced by continued expansion in others (such as social security and health); and it continued to press ahead with voluntary control to reduce inflation through the 'social contract'. To some extent these policies were successful, for inflation did start to fall after 1976, although the world-wide recession within which Britain was then operating meant that stimulating economic growth was not so easy to achieve.

However, the ability of the government to sustain its voluntary pay and prices policy was subject to significant political challenge at the end of the decade as many trade unions, especially those representing public sector workers, rejected the social contract and went on strike for higher wages. The public sector strikes of 1978 and 1979, which halted many public services in local authorities and hospitals, were dubbed the 'Winter of Discontent' by media critics; and they undoubtedly lost the government much political support. In the election which followed in 1979 the Labour Party was defeated, and a new Conservative government, under the leadership of Margaret Thatcher, was elected to power. Thatcher was an outspoken supporter of the policy prescriptions of the New Right and was much more willing than Labour had been to embrace the recommendations of the monetarists, and also to reject Keynesianism.

In the early 1980s, therefore, the shift in economic policy away from Keynesianism became both more determined and more far-reaching; and it was accompanied by changes in social policy too. The Thatcherite wing of the Conservative Party was closer to the welfare ideology of the New Right than to the Middle Way collectivism that had characterised previous administrations. Thus restrictions in overextensive state welfare provision were viewed as desirable goals in themselves and not merely as the necessary consequences of stricter economic policy.

Stricter economic policy was nevertheless pursued in the early 1980s, with monetarist controls aimed at reducing inflation now identified as the major feature of policy planning. In fact inflation rose immediately after the Conservative election victory, partly because of a concession to the public sector wage demands and a shift from direct to indirect taxation resulting in a big increase in Value Added Tax (VAT), which together pushed up both wages and prices. After this inflation did fall significantly, reaching a low of 3.7 per cent in 1983 (Peden, 1985, p.215).

However, the economic growth that was supposed to follow from the shift towards financial constraint and freedom for the private market did not materialise. In the early 1980s the international recession was generally getting worse rather than better, in particular as a result of another OPEC oil price increase in 1979. By the 1980s, of course, Britain was itself an oil producing and exporting nation and this did begin to provide much needed revenue for the country. Yet, despite it, the balance of payments began to decline dramatically, with manufacturing exports being particularly hard hit. Manufacturing industry in Britain experienced its worst ever period of decline during the early 1980s, with the effects of international recession being compounded by the government's policy of privatisation and the withdrawal of public support for industry, aimed ostensibly at restoring private incentives within a free market. The effect of this was a shift into the red in the balance of trade in manufactured goods between Britain and the rest of the world by the mid-1980s, and a catastrophic decline in manufacturing employment and output, especially in the heavy staple industries such as steel and coal.

Thus in the 1980s, although inflation declined, unemployment rose to two, and then three, million, with many of those leaving (or seeking to enter) the labour market facing the prospect of never securing permanent employment again. This of course created pressure on government expenditure on social security to support the new army of unemployed and, ironically, despite the espoused aims of government, public spending continued to grow; in particular, it grew as a proportion of a now declining GDP (Peden, 1985, p.225).

In the face of international recession, therefore, it appeared that – even if it was able to control inflation – monetarism, too, was unable to deliver economic growth. In fact, the ability of government to pursue an effective monetarist policy was proving to be much more difficult than some of its anti-Keynesian supporters had initially supposed. Monetarism required exercising control over the supply of money in the economy. This immediately raised the problem of deciding, or defining, what the supply of money was, and different definitions were in existence. A narrow definition (M1) included only those notes and coins in circulation in the country; but the government of the 1980s preferred to use a broader definition (M3) that also included all money held in deposit in banks and savings accounts.

However, even *calculating* the value of M3 was inevitably a problematic exercise, and *controlling* it proved to be much more difficult; especially as the main lever over which the government supposedly did have control, public expenditure, was continuing to rise. The financial planning targets for control of the money supply in the early 1980s were thus continually revised and, in the mid-1980s, they were finally abandoned. With the British economy deeper than ever in recession in the early 1980s, the most obvious conclusion was that the monetarist strategy for growth had rather rapidly failed.

Supply-side strategy

Despite the rhetoric of financial control and the very real desire of the Thatcher governments of the early and mid-1980s to curtail public expenditure, at least on welfare services, their commitment to monetarism was in practice always rather faltering, and by 1985 had been officially abandoned. The government had been forced to face the reality that without economic growth, financial stringency was barely achievable and in any event was of debatable value. Thus the priority became the need to stimulate economic growth. With her strong New Right leanings Thatcher was unlikely to look to a return to Keynesianism in order to achieve this and, perhaps fortunately, evidence from a newly resurgent US economy in the mid-1980s suggested that this might not in any case be necessary.

Implicit in New Right thinking was the plea for a return to the free market of classical economics that critics such as Friedman (1962) argued had been progressively destroyed by Keynesian interventionism and welfare-state social protection. If economic growth was to be restored, the argument ran, freedom must be returned to the market. This twentieth-century *laissez-faire* is sometimes referred to as neo-classical economics but, following the terminology and the policy developments pursued along these lines by the Reagan administration in the USA in the 1980s, it was also called a *supply-side strategy*.

Supply-side economics, as the name suggests, implies something of a reversal of the demand-led strategies for growth proposed by Keynes. Demand-led strategies required government manipulation of the economy in order to stimulate growth. This was now referred to as *macro* management and it was argued to be ineffective. Instead, the neo-classical economists argued, governments should withdraw from macro management and restrict public intervention in economic development to *micro* level strategies to respond only to particularly serious problems or blockages. Thus the Keynes/Beveridge control and protections should, as far as possible, be removed to restore the incentives to private capitalist investors to produce new goods and services in the expectation of making a profit. Incentives for profits would therefore stimulate supply, and increased supply would lead to a growth in employment, and thus greater demand, which would stimulate yet further production for supply: a virtuous circle operating in the reverse of the direction put forward by Keynes.

The withdrawal from macro management, however, included more than just the limited privatisation and cuts in subsidies pursued by the Thatcher governments in the early 1980s. It required a removal of controls over the movement and investment of capital, the freeing-up of financial markets, the withdrawal of restrictions on credit, the repeal of protections and regulations governing employment conditions and wage levels, the reduction in the rights and powers of trade unions, the privatisation of state assets, and (perhaps most importantly) the cutting of taxation levels. Critics and supporters referred to this as 'rolling back the boundaries of the state'; and, of course, it had implications for social, as well as economic, policy as significant cuts were implied in welfare services such as housing, education and social security benefits.

The development of micro-level interventions as a new role for government economic policy was perhaps less significant than the withdrawal from macro management in supply-side economics. Nevertherless they included a new role for the Department of Trade and Industry in acting as technical adviser and assistant to private industry and for the (then) Department of Employment in providing targeted training and advice to vulnerable groups among the unemployed. The idea was that government should respond to the needs of the market rather than the other way round.

By the mid-1980s, moreover, it appeared that the supply-side measures that had worked previously in the USA were also being successful in restoring growth to the British economy. British GDP began to grow, reaching an average of 4 per cent growth a year in the mid- to late 1980s. As a result, although public expenditure itself continued to rise, it began to decline as a proportion of GDP after 1982–3 (see Figure 13.1). Unemployment, although still high by previous standards, also began to fall as new jobs were created, especially in the rapidly expanding service sector, which included such things as banks, insurance, communication technology, catering and leisure.

In fact the growth in the British economy was so rapid in the late 1980s, even by international standards, that government supporters began to heap praise upon the 'economic miracle' that the shift in policy direction had secured. At the height of the boom in 1988, after the Conservative Party's third election victory, the Chancellor, Nigel Lawson, continued the supply-side stimulation with wide-ranging tax cuts, especially for the wealthy from whom the higher rates of income tax were removed. Neo-classical economics appeared to have proved, finally, that Keynes was wrong after all.

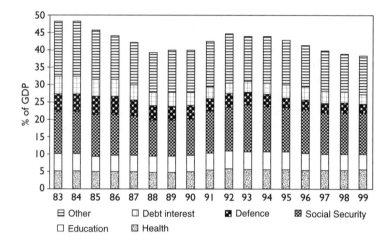

Figure 13.1   Government spending as a percentage of GDP, 1983/84 to 1998/99
Hills (2000), Figure 4

Source: HM Treasury (2000b), Table 4.4, and earlier equivalents.

QUESTIONS: COMPREHENSION

■ What is inflation, and why did it become a problem within the British economy in the 1970s?

■ Why do monetarists believe that controlling public expenditure will promote economic growth, and why were they unable to achieve this in Britain in the 1980s?

■ What was meant by a move from *macro* to *micro* state intervention in the economy in the 1980s, and to what extent did it involve a repudiation of Keynesianism?

Globalism and recession

Despite its apparent success there were serious problems, and indeed contradictions, at the heart of the supply-side boom in the British economy in the late 1980s. For a start, as we have mentioned, public expenditure growth had not been contained, even though it was no longer growing more rapidly than the economy itself. Furthermore, even this limited growth was being artificially restricted by the high revenue now being received from the sale of North Sea oil and by the receipts that the government was able to secure from its major privatisations of government monopolies in such things as gas, electricity and water supply. In this context tax cuts could be sustained as long as the economy continued to grow rapidly; but if it did not then public borrowing would be bound to rise again.

In addition, although unemployment was falling, it still remained well above two million and the government continued to accept no responsibility for seeking to reduce it further if the market itself was unable to do so. Unemployment also was increasingly unevenly distributed throughout the country, with the highest levels being found in the still declining industrial areas in central and northern England and Scotland. This was because manufacturing industry was still producing much less than it had been in the 1970s or 1960s and, even where production levels were increasing, this was usually a result of improved machinery or methods rather than a larger workforce. Much of the growth of jobs, therefore, was in the service sector and was concentrated in the South East of England. Although some of these jobs were well paid and highly skilled, many were menial tasks undertaken for very low pay in restaurants or shops and were increasingly available only on a part-time and/or a temporary basis. Both socially and geographically, therefore, the economic trends of the 1980s had produced only partial success with greater divisions within British society, growing affluence for some being mirrored by growing poverty and inequality for others.

Britain's 1980s' boom was not only partial, however; it was also very fragile. Increased supply of goods and services had been met by increased demand. But the growth in demand had been very rapid, and in practice much of it had been fuelled by the private credit that was now much more widely available as a result of deregulation. Furthermore, this increased demand did not entirely support increased production at home. Partly because of the poor condition of British manufacturing industry, and partly because of the wider international market in which Britain was now forced to operate anyway, increased demand led, as it had done before, to a major increase in imports. The result of this was a continuing, and growing, balance of payments deficit, which was made worse by the tax cut stimulation of the economy in 1988.

Ironically, the real problem was that the British economy was growing too rapidly and, in an international context, with a balance of payments deficit, this could not be sustained. The evidence for this non-sustainability was growing international pressure on the value of the pound, which was of course now floating on the international currency markets (although, in the 1980s, the policy of the government had been to keep its value as close as possible to that of the strongest European currency, the Deutschmark). In the late 1980s the government formed the view that something had to be done to control economic growth; and, since the major motor for this was the rise in private credit, the interest rates for the cost of borrowing money were significantly increased.

As a result of these pressures the pace of change in British economic policy in the early 1990s was swift, in particular because the massive boom of the late 1980s came rapidly to an end. The increased cost of borrowing due to high interest rates halted the rise in credit (although in any event this could never have been sustained indefinitely) leading to a major reduction in demand. This reduction was made worse, temporarily, when the government joined the EU's exchange rate mechanism (ERM) which *required* it to guarantee the value of the pound against other European currencies (in effect still primarily the Deutschmark) at a level which British economic performance did not justify.

This resulted in further interest rate rises, which further deflated demand; and in the end the pressure became too great. Following a shift of policy across the space of eight hours in one day Britain withdrew from the ERM and the pound was floated once again. After this interest rates were reduced, in the hope of stimulating demand once again, but without much success (especially as, in order to minimise growing public borrowing, the government despite – its continued rhetoric to the contrary – was forced to raise taxation levels, primarily through increased indirect taxes such as VAT).

Thus the boom of the 1980s was followed by a sharp recession in the 1990s, when GDP again declined and unemployment once more passed three million. While, however, it had been manufacturing workers in the Midlands and North who had lost their jobs in the 1980s recession, it was the service workers in the South who became redundant in the 1990s as the expansion in these jobs proved to be rather short term. Therefore, while many of those who remained in employment continued to enjoy relatively high standards of living, the social and economic divisions in society continued to grow. If the recession of the 1970s had proved Keynes wrong, and we could not *spend* our way out of a recession, the recession of the 1990s seemed to prove that neo-classical economics was also flawed, and that we could not *borrow* our way out of one either.

In fact the major lesson to be learnt from the economic policy changes of the 1970s, 1980s and 1990s is that Britain had by then become a part of a much bigger, and more powerful, European and world market, on which the British government, no matter what policies it adopted, could have only limited impact. In this world market too this was a period of rapid and far-reaching change. International economists talk of a transformation here from *Fordism* to *post-Fordism*, by which is meant a decline in the importance of the mass-production manufacturing process (associated with Ford Motor Company which developed the first mass-produced automobile) and a growth in the development of small businesses and specialist manufacturers producing small-volume goods for particular market needs.

The effect of these changes, it is argued, is a decline in manufacturing employment, especially in the older industrial countries, and an increase in specialist production methods that might result in employment which is part-time or temporary. These changes in manufacturing are accompanied by the growth of employment in the service sectors in all welfare capitalist countries. However, this employment is often low skilled and low paid and, where accompanied by deregulation of labour markets, leaves these workers with fewer rights and protections than had been enjoyed by the workers engaged in mass production in the past.

This restructuring of both investment and employment has resulted in instability on a global scale, and has been one of the major causes of the series of recessions that affected most industrial economies over the last quarter of the last century. In the face of these recessions most governments, even those with strong welfare states such as Sweden, had to adjust economic policy planning and, in particular, to cut back on planned growth in state expenditure and social protection. Seen in this context, therefore, the changes experienced in Britain are but one example – albeit in practice a rather extreme one – of a more general international drift in economic and social policy.

The Third Way

The recognition that economic development in the twenty-first century requires government to adopt policies which will maximise economic competitiveness within the global economy has been a central feature of the economic and social policies pursued by the New Labour governments in Britain since 1997. The Chancellor, Gordon Brown, made clear early in the first term of office that he regarded the maintenance of low inflation and stable economic growth as the key to underpinning all aspects of private and public investment and expenditure. In other words, managing the economy to secure growth must come first; this is, sometimes referred to by Brown, and his critics, as economic 'prudence'. This was not Keynesian demand management, however. Brown also made clear that he accepted the importance of control over inflation as the key driver of economic stability, and that only from such stability could other goals, such as moves towards full employment or improvement in welfare services, be achieved. He also shared the view, common amongst many economists by the 1990s, that the most effective way to control inflation, and growth, was through the setting of appropriate levels for the rates in interest charged on borrowing in the economy: when inflation and growth were low, low rates of interest would encourage borrowing to support investment and expenditure; if rapid growth was leading to a rise in inflation, then higher interest rates would reduce borrowing and hence expenditure and so stabilise the economy.

What is more, Brown conceded that governments were not necessarily the best judges of the appropriate levels for interest rates, as they may be tempted (as most in the past had) to resort to interventionist actions to boost growth imprudently to meet short-term pressures to reduce unemployment, to cut taxes or to increase public spending, leading to the 'stop/go' policies of the 1950s and 1960s and the booms and recessions of the 1980s and early 1990s. Stability was best ensured, the Chancellor argued, if decisions about interest rates were taken by impartial economists; and so, shortly after the 1997 election victory, he passed decisions on rates to a committee of the Bank of England, comprised of economic experts from different sections of the economy, which met on a monthly basis to set rates for the following month. The effect of this was to transfer a significant aspect of economic power to outside government; and the evidence of the following few years was that this had been a successful move.

At the turn of the century Britain was experiencing slow but steady economic growth. Inflation remained low, and so interests rates were kept low (both in fact generally lower than at any time since the 1960s). Unemployment fell significantly, dropping below a million by 2001 for the first time in almost 30 years. The proud boast of the government was that by making economic management the key political priority (Brown's prudence) they had succeeded, where past Conservative and Labour governments had failed, in providing a stable economic base for policy development. In this it also appeared that, unlike in the 1970s and 1980s, Britain was performing more effectively than many of its economic competitors, with higher growth and higher employment than most of its EU neighbours and a return to a positive balance of payments for the first time since the 1980s (Thomas, 2001, p.52).

There was a price to be paid for such economic prudence, however. For a start, the policy priority accorded to economic management further increased the political power of the Treasury within government. The Treasury has, of course, always been the most powerful arm of government, and has exercised both direct and indirect influence over other aspects of policy planning, including provision for welfare (Deakin, 2000). However, Brown's powerful personal position within the Labour government (he is seen by most pundits as most likely to succeed Blair as Labour leader), and the determination of the government to make all policy decisions conditional upon their not undermining the pursuit of stable economic growth, have made this dominant position even stronger and further reaching. For instance, it was the Treasury which led many of the tax and benefit reforms introduced by Labour, with policy documents published here and policy planning following a direction explicitly approved by Brown.

More generally, however, the prudent approach to economic management has dominated the policy agenda of the Labour governments since 1997. For the first two years after 1997 Labour pledged to remain within the public spending limits set by the previous Conservative administration, with the result that in relation to a growing GDP overall levels of public expenditure fell (Burchardt and Hills, 1999, p.44). Brown also aimed to control and reduce public borrowing, abandoning the old PSBR in favour of a new measure, the public sector net cash requirement (PSNCR), and sought to adhere to the 'golden rule' that over the economic cycle government would not borrow to finance current expenditure but only capital investment (such as new public buildings), and here only where such expenditure could be afforded (and in places matched by private investment). The effect of this was to reduce levels of public borrowing for the first time since the end of the 1980s (Thomas, 2001, p.52).

Following the two years of fixed expenditure the government introduced a Comprehensive Spending Review (CSR) to plan public spending over a three-year cycle. The first of these in 1998 led to commitments to raise significantly public spending on health and education in particular, and this was followed by further such increases in a later CSR in 2002. By the early years of the new century, therefore, the government was able to claim that their prudent approach to economic management had underpinned a major growth in public expenditure on welfare services, which was not financed by either public borrowing or major tax increases (although some tax increases were made, notably the increase in National Insurance to fund new health spending in the 2002 budget).

Further changes to taxation policy in the early twenty-first century, in particular the extension of tax credits to the lower paid, also began a minor redistribution of resources from rich to poor within the country, reversing the trend set in the opposite direction by the Conservative governments of the 1980s and 1990s. To some extent, therefore, it could be argued that the new Labour governments were able to find a 'third way' forward for economic and social policy, within which stable economic management could underpin improved welfare services and limited redistribution of resources to those at the bottom of the income distribution, and without a return to the Keynesian interventionist role for government championed by most post-war Labour administrations.

However, even such prudent economic management is susceptible to changes in broader economic development. Significant downturns in economic growth in many advanced industrial countries (notably the USA) in the early years of the new century led to reductions in growth in the UK too, and a consequent failure of the UK economy to meet the targets planned by government. In the short run this led to major extensions in government borrowing to meet public expenditure commitments, but whether these could be sustained in a continuing economic trough has been questioned by some critics.

Furthermore, it could be argued that in any event the government's new Third Way still involves a significant element of continuity with the supply-side economic policies of the previous Conservative administrations. Supply-side measures have been at the forefront of employment policy (see Chapter 7), and have been the justification for much of the additional investment in education in order to equip the economy with a well-qualified workforce. And more generally, the recognition that governments cannot, and should not, seek to intervene to counteract the more general trends of global economic development, but rather should act only to improve competitiveness and encourage economic growth (with social policy improvement following on the back of this), involves a large measure of agreement with previous supply-side rejections of Keynesianism and the 'relegation' of government to the role of economic management.

The impact of global economic forces has certainly made it more and more difficult for individual countries to pursue economic and social policies that undermine their international competitiveness, and this has led to policy change in most advanced industrial nations in recent times, including Sweden and the other strong social democratic welfare states. And, as we shall discuss in Chapter 14, these international economic pressures have led to more extensive international planning of economic and social policies more generally. However, they do not remove the power of governments to undertake social and economic planning at national level, as the changes pursued by the Labour governments after 1997 make clear. How economies are managed involves political decisions about economic and policy priorities; as we have seen here, this interplay between economic development and policy planning has been critical in shaping the policy environment in the past and will continue to structure the future development of social policy in Britain, as well as in all other nations.

QUESTIONS: COMPREHENSION

- To what extent did the recession of the 1990s prove that the country could not *borrow* its way out of recession?
- Why did the Labour government transfer the setting of interest rates to the Bank of England Monetary Policy Committee?
- To what extent is Labour's Third Way a departure from previous principles of economic policy planning?

QUESTION: REFLECTION

- Have the failures of past models of economic policy planning taught us that economic forces cannot be managed by government intervention?

FURTHER READING

An accessible and wide-ranging review of the British economy in the late twentieth century is provided by Hutton (1995). Balls and O'Donnell (2002) is an up-to-date discussion of recent government economic policy. For a longer-term analysis of Britain's economic problems and political responses see Gamble (1994). Hills (1993) provides a good, if dated, guide to how economic policy informs future public welfare planning.

International and European Influences

14

SUMMARY OF KEY POINTS

- Global economic forces now influence economic and social policy planning in all countries, although the extent of this influence is much disputed by commentators.
- Global agencies now play an influential role in determining the development of social policy in many nations.
- Comparative analysis of different 'welfare regimes' has helped to extend understanding of the international context of social policy.
- Policy transfer is the adoption of policy ideas from one country into another. In recent times Britain has adopted policy ideas from the USA and Australia.
- The European Union (EU) was initially developed to promote economic collaboration in Western continental Europe. Since then it has extended across all of Western Europe.
- Social policy regimes within the EU are diverse, but all member nations are committed to elements of joint policy planning and coordinated policy practices.
- Social policy within the EU has developed through a series of phases, with shared policy planning becoming more extensive in each phase.
- EU social programmes target resources on to regions within the Union with acute social and economic problems, thus leading to a redistribution of resources across (and within) nations.
- Since joining the EU in 1973 Britain has been a reluctant partner in European initiatives, and both the Labour and Conservative parties have been divided in their views on EU partnership.

The global context

The primary focus of this book is on social policy in the UK. Most social policies affecting the lives of UK residents have been developed within the country on a national basis by the British government, or at a local level by other agencies or authorities with devolved powers from national government; and by and large social policy has been studied and analysed at a national level. As we have already discussed, however, in both economic and social terms Britain is no longer, if it ever was, an isolated national social entity.

The lives of the British population are affected by international social and economic forces; and the ability of the British government to develop policies to respond to these forces is constrained by our relations with other nations, both politically and economically. Furthermore, the policies that are pursued by the British government are likely to be informed by the knowledge and experience of policy developments in other countries. We are not only affected by the actions of our international friends and neighbours; we can also learn from them. Thus social policy in Britain, like economic policy, has an international context, and overall this context is a broad and far-reaching one.

As we discussed in Chapter 13, much economic development now takes place on a global scale. Large international corporations, such as Microsoft, Coca-Cola, or General Motors, produce and distribute goods and services across the world. The scale of their economic activity is vast (the larger corporations have annual turnovers much greater than that of many countries) and their economic power and influence is a significant factor in shaping the economic climate both globally and within the individual countries within which they operate (or do not!). This globalisation of economic activity has led some to argue that it is these international economic forces that are now the prime determinants of economic and social policy development in all nations, because all nations must adapt their domestic economic and social policies to ensure that they can compete within the global economic market.

The argument about the extent to which global economic forces do shape national economic and social policies is a complex one, however. Although some commentators have argued that globalisation has forced a significant restructuring of social policy in all states (Mishra, 1999), others have argued that in practice there is little evidence that national policy making has been significantly altered by global forces (Pierson, 2000). In reality, of course, the situation is likely to be somewhere in between, with all countries recognising the need to adapt policy to global economic forces (as the current UK government clearly acknowledges), but with different political traditions and welfare structures leading to different responses within different welfare contexts, which is sometimes referred to as 'path dependency' (see Sykes, Palier and Prior, 2001).

We shall return shortly to discuss the extent to which these different contexts can themselves help us to understand the international context of social policy development, but it is important also to recognise the importance of another dimension of the global context of policy making, and that is the role and influence of international economic and social policy agencies. For some time international agencies have sought to influence, or even determine, policy making across nations, most obviously perhaps through the United Nations (UN), which was established after the Second World War to prevent future international conflict and promote international relations. Although the UN remains largely a political and strategic body, it has developed a range of initiatives to promote and support international social policy activity, such as the United Nations Development Programme (UNDP) and the International Children's Fund (UNICEF); and, although mainly operating in developing nations, these initiatives have also had an impact in industrial states such as the UK.

In addition to the UN, however, there is a range of other international agencies with an interest in seeking to support, and to shape, social policy making across nations. These include the Organisation for Economic Co-operation and Development (OECD), the International Labour Organisation (ILO) and the World Health Organisation (WHO). All of these gather data about policy development across member nations (they are useful sources of information for comparative policy analysis), but also seek to use this knowledge to influence policy development within nations: for instance, through the work of the WHO in preventing the spread of disease and setting standards for promotion of health.

Whilst the WHO and the ILO focus specifically on social policy there are other agencies which, although they are mainly concerned with the planning and support of economic development, also have the power to wield both a direct and an indirect influence over the development of welfare planning. For a start the world's most powerful industrialised countries now meet regularly to plan and coordinate international economic policy development at a general level (usually referred to as the G8 Summit). More specifically there is the work of the World Bank and the International Monetary Fund (IMF), who can support international investment and development within nations (World Bank) or to nations (IMF), and who in doing so generally have a clear view about the social policy priorities which they wish to promote (see Deacon, Hulse and Stubbs, 1997); for instance, we discussed the influence of the IMF on British economic and social policy in the 1960s and 1970s in Chapter 13.

B Deacon (2003; and Deacon, Hulse and Stubbs, 1997) provides a useful guide to the increasingly influential role that these major international agencies now have in shaping the development of social policy across the globe; and, although much of their activity has been concentrated in the developing nations and former communist states, it would be unwise to underestimate their influence, especially indirectly, in more developed nations such as the UK. This is also true of those international agencies that are not established or supported by governments, but nevertheless operate to influence social policy and respond to social needs on an international scale. Sometimes referred to as international non-governmental organisations (NGOs) these include major charities such as Oxfam, Christian Aid and the Red Cross, who influence policy and practice across the globe. Like the government agencies these organisations operate in both developed and developing nations (for instance, Oxfam has an extensive anti-poverty programme within the UK).

At the beginning of the new century, therefore, the global context of social policy development is one in which international forces and international agencies are exercising an ever-growing pressure on policy development and delivery in all nations. The pressures of globalisation do not mean that, as a result of some inevitable global convergence, all national policies will move closer and closer to one common denominator, set by the World Bank or the IMF; but they do mean, as the UK government recognises, that policy making within individual nations must respond to this international context and the pressures and opportunities that flow from it. It is, of course, partly for this reason that comparative analysis of social policy occupies such a key role in academic study today, and such analysis can help us to understand better the way in which British social policy relates to, and is influenced by, developments in other countries.

Welfare regimes and policy transfer

Comparative social policy is now a well-developed element within the study of social policy and encompasses a number of different levels of analysis. There are studies providing a guide to the policy context in different countries (Alcock and Craig, 2001), studies exploring aspects of social policy across different countries (Clasen, 1999) and studies examining the international policy context and trends in policy planning (Castles, 1998). There are also those who have sought to provide a theoretical framework for analysing (and measuring) the different types of policy development found within different national contexts in order to explore the extent to which we can explain (and predict) national policy development by setting this within a broader international framework.

It was Titmuss himself who was one of the first social policy academics to attempt to produce such a framework with his three models of social policy (Titmuss, 1974; and see also Alcock *et al.*, 2001, Part 5):

- Model A – the residual welfare model
- Model B – the industrial achievement-performance model
- Model C – the institutional redistributive model.

However, this tripartite framework was developed much further by the Scandinavian academic Esping-Andersen in the 1980s (Esping-Andersen, 1990). Based on empirical research using data on welfare activity in 18 advanced industrial countries from the OECD and other international agencies, and drawing upon analysis of political trends within a number of exemplar nations, Esping-Anderson constructed a tripartite typology of what he called 'welfare regimes'. In particular he argued that two key features could provide a guide to the differences between different types of welfare state. These were:

- decommodification (the extent to which welfare protection was provided by non-market providers)
- stratification (the extent to which access to welfare was determined by social class).

From this he drew up a rank order of the states that he examined according to their score on a decommodification index (Esping-Andersen, 1990, p.52), and argued that these could be broken down into three distinct clusters (regimes) with different types of welfare provision, resulting from the different political contexts of the countries within these. The three regimes which he identified were the social democratic, the corporatist and the liberal; and he also selected three countries which could provide examples of each of these: Sweden, Germany and the USA respectively (see Table 14.1).

Table 14.1   Characteristics of welfare regime ideal types

	Sweden	**Germany**	**USA**
Regime	Social Democratic	Corporatist	Liberal
Political base	Broad-based compromise	Employer/Worker coalition	Free market
Service type	Universal	Occupational	Residual
Public expenditure	High level	High level	Low level
Labour market	High employment High wage	Low employment High wage	High employment Low wage

Source: Alcock and Craig (2001), p.19, Table 1.2.

Esping-Andersen's typology of welfare regimes has dominated comparative analysis of the international dimension of social policy since its first publication in 1990, primarily because it provided a framework for comparison to be made between structures and trends according to fixed and measurable criteria, whereas much previous comparative research had merely described the welfare characteristics of different countries. Esping-Andersen himself later used the model to examine the ways in which different regimes were responding to the pressures of globalisation in the early 1990s (Esping-Andersen, 1996); he concluded that different regime types did respond in different ways, which challenged the globalisation convergence thesis mentioned above.

Others have also adapted and developed his approach to extend the framework to other national and international contexts. In particular this has led a number of authors to argue that there may in practice be more than three regime types across the developed world. For instance, Leibfried (1993) and Ferrera (1996) have suggested that there might be a fourth type within Europe associated with the more limited public welfare nations of the 'Latin Rim' (Spain, Portugal and Greece). Castles and Mitchell (1991) identified another regime in the largely means-tested welfare systems of Australia and New Zealand; and other regime types have been suggested in the former communist countries (B Deacon *et al.*, 1992) and the 'tiger economies' of the Pacific Rim (C Jones, 1993). There have also been those who have criticised Esping-Anderson for limitations within his theoretical framework and data base: for instance, Lewis (1992) argued that he ignored gender dimensions within welfare provision and that these could have altered the construction of his regimes.

Nevertheless the welfare regime approach has become well established within social policy analysis, and the fact that most commentators now argue about extensions or criticisms of Esping-Andersen's work suggests that his basic approach remains influential. Welfare regime theory permits us to compare the different structures and characteristics of different welfare systems. This can help us understand our own country, and its regime, better, and can also mean that lessons can be learnt about future policy development from those regimes which have approached similar problems in different ways, and perhaps with more success. Policy development in one country, such as the UK, can therefore be influenced by our knowledge of development elsewhere. However, this does not just happen at a general level; it can also take place with specific policy ideas and initiatives, where these are developed in one country and then copied elsewhere.

The copying of initiatives developed in one country by another is now referred to as *policy transfer*, and it has become an important feature of recent comparative policy analysis and political theory (see Dolowitz and Marsh, 1996; Dolowitz *et al.*, 2000). Of course, the adaptation of policy ideas from one country to another is hardly a new one; the social insurance developed by Bismarck in Germany in the later nineteenth century was copied in many other countries over the next century and the British NHS of 1948 provided a model for public health services across the world. However, it is only more recently that such policy transfer has been studied and researched as a form of policy making, and that the full range of its advantages, and disadvantages, has been more widely discussed.

Over the last decade or so there have been some important examples of policy transfer openly pursued by the UK government. The Child Support Agency, introduced by the Conservatives in the early 1990s, was modelled in part upon similar provision which had been operating in Australia. The close ideological links between the British and US administrations at the turn of the century, notably the similar views of Tony Blair and the then US President, Bill Clinton, led to Britain adopting a number of American policy initiatives in the area of employment policy, with both the New Deal and the working tax credit (see Chapters 7 and 2) being based upon similar US programmes (see Dolowitz, 1998; A Deacon, 2000).

The influence of Australian and American practices on UK policy making is in part a consequence of the close political and linguistic links between the countries, themselves a consequence of the fact that both in the past were colonies in the former British empire. Britain also has close geographical and cultural links with continental Europe, however; and in the latter part of the last century in particular, these links began to encourage policy transfer and policy development within Europe too. Of course this European policy development is now dominated by the policies and practices of the European Union (EU), which provides a much more formal, and more powerful, supranational control over economic and social policy planning within its member states.

QUESTIONS: COMPREHENSION

- In what ways do global agencies now shape international social policy?
- What did Esping-Andersen mean by 'welfare regimes', and how has this notion been developed by later comparative social policy commentators?
- What is 'policy transfer', and how has it influenced policy development in the UK?

QUESTION: REFLECTION

- Can national governments ignore global economic forces in the planning of social policy?

Social policy in Europe

The EU is not the only international agency influencing social policy in Europe. The *Council of Europe* is a broader-based body, initially covering the whole of Western Europe and now including also the former communist Eastern nations, with a membership of almost 40 countries. It acts to promote human rights amongst its members and established a European Court of Human Rights with supranational authority. It has also sought to influence social policy through the establishment in 1961 of a Social Charter embodying rights for workers and citizens which member nations can (but do not have to) take up (Brewster and Teague, 1989, p.10). Because of this largely voluntary coordination the Council has not been as important in influencing social policy in Europe as the EU, which for its members at least is a club within which members must agree to share in the policy making and abide by the rules developed.

The EU emerged from the reconstruction of Western Europe which took place after the end of the Second World War. To prevent the political and economic competition which might lead to further wars, the major nations of continental Western Europe decided to join together to share and to plan economic development; and since then they have been joined by many of the other Western European nations, including Britain. What started out as a community of nations sharing economic planning has developed into a single European market for goods and services, capital and labour, with a European legislature and a massive bureaucracy responsible for a wide range of international initiatives and a (largely) single European currency. Since its establishment in the 1950s the EU has been growing in scale and influence, and since Britain joined in 1973 this influence has shaped the way economic and social policy has developed here, too; indeed, in the three decades since then the influence of the EU has become ever more pervasive.

There is now an extensive literature on social policy development within the EU both examining the development and operation of the EU (Geyer, 2000; Hantrais, 2000; Kleinman, 2002) and exploring the more general trends in policy making in the member nations (George and Taylor-Gooby, 1996; Bonoli, George and Taylor-Gooby, 2000). What these and other authors point out is that European social policy analysis must take account of the different understandings and structures of social policy within the different countries since there are various different welfare regimes operating within the EU. There are a number of dimensions to this difference, or *diversity* as it is generally called, but (as can be seen in Figure 14.1) broad variations can be seen simply by looking at overall spending levels and the relation of these to GDP. What is more, Figure 14.1 reveals that this diversity has become more pronounced as the EU has grown, with the later members exhibiting an ever wider range of spending patterns, and this will be accentuated even further when the new accession countries in Eastern Europe have joined.

Such diversity is in part a product of the different ways in which social policy is conceived within the different member nations. In Britain social policy has traditionally been associated with the planning and delivery of the major welfare services, such as education and health (see Chapters 2–6). In some other European countries, however, social policy practice also includes employment

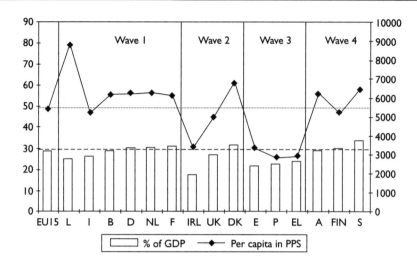

Figure 14.1 Social protection expenditure in EU member states, as a percentage of GDP and per capita in proportionate personal spending, 1997

Source: Hantrais, (2000) p.31, Figure 2.1; data from Eurostat (2000), Table 1 and Figure 2.

relations and employment rights, family structure and family support, industrial training, health and safety, and other activities that clearly are policy driven and do affect the lives of all people, but which have not been subject to policy analysis, or in some cases even policy planning, in Britain. These differences can make comparison difficult. They have also, however, led to some conflict over the proper scope of EU social policy influence (for instance, attempts by the EU to regulate employment rights under the rubric of health and safety measures have led on occasions to opposition from some countries, in particular the UK).

The more general differences between welfare regimes pose more significant problems for the broader development of EU policy making. One of the original aims of the founder nations of the EC was the eventual *harmonisation* of welfare provision within a single European model, perhaps as a precursor to a *federal* European state that could plan social and economic policy across the existing member nations. This is still the hope of some EU members but, as the wider range of welfare regimes now included within the Union reveals, it has become a more and more distant goal as the Union has expanded and diversified. Furthermore, the hope that there might be a gradual convergence towards the corporatist, labour-market and family-based protection of the north-western continental regimes now seems to be contradicted by recent moves towards a more liberal or residual regime in Britain, and by fears in Denmark and Sweden that their more comprehensive and universal welfare state should not be watered down by European pluralism.

In the more immediate term, therefore, the goal of harmonisation has effectively been replaced by a policy of convergence: a more limited commitment to the development of shared, or European-wide, social policy initiatives around particular issues of international importance or in areas where standardisation of practices will ensure fair competition between nations within a single economic market. However, even this level of convergence is contradicted to some extent by another key EU principle: subsidiarity.

Subsidiarity is based on the German practice of seeking to devolve decision making and initiative taking to the smallest possible local base, thus encouraging participatory activity rather than top-down state paternalism. This strategy is supposedly now being replicated throughout the EU. However, it has often been understood by some member states (notably Britain) to mean that policy decisions taken by national governments are preferable to international directives from the EU Commission, which in effect means that federalist tendencies can be resisted at a national level.

Harmonisation and subsidiarity are political principles. They have been important in shaping the development of policy making within the EU, but they have not been the only factors. The primary aim for the initial establishment of the Union was the pursuit of collaborative economic development, as we shall discuss below; and the result of this is that economic development within Europe has also created pressures for social policy planning to deal with the consequences of this.

One of the consequences of economic planning and development taking place at a European level has been the concentration of the power, and the advantage, of economic development into a small central core within the EU, sometimes referred to as a *golden triangle* based between Frankfurt, Paris and Milan. As this has happened the more peripheral regions, including much of Britain, have experienced relative economic decline. This can only be counteracted by the use of European-wide social policy initiatives to redirect resources and investments towards these peripheral areas, and, as we shall see, this has become a key feature of EU social policy action and has led to a growing role for the EU in promoting regional economic and social development.

The concentration of economic power and benefit is not, however, the only broader social policy implication of collaborative economic development within the EU. There are also fears that employers within the Union seeking to reduce costs through the use of cheap labour will transfer capital resources around the new Union in order to employ those workers with the worst pay and conditions, and the least expensive social protection (a process sometimes referred to as *social dumping*). The effect of this over time could lead to a general downward drift in conditions and protections throughout the Union if all countries or regions ended up seeking to compete with each other by lowering standards. Again, a response to this requires European-wide commitments to minimum standards and enforceable rights for workers, and this has been a major factor in promoting the regulation of employment and other rights through initiatives such as the Social Charter.

A reverse tendency to the problem of social dumping is the accompanying fear of *social tourism*. Workers, or more especially non-workers, in disadvantaged regions with poor social protection are likely to be encouraged to exercise the rights which they enjoy within the EU to move around within the Union in order to seek improved protection in other countries where this exists.

Thus those nations with better social welfare protection may find increased pressure of demand on these protections from the mobile population of countries with less well-developed social services. This is a fear that has in part been responsible for restrictions on social security entitlement in Britain for those not 'normally resident' within the country. However, only enforceable European-wide planning and European standards could counteract these tendencies effectively across the Union, providing yet another source of pressure for integrated social policy development.

When viewed in this light, the greater integration of European social policy across the member nations of the new Union seems to be an inevitable process and, from the point of view of the majority of workers and citizens throughout the Union, a desirable one; for without the attempt to guarantee social standards across the member states, there may be pressure on all governments to reduce protection in order to secure short-term economic advantage. Economic concentration has therefore inevitably been followed by social concentration and an ever more extensive role for EU social policy making, as the development and structure of the Union reveals.

The development of the European Union

The history of the EU is primarily a story of the gradual development of European cooperation from the limited goals of the original six members in securing some shared political vision and economic regeneration after the ravages of the Second World War, to the federalist ideals of a European super-state that could be the world's most powerful economic block – and most progressive social regime – in the twenty-first century. This is a process during which the EEC, as it was first called, has expanded in size and at the same time has increased the extent and depth of its activities and aspirations.

The expansion in size has seen the Union grow from six nations to 15, with the pace of expansion becoming increasingly rapid towards the end of the last century:

- *1957* France, West Germany, Italy, Belgium, the Netherlands, Luxembourg
- *1973* UK, Ireland, Denmark
- *1981* Greece
- *1986* Spain, Portugal
- *1995* Austria, Sweden, Finland (Norway voted not to join).

In the early years of the new century the EU will expand further when a number of the countries in Eastern Europe are granted membership of the Union, including the Czech Republic, Estonia, Hungary, Slovenia and Poland, plus Cyprus and Malta. The principle of such further extension has now been agreed by the current 15 members, although the consequences of such an expansion for both economic development and political process are likely to alter significantly the balance of EU policy making.

Before the EEC proper was established by the *Treaty of Rome*, signed by the original six members in 1957, the same countries had already embarked on limited joint economic planning to deal with socio-economic consequences of industrial change in the form of the European Coal and Steel Community, which followed the *Treaty of Paris* of 1951. The Treaty of Rome, however, established a much more extensive base for joint economic development. There was a total of 248 articles in the treaty covering a wide range of matters of shared concern or commitment, although most focused on economic policy (Hantrais, 2000, ch.1).

The Treaty of Rome began what can be categorised as the *first* phase of development of social policy within the EEC/EU. This period ran from 1957 to 1972 and was characterised largely by the promotion and regulation of movement between labour markets within the new community. At this time such social policy activity as existed was closely tied to the broader aims of economic development within the six member states with no specific social goals being pursued (hence the focus on labour mobility).

The *second* phase of development, from 1973 to 1984, following the first expansion of the Community, saw a more extensive concern with employment-related social rights across the member nations. There were attempts to harmonise and upgrade basic employment rights: for example, in the areas of equal pay and equal treatment for men and women. This period also saw the implementation of the Community's first social action programme which was begun in 1974. Although it was outside the formal treaty commitments, this had the political support of all members and resulted in a number of important new community-wide initiatives, such as an anti-poverty poverty programme, and the establishment of community agencies to monitor and develop social issues, such as the European Foundation for the Improvement of Living and Working Conditions which was established in Dublin in 1975.

The *third* phase of development followed the accession of the Frenchman, Jacques Delors, to the Presidency of the Commission, and ran from 1985 to 1992. Delors is credited with developing a social dimension to supplement the focus on economic development that had always dominated the EC (or *l'espace sociale*, as it was called in French). So at the same time as economic planning was drawing closer together – notably through the commitment of most nations to a European exchange-rate agreement (the European Monetary System, EMS) – social commitments to workers' rights were also placed on the EC agenda, and the range of scope of Community-wide social programmes and initiatives was expanded.

In 1985 high-level talks on socio-economic issues were held at Val Duchesse in Belgium and, following this, new legislation (the Single European Act) was signed by all countries in 1986. The Act emphasised a commitment by the Community to social cohesion as a corollary to economic cohesion, and European activities in the social field were considerably expanded. The idea of social rights for citizens within the Community was taken further in 1989 by the drafting of the *Community Charter of the Fundamental Social Rights of Workers* (the EU Social Charter: see Grahl and Teague, 1990, p.211).

The EU charter was similar in some ways to the earlier Social Charter developed by the Council of Europe, and it similarly focused primarily upon rights at work. It echoed the continuing domination of economic concerns over social issues within the Community and the fact that the labour-market focus remained the major focus of social policy in the most powerful nations of continental Western Europe. Like the Council of Europe Charter, the EC Charter was not legally binding on members. However, at Strasbourg in 1989, it was adopted by all member states, with the exception of the UK, and has sometimes since been referred to as the *social dimension* of the Single European Act.

The 1980s also saw a much increased use of EC structural funds and community-wide initiatives, such as the poverty programmes, to secure social policy goals and, in particular, to attempt to mitigate some of the deleterious consequences of the economic restructuring which followed the concentration of economic growth within the core of the Community. Knowledge about these social changes was also a much more important feature of the EC agenda, not least because of the increased activity of Community agencies such as the statistical office, the Dublin Foundation and some of the newly established *Observatories* examining issues such as ageing and social exclusion; these EC-wide agencies began to provide the Community with more extensive and detailed information about social and economic trends, both within and across member states.

However, concern with social and economic trends within the community became even more significant in the *fourth* phase of development, which began after the creation of the Single European Market in 1992 and continued with the signing of the *Maastricht Treaty* that year, which formally transformed the EC into the European Union. The creation of the single market was the logical conclusion of the plans for economic cooperation that had begun in 1951. All trade and tariff barriers between member states were removed; goods, labour and capital could now move freely from one country to another. For employers and employees, therefore, national boundaries within the Union no longer had any practical significance.

There was some opposition to these further extensions of EU policy influence within the Maastricht Treaty, however, fuelled in part by concerns that moves towards more extensive economic and political union would now be likely to develop more rapidly. Denmark initially voted against adoption of the treaty; but the most vociferous opposition came from the UK, led by John Major. Britain secured an arrangement which permitted it to opt out of the creation of the single European currency envisaged by Maastricht, and to opt out of endorsement of the Social Chapter, which (through a separate Protocol to the treaty) committed the member states to implementing the Social Charter (Hantrais, 2000, p.11). As we shall see, Britain has always been a somewhat reluctant participant in the moves towards greater harmony of economic and social policy planning within the EU, and at Maastricht it was clear that not all member states were always going to be able to agree on the pace and direction of policy change.

This disagreement did not prevent the Union pressing ahead with economic and social policy reform, however, including the publishing of White Papers on Growth and Competitiveness (European Commission, 1993) and Social Policy (European Commission, 1994). The social policy White Paper maintained the formal priority on employment rights and job creation, but also argued that the

EU should work more generally to preserve and develop the European social model; and following this a series of social action programmes were developed by the Commission (Hantrais, 2000; Kleinman, 2002).

After the 1997 UK election the new Labour government adopted a much more participatory stance towards EU policy making. The new government acted quickly to endorse the EU Social Charter and in 1997 signed the *Treaty of Amsterdam*, which consolidated this and a number of other social policy measures into the main body of the EU Treaty. Nevertheless Britain did not join with the majority eleven member nations in the establishment of formal monetary union in January 1999, and neither did it join the new European currency (the *Euro*) introduced in January 2002.

At the beginning of the twenty-first century, therefore, it has become clearer that there are differences of opinion about the extent and depth of European integration that should be pursued within the EU. This is likely to be extended further when the candidate nations from Eastern Europe are admitted to membership. Some commentators have talked about the need to develop a 'twin track' approach to policy making within the Union, permitting those that want to take integration further to do so, even if some others do not wish to participate in this. Such a principle may in practice be little more than a recognition of the political reality of national interests, of course, and once recognised may lead to the identification of more than two tracks as accommodation of the different interests of different members is sought within an ostensibly single planning framework.

QUESTIONS: COMPREHENSION

- What are the obstacles to the harmonisation of social policy within the member nations of the EU?
- What is 'social dumping', and why has it been important in the development of EU social policy?
- What was *l'espace sociale*, and how did it transform social policy making within the EU?

QUESTION: REFLECTION

- To what extent will the further expansion of the EU make it more difficult to achieve harmony in social policy planning across the Union?

The institutions of the European Union

The problem for this single planning framework is that the EU, and the EEC which preceded it, is constituted by the coming together of initially separate member states, and is still predominantly run – or 'governed' – by the representatives of the member governments. The EU is an association of member nations rather than a separate political entity, as the Federal government of the USA is. The forum for the meeting of these representatives is the *Council of Ministers* (meeting in Brussels) consisting of the relevant ministers, depending on the business in hand, from each country. The heads of government also meet twice a year to take major policy decisions. The presidency of the Council rotates on a six-monthly basis between all the member states, providing an opportunity for all the different influences to be brought to bear at different times.

The Council determines policy for the Union. However, policy development is generally based on the proposals made by the *European Commission*, which in effect operates as a kind of civil service for the Council. The Commission is also based in Brussels and comprises a vast administrative network, led by permanent Commissioners appointed by each member state, and a President (at present Romano Prodi, an Italian). The Commission initiates and implements EU legislation, which is approved by the Council. An early example of this process in the social policy field was the approval by the Council of Commission recommendations for *directives* on equal pay and equal treatment between men and women in the 1970s. These then became binding on member governments, forcing some (such as the UK) to alter legislation in their countries to bring it into line with the directive.

The vast administrative machinery of the Commission is divided into a number of departments, or Directorate Generals (DGs), with responsibility for different aspects of EU policy development and implementation, the main one in the social policy area being DGV, which is responsible for employment, industrial relations and social affairs. The Commission has also established a number of other bodies operating to develop, implement or monitor policy on a community-wide basis. These include the EU statistical service (*Eurostat*), the research *Observatories* comprising academic representatives from all member states (such as the Observatory on National Family Policies) and various European *Centres* (such as the one for the Development of Vocational Training, CEDEFOP, in Berlin).

If the Commission is the EU's civil service, then the *European Court of Justice* (sitting in Luxembourg) is its judiciary, acting as the guardian of the treaties and the enforcer of legislation and directives. The court is controlled by judges appointed for six-year terms of office and it operates as an autonomous legal system over and above the legal systems of the different countries. All citizens, and member states, can use the court; and, if the court finds a country to be acting in breach of treaty commitments, that country must change its legislation to comply (as happened in the UK to equal pay legislation in the 1970s).

In terms of constitutional theory, therefore, we might expect that the *European Parliament* (sitting in Strasbourg) would be the legislative body of the EU especially as, since 1979, its members have been directly elected by all EU citizens. However, the member governments have not ceded any real political power to the European Parliament and continue to exercise control over all major policy making through the Council of Ministers. In practice, therefore, no new legislation can be initiated in Strasbourg. Nevertheless, the Parliament does have something of a blocking power, since it can refuse to support a Commission proposal; and it can also require the Commission to answer questions or supply information. Furthermore, as the Union develops, it seems likely that the powers of the Parliament will expand.

The other major EU social policy institution is the *Economic and Social Committee*, which comprises direct representatives of employers, workers and other interest groups throughout the community. Like the Parliament, the Committee has no power to initiate legislative change but it does provide a forum for consultation and representation on a range of social and economic issues (including, for example, the social action programmes and the Social Charter). In effect, the Committee has something of a 'watchdog' role situated within the complex set of institutional checks and balances which seek to ensure that policy making within the EU follows the wishes and interests of a broad spectrum of the population across the community. It is also an example of the formal commitment within the EU to a corporatist approach to policy making which seeks to involve these different major interests (sometime referred to as the *social partners*) in policy-making processes.

European social programmes

As the EU has developed from economic cooperation to social partnership, the concern of the Council of Ministers, and more especially the Commission, has focused increasingly upon the European-wide implications of the economic development that the Union has fostered, and in particular the deleterious social consequences of this and the inequitable distribution of these consequences throughout the different member nations. What is more, the development of European Centres and Observatories to examine these social trends has created internal pressure within the Commission to act to redress some of the worst and most pressing of these developments; and this in turn has resulted in proposals being brought before the Council for action at a European level. The result of this pressure has been the establishment of an increasingly extensive and far-reaching set of community-wide social policy initiatives, or programmes, designed to counter – or at least to alleviate – the growing social problems that have been identified.

The main initiatives used to counteract the consequences of social and economic restructuring have been the *European Structural Funds*. There were initially three separate structural funds (Kleinman, 2002, ch.5):

- the *European Social Fund* (ESF) for employment and training initiatives
- the *European Regional Development Fund* (ERDF) to improve infrastructure in depressed regions
- the *European Agricultural Guidance and Guarantee Fund* (FEOGA) to assist in rural change and development.

However, after the Single European Act, these separate funds were extended and integrated in order to maximise their impact within member states, and after Maastricht they were extended further to include a new Cohesion Fund. In effect, the funds now operate as one general programme for employment, infrastructure and agricultural change, providing support for projects initiated or supported by national governments in areas of established social need. The targeting of funds is now determined by the designation of specific regions within countries as priority areas for European support, against a series of criteria, or objectives, agreed by the Council. In effect therefore it is a major programme for regional redistribution within the Union, intended to counter-balance some of the effects of the geographical concentration of economic development. In the last century there were seven such objectives, distributing resources across a wide range of areas across the member nations. However, since 2000 these have been reduced to three (Kleinman, 2002, ch.5):

- *Objective 1* – the most deprived areas
- *Objective 2* – areas facing industrial decline, rural areas, urban areas and those affecting by fishing industry decline
- *Objective 3* – assistance to education, training and employment.

Spending on the structural funds grew rapidly in the latter years of the last century to over €32 billion, more than a third of the EU budget (although it is expected to decline over the next few years: see Kleinman, 2002, p.114). In the 1990s most of this spending also went to the first two objectives, covering around one-half of the EU population, although the proportion covered by the first two objectives will decline under the new regime in the new century.

The development of the social programmes is also likely to be affected significantly by the extension of EU membership to the candidate nations in Eastern Europe. These countries already face more serious problems of economic decline and industrial restructuring than most of even the poorer areas of Western Europe, and ironically membership of the Union may only serve in the short run to accentuate the gap between them and the prosperous 'golden triangle'. The programmes to promote economic and social development through regional redistribution may therefore have to reassess their priorities and to recognise that even further elements of redistribution within European social policy practice will be required in an expanded EU.

Britain in the European Union

As we have seen, Britain was not a member of the original 1951 Coal and Steel Community or of the EEC which was established by the Treaty of Rome in 1957. During the 1960s the British government sought to alter this isolation and applied on several occasions to join the Community, but their application for entry was vetoed by France; so when Britain did eventually join in 1973 it was after a decade of waiting. Thus it might be expected that there was widespread political support and enthusiasm for membership and future European cooperation within the country. However, this was not the case.

In the 1970s the Labour Party, which was in government from 1974 to 1979, was split over the question of EEC membership. Partly in order to quell the divisions within the party, the Prime Minister, Harold Wilson, organised a referendum in 1976 on the question of whether or not to continue membership. This resulted in a significant majority in favour of continuation, thus isolating Labour's anti-Europeans. Some of this early Labour opposition to the Community was based on its initial predominantly economic focus and narrow labour-market concerns. When this focus began to change, with the development of a stronger social dimension in the 1980s, the Labour Party (now in opposition) adopted a much more united policy of support for the EU, which has largely continued since the 1997 election.

At the same time in the 1980s, however, the Conservative Party in government began to divide over Europe. A significant, and vocal, minority of Conservative MPs became overtly hostile to the extending powers and influence of the European Commission, in particular in the social policy field. Some of this hostility was also shared by the Prime Minister, Margaret Thatcher, who led Britain into a much more oppositional role within the Council of Ministers, frequently speaking out against new policy initiatives and far-reaching federalist plans. Britain did not join the European Exchange Rate Mechanism in the 1980s, preferring to pursue a separate monetary policy; and, although this changed with membership being agreed in 1990, Britain quickly withdrew again when the 1990s recession began to bite (see Chapter 13). British reluctance to participate in further EU development continued under Major with the opt-out arrangements over the single currency and the Social Chapter at Maastricht in 1992.

In the new century the Labour government's more positive approach towards EU participation has meant that for the first time since joining in 1973 Britain has a government that is largely committed to the maintenance of an active role in EU policy making and to ensuring that Britain's economic and social development is closely tied into that of its co-members on the continent. This has meant that social policy initiatives such as the Social Charter have now been implemented in the UK: for example, an EU directive on working time now regulates the maximum number of hours that most workers can be required to work each week and provides for a minimum paid holiday entitlement. It has also meant that Blair and the other government ministers are more willing to discuss and agree to further programmes for social action within the Council of Ministers, and so to a continued extension of EU social policy practice.

Despite this, however, Britain remained outside the single currency in 2002, and has remained reluctant to fix a date for entry into the new 'Euro zone', arguing that this will only happen when the indicators reveal that it is in the country's economic interest to do so, and only if a majority support the move in a national referendum. How long Britain will be able to maintain this relative isolation is, of course, a matter of judgement. Membership of the EU has sometimes been likened to travelling down a one-way street: one may be able to slow down or even stop, but once in the street one cannot turn round and go back.

QUESTIONS: COMPREHENSION

- To what extent is the EU is an organisation of nations rather than citizens?
- What are the EU social programmes, and how have they sought to redistribute resources within member nations?

QUESTION: REFLECTION

- Why has Britain been such a 'reluctant' member of the EU?

FURTHER READING

The impact of globalism on social policy, in particular as it affects Europe, is discussed in the papers in Sykes, Palier and Prior (2001). Deacon, Hulse and Stubbs (1997) provide a useful guide to the growing role of international agencies in the development of policy. The most useful book on the structure and operation of the EU is Hantrais (2000), now in its second edition; and Kleinman (2002) provides a good discussion of social policy development within the EU. EU documents can be accessed through their general website at **www.europa.eu.int**. There are two useful websites providing a forum for information on global social policy, **www.globalpolicy.org/socecon** and **www.worldforum.org**.

Devolution and Local Control

SUMMARY OF KEY POINTS

- The UK is only in part a 'United Kingdom'. There is significant devolution of policy-making powers to Scotland, Wales and Northern Ireland.
- There is also some devolution of social and economic planning to Regional Development Agencies in England, and elected Regional Assemblies are under consideration.
- Local government became established in Britain by the end of the nineteenth century. However, Britain retains a relatively unitary and centralised state structure.
- Local councils played a key role in the development of much economic and social policy provision, although the extent of local government powers was in decline throughout much of the last century as the balance between central and local control of policy planning shifted.
- Local authority income is made up of local taxes (Council Tax), charges for services and grants from central government.
- In the 1980s cash limits and cutbacks in government grants were used to control local government, leading to conflict with central government over the extent of local autonomy over service planning.
- Further reductions in local autonomy have followed from the contracting-out of some local services and the imposition of audit and inspection of local services.
- The different electoral bases of central and local government have been a source of conflict between them, usually flowing from differences in party political control in each.
- Local governance has meant a shift in the role of local councils from service provision to that of *enabling* authorities.

Devolved policy making

Most discussion and analysis of social policy in Britain focuses upon policy making at the national level and the role of the national government in determining and delivering public policy. However, policy making and policy delivery do not just take place at a national level. As we saw in Chapter 14 there are external international pressures on UK policy development, which restrict the power and freedom of the British government. There are also restrictions on national policy making which flow from structures and pressures within the nation, however. Indeed the British state has always had an internal political structure within which political power and policy-making authority does not always reside at a national level; and in recent times this devolved structure for policy making and policy delivery has become more accentuated and more diverse across a range of geographical and political dimensions.

For a start, as we saw in Chapter 8, the UK is only to some extent a 'United Kingdom'. It is comprised of the separate nations (or subnations) of England, Scotland, Wales and Northern Ireland. These separate nations have always had some level of autonomy from the British government in Westminster and Whitehall (for instance, in Scotland there has always been a separate legal system with different courts and a separate judiciary operating under significantly different legal principles, at least in some areas of law). Towards the end of the last century, however, there was increased pressure from Scotland, Wales and Northern Ireland for greater autonomy from the UK government in policy making and service delivery; indeed, there were political parties arguing for complete independence which attracted significant (though only minority) support in elections.

The UK government had always had separate offices overseeing public policy in Scotland and Wales, and in Northern Ireland there were a number of separate administrative structures controlling policies such as housing and education across the province; but these offices had largely been responsible for policies decided by the national government in Westminster. In 1999, however, the new Labour government moved beyond administrative separation to introduce genuine devolution of policy-making powers to separate elected bodies in these three countries. In Scotland this took the form of a new Scottish Parliament with legislative powers in certain designated areas. In Northern Ireland an elected Assembly, also with restricted legislative powers, was established as part of the power-sharing agreements flowing from the Good Friday peace process. In Wales an elected National Assembly was set up with lesser secondary legislative powers, requiring parliamentary approval in Westminster for any changes to primary laws.

The different constitutional position in each of these three countries is the product of the different political and institutional structures already operating within them and the varying strength of feeling on devolution expressed in referenda held there before formal devolution took place. They make understanding the different political and policy developments within the UK an ever more complex issue, which we can only briefly refer to here. The result is that the political and administrative structures are somewhat different in each of the three countries (see Adams and Robinson, 2002; Parry, 2003). In Scotland and

Wales there are separate coordinating bodies implementing devolved policy powers, known as the Scottish Executive and the Welsh Assembly Government (based on the former Scottish and Welsh Offices). In Northern Ireland there are a number of separate functional departments, such as education and health, with some coordination provided by the Office of the First Minister and Deputy First Minister.

In all cases, however, the range of policy matters devolved to the separate administrations is similar and includes education and training, health, social services, housing and planning, and local government (see Adams and Robinson, 2002, pp.16–19). In all these areas devolution has already led to some significant departures in policy development: for instance, the decisions to provide free higher education tuition and universal free long-term care for vulnerable adults in Scotland, and the abandonment of school performance league tables in Wales.

Devolution to Scotland, Wales and Northern Ireland leaves unresolved, of course, the question of what should happen about policy making within England, the largest country in the UK with 85 per cent of the population. In practice nothing much has really changed here, with the British Parliament being the legislative body for England on those issues where elsewhere power is devolved to the new national bodies (which has led to some political conflict over the role Scottish, Welsh and Irish MPs in Westminster should play in determining legislation to be applied only to England). However, the size of England itself has led to increasing concern about the extent to which policy making and delivery could also be devolved here; and since 1997 the Labour government has begun to develop some new elements of policy of devolution within England. For instance, the introduction of the new office of the Mayor in London has resulted in the pursuit of some separate policy initiatives, such as congestion charging on roads in the capital. Other local areas have also been given the power to establish mayors, though not many have done so and none would have the extent of power wielded in London, where the mayor's office is the only base for policy planning across the capital.

Devolution has also been taking place to some extent at regional level in England, however. Regional government has never traditionally played any significant role in political or policy practice in England, or in the UK more generally. By contrast regional government can be found in a number of advanced industrial countries, including some in the EU; and regional planning has been a significant feature of EU social policy activity, particularly in the context of support for economic and social regeneration, where it is regions which are the focus for EU finding (see Chapter 14). Nevertheless some elements of regional policy development had begun towards the end of the last century with the establishment by the previous Conservative administration of Government Offices for the Regions (GORs) to coordinate some aspects of policy development and delivery at regional level within the country.

The GORs reflected a recognition that, in some policy areas at least, national planning was unable to respond to the different needs and circumstances of different parts of the country; and that the local government structures that we shall discuss below were focused too specifically upon their own local area to be able to address broader regional trends. The Labour government has taken this further with some element of devolution in policy practice being extended to the English regions. In each region a Regional Development Agency (RDA) has been established, many taking their name from the region itself (such as *Advantage West Midlands*). The RDAs are supported by the GORs and have responsibility for some limited aspects of policy delivery: for instance, they manage the Single Regeneration Budget programme support for economic and social regeneration projects in the region. At present the RDAs are appointed bodies, mainly comprised of representatives from the constituent local authorities, and their development has been a rather top-down process steered and managed by central government. A move to elected regional assemblies would provide a more bottom-up and democratic basis for regional government and is likely to follow if present commitments to devolution are maintained even though, of course, this would further complicate the distribution of power within the country and could accentuate some of the dilemmas surrounding the relations between central and local government which have been a significant feature of policy development over the last century or more.

QUESTIONS: COMPREHENSION

■ What are the main policy areas now devolved to separate national administrations within the UK, and what have been the consequences of this for policy development?
■ To what extent is policy making devolved to regional level within England, and how is this pattern changing?

QUESTION: REFLECTION

■ Will devolution lead to end of the British welfare state?

The central–local dimension

The recent moves towards the devolution of policy making to subnational and regional bodies in the UK has largely been the result of a top-down transfer of power from central government. However, a longer historical review of the development of public services in Britain reveals that it is local initiatives that have frequently been the driving force behind the establishment and extension of many major services, and that the local administration and delivery of services is still a major operational feature of modern welfare provision. Indeed in many ways it would be more accurate to say that modern British welfare has its roots in the initiatives and activities of local, *rather* than central, government within the country.

The history, and current state, of the relationship between central and local government in the development of welfare services is, however, a complex – and at times a conflictual – one. In particular in organisational terms, the extent of devolution of power and responsibility that can be made to the local level is fraught with difficulties and contradictions. For instance, if local administrators have the power to determine the shape, or size, of local services, how can consistent standards of service for users be maintained between different areas? And, if local responsibility for services is based upon the power of locally elected representatives, does this not provide a basis for political conflict between local and central government? Both of these are problems that dogged the relationship between central and local government in Britain in the latter half of the twentieth century, as we shall see. As a result the central–local dimension of social policy development is both complex and fraught and, as a consequence of this, it is also constantly changing. The current distribution and operation of responsibilities are the products of such a process of change.

In examining the central or local balance of policy control, however, it is important to distinguish between the local administration and delivery of welfare (or other) services and the local government of such services. Of course, most welfare services are delivered, and thus *administered*, on a local basis, even where all aspects of policy and practice are determined directly by central government. Citizens using such services on a day-to-day basis are likely to have access only to their local area office. However, for services which are governed nationally, this local administration of central welfare services is merely an organisational feature of the structure of delivery to users, who need a local point of contact with those providing the service (for instance, the local benefits office or jobcentre provides a base from which claimants can pursue their entitlement to social security benefits).

By contrast the local *government* of welfare services means that these are the direct responsibility of a set of politicians elected by the local population, operating with powers and duties that are quite separate from those of national politicians in the central state, and which may even conflict with these. For instance, education services, although they are constrained by statute to provide certain standards in teaching and learning, are controlled by local councillors who can set the policy priorities for development and delivery of these within their local area; and local authority housing has been planned, designed and built according to policies set by local politicians, sometimes against central government priorities. Local government is therefore a separate sphere within the state, with a guaranteed constitutional status (once referred to by one commentator as the 'local state': see Cockburn, 1977).

In fact, most welfare capitalist countries have local, as well as central, state machinery as a constitutional feature of their political make-up, and these enjoy clear, yet delineated, powers over both policy development and implementation. The central–local political divide is a widespread international phenomenon; and in comparative terms this divide can take a number of different forms. In particular it is important to distinguish between two broad categories of central–local structure:

1. *Unitary* states have a central government which has historically been the major political base of the country and has the exclusive power to legislate and thus determine the broad structure of policy throughout the country, although in unitary states some powers and responsibilities are usually

devolved by legislation to local government. Leaving aside for a moment the devolution of powers discussed earlier, the UK is an example of a unitary state; and within the UK central government politicians have greater power and influence than local politicians.

2. *Federalist* states are generally the product historically of the coming together of a number of smaller administrative regions, each initially with their own autonomy; and, although there is now a central government covering all such regions, this autonomy is preserved to some extent (for example, by the retention of law-making powers by local states). The USA is the major example of a federalist state, where law-making powers over major aspects of social policy are retained by individual states despite national union. Here, by contrast, the power of local state politicians is such that they are considered some of the most important political actors within the country.

However, even between unitary states the extent and amount of devolved power and control varies significantly. For instance, in Europe, countries such as France and Germany have devolved control to local government to a much greater extent than is the case in Britain, with the German *Länder* appearing in some cases to have almost as much power as American *states*. In fact, in such comparative terms Britain is not just a unitary state, it is one of the most centralised; and it has become more and more centralised as its welfare services have developed.

The development of local government

The history of local government in Britain, in the context of social policy, is one of structural stagnation, and yet policy initiative. It is also a story of rapid local growth followed by a gradual loss of powers to central government, although this is a much more complex and fluctuating picture than it is sometimes presented as being. For instance, especially since the Second World War, the loss of powers has been accompanied by a significant growth in local government expenditure; and in recent years the centralising thrust of national government policy has been counteracted by the extension of local political activity into new and innovatory areas. As Stoker (1991) argued in his textbook on local government, the view of the development of local government as a history of decline is at best a one-sided one.

The rise of local government in Britain was initially closely linked to the growing impact of the process of industrialisation. The creation of new, large, urban populations led to local problems, to which the existing minimalist central state was unable to respond. The initial reaction of central government to this was to establish bodies at a local level, such as the Poor Law Boards and the Improvement Commissioners, to deal on an ad hoc basis with different social problems as they arose. In 1835, however, elected municipal councils were established in the new urban towns and cities. As the century progressed, these authorities gradually acquired responsibility for a range of local social services, such as health and housing. At the same time, however, the ad hoc bodies continued to grow, in particular through the establishment of School Boards to run local primary schools.

In 1888 local government was extended by the establishment of county councils in rural areas and municipal borough councils in the larger non-industrial towns. A separate London County Council covering the whole of the London metropolitan area was also established, providing some much-needed coordination over local services within the capital. Between 1894 and 1899 this structure of local government was completed, and in places revised, in particular through the creation of new multipurpose authorities (district councils) operating below county councils in rural areas and with responsibility for a separate set of powers and services. Similar developments also took place in Scotland. Thus throughout much of the country there were, by the end of the nineteenth century, two tiers of local government, with a larger county council including within it a number of smaller district and parish councils with various powers over different services. In the larger urban towns and cities, however, there was unitary political control within the municipal borough council.

The structure that emerged from the 1890s was thus a complex – and frequently overlapping – one. Nevertheless, it remained throughout the first three-quarters of the twentieth century and was not reformed until 1974 (1975 in Scotland), following the recommendations of the Maud Committee of 1967. Since then, however, structural reform has taken place each decade with some authorities being abolished in the 1980s and a range of others restructured or abolished in the 1990s.

In the early part of the twentieth century, however, despite an unchanging structure, local government initiative and influence within social policy grew dramatically. During this period the functions of local government also changed and expanded:

1. Control of health, highways and housing remained but the latter grew significantly in importance after the development of municipal housing for rent in the 1920s.
2. Local councils controlled and developed major infrastructural services such as gas, water and electricity.
3. In 1902 the School Boards were abolished and control over education passed to local authorities.
4. In 1929 local authorities acquired responsibility for Poor Law relief and for local hospitals and their responsibilities for children were expanded.
5. Finally, by the late 1940s local government had acquired more general control over all physical development through responsibility for town and country planning.

The first half of the last century was therefore a period of municipal enterprise and municipal development, influenced by the pioneering work of Joseph Chamberlain who, as leader of Birmingham, the largest local authority in Britain, oversaw a massive growth in local services and proudly boasted that the lives of all citizens of the city had been 'improved' by the council's achievements. The model of Birmingham was followed in particular by a number of other larger municipal authorities, for whom the power, for example, to build local authority housing allowed them to transform both physically and socially the circumstances of local people. This resulted in a massive growth in the extent of local government activity; and between 1900 and 1938 local authority expenditure increased fourfold.

The period up to the beginning of the Second World War is sometimes referred to as the heyday of local government in Britain, because it was a period of almost uninterrupted expansion on all fronts and was followed after the war by the gradual loss of many of the functions that had been created and developed in this early period. In one sense this is clearly true.

1. Control of gas and electricity was lost in 1947.
2. Control over mainstream health services was lost in 1948 when these were transferred to the NHS.
3. Control over water services was lost in 1962.
4. Control over ancillary health services was lost in 1974.
5. In the 1980s control over housing, education and personal social services was much restructured and reduced (an issue to which we shall return later).

This loss of local government services during the post-war period was made all the more significant because this was the period of the major growth of state welfare in Britain. For the Labour government of 1945–51 in particular, the vision of social policy development was one of national, rather than local, responsibility for the welfare of citizens. This can be seen most obviously in the establishment of the NHS, which took much responsibility for health provision away from local government, and of the social security system (National Insurance and National Assistance), although many functions here had effectively been lost in the 1930s.

In practice there was little effective voice from local government within the post-war Labour government and the implicit distrust of the local state to deliver national services evenly on a high-quality basis was undoubtedly compounded by the rather outdated structure within which it was trapped. Yet, although there was pressure from some quarters for reform of local government structure, this was never accorded sufficiently high political priority during the welfare reform years of the early post-war period (Stoker, 1991).

However, the centralising tendencies of the post-war period can be overexaggerated. Of the five major welfare services, three (education, housing and personal social services) remained – or, in the case of social services were placed – in local government hands. For instance, as we saw in Chapter 3, the Education Act of 1944 was the first of the welfare reforms and it placed almost total control over the establishment and running of primary and secondary schools on local government; this situation was to lead to conflict in the 1960s and later, when central government sought to change the structure of secondary education in particular, and many local councils refused to implement the required changes.

Before the reforms of the post-war period, education and housing had already become established as the major items of *expenditure* for local government (Dunleavy, 1984, pp.52–4). Throughout the 1950s and after, the rapid growth of these services fuelled a continued growth in local spending, with the result that, even though functions had been lost, local authority expenditure continued to increase (both absolutely and in proportion to overall national expenditure growth). Between 1955 and 1975 local authority expenditure increased threefold, and rose from 28 to 30 per cent of overall public expenditure. Furthermore, much of this expenditure was represented by an increase in employment in local authority services (Stoker, 1991). In terms of Keynesian economic policy, therefore, local government remained a central feature of both service delivery and the generation of economic growth.

Alongside the continued increase in local authority expenditure in the immediate post-war period, however, was a shift in the financial base for such expenditure, although this shift had already begun to take effect before the war. Local authority expenditure was, and still is, financed by income from three sources:

- local taxation raised by councils (initially these were *rates* paid by property owners and based on property values, but since 1993 they have been replaced by a similar *council tax*).
- the *charges* that authorities make for some of the services which they provide, such as adult education classes, planning applications or domiciliary care services.
- a share of national taxation revenue to cover some of the costs of local services, provided by *grants* from central government.

Originally the local development of services had been financed primarily out of local taxation through the rates, with central government money constituting only a minor source of income, and charges (providing around 30 per cent) somewhere in the middle. The role of charges has remained more or less constant, although the range and scale of charges began to grow in the 1990s. But the relative balance between rates and grants has changed dramatically, with central government grants replacing rates as the major source of income by the 1950s. The reason for this was the greater importance of national services, locally governed, such as education and housing, within local expenditure; the concern of central government was to ensure that adequate provision of these services was secured in all areas. However, the consequence of this was to provide central government, potentially at least, with much greater control over local government through the provision of central grants. This was a factor that was to become of major significance in the changing relationship between central and local government from the 1980s on.

Between the 1950s and the 1970s, therefore, the gradual expansion of the welfare state was mirrored by a gradual expansion, and enhancement, of the role of local government. Not only did the numbers of teachers, planners and social workers grow, but so too did their professional prestige and influence. With the support of their increasingly powerful public sector trade unions, local authority employees enjoyed secure employment and extensive (and some would say paternalistic) control over local services. So, although functions had been lost, it is these post-war years that were perhaps the real heyday of local government (at least in the social policy field).

Towards the end of the 1970s, however, this began to change. As we have seen, the major fuel for local government expenditure and influence was by this time the provision of welfare services; the freezing, followed by cutbacks, of these services after the onset of recession was therefore bound to lead to pressure for reductions in local authority spending and local authority influence. In the late 1970s cash limits were set for all public expenditure, including house building and education spending; and in the 1980s these cash limits became cash cuts. As we shall discuss shortly, the attempts by central government to secure reductions in local government expenditure on welfare service in the 1980s led, in practice, to major conflicts between central and local government, fuelled by the party political differences between Conservative central government and the Labour controllers of many of the major local authorities. And as a result of this a number of significant changes in the relationship between central and local government were introduced in the 1980s, in particular to restrict central financial support for local government services.

Throughout the earlier post-war period central support had taken the form of a *Rate Support Grant* (RSG) from central government to supplement local rates and to ensure that service spending commitments could be met. The problem with this was that it left the determination of local commitments in the hands of local government, and thus cuts in the RSG would tend to be perceived by local government, and local people, as cuts in service commitments. Thus it was replaced after 1980 with a regime of financial support determined on a standardised basis through the use by central government of a list of indicators of local service needs. This was called the *Grant Related Expenditure Assessment* (GREA). It was determined directly by central government and, in a climate of cuts, it was frequently well below the assessments of need made within authorities by local politicians.

The initial response of many authorities to the reduced levels of central support through GREAs was to increase local rates in order to maintain services at the levels that they felt were necessary. This, however, meant the government's overall targets for reduced public expenditure were still not being met because, in effect, they were thwarted by the continued spending of local authorities. Central government therefore sought to control the powers of local authorities to expand expenditure through increased local rates.

At first this was attempted by setting spending targets for authorities, which were enforced by reductions in the government grant if the targets were exceeded. But this did not prevent some authorities defying the government by exceeding the targets and paying the penalties through yet further increases in the rates. The government therefore sought to prevent rate increases altogether in some authorities through the introduction of *rate capping* (setting a limit on the amount of increase in the local rates); but even this was difficult to enforce in practice, and was unpopular with local electorates. So eventually the whole rating system was replaced by a new form of local taxation, the *community charge* (or 'poll tax'), which was paid by all individuals living in the area, who, it was thought, would thus be less willing to vote to elect high-spending authorities.

In fact the community charge proved to be a hopelessly ineffective and widely unpopular form of local taxation. It was difficult to collect money from all individuals and it provoked popular resistance to payment in many areas. It came into force in 1990, but by 1993 had been replaced by the new *council tax* based, as the rates had been, on payments made by all property owners or occupiers. By the 1990s the GREA had also been replaced by a reformed, but similar, form of centrally determined expenditure calculation called the *Standard Spending Assessment* (SSA). By this time central control over local expenditure was much more effective and, of course, had much reduced the political and policy-making powers of local government. Despite the change in government in 1997, this trend has continued under Labour with both central grants and local taxation heavily controlled by national government.

During the 1980s, however, local government did not just experience reductions in its expenditure base; there were also attempts to remove important aspects of service provision from authorities, primarily though measures requiring or encouraging the privatisation of local government services. This process was begun, most dramatically, in 1980 by the granting to council house tenants of the 'right to buy' (discussed in Chapter 5). Later there was the provision for whole estates to opt out of local authority control, and similar powers were also given to local schools (see Chapter 3). In addition to this opting out, local authorities were also required to offer certain services, such as cleaning or refuse collection, to commercial operators through a process by which contracts for the delivery of local services were put out to tender on the private market. This was extended further in the 1990s to a wider range of local services, including housing management. In some cases these contracts were 'won' by the existing local authority workforce, in competition with commercial tenders. However, on occasions they were not; and in such cases service provision was removed from direct local government control.

Unlike the earlier losses of functions in the 1940s, this reduction in the scope of local government in the 1980s and early 1990s was somewhat piecemeal in its effect, with the extent of opting-out and contracting-out varying from one authority to another. In general it was also nowhere near as extensive as some of the protagonists of the 'contract culture' on the political right (both in and out of government) might have hoped, and in most cases services remained in the hands of local government. Nevertheless, it was a further accentuation of the gradual trend towards a reduced role for the local control of service provision, and little has been done to reverse it by the Labour government since 1997.

The right for schools and housing estates to opt out of local control remains and, as we saw in Chapter 5, in the case of housing this has led to some significant transfers out of council control. Compulsory competitive tendering for service provision has been abandoned and replaced by a new duty on authorities to secure *Best Value* in the provision of local services. This is a judgement of quality as well as quantity (or cost) and is intended to lead to a gradual improvement in service standards. However, in keeping with Labour's Third Way approach to policy development, it is intended to operate within a mixed economy of service provision in which the best services may be delivered by private or voluntary sector providers rather than local government departments.

Best Value is part of a more general pressure from the Labour government to 'modernise' all aspects of local (and central) government. The White Paper outlining this talked about the need for local government to aim for continuous improvement in local services, to put the needs of local people first and to work in partnership with other national and local agencies (Department of the Environment, Transport and the Regions, 1998). As we shall see in Chapter 18, partnership working has become a key element in Labour's new approach to the delivery of social policy; and the government's concern to improve services has led to much more widespread use of audit and inspection of providers, including those in local government. The effect of all of these changes, however, has been to accentuate further the control of central government over local government. The hostility between central and local government in the 1980s has now largely dissipated, but it is clear that central government suspicion and mistrust remains; and at the beginning of the new century local government's social policy powers are more limited and controlled than they have ever been.

Local authority structures and powers

One of the problems for local government in its struggles with central government over the devolution or the centralisation of powers has been the complex, and frequently outdated, structure of local authority organisation across the country. The structure of local government is the product of historical process. It is not, therefore, the product of logical planning; and, despite a number of supposedly comprehensive reviews (especially in the latter part of the last century), it has remained dominated more by current vested political interests than by any future vision of the proper role for localism.

In reality, of course, what might properly constitute the 'local' area for the purposes of devolved government or community control is far from clear. The local dimension is perhaps best seen as something of a continuum rather than a clear-cut distinction; it ranges from the small village or neighbourhood community (where in theory at least everybody knows everybody else), through the parish or small town, to the city, county or metropolitan area, and then to the region, although in Scotland, Wales and Northern Ireland these distinctions are not so complex:

Smallest neighbourhood	Parish	District	City	County	Largest region
Belgravia	*Beverley*	*Bedford*	*Birmingham*	*Berkshire*	*East Midlands*

There has never been local government at neighbourhood level in Britain, although – as we shall see in Chapter 18 – there is now a significant amount of policy delivery aimed at neighbourhoods in some areas. At parish level, however, local councils have existed in rural areas since the nineteenth century and most remained after the local government reforms of 1974, although their powers are very limited (Elcock, 1982, pp.35–7). District councils cover all towns and some smaller cities, and usually share the powers of local government with the county council which extends over a number of district areas. Larger cities, however, often have single local authorities which enjoy the full range of local powers. As we discussed earlier there is no tier of regional government at present in the UK, although the English RDAs do carry out some policy functions.

Thus the structure of local government does not follow the simple logic of devolution of different powers down to different local levels on a consistent basis. In particular, since the changes made by the abolition of the metropolitan counties in the major urban areas, such as London and Merseyside, in the 1980s, there has been a somewhat arbitrary divide in England between those large industrial towns and cities, such as Newcastle or Oldham, and the London boroughs, such as Islington or Tower Hamlets, which have unitary authorities providing all local government services, and those more predominantly rural areas where powers are divided between a district council and a larger county council. Until the 1990s county councils also included some large cities, such as Bristol or Nottingham, which were larger than some of the single-tier authorities in places like Oldham. Beginning in 1996, however, most of the larger towns and cities were given single-tier status although dual authorities remained throughout the rest of the rural areas in England, despite initial hopes in some local government quarters that this dual structure might have been abandoned altogether. In Scotland and Wales, however, all the larger regional and county councils have been removed and replaced with smaller unitary authorities.

Since the mid-1990s reforms local government has remained a mixture of single-tier authorities in the larger towns and cities (plus the London boroughs and Scotland and Wales), where all locally devolved powers are concentrated in one elected council body; and dual-tier authorities in the predominantly rural counties in England, where some powers (such as housing) are the responsibility of a local district council and others (such as education and social services) are the responsibility of a larger county council covering a number of districts. In Northern Ireland, however, local government has considerably fewer policy powers, with policies in education, social services and housing being determined by separate national bodies.

Despite the loss of services to central government mentioned earlier, education, housing and personal social services have remained in local government hands. In addition to these local authorities also have responsibility for a range of other service provision, which, in part at least, is encompassed within the field of social policy. These include leisure services (such as sports facilities, museums and parks), consumer protection, maintenance of highways and street lighting, and emergency services (such as policing and fire fighting). The latter services, however, are under the control of separate bodies of councillors sometimes covering more than one authority in urban industrial areas; and the Metropolitan Police (in London) and the Royal Ulster Constabulary (in Northern Ireland) are separately controlled by statute.

Furthermore in the latter part of the last century local authorities in some areas began to expand their range of interest and activity into new areas of policy action. This was particularly the case with the large urban authorities mainly controlled by the Labour Party. In the 1970s and 1980s many of these areas experienced significant economic decline as the manufacturing and other heavy industries based in them declined, and with this decline came serious social and economic problems. Levels of poverty and deprivation increased and economic opportunities decreased. This prompted some authorities to take a proactive role in seeking to combat local poverty and promote economic development.

In the 1980s a number of the larger metropolitan councils began to develop a range of measures to assist those experiencing poverty in their area, including setting up welfare rights services to advise on benefit entitlement and credit unions to alleviate levels of indebtedness (Balloch and Jones, 1990). In the 1990s these kind of activity had spread to many district and county councils too, many of whom began to adopt formal 'anti-poverty strategies' (Alcock *et al.*, 1995). Many of these authorities did not just aim to combat poverty, however, but also sought to foster and support local economic development; for example, many large cities such as Birmingham, Manchester and Sheffield set up new departments to coordinate efforts to promote local employment and economic development, providing training for local workers and assistance for local businesses. As we shall see, in the 1980s and 1990s these activities were conducted against a backdrop of conflict with a central government which did not see a role for government in poverty prevention or social regeneration. However, after the election of the Labour government in 1997 these new policy dimensions began to infuse national policy planning too, and were openly encouraged and promoted by central government. National policy initiatives to foster local social and economic development now include partnership working between local authorities and national government, and in the Local Government Act 2000 authorities were given the power to promote explicitly economic and social improvement in their area.

The structural divisions between local authorities and the distribution of powers to local government does in itself pose problems for the management and delivery of services, however. For a start the delineation of local authority areas is controversial issue. Lines must be drawn on a map between authorities, and wherever they are drawn they are likely to lead to boundary problems. For instance, families living near the boundary of one authority might wish to send their children to a school nearby in a neighbouring authority. Prior to the education reforms of 1988 they would not have been able to do this; and today they still may not, in practice, if the neighbouring authority will not accept children from another local council. Similarly, an urban local authority wishing to demolish the inner-city slums and rehouse their inhabitants in new housing estates in the countryside may be unable to build such houses because the neighbouring countryside it wishes to use is part of a different authority. In some cases neighbouring authorities are able to cooperate successfully over issues that cross their respective boundaries – in London in particular this is common and essential – but it does not always happen; and in practice it requires both careful management and political support.

Cooperation between authorities is required in rural areas where powers are shared between county and district authorities. To many local people here, the difference between the county and the district authorities in their area may be an obscure, and even an unjustifiable, one. All they know is that they need to contact different officers in different council buildings, probably in different towns, in order to make use of different local services; and, if the officers of these two authorities whom they contact turn out to know little or nothing about the structures or workings of the other (a not uncommon problem), this is unlikely to extend the popularity of local government to local service users.

If they are in conflict (which sometimes they are), it is likely to make the practice of local accountability both a negative and a frustrating one.

The experience of local government is not always as positive as some politicians and policy makers might wish to believe, therefore. The idea of local government accountability is based upon the assumption that local elections provide a basis for communicating the views of local people to the local councillors who represent them, so that these councillors can then ensure that the officers providing the services follow the dictates of the local electorate. However, the political process of local government does not always operate in such a directly responsive way to pressures of local democracy. In a number of authorities councillors from one particular political party have been in control of local government for decades or more, and in such cases they often rely heavily on the advice and guidance of the senior officers within the authority rather than on any changing views among their local electorate.

Partly because of the rather limited nature of democratic accountability, therefore, local authority services have often in practice been developed within highly bureaucratic, and heavily paternalistic, frameworks. A typical example of this would be the local housing department of the 1960s or 1970s with its long waiting lists for new properties and its strict controls over the rights and responsibilities of tenants, even down to the colour of paint on their front doors. In circumstances such as this the attractions of the local control of welfare services may turn out to be more apparent than real, and this in part explains the conflicts between central and local government that became more acute towards the end of the last century, and the moves towards a different model of 'local governance' which has developed at the beginning of the new one.

QUESTIONS: COMPREHENSION

- What is the difference between the local administration of welfare services and the local government of these?
- To what extent has the history of local government been one of a gradual decline in local autonomy over policy planning?
- How did central government seek to control local government spending in the 1980s and to what extent were they successful in this?

QUESTION: REFLECTION

- What do you think would be the best geographical basis for local policy planning to take place within?

Central–local conflict

Within any democracy political conflict is inevitable: indeed arguably it is desirable, for it is evidence of healthy political debate. However, the separate electoral base for local government from central government creates a specific context for potential political conflict between the two, since there are likely to be a range of issues, particularly those relating to local government powers and resources, over which they may not agree. Furthermore, these conflicts are likely to be exacerbated in a party political electoral system, where at different times different parties may be in control of different levels of central and local government.

Despite this potential, however, the history of local government is not in particular a story of party control and party conflict. Even by the time of the Maud Committee of 1967 only around 50 per cent of local authorities were under party political control (Stoker, 1991, p.37), with the majority of these being in the larger urban areas. Since that time, however, local government has become much more widely politicised and now control of virtually all councils is the subject of party political struggle and competition, although often competition has to be followed by compromise and cooperation if the election is 'hung' and no one party is successful in winning enough council seats to exercise overall control.

If, however, party control is a relatively new phenomenon for many rural authorities, it is a much more established tradition in the larger urban areas. Following the lead in municipal development taken by Birmingham in the early part of the twentieth century, many of the larger city authorities elected parties into power based upon radical manifestos for local development. The Labour Party in particular was instrumental in using such local government manifestos as an early base for demonstrating the potential achievements of democratic socialism. In cities such as Sheffield, where Labour exercised control on an almost uninterrupted basis from the 1920s to the 1990s, a programme of 'municipal socialism' based on public house building and infrastructural improvement was pursued by the new council regimes of the early half of the century (Blunkett and Jackson, 1987).

Of course the local pursuit of municipal socialism was likely to bring such Labour councils into conflict with a Conservative-controlled central government, for whom such socialism was definitely not a part of the political agenda. In the 1920s, for instance, conflict arose in a direct form within the London Borough of Poplar (now Tower Hamlets) where the Labour council was pursuing a policy of paying higher wages to its workers and higher levels of poor relief to its benefit claimants. This led to legal action being brought against the council as a result of which some councillors were eventually sent to gaol. Although the imprisonment of elected representatives in Poplar was a rather extreme consequence of such political conflict, other authorities, too, pursued radical policies that did not have the support of central government and resulted in political conflict with it. This form of local political challenge began to be referred to as *Poplarism* (Ryan, 1978; Holman, 1990).

After the war, however, the welfare state reforms of the 1940s removed some of the political impetus for Poplarism from local government, as the major concern of central government at that time became one of ensuring that recalcitrant Conservative local authorities were required to meet national standards of service delivery in areas such as education and housing. Since then, however, the growth in the size and importance of these local authority welfare services has been accompanied by an increasing politicisation throughout local government and, as a result, conflicts between central and local government have again become common. In the 1960s there was conflict between the Labour government and a Conservative authority over comprehensive schooling in Tameside, near Manchester (Finch, 1984, p.55), and in the 1970s there was conflict between the Conservative government and a Labour authority over increases in council house rents in Clay Cross, in Derbyshire (Elcock, 1982, pp.48–9). In the 1980s, however, the politicisation of local government, and the conflicts between local and central government, reached new levels. In particular, in the large urban councils, where Labour had traditionally been in control, there was a dramatic move to the left in many areas at the same time as the central government, under Conservative control, was moving to the right.

Commentators referred to this shift as the development of a new *urban left*, committed, as their predecessors in Poplar in the 1920s had been, to the development of a kind of 'local socialism' (Boddy and Fudge, 1984). This urban left began to exercise power in the West Midlands, in Manchester, and in London boroughs such as Hackney and Lewisham, and, most notably, in Sheffield, under the leadership of *Blunkett*, and in Greater London, under the leadership of *Livingstone*. The latter two figures in particular became dominant spokesmen for the new local politics of Labour. Blunkett wrote about the renewed importance of local democracy (Blunkett and Green, 1983; Blunkett and Jackson, 1987); and Livingstone was instrumental in extending the range of local government activity in London to cover economic development, support for minority groups and local anti-poverty initiatives. Both were interviewed in Boddy and Fudge (1984, pp.242–83). Both have also since remained prominent in national and local politics, Blunkett becoming a key member of the Labour cabinet after 1997, and Livingstone becoming a Labour MP and then leaving the party to become the first elected Mayor of London.

The conflict between central and local government in the 1980s was not a struggle of equals, however; and, as with the Poplarism of earlier eras, it was a conflict that central government was ultimately better placed to win. Throughout the 1980s therefore central government acted to restrict the activities of local government and to prevent it mounting an effective challenge to national policy priorities:

1. Grants to local government for service provision were cut.
2. The power to raise money through the rates was restricted and rates were finally abolished.
3. Local government political campaigns against central government policy were made unlawful.
4. New service initiatives developed by some authorities in defiance of government were stopped, such as the subsidisation of public transport, begun in Sheffield and copied in Greater London in the 'fares fair' campaign which reduced tube and bus fares in the capital.
5. Some authorities, notably the Greater London Council itself, were abolished and their powers transferred to smaller authorities.

The overall affect of this was to reduce the political clout of local government, and to cast doubt over the political effectiveness of local democracy.

If locally elected councillors could not pursue the policies on which they had secured a mandate from their local electorate where this contradicted the policies supported by central government, then to what extent did local democratic control over local services have any effective meaning? This is a question which raises fundamental questions about the nature of local democracy and the role of local government which have been taken up by the new Labour government after 1997 as part of their modernisation of government and policy making more generally.

Local governance and the enabling authority

The declining powers and influence of local government over the last 20 years or so have been accompanied by a decline too in the apparent support for local democracy. The turn-out in local elections has generally decreased, and it is well below that in national elections with only one-third or less of those entitled to vote doing so (far fewer than in most other European countries). It is even difficult in some cases for parties to find candidates to stand for election in their local wards, so that in a small number of wards councillors are elected unopposed. This low turn-out and shortage of councillors is accentuated in some authorities where one political party has enjoyed a long period of unchallenged political dominance. Here local democracy has become simply the practice of local party politics. This has occasionally led to high-profile cases of corruption amongst local politicians who have abused their powerful positions to pursue their own financial interest; but more commonly it has often meant that local policy making and service delivery have become dominated by the senior officers of the local authority departments, with elected members largely acting as 'rubber stamps' for the policies developed by local officials.

By the end of the last century this had led some commentators to talk about a 'democratic deficit' within local government in the country, where electoral democracy was no longer acting as an effective control over the development and delivery of local services and the role of local democratic control required some rethinking (King and Stoker, 1996). Critical to this rethinking has been the notion of a move from local government to local governance as the guiding principle of local democracy and local service delivery (Cochrane, 1993; Clarke and Stewart, 1999).

The idea of *governance* is in fact much broader than the operation of local democracy in the UK. It has been used to describe a more general recognition within political science and political practice that the factors influencing the exercise of policy-making powers are (and should be) more that just the responsibility of elected politicians. It has been widely adopted in the USA and has been central in influencing national thinking about public policy making and public management in the UK, especially after 1997 (see Chapter 18 below, and Newman, 2001). The critical issue, for local governance, however, is the acceptance that responsibility for public service provision does not necessarily imply direct of provision of these, or direct accountability of providers to elected local councillors; rather, the role of local government is that of ensuring that appropriate services are delivered to meet the needs of local citizens (hence the Best Value mandate).

This requires a new approach to policy planning and the development of positive measures to assess local need. Rather than assuming that existing services are effective, councils have commissioned audits of need and have engaged in consultation with local users and citizens. It also requires collaboration and partnership working with other local providers of services (public services such as the NHS as well as voluntary sector and private bodies), and a recognition that it is through appropriate management and the development of a mix of service providers that the needs of local citizens will be met. Overall this has been characterised as a shift in the role of authorities from that of providers to that of *enablers* (Clarke and Stewart, 1988 and 1999).

As enablers local authorities work with other public, private and voluntary agencies in their area both informally and formally, through partnership bodies and interagency agreements. The structure and operation of these relationships vary from authority to authority though there are many common features. For instance, joint working is required by local social services and health trusts over community care provision (see Chapter 6), and since 2002 all local authorities in receipt of Neighbourhood Renewal funding have been required to establish Local Strategic Partnerships (LSPs) to bring a range of local agencies together to oversee economic and social development planning. The new LSPs are an interesting example of the differences between local governance and previous models of local democratic control. Within these partnerships local authorities are only one party, and decision making is based upon consensus and collaboration between a number of different interests, all of which have some measure of influence or control over local policy provision. Where this works well such collaboration – local governance – should lead to improved provision for citizens across a wide range of local needs, beyond that which could be achieved by individual partners (even local councils) acting alone.

Another dimension of this shift in local government has been a move away from the emphasis on electoral democracy (somewhat discredited by the poor turn-out in local elections) towards the promotion of 'deliberative democracy'. This too is a complex issue extending far beyond UK local government, but in simple terms the idea is that the involvement of local citizens in service development and the accountability of providers to users should be pursued through the establishment of methods of direct consultation with local people, rather than (only) through the electoral process. Such consultation can take a variety of forms including local committees of residents, service fora where representatives of local user groups can meet, and citizens' panels or citizens' juries where the views of a random sample of local people can be gauged. The Local Government Act of 1999 required all authorities to engage in such formal consultation with local interests and encouraged the establishment of local fora to act as the settings for democratic debate.

The 1999 Act also imposed other changes on local government, requiring all councils to move away from their previous organisation and management based upon separate committees responsible for different service departments to the establishment of central 'cabinets' with overall strategic and planning powers, perhaps working with a local directly elected mayor. Most authorities have been slow to move towards the mayoral model although there have been some high-profile mayors elected, most notably in London. The greater centrality of planning and decision making has significantly altered the structure and practice of local government democracy, however, making local authorities more like strategic planning agencies than local parliaments.

Local or central control?

The moves towards governance and enabling have altered the role and the practice of local government over the most recent past; and many of these changes have been imposed on authorities by central government. Nevertheless, in some ways they have resulted in an enhancement of the profile and influence of local government and an improvement in its relations with central government. This has also been reinforced by the increasing willingness and ability of local government collectively to coordinate and develop its role in the democratic and policy-making process. Local government now has an effective national voice, provided by the Local Government Association (LGA), a representative body of all local councils in England (with similar bodies in Wales and Scotland). There are also national agencies providing advice, support and training across authorities, notably the Improvement and Development Agency (IDeA), formerly the Local Government Management Board.

Despite these developments, however, local governance in the twenty-first century is likely to be very different from the local government of the twentieth century. Overall the trend of recent changes has been to confirm, and accelerate, the previous drift of powers and responsibilities away from local government. Conflict with central government may have been replaced by partnership; but (as with some local partnerships, too) it is far from a partnership of equals, and central government intervention in local government practice has become ever more extensive. At the same time, however, this centralising drift is complicated by the moves towards devolution and regional autonomy discussed earlier; and this suggests that the changing balance between central and local control of the policy process may continue to be a more contradictory story than simply the aggregation of power by national government.

As we suggested earlier there is an inevitable tension at the heart of relations between central and local control over the provision of social policy; and both past and recent changes in the structure and practice of relations between central and local government have been largely informed by attempts to secure an appropriate balance between the contradictory pressures of central and local control. Of course there is no right answer to this challenge, and there is likely to be much disagreement about what the balance should be in any particular area, not least between those involved in central and local government themselves. What is clear, however, is that a balance must be struck, and that the way in which it is will be critical in determining the future development and delivery of all welfare services.

QUESTIONS: COMPREHENSION

- To what extent has political conflict between central and local government led to central government taking more control over local affairs?
- What are 'enabling authorities', and to what extent has the development of these improved the delivery and accountability of local welfare services?

QUESTION: REFLECTION

Local control ensures a closer relationship of accountability between local people and those providing services to them; it permits knowledge of local conditions and local preferences to inform policy development and delivery; and it encourages a strong sense of identity and community to support local initiatives.

Central control can be more efficient, ensuring economies of scale and uniformity of services throughout the country so that school children in Birmingham get as good an education as those in Bournemouth; and it can permit redistribution of resources from wealthy areas to poorer areas to prevent geographical inequalities being replicated in local service provision.

- How can we strike an appropriate balance between these different costs and benefits?

FURTHER READING

The literature on the devolution of policy at national level within the UK is still developing, but Adams and Robinson's (2002) collection provides useful information on a range of recent developments. The history of the development of local government is covered in Stoker (1991); and Wilson and Game (2002) provide the most comprehensive guide to current structures and issues. For a broader discussion of governance at local level see Leach and Percy-Smith (2001). The website of the Office of the Deputy Prime Minister houses documents on regional and local government in England: see **www.odpm.gov.uk**. For developments in the devolved administrations see their separate websites: **www.scotland.gov.uk**, **www.wales.gov.uk** and **www.northernireland.gov.uk**. The Local Government Association has a useful website, **www.lga.gov.uk**; and more general discussion of local government issues can be found on **www.lgiu.gov.uk**.

Part
IV

Issues

Social Divisions

SUMMARY OF KEY POINTS

- Britain is a divided society in which the experiences and needs of different social groups are varied and diverse, and may even come into conflict.
- Class differences linked to economic status continue to divide British society, although social policy has acted to reduce some inequalities between classes and to promote mobility across classes.
- Gender inequalities within social policy have flowed in large part from the assumptions about the different roles of men and women in employment and family structures underpinning most of the welfare reforms of the last century.
- Britain is a multicultural society with a wide range of different ethnic groups whose differing needs and circumstances are not always recognised within the provision of welfare services.
- Racism directed at Britain's black population has led to discrimination and disadvantage within welfare provision.
- Families with children are disproportionately disadvantaged with around one-third of children in poverty compared to around a quarter of adults.
- Ageism within social policy planning has led to assumptions about the 'dependency' in old age and to concerns that the growing proportion of older people in society will constitute a burden on future generations.
- Disability covers a wide range of different circumstances and needs, but generally means that people with disabilities need support to reach the standards of living enjoyed by others, yet disabled people are more likely to be unemployed and poor.

A divided society

We usually conceive of British society, or indeed any society, as providing a uniform social structure in which we all live. Within this social structure we are bound together by a common democratic and political structure and by a shared cultural experience and heritage, exemplified perhaps most strongly in modern times by the national media (television, radio and newspapers) which provide us with so much of our knowledge of the rest of our social world. In particular, from the point of view of social policy, we are also subject to the same policy provisions and legal rights and responsibilities.

However, as some sociologists are quick to point out, this mono-dimensional and *functionalist* model of British (and other) societies is in fact a rather partial one, and in many senses is a fundamentally flawed one. While there may be much that unites us as British citizens, there is also much that divides us. We have different histories, cultures and circumstances, which have shaped our individual lives and our social relations, and as a result we do not all have similar needs and interests and our experiences of the supposedly shared welfare services state is in practice a widely varying one. Against the assumption that society follows a functional model, therefore, sociologists argue instead that we should adopt a *conflict* model. A conflict model highlights the different circumstances and different experiences of social groups within society in both the production and consumption of resources, and recognises that the needs or interests of some will conflict with those of others. From such a perspective, the development and the consumption of welfare services is not a product of improved social functioning, it is a focus of social struggle.

In a broad sense, of course, both approaches have some truth in them. We do all share a social and cultural context as British citizens; yet at the same time we are members of different groups with different and sometimes conflicting interests. However, where there may have been a tendency in some of the more traditional social policy and social administration literature to emphasise the shared – even supposedly universal – nature of welfare services (Crosland, 1956), there is now an increasingly widespread recognition in social policy debate of the fact that we live, and function, within a divided society (F Williams, 1989).

In understanding the development and operation of social policy, therefore, it is essential to recognise, and to study, the issue of social divisions. The social groups to which people belong will structure their experience of social policies, and the political processes by which policies are developed will be determined by the differential power and influence of different groups. Furthermore, these experiences and processes are intertwined: marginalisation or exclusion from the process of policy making is also likely to lead to disadvantage or discrimination in the receipt of services. However, in Britain, as in most other advanced capitalist countries, welfare has in practice been constructed largely by certain social groups, who have consequently benefited disproportionately from it. The model of universalism on which it is supposedly based is therefore essentially a flawed one and needs to be replaced with a recognition of diversity and difference.

The most widely recognised and debated social division is probably that of social class. Class is also still the most important social division, although in modern welfare capitalist societies class differences have become more complex. Class divisions are a way of making sense of the inequalities of socio-economic circumstances within society by reference to people's position within the labour market or production process and, as we shall see, such divisions have long been debated and argued about. However, inequalities are not just the product of the labour and production processes: class differences also arise from consumption patterns, and in addition there are broader aspects of inequality than simply cash income and access to material resources. Social status, life chances, life choices, and cultural freedom are also inequitably distributed, and differences here are not only structured by the economics of class.

Gender differences clearly affect all of these issues, as well as structuring economic inequality independently of class. In a multicultural and multiethnic society such as Britain differences in racial or cultural background also lead to a range of inequalities, although here, as we shall discuss, it is often the rac*ism* which reacts to such differences which is the cause of the inequity and disadvantage. Gender and 'race' were discussed by F Williams (1989) in her critical review of social policy, where she argued that they had largely been ignored by both academic analysis and policy development. However, there are other divisions, too, that have also remained hidden in – or hidden from – social policy debate.

Differences of age can also affect both involvement in, and experience of, welfare services, as do differences of physical ability, or disability, and we shall discuss these further below. Sexual orientation may also influence experience of social policies, especially perhaps since the growth of AIDS. Family circumstances, language differences, geographical differences and many other circumstances also lead to different needs and experiences. Indeed in all sorts of ways we are divided from each other through our membership of different social groups, with their different experiences and different needs.

Furthermore, as we shall also examine below, welfare services are not only affected by social divisions, they also frequently reaffirm and reinforce these divisions. Indeed, the structure of welfare provision itself may *create* social divisions. For instance, as authors such as Dunleavy and Husbands (1985) have argued, the consumption of welfare services can create *consumption cleavages* between different user groups, such as the different material interests of owner-occupiers and tenants within different sectors of housing provision. The receipt of services from different providers itself also creates divisions, such as those between pupils in 'public' (private) schools and pupils in the state sector. Finally, the very process of delivering services creates divisions and conflicts of interest between the providers of services and the consumers of them, starkly symbolised by the plastic screens once found in benefit offices separating staff from the claimants who came to see them.

As we discussed in Chapter 12, recent *postmodernist* theorising in social science has stressed the complex nature of such social divisions and social processes within welfare capitalist societies. Postmodern society, they argue, is characterised by complexity and diversity, which cannot be captured by either functionalist or class conflict models of social structure. The contributors to a recent book on social divisions (Payne, 2000) discuss a number of the diverse social groupings to be found in current British society, and some of the more important ones for social policy analysis are summarised here.

QUESTIONS: REFLECTION

- To what extent do you think that the experience of welfare services is likely to be influenced by social divisions within British society?
- Are some social divisions more significant than others in social policy terms?

Class

Theoretical and empirical debate about the structure of social class in Britain, and other modern societies, is both wide-ranging and longstanding. Indeed it is probably true to say that the concept of class is one of the most critical, and most contested, issues in social science, although a useful guide to major perspectives is provided by Crompton (1998). Theoretical differences over how to define, and how to determine, social classes have their roots in the major theoretical traditions stemming from the work of Marx and Weber, the former arguing that social class is determined only through relationship to the means of production, and the latter arguing that differences of occupational status are also important in separating people into different classes (Sarre, 1989, pp.84–96). More recent sociological analysis has been taken up by Goldthorpe (Goldthorpe and Hope, 1974), who developed a hierarchy of divisions based upon occupation, from managers to agricultural workers, and EO Wright (1985 and 1989), who developed the Marxist approach to produce a list of classes based on ownership and control of property.

Within the UK, however, there are also some official classifications of class divisions, which in practice are widely used for empirical measurement and to inform policy planning. These include the Registrar General's scheme (shown below) and a more extensive and sophisticated classification called the Socio-Economic Group (SEG) scheme:

I	Professional and managerial
II	Intermediate middle class
III(N)	Skilled non-manual
III(M)	Skilled manual
IV	Partly skilled
V	Unskilled

The classes shown here are obviously in a hierarchical order. Those at the top have most wealth, privileges and power; and the unskilled workers at the bottom are likely to have low wages and little wealth. This reflects traditional Marxist and Weberian notions of differences in property and status. This hierarchy of categories is not watertight or fixed, of course. For instance, some factory workers are now paid much more than some teachers; and in particular the relative size of the different classes has changed, with most commentators agreeing that over the latter part of the last century the size of the manual and unskilled classes (the working classes) declined and the size of the non-manual and professional classes (the middle classes) increased (Crompton, 1998).

Furthermore, because the classification is based upon work it ignores those outside the labour market altogether (for instance, pensioners and the unemployed). Some have argued that as a result of de-industrialisation and the restructuring of the labour market a more or less permanent group of people who are unemployed or can only get limited part-time and/or temporary jobs has been created, and that this group now constitutes a separate social class, the 'underclass', with little or no resources or power. The existence of such an underclass is actually a much contested issue within sociology and social policy, with some commentators suggesting that members of the underclass have cut themselves off from the rest of society by their unwillingness to seek employment (Murray, 1996), although the evidence from sociological studies suggests that this is not the case and that the existence of a separate underclass may be impossible to establish empirically (D Smith, 1992; Morris, 1994).

It is not only the case that class categories are changing, however. Membership of social classes is also subject to change. In most societies there is likely to be significant *class mobility*, with individuals moving up, and down, between classes. For instance, someone from a working-class family may, through achievement within the education system, secure a job in the professional middle class or may start up a successful business; conversely, someone else may see their business fail and may become unemployed and unable to secure future permanent work. Class mobility is, in part, the means by which such a hierarchical class structure retains a level of legitimacy within any society (we all might hope one day to join the higher classes). Such mobility, and the gaps between social classes, have also been the major foci of social policy development.

The introduction of welfare provision through social policy in Britain was clearly intended by some of its promoters to *reduce* the inequalities between class categories. For instance, social security policies were intended to prevent an underclass developing as an impoverished group cut off from the rest of society; and the National Health Service (NHS) was intended to provide equal medical care and cure to all, reducing the differences in health and illness that might otherwise exist between classes. However, social policies may also promote social *mobility* by making it easier for people to move between classes, especially in an upward direction. For example, one of the aims of education provision has been to ensure that all are given an equal opportunity to reach their full potential in learning, and thus progress to a potentially higher class status than they might otherwise have achieved.

However, the continued existence of stark divisions of class within welfare capitalist countries such as Britain suggests that social policies have not been effective in achieving such goals. Social security may have prevented extreme hardship, but the low level of benefits that it provides still means that those dependent on them live at standards significantly below those of the majority of the working population. Indeed, in relative terms the position of social security claimants remained more or less constant as a proportion of average wage levels throughout most of the last century in Britain (Atkinson, 1990). And, despite the success of the NHS in providing free health care for all, class differences in morbidity and mortality rates have remained, and even expanded (Shaw *et al.*, 1999).

That welfare services have not succeeded in removing class differences is not really such a surprising conclusion to reach. Social policy in welfare capitalist societies such as Britain has been constructed and implemented within a continuing complex and divided socio-economic structure. Those in positions of power and wealth within such a structure have obviously sought to ensure that these privileges are not destroyed by the development of improved welfare for all. To put it simply, welfare services have been in part a victory for the lower classes; but they have also been in part a benefit conceded grudgingly by those higher up the social order.

Furthermore, the development of welfare services themselves, while delivering benefits to users and securing (sometimes well-paid) employment for providers of services, has also created its own differences of power and privilege. Within the health service, for example, hospital consultants and hospital managers have become influential arbiters of people's health needs, involving decisions even over life and death. And yet at the other end of the spectrum a new section of the lower working class, such as hospital cleaners and porters, has been created, often with lower pay and poorer conditions than those working in private industry.

Thus class differences may have been influential in creating pressure for the development of social policy in welfare capitalist countries; and class structures have been significantly affected by the development of welfare provision within all such countries. However, class differences have not been removed by social policy, and it would not be at all realistic to have expected them to be.

QUESTIONS: COMPREHENSION

- To what extent has social policy aimed to remove inequalities in housing, health and education between different social classes?
- What is 'social mobility' and to what extent has it undermined the significance of class differences in determining life chances and welfare needs?

Gender

Gender differences, in particular the greater power and privilege of men over women, are as deep-seated and as longstanding as differences of class in British society, and in other countries too. These differences have not only survived but have also in part been accentuated by the development of welfare services, and they remain central to our understanding of the operation of these. However, unlike class, gender has not always been a central feature of debate about the development or the delivery of welfare services. In an early feminist critique Wilson (1977) argued that the different experience of welfare for women had frequently been marginalised in mainstream social policy debate; and the concern with gender difference and inequality has been taken up by other feminist writers since (Hallett, 1996; Pascall, 1997; Watson and Doyal, 1999).

This is because, in a society in which men hold most of the dominant positions of power and influence, it is also men who have dominated the development, and the study, of social policy. But there has been a growth of academic interest in the gender dimension of policy development and delivery, and a growth in the political activity of women seeking to challenge male domination of our social services. Thus we now know much more about the different experiences, and needs, of men and women within welfare capitalist societies; and what we know confirms feminist suspicions that gender inequalities remain sizeable and significant, and that within this it is women who are disadvantaged.

The different circumstances and experiences of men and women are deepseated features of society and extend much beyond the development and delivery of social policy. The context of social policy provision within the UK, and most other advanced industrial societies, has been in particular influenced by assumptions about family structure, labour market participation and the roles of women which underpinned the development of most welfare services during the welfare reforms in the middle of the last century. These can be captured in the notion of the 'male breadwinner' model of work and family life.

In this model family life is presumed to be stable and based on married couples and their children. Within such families men work in the labour market and earn a wage which supports their wife and children, and women stay at home to care for the household and look after the children. This was the model which informed Beveridge's plan for social security. His assumption was that married women's main role would be as housewives and mothers within the family, and that they would therefore make 'marriage their sole occupation' (Beveridge, 1942, p.49). He thus excluded married women from insurance protection within his social security proposals through the offer of reduced contributions without an entitlement to benefits, because he assumed that their husbands would be able to provide income support for them. In fact since then commitment to equal treatment, in part led by EU directives, has removed the separate treatment of married women within social security and ensured that women and men have a formally equal status, although many older women who only paid the reduced contributions still experience exclusion from National Insurance (NI) benefits such as pensions.

The assumptions which Beveridge made about women's family 'responsibilities' extended beyond social security, however. The provision (or non-provision) of nursery education and care for young children and the organisation of the school day and school year for older children all assume the availability of someone at home to care for children outside school hours, and in the vast majority of cases it is women who do this. And, as we discussed in Chapter 6, community care within health and social services is predicated upon the availability of carers to provider informal care in cases of both acute need and chronic illness, and this burden too predominantly falls on women.

Of course, the male breadwinner model has always been a mythical characterisation of family life and the roles and responsibilities of men and women. Even in the immediate post-war period when Beveridge's reforms were introduced, significant numbers of married women engaged in paid employment, and by and large did so because their income was critical for the survival of the family. Since then the participation of women within the labour market has been steadily growing, with over three-quarters of women aged 25–44 economically active in the late 1990s and married women with children constituting the fastest growing group; by contrast, in recent years activity rates amongst men have actually begun to decline (Abbott, 2000).

Women's participation in the labour market has not been without its problems, however. For a start women do not enjoy equal status or equal pay within the labour market. In the 1970s women's average wages were only about 55 per cent of men's; and, although this led to the introduction then of legislation to promote equal pay and prevent discrimination against women at work, that proportion had only risen to around 75 per cent by the end of the century (Abbott, 2000, p.79). This is largely because many of the jobs into which women have been recruited are different jobs from those traditionally done by men. Within the labour force women are *horizontally* segregated from men (they are doing different jobs) and are *vertically* segregated from men (they are generally at lower grades in the career structure).

These differences in women's employment circumstances have not been altered significantly by the development of welfare services. Indeed, to a large extent the growth of welfare provision, including in particular state welfare, has often reinforced occupational segregation through the creation of jobs that have been occupied almost exclusively by women, such as nurses, primary school teachers or social workers. In Britain these jobs have usually been associated with low status and low pay compared to those occupied characteristically by men, such as doctors, lecturers and service managers. Thus, while welfare services have created employment opportunities for women, they have also reinforced employment inequalities, although in some other countries (for example, Sweden) such occupational inequities are much less marked.

Women's position in these labour markets in part reflects their assumed responsibilities for family and community care of course. As we saw in Chapter 11, the costs of caring do extend to disadvantage in other aspects of economic activity; and in practice, despite the false picture presented by the male breadwinner model, it is still predominantly women who forgo employment and career opportunities to undertake unpaid caring work. This is now recognised to some extent in social policy planning through the encouragement of employers to recognise the caring commitments of women (and men), now referred to as the promotion of 'family friendly' employment; and through financial support for some of the costs of child care by child care credits for low-paid workers. But there is still some way to go before policies such as these reverse the disadvantage that women have experienced in labour markets or have much effect in shifting the burden of family responsibilities to men.

The inequality and disadvantage that women experience in the labour market also has other consequences for their experience of social policy provision. With lower pay women are less able to purchase private welfare services, such as private pensions or health care. They are also more likely to be dependent upon means-tested welfare services, notably social security benefits. Although the majority of benefit claimants are still men (because in family units it is still predominantly the man who claims benefit for the household), more women depend directly or indirectly on benefits and are more likely to be in those groups experiencing the lowest benefits and the longest periods of dependency, notably lone parents and single pensioners.

Where women are dependent on the incomes received by their male partners, and where both are unemployed or where only the man is the breadwinner, there is an additional problem of dependency. Research by Pahl (1989) has revealed that within family units resources are not always equally distributed between women and men, with women generally receiving less; and, as some of the commentators in Glendinning and Millar (1992) demonstrate, this sometimes results in greater risk of poverty for women. This can be continued, and even compounded, where women are separated from their partners, especially where they have dependent children, because of the difficulties many experience in getting maintenance payments from former partners. Women's experience of poverty and deprivation is therefore different from men's, in particular because of the different dimensions of dependency which frequently underpin it.

In other areas of welfare, too, women's circumstances and needs may sometimes be different from men's. In education there have always been a significant number of schools providing single sex education on the grounds that the educational needs of boys and girls are different, although here, and in co-educational schools, the current evidence is that in school achievement girls generally do better than boys. In health some of women's different needs are self-evident (for instance, around fertility and child bearing); here, too, women-only services have been developed, sometimes extending to a wider range of women's health needs as in 'well women's clinics'. These latter examples are more positive indicators of the role of gender difference within social policy provision. More generally, however, the picture is one of inequalities and disadvantages within which women lose out to men, both in the development and delivery of services as policy makers or providers, and in receipt of services as benefit claimants or home carers.

QUESTIONS: COMPREHENSION

- What is the 'male breadwinner' model and how accurate a picture was it of the employment and family structures of the last century?
- What are 'family friendly' policies and to what extent do they challenge the roles of men and women assumed within much welfare provision?

Race

The importance of racial or ethnic differences in the experience of welfare services has, like those of gender, been marginalised within mainstream social policy. This marginalisation is now being exposed, and challenged. Like class, however, debates over divisions of 'race' depend to some extent upon how racial differences are perceived and defined and, more importantly, upon how the whole issue of race – or racism – is approached.

Britain is, and always has been, a multiracial and multicultural society, as flows of immigrants and emigrants have altered the composition of the indigent population. In the nineteenth and early twentieth centuries people came to Britain from Ireland, and Jewish emigrants arrived, in particular from Eastern Europe. Following the Second World War, Europeans, notably Poles, established themselves in Britain, and immigration was encouraged from Britain's former imperial colonies, such as the West Indies, India, Pakistan and Bangladesh. Immigrants have also arrived at different times from Africa, the Middle East and the Far East; and, since Britain's membership of the EU, significant numbers of people have come to this country from other member states.

There is thus a wide range of ethnic minority groups in the UK, some of whom have retained, or developed, relatively close community ties among themselves. Many of these ethnic minority groups have also been subject to discrimination and ill-treatment by other sections of the indigent population. The Irish, Jews, Poles, Pakistanis, and others, have all been the victims of negative attitudes and hostile reactions. These ethnic differences have also sometimes been reflected in disadvantage within welfare services. However, there has been a significant difference between these disadvantages and the discrimination experienced by the black immigrants who came from Britain's former colonies to settle in the UK in relatively large numbers in the 1950s and 1960s. These immigrants were readily identifiable because of their black (or brown) skin colour and this became a source of hostility – and identity – that was independent of, or additional to, any other cultural or ethnic differences.

The hostility to black people coming to live in Britain is *racism*; it extends not only to immigrants but to all black people living here, an increasing proportion of whom, of course, have been born and brought up as British citizens. The racism that black people in Britain experience is thus not the same thing as reaction to ethnic differences, in part of course because it is quite independent of any such differences. The distinction that it creates is one between black people and white people, in which the former, whatever their origins, are frequently seen as undeserving interlopers. Despite recognising the differences of ethnic and cultural background that exist within the country, therefore, it is this racist distinction between black and white that became the major force dividing the British population on the basis of race in the latter half of the twentieth century, and that remains most important for our understanding of divisions within welfare services. It means that the focus of our analysis is thus not *race*, but racism (Solomos, 1989; Law, 1996).

This racism is in large part a product of the recent history of black immigration to the country. Although immigration from the former British colonies in the Commonwealth was encouraged in the 1950s in order to boost the labour force, including filling (mainly low-paid) jobs in the growing welfare services, in the mid-1960s recruitment even to low-paid jobs in Britain began to decline and, after legal changes in 1962, immigration was restricted to those who could first demonstrate a guarantee of a job on arrival. As the boom turned to recession in the 1970s, it was mainly only spouses and children joining their relatives here who were able to secure entry to the country. This process of restrictions on immigration has in itself created many problems for black people who have had difficulty proving their rights of entry into Britain (Moore and Wallace, 1975). However, it has also compounded the problem of anti-black racism, which was already present among the white British population, providing fuel for the suspicion that black people do not 'belong' in the country.

This suspicion has spilled over into the delivery of both public and private services to black people, operating in practice to restrict their access to them. For example, where services are only available to those with a legal right of residence in the country, the suspicion that black people may be illegal immigrants without such a right means that those delivering services may unjustifiably extend suspicion of non-entitlement to all potential black service users (for instance, in the requirement on black claimants to produce their passports as evidence of entitlement to social security benefits as documented by Gordon and Newnham, 1985, in the 1980s).

The exclusion of black service users from welfare provision in Britain is not, however, just a product of racist discrimination fuelled by suspicion of illegal immigration; at a more general ideological level it runs much deeper than that. The development of services within the 'welfare state' of the post-war era was very much a product of the national (and nationalist) politics of the time. The political struggles which underpinned the reforms were dominated by the political parties and campaigning organisations of the white British population. The welfare state was a (white) British achievement, and most of the black people resident in Britain in the 1960s and 1970s arrived in the country after the establishment of these national welfare services. This invited an assumption by some that Britain's black population had not contributed to the development of the country's welfare services and thus were not *entitled* to use them. From such a (racist) ideological perspective the welfare state was not intended for black people in Britain, and as a result their attempted use of it justified both suspicion and discrimination (a view which now underlies some of the hostile attitudes towards asylum seekers amongst both policy makers and the popular press).

In the case of entitlement to some services such an exclusion was not just a product of certain ideological attitudes, it was also incorporated into the eligibility criteria for access to services. For instance, as we saw in Chapter 2, entitlement to NI benefits, in particular pensions, was based upon past contributions made through employment. Immigrants coming to Britain late in their working lives would be unable to establish full contribution records and so would not secure full benefit entitlement. Similar indirect exclusion occurred in housing policy where waiting lists for public sector tenancies disadvantaged those who had only recently moved into the area, forcing black people into poorer and less secure properties in the private sector. In both of these cases rules and practices controlling access to welfare services did not *directly* discriminate against people on the basis of skin colour: NI contribution conditions and council house waiting lists technically applied equally to all. However, they did constitute a form of *indirect* (or *institutional*) racism, because of the much greater likelihood that black people would experience reduced access as a result of them.

One of the effects of such institutional discrimination was that Britain's new black population of the 1960s and 1970s was unable to benefit equally from the social services which had been developed within the national welfare state, and thus were forced into greater dependency upon means-tested benefits and greater reliance upon poor quality inner-city housing. Together with their concentration in certain sectors of the labour market, this meant that black populations were thus not evenly distributed on a geographical basis throughout Britain. In practice they have lived and worked in particular urban areas, such as London, the Midlands, Lancashire and West Yorkshire; and within these urban areas have been concentrated in poorer, inner-city districts where housing conditions, and other service provisions, are much below the average.

Such race, or ethnic, concentration is common in most other welfare capitalist countries, too, and it is particularly stark, for example, in the USA. However, it also further compounds the discrimination and disadvantage experienced by the black people living in such inner-city 'ghettos'. The reduced access of black people to welfare services is thus compounded by their geographical isolation within such local communities and fuels direct racism against black residents here, as the violence and riots in some northern towns and cities in the early twenty-first century revealed. The discrimination and exclusion flowing from immigration has thus become a structural feature of the disadvantage that many black people experience, as well as continuing the source of racist suspicion of them.

In addition to the direct and indirect racism experienced by black people there are some other examples of disadvantage within welfare services linked to ethnic and cultural differences within Britain's black population. For instance, there have been difficulties in accessing health service provision for diseases specifically affecting black groups, such as sickle-cell, rickets and hepatitis; and there has sometimes been reluctance to recognise and provide for religious or cultural differences in education, such as the need for Muslim children to have halal meat in school meals and to subscribe to strict dress codes in girls' clothing.

Some of these problems have led black groups in the country to develop separate welfare services, designed to meet the needs to which public welfare services cannot, or will not, respond. Separate provision can be found in the voluntary and community sectors, where there are large numbers of black and ethnic minority organisations serving both distinct ethnic communities and particular service needs. Separate provision has also been sought within state welfare services, most notably in the attempts to use the provisions for opting out of local authority control discussed in Chapter 3 to establish schools providing education for Muslim or other specific religious or cultural communities.

There are problems with the development of separatist provision for black and other ethnic minority communities within welfare services, however. In general they can operate to confirm, rather than reduce, divisions between black and white users of welfare, and further fuel racist suspicions amongst white service providers. They can also perhaps promote the misleading assumption that, because of the existence of separate provision, changes in existing public services are either unnecessary or not worthwhile. The real issue here perhaps is how to secure an appropriate balance between exposing and combating the racism within existing welfare services, whilst at the same time recognising and supporting separate provision where this is actively sought by different communities; but this is a balance which has thus far operated against the interests of most black people in Britain.

QUESTIONS: COMPREHENSION

- What is 'institutional racism', and to what extent is there evidence of this within the delivery of welfare services in Britain?
- Is the separate development of black and ethnic minority voluntary activity a result of the failure of public welfare services to recognise the particular needs of different ethnic groups?

Age

Discrimination by age adversely affects both the young and the old. Children, of course, are unable to provide for themselves and so they must be supported by others; they thus need welfare services. In Britain, as many other countries, the expectation is that these services will be provided predominantly on an informal basis through the family, and this is largely what happens in practice, except for the provision of free state education. However, families need support to care for their children, especially where income is low; and the cost of providing for children is likely to push such families into deprivation.

The costs of providing for children within families were a major focus of social policy campaigning in Britain in the interwar years, resulting in the introduction in the 1940s of family allowances to cover some of the costs of family child-rearing (Macnicol, 1980). Family allowances, and the former tax allowances for children, have now been replaced by *child benefit*, a direct subsidy towards the additional costs of children. However, child benefit does not (and is not intended to) cover all of the additional costs that families face in providing for their children, and additional support is now provided for low-income families by the tax credits and other measures discussed in Chapter 2. Families with children therefore still experience higher rates of poverty than adults (Howard *et al.*, 2001), and the government has committed itself to addressing this problem by reducing levels of child poverty and removing it altogether by 2020.

Discrimination against the young in social policy is not, however, as marked as discrimination against the elderly. Older people experience a range of disadvantages within policy development and delivery which are the direct result of assumptions that younger policy makers make about their circumstances and needs. It is only relatively recently that the particular problems experienced by older people as a result of 'ageism' within social policy have been widely debated and analysed, however. It has now developed as a specific area of study called *gerontology* and, in their collection of papers on ageing and social policy, two leading gerontologists (Phillipson and Walker, 1986) discussed a number of the important aspects of age discrimination within welfare, in particular the myths about dependency and need in old age.

The myth of dependency is based upon a fear among policy makers that the growing numbers of elderly people will constitute a financial burden upon the rest of the population, as a result of which provision for them needs to be curtailed. Certainly the numbers of older people in society have been growing in Britain, and in most other developed countries, throughout the twentieth century, and they are set to increase further in the early twenty-first century (see Table 16.1). This is in large part, of course, a product of the success of other social policies in prolonging life expectancy. At an individual level it is no doubt welcomed by all; but at a collective level it changes the balance of age distribution within the population.

Table 16.1 The rising proportion of older people in the UK

Percentage of population aged:	1971	1991	2001	2021
16–64	58	61	62	60
65 or over	16	18	18	21
75 or over	5	7	7	9

Source: National Statistics, 2002, and Government Actuaries Department.

In the early half of the last century the growth in numbers of the elderly was not seen as a social problem, and older workers were often valued for the experience that they could share with new recruits. However, two policy developments in particular have conspired to change the value placed on age and experience: these are the provision of pensions for older people as a substitute for wages, and the establishment of retirement as a means of removing older people from the labour market. Retirement is now a well-established life course event. Men expect to retire, or are required to retire, at 65 and women at 60, although women's retirement age is being raised to 65. With high levels of unemployment in the last quarter of the last century, however, many men and women working in areas where labour was at a surplus were persuaded or coerced to take earlier retirement in order to leave jobs for younger people, or effectively retired early themselves after becoming unemployed in their fifties or sixties, thus extending retirement to earlier years.

Retirement is seen as justified by many, and may be welcomed by some, because pension provision means that those who do retire can continue to enjoy an income after employment. As we saw in Chapter 2, state pensions are a central feature of the social security system. They have also (since the latter part of the last century) been supplemented by many with private or occupational pension cover. For those with a significant private pension entitlement retirement, even early retirement, can be a time to enjoy the material benefits acquired throughout a working life. There is even an acronym used to describe such relatively affluent pensioners: *Woopies* (well-off older persons).

In fact, however, such better-off pensioners are only a minority of older people in Britain today. Most have little or no private pension income and depend entirely on the state benefits to which they are entitled. The value of the basic state pension has been falling in recent years in relation to average earnings. Some more recent pensioners are entitled to an earnings-related supplement to the basic pension, but this is determined by the NI contributions made and many are excluded from it. Those on the basic pension therefore are likely to be living in or near poverty and may be entitled to a means-tested supplement, now called the Minimum Income Guarantee, although it is suspected that many who may entitled do not claim this. For these pensioners the experience of old age is likely to be characterised by poverty rather than plenty, and poverty in old age has been the most significant feature of inequality and deprivation in Britain throughout most of the last hundred years.

Despite the current poverty of many pensioners, however, the growing numbers of older people, and in particular the growth in the proportion within the adult population of those over pension age, has led to concerns about the ability of society to be able to afford the pensions which future generations of older people will need and expect. Most importantly, if current levels of poverty in old age are to be reduced in the future, then more generous pension payments will have to be made to a wider range of people within a growing older population. It is this dilemma which has behind the pension reforms introduced by the Labour government discussed in Chapter 2, the essence of which is to require most current workers to take out private pension protection and to provide an improved state pension for those on low wages only.

Calculating the financial costs of future pension provision is a complicated, and much disputed, exercise in policy planning (Bonoli, 2000). Current debates largely focus on the appropriate balance between state-funded support and private pension investment, although looking more broadly all future pensions will have to be paid out of future economic resources, and will thus depend on future economic performance. If economic growth continues then paying higher rates of pension to older people may not be a problem, and if economic performance declines then no private pension investment is likely to be able guarantee its value in a falling market (see Hills, 1993). Seen in this context the concern over the 'burden' of future pensions for older people is a question of future social and economic justice rather than an imposition on current working people.

This myth of the financial burden of older people on the rest of society has been accompanied by another element of ageism, the myth of service dependency. This is the assumption that older people have more extensive, and more expensive, welfare needs than the rest of the population; and that as a result they are less able to provide for themselves and more likely to require support from social services. Underlying this assumption is the presumed frailty of older people and their consequent need for health and personal care. While it is true that older people do consume a larger proportion of health and personal social service spending than the younger population (McGlone, 1992), this is because when people are older they are more likely to experience physical disability, especially over the age of 75. In other words, their welfare needs arise because of physical or other disabilities, not because they are old. This is a crucial distinction; yet it is unfortunately frequently disguised in the classification, by health and social service providers, of all older service users as *elderly* even though the services that they use are based upon their specific and identifiable needs for care or support.

In fact, the majority of older people do *not* have extensive needs for health and social services. More than half of those over 65 do not have any disability and a further 20 per cent have only slight disability; even among the over-75s, over one-half have no disability or only slight disability (Phillipson and Walker, 1986, p.8). The vast majority of older people live alone, or with partners, in private homes within the community. Furthermore, despite retirement, many older people still are still engaged in part-time paid work, and most are capable of employment. Also many undertake voluntary work; and virtually all, particularly women, continue to do unpaid work in the home and family. Indeed, Finch (1989) found that older people were generally the givers, rather than the receivers, of informal services within families. The discrimination against older people within social policy, therefore, and the fears of the 'burden' of an ageing population, may both be seen as products of social policy rather than problems for it.

QUESTIONS: COMPREHENSION

- Why are older people more likely to experience poverty?
- Why is it argued that the growing numbers of older people will impose a burden of dependency upon the future working population?

Disability

Discrimination and disadvantage experienced by people with disabilities is, like that experienced by the other social divisions discussed above, a longstanding feature of policy development and delivery in Britain. Like race and age, however, disability has frequently been absent from mainstream social policy debate and analysis, even in relatively recent times; thus the policy implications of recognising the importance of disadvantage among the disabled are still sometimes ignored in the study of social policy.

As in the case of older people, too, the numbers of people with disabilities has been growing, although again this is largely a product of more general successes within social policy which should be welcomed. Furthermore, the increased consciousness of disabled people of their disadvantaged state, and their more vocal demands for services, have challenged the paternalistic approach towards disability that had often characterised service provision in the past (Campbell and Oliver, 1996; Oliver, 1996). Such paternalist approaches have generally characterised disabled people as the clients of welfare services, whose needs are provided for by others on the basis of professional assessment. The new political campaigners for disability, however, present themselves as citizens with rights, which they are demanding, but are being denied by discriminatory practices and inappropriate professionalism among service providers. Disability is thus forcing itself into a different place on the social policy agenda.

From a policy perspective, however, there are some definitional problems of both an analytical and a practical nature that complicate the debate about policy development for people with disabilities. Most fundamentally, there is no clear agreement about what constitutes a disability, or what degree of disability is likely to lead to disadvantage. Clearly degrees, and consequences, of disability vary widely from a minor loss of functions or physical features, which may often be undetected by others, to complete paralysis and dependency. This has resulted, for instance, in attempts to classify degrees and types of disability, such as the social security regulations which provide a percentage scale which is used to determine the amount of benefit due to people with certain disabilities, and the elaborate definitions of care and mobility needs which are used to determine entitlement to benefits intended to meet the extra costs associated with such disabilities (notably the Disability Living Allowance, or DLA).

These issues were explored by the Office of Population Censuses and Surveys (OPCS) in the 1980s; it distinguished between different categories of disability and found over 6.5 million people in Britain with some disability and almost 250,000 in the most dependent category (see Dalley, 1991). Part of the disadvantage of much disability is obviously a result of the loss or impairment of function which disabled people experience: for instance, blindness or paralysis mean that people cannot readily move around without guidance or assistance. Of course there are aids, such as guide dogs or wheelchairs, that can help to overcome such problems, but such aids cost money to purchase and maintain; in effect they mean that people with disabilities frequently require a larger income to enjoy the same standard of living, or quality of life, as others.

These extra costs of disability were recognised and discussed within the OPCS survey; they calculated these at between £5 and £12 a week at 1985 prices for those in the most disabled categories, although these figures were disputed by some disability campaigners (Large, 1991). These additional weekly costs suggest that people with disabilities will need to receive relatively high incomes, or significant support in the form of cash benefits or service provision, to maintain a similar lifestyle to others. In fact, however, people with disabilities generally have lower, not higher, incomes than the rest of the population, primarily because they experience inequality and discrimination within the labour market. Less than one-third of disabled people of working age are in paid employment, compared to over two-thirds of the general population; and even where they are in employment, disabled people earn, on average, lower wages (Dalley, 1991). Legislation to outlaw discrimination against disabled people was introduced in the 1990s, along similar lines to that applying to gender and race discrimination, but it is unlikely that is has had much effect in shifting the balance of employment opportunities.

Their relative exclusion from, and disadvantage within, employment thus means that people with disabilities are more likely than others to be dependent upon benefits. There are specific benefits targeted at the needs and costs experienced by disabled people. These include higher rates of standard benefits for those who are out of work due to chronic sickness or disability, such as incapacity benefit (formerly invalidity benefit, which was actually paid at an even higher level), and additional non-contributory benefits aimed at meeting the extra costs of disability, such as the Disability Living Allowance which includes payments for the costs of providing mobility and home care. None of these benefits is paid at a very generous level, however, and they do not bring the majority people with disabilities anywhere near the average income levels enjoyed by the bulk of the rest of the population. Yet evidence suggests that even some of these benefits are not claimed by all of the disabled people who may be entitled to them, in part because of their highly selective focus on specific disability needs and the complex process that must be undertaken to claim them; and many disabled people are therefore dependent upon income support (Walker and Walker, 1991).

Inadequate incomes could be compensated, in part at least, by the provision of services for people with disabilities. Statutory requirements are placed on SSDs for the provision of services for disability through the Chronically Sick and Disabled Persons Act 1970 and the Disabled Persons Act 1986. In the 1990s much of this service provision was restructured as part of the planning of community care discussed in Chapter 6. Where community care practice has given disabled people the ability to shape the development and delivery of packages of care and support for them this has increased their power as service users to some extent, and may even have improved their quality of life. However, the limited financial resources available for much community care has often resulted in reliance being placed on informal providers, further accentuating the family pressures that many disabled people and their caring relatives experience; and in greater expectations being placed on disabled people to purchase private services, or pay charges for public services, out of their (generally low) private incomes.

The disadvantages flowing from inadequate income and lack of services are compounded for many disabled people by their daily experience of the frustrations and exclusions of living within an able-bodied world. Lack of wheelchair access keeps many disabled people out of public buildings; lack of information in other than written form keeps blind people underinformed about events and services. Other barriers and exclusions exist throughout all public and private service provision. But, of course, it is quite wrong to conclude from this that it is their disability which prevents people from participating equally with their able-bodied colleagues and neighbours. The Houses of Commons and Lords, the main seats of government in Britain and arguably the most powerful policy-making institutions in the country, contain members in wheelchairs and members who are blind and deaf: these politicians are no less capable or effective than their colleagues as a result of these disabilities, because they have the resources to ensure that, with appropriate support and assistance, they are able to avoid or overcome the barriers they face. These policy makers are high-profile examples of the fact that it is the barriers to participation, not the conditions of disabled people, that are the cause of the disadvantage and discrimination experienced by them, and that these barriers can be overcome, by some.

QUESTIONS: COMPREHENSION

- Why do disability campaigners argue that much welfare provision for disabled people is paternalistic?
- Why, despite the existence of services and benefits for people with disabilities, do many continue to experience discrimination and disadvantage?

FURTHER READING

A general guide to the different social divisions in British society is provided by the contributions to Payne (2000). Williams (1989) was the first comprehensive analysis of the role of gender and race in structuring the experience of welfare. Lavalette and Pratt (2001) provide a conceptual critique of welfare policy with contributions on feminism, racism, ageing and other related issues. Differences in the outcomes and experiences of policies are discussed in Saraga (1998).

Paying for Welfare

SUMMARY OF KEY POINTS

- Welfare services must be paid for, although patterns of spending, including public spending, vary widely across different welfare capitalist countries.
- Some economists have argued that there is a 'trade-off' between the goals of equity and efficiency in the funding of welfare provision, although this is disputed by others.
- Public spending includes subsidies paid to low-income earners, although where these take the form of tax credits they do not appear in public expenditure accounts.
- Public spending decisions are announced in the annual Budget and are also subject to planning over a three-year period within the Comprehensive Spending Review.
- Public expenditure redistributes resources *vertically* (between social groups) and *horizontally* (across the life course of citizens).
- Taxation includes both *direct* taxes on incomes and *indirect* taxes on the purchase of goods and services.
- Fees are charged for most private welfare services, and charges now play a significant role in raising revenue from the users of some public welfare services.
- Charitable giving can take a number of forms; it is important to voluntary sector welfare providers but may also be used to support public welfare services.

The cost of welfare

The economic context in which social policies are developed and implemented is important in determining the scale and the scope of welfare services. As we discussed in Chapter 13, economic trends influence both the need for social services and the ability of a country to afford to provide them; and thus the shifting patterns of economic growth in Britain, and elsewhere, over the last century or more have had a significant impact in controlling the development of social policy. At the same time, however, it is now widely recognised that the provision of welfare services can also influence the patterns of economic growth: both directly, by providing employment in welfare services, and indirectly, by stimulating demand for goods and improving the quality of the workforce. Social and economic policy interact; therefore they need to be planned and developed together and, in practice in Britain and elsewhere, this is just what happens.

This means recognising the important role that welfare plays in securing economic growth; but it also means planning to ensure that the costs of welfare services are identifiable and measurable, and can be met from within current economic resources. For, even though welfare services may be desirable in both social and economic terms, they still have to be funded. Welfare costs money; or at least it consumes resources, whether or not those resources are provided in the form of cash. Thus the money, or the resources, must be identified and collected and must be distributed to those providing, or consuming, welfare services. In all cases, therefore, the study of social policy involves not just undertaking an examination of the structure and the use of welfare services but also understanding the means of *paying for* these.

Welfare services must be paid for in all countries; however, comparative analysis reveals that in practice the amount of resources allocated to welfare does vary significantly across different countries and over time. Table 17.1 compares the different proportions of GDP spent on social protection (education, health and social security) in a number of major European countries in the latter half of the last century. In all there is a pattern of growth in the spending, but there are also major differences between high-spending countries, such as Sweden, and lower-spending countries, such as the UK.

Table 17.1   Public expenditure on social protection as a percentage of GDP

	1960–9	1970–9	1980–9	1990–3
France	16.1	21.1	27.5	27.5
Germany	19.1	22.5	25.3	27.2
Italy	15.0	19.7	22.4	24.3
Spain	n.a.	n.a.	18.3	n.a.
Sweden	13.2	21.1	33.3	36.6
UK	11.5	14.9	22.8	23.4

n.a. = not available.

Source: Bonoli, George and Taylor-Gooby (2000), p.125, Table 6.1 (OECD (1994a), Table 1a and 1b, pp.57–61).

These comparisons are based on OECD data. A comparison between a wider range of countries based on local data revealed a broader spread of proportionate spending in the 1990s from 36 per cent in Sweden to 18 per cent in Australia and only 13.7 per cent in Japan (Alcock, 2001, p.20), although again the trend over time in most countries was upwards. Different countries are therefore paying very different amounts for the welfare services that they have developed.

The picture is more complex than these broad comparisons suggest, however. This is because there is variety not just in how much is spent but also in how this money is collected and distributed. Different models for financing and distributing welfare are also likely to produce differences in the structure, and the effectiveness, of welfare services; and these are independent, at least in part, of overall costs. In other words, the same overall amounts of resources can be spent in different ways, some of which may deliver similar, or better, services for the same cost. Thus comparisons based only on overall expenditure may not tell us much about the extent of welfare; we need to look in addition at how effectively the money is spent.

The debate about the effective use of resources in providing welfare services has sometimes been presented as a balance, or a conflict, between 'equity' and 'efficiency' in paying for welfare:

1. A concern with the *equity* of welfare services focuses attention upon whether services are provided adequately to consumers and, in particular, whether individual needs for social protection are being met.
2. A concern with *efficiency* focuses attention upon whether the resources that are consumed in service delivery are being used for maximum effect and at minimal cost.

Economists have sought to evaluate the effectiveness of services in quantifiable terms, by contrasting equity gains with efficiency costs. They have sometimes suggested that pressure on efficiency resulting from the broader context of economic growth means that there is an inevitable 'trade-off' between the two, in which equity gains must be scaled back to meet the need for more efficient use of scarce resources for social protection (Okun, 1975). However, as Le Grand (1990) pointed out, the inevitability of such a trade-off is in practice a misleading notion, for the goal of securing equity in the meeting of needs is rather different from the aim of ensuring that the delivery of services is cost-effective. Pursuing efficiency can result in the maintenance of quality at reduced cost (Le Grand, 1993). Thus it does not also prevent the securing of equity; indeed, arguably improved efficiency in service provision could contribute to greater equity.

Certainly attempts to contrast the two in quantifiable terms, and to set the costs of one against the other, are fraught with both conceptual and practical difficulties. Economists may argue that judgements about how, and how much, to pay for welfare should be subject to efficiency criteria; but efficiency alone cannot be the basis for making judgements about paying for welfare, for we also need to determine the social policy goals for which services are developed and delivered. Therefore efficiency and equity are twin goals for social policy that must be considered together, not mutually exclusive poles that we must choose between.

Public expenditure

Whatever the aims or the outcomes, however, economists all agree that public expenditure on welfare provision has been growing in the UK over recent decades. Indeed as we saw in Table 8.1, there has been a consistent pattern of growth over the last hundred years, both in overall levels of spending and in the proportion of GDP taken up by this. This is despite the overt attempts by the Conservative governments of the 1980s to contain, and even reduce, the growth in welfare spending (although, as Table 8.1 reveals, they did slow the proportionate growth against GDP to some extent in this decade).

Public expenditure has grown in part because it is more effective, and more efficient, at providing for many social needs than the previous provision within the private market or voluntary sector: what economists would call the effect of *market failure*. But it has also grown because a wider range of social needs and public services have resulted in demands for overall improvements in collective welfare: what economists would call the impact of *public choice* (Glennerster, 1997, ch.2). Increased public expenditure thus reflects both growing demands for welfare services and limitations in the supply of services from other providers. In practice, however, this growth in expenditure has been a more complicated phenomenon than simply an increase in the scale of publicly provided services, and its relationship with private and voluntary welfare is also more sophisticated than a simple model of public take-over might imply.

Public expenditure can be used to cover the direct costs of providing services. This is the pattern for many well-known public services: schools and hospitals are built with public money, and teachers, doctors and nurses are paid to deliver education and health services. Many of these services are not exclusively funded by the state, however. Private investment is now used in partnership with public funding in the building of new hospitals under the private finance initiative, and charges are levied on users for some aspects of health and education, such as medical prescriptions and some school activities.

Within the public funding of these services there is also a distinction between the allocation of resources to the *providers* of the services, such as the schools or hospitals, and the distribution of resources to the *purchasers* of those services. As we saw in Chapter 9 the recent development of quasi-markets within state welfare has led to a shift in the distribution of public spending through purchasers rather than providers. There are some limits to this distribution, however. In health and social services in particular it is other state officers (doctors and social workers) rather than service users themselves who actually receive and control the funding. And in education it is still schools, rather than children and their parents, who have the final power to allocate places; the idea of providing cash (or equivalent) vouchers to parents, which could be 'spent' in any education setting, has never been taken up.

In other areas of spending public resources do go more directly to purchasers, however. For instance, housing benefit paid to low-income tenants is a form of public spending on housing distributed to the purchasers of rented housing, both within the public and private rented sectors. In effect such benefits are a form of state subsidy towards the cost of meeting their housing needs for those without the means to purchase this themselves either from public or private providers. Such subsidisation extends to the provision of other forms of means-tested support for poor service users (for instance, the free school meals and free prescriptions provided to some low-income families and benefit claimants). Benefits such as these usually go to those at the bottom of the income scale. However, the use of tax credits to reduce the tax liability of those purchasing certain services, such as private pensions or private child care, are also an indirect form of public subsidy, and they may extend more widely up the income scale.

The use of tax credits has been developed significantly by the Labour government since 1997, in particular to subsidise the costs experienced by low-wage families (for instance, through the child and child care credits). However, tax credits have a longer history. In the past they have been used as a form of subsidy for private pension contributions or the interest payments on private mortgages, and traditionally have often been of most benefit to the better-off who are more likely to be paying tax and buying such services. Titmuss famously referred to this form of public spending as 'fiscal welfare' (Titmuss, 1955), and argued that it involved a disguised distribution of resources to these better-off taxpayers. It has also often been hidden from analysis of public spending because, as income not received by the state rather than money spent, it is not included in official calculations of public spending. Nevertheless, as a form of individual subsidy, tax credits are just as important as the benefits paid to people directly, and are now widely used by government.

The use of public funding to purchase services outside the public sector extends beyond individual subsidisation, however. Public funds are also allocated directly to those providing services within the private and voluntary sectors. As we saw in Part II, this funding of non-state providers can take the form of *grants* of public money to organisations which offer to use this to provide particular services to citizens, a common form of funding for many voluntary sector service providers. It can also take the form of *contracts* between non-state providers and public funding agencies for the delivery of specific service packages. Such contracts have become increasingly common in recent years, both with commercial providers (such as the private companies now providing hospital catering or local refuse collections) and with voluntary sector organisations (such as those providing home care services or residential homes for vulnerable adults).

It is not just where public expenditure takes place which matters to social policy, of course: there is also the question of what public money is spent on. Decisions on the distribution of public spending are taken by the government. This is done on an annual basis in the national Budget, which also contains decisions about the raising of revenue to pay for the planned spending; although in practice each annual Budget statement concentrates mainly upon those decisions that involve major changes in planned spending or departures from past policy, for in large part future spending commitments are determined by past policy developments and the activities and organisations established to deliver these. We cannot just decide to stop funding schools or hospitals, and indeed any significant change in spending patterns is likely to take some time to establish and operate. As a result of this the Budget statements often contain spending or taxation decisions which will not become operational for months or even years, and such forward planning has become more common in recent Labour government budgets.

Forward planning in policy development can also take place through the normal process of legislative change: for instance, the 1986 Social Security Act introduced significant changes to social security spending, which in fact did not come into effect until 1988 *after* there had been a general election. Since 1997, however, the government has sought to engage in a more general strategic planning of future public expenditure commitments which aims to align these with planned policy developments and other political commitments. This is called the Comprehensive Spending Review (CSR) and thus far it has taken place twice, planning expenditure over a three-year time horizon. The first CSR outlined expenditure plans for 1999 to 2003, and a second CSR took place in 2002 outlining spending up to 2006. In both cases large increases in spending on health and education were promised. The CSR is intended to lead to a more stable planning environment for public spending and policy development, although of course it is dependent upon future economic activity meeting the predicted targets set by the Chancellor in the planning process; in a changing global economic environment this may not always turn out to be the case. The distribution of public spending thus reflects past policy commitments and current shifts in spending plans. In 2003 this led to the distribution of funding revealed in Figure 17.1.

Despite the big increases in spending on health and education under Labour, social security remains by far the largest single element of public spending on social policy. It has also been growing consistently over the last two decades or so as the numbers of pensioners, unemployed and other claimants has generally

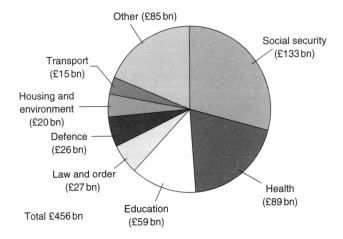

Figure 17.1   Public expenditure in the 2003 Budget

increased. The shift of some benefits to tax credits, is now having some effect in slowing this growth, as have recent reductions in the numbers of the unemployed, although as we said the greater use of tax credits is really concealing the amount of redistribution through the state which takes place across the tax and benefit systems, and this is greater now than at any point in the past.

The effect of public spending in redistributing resources within society is perhaps one of the main policy objectives of social policy planning. It was a key theme of Titmuss's early analysis of the role of public expenditure planning (see Alcock *et al.*, 2001, Part 3). Despite the assumption by many that such redistribution would generally benefit those at the bottom of the social scale, Le Grand (1982) produced a famous analysis of spending which suggested that much of it actually went to the middle classes. However, more recent analysis of the impact of a wide range of public spending commitments suggests that overall there is a significant redistribution of resources towards those in the lower parts of the income distribution within society (see Hills, 2003), despite the fact that key major services such as health and education continue to be available on a universal basis.

Hills (2003) also points out that public expenditure operates to redistribute resources in another way, *horizontally* (over the life course of citizens) as well as *vertically* (between social groups). This is most obviously the case with payments such as pensions and child benefits, but it also applies to much of education and health spending too. Horizontal redistribution is also effected by the impact of taxation with direct taxes, such as income tax and NI contributions, being paid predominantly by people during their working lives only. The overall impact of such horizontal redistribution is quite significant. For all of us public spending has the effect of shifting resources across our life courses as our needs and circumstances change; and some of these changes have been analysed and quantified by researchers using financial models to track the dynamics of life cycle redistribution (see Falkingham and Hills, 1995).

QUESTIONS: COMPREHENSION

■ What is meant by the notion of a 'trade-off' between the goals of equity and efficiency in the funding of welfare services?

■ What is 'fiscal welfare', and to what extent does it disguise disproportionate benefits for the middle class from the distribution of welfare services?

QUESTION: REFLECTION

■ What are the advantages and disadvantages of annual budget planning within social policy?

Sources of funding

In his work on the funding of welfare services Glennerster (1997 and 2003) argues that the sources of funding are as important in influencing the operation of social policy as are the ways in which money is spent. In this context he distinguishes between three main sources of funding: taxation, fees or charges and gifts or charity. To some extent these three different sources reflect the differences between the three organised sectors of welfare provision: the state, the private sector and the voluntary sector. However, in practice, their use is more complex than such a simple three-way division, for funding of state services includes both charges and charity, and, as we have seen, taxation is used to support both private sector and voluntary sector services. The mix of funding is thus as complex as the mix of services, if not more so, although state funding (financed through taxation) remains the most important source both in terms of its impact on taxpayers and its support for a wide range of service provision.

Taxes

Taxes are a compulsory payment to the state which are used by government to fund public expenditure. The most widely known tax is probably income tax, which is fixed as a proportion of earned income: 22 per cent at present in the UK. In most cases this is deducted at source from people's income by their employers, who then pay this over to the Inland Revenue (the taxation arm of the Treasury). Income tax is a common form of taxation in most countries, and it remains the largest source of taxation revenue in the UK; but it is not the only form of taxation – far from it. As Figure 17.2 reveals, income tax comprises a minority of the total taxation income within government budget planning.

Most commentators distinguish in particular between direct and indirect taxation. *Direct* taxation is tax on income and includes NI contributions. By and large this means that those with larger incomes pay more tax (sometimes referred to as progressive taxation), especially where higher rates of tax are levied on higher levels of income: in the UK taxpayers on higher incomes pay tax at the rate of 40 per cent on some of their income. *Indirect* taxation is tax on the

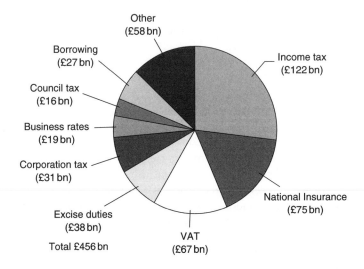

Figure 17.2   Distribution of tax funding in the 2003 Budget

purchase of goods or services. The main indirect tax is Value Added Tax (VAT), which is levied at 17.5 per cent of the costs of most goods and services. Because everyone must buy such goods, indirect taxes fall more broadly across the income range and may even be regressive, comprising a larger proportion of the incomes of lower-paid people who generally spend all of their income rather than saving or investing it.

There are some other important distinctions within taxation. Although most taxes simply contribute to overall public expenditure, it is possible for taxes to be linked to specific areas of spending. This is called ear-marked or *hypothecated* taxation, and the only significant example in the UK is NI contributions which are placed in the NI fund and used to fund insurance benefit expenditure (although to some extent council tax is also hypothecated, or at least is restricted to those activities under the control of local government). Some indirect taxes are intended not only to raise revenue but also to influence social behaviour. This applies particularly to the additional taxation on tobacco and alcohol (much higher, for instance, in the UK than in most other European countries), but it also applies to taxation on fuel (especially petrol), which is intended in part to reduce road usage and atmospheric pollution.

Payment of taxes is compulsory and, in theory, should be popular for they supply the funding for the services that the electorate have decided they want the government to provide. There is, however, a strong ideological current of hostility to taxation; and this was encouraged in the 1980s and 1990s by Conservative government claims that there was a need to reduce tax burdens in order to 'return' control over spending to individual earners and so, it was argued, stimulate economic growth. This hostility to taxation remains wide-spread at the beginning of the new century, at least according to opinion polls, and has been accepted by Labour as a reason for seeking to avoid increases in (especially income) tax even in order to pay for improved public service provision. Despite this hostility overall levels of taxation have grown in this country, as elsewhere, in order to fund the growing commitment to public spending discussed above. Important though taxation is, however, it is not the only source of funding for welfare services.

Fees and charges

The provision of most private welfare is based upon the payment of a fee, calculated to cover the cost of the service provided, and perhaps to include an element of profit for the owners of the service. However, access to public services, too, sometimes involves the payment of a fee. For instance, fees are charged for the use of leisure services, such as public swimming pools; and sometimes fees are charged for welfare services too, such as adult education classes. However, it is more common for payment by consumers of public services to take the form of a charge rather than a fee, the difference being that a charge is not intended to cover the full cost of providing the service but requires users to make a contribution towards such costs.

Charges have existed for a long time in state welfare services although their role was initially a minor one, with most services being provided free to users.

The payment of charges for prescriptions for drugs was introduced in 1951, very soon after the National Health Service (NHS) itself had come into operation in 1948. This was a controversial measure at the time, leading to the resignation of the health minister, Bevan. Nevertheless, charges for prescriptions have (apart from a brief period in the 1960s) remained ever since; and in recent years the level of the charge has been dramatically increased. Furthermore, charges for other services, such as dentistry and optical treatment, have also been introduced, and in more recent years the use of charges within other areas of public policy provision, such as education and social services, has also been growing. As we saw in Chapter 6 these include charges for residential, day care and domiciliary services within social services.

Although the scope of charges has been increasing, however, the structure of charges and charging policies has remained uncoordinated and, as a result, somewhat complex. The types of charges used by public service providers vary, with some making flat-rate charges to all service users and others grading charges either according to the level of service use or according to the circumstances of the client. The levels charges are fixed at also vary widely. Some charges are based on an attempt to secure an approximate contribution to the cost of the service provided but some have been priced at quite nominal levels, perhaps not even recovering the cost of collecting them.

The growth in charges within state services has largely been the product of reductions in the provision of direct public funding base for such services. However, the use of charges for services does serve purposes other than revenue-raising from consumers. Charges can reveal the real preferences and priorities of consumers, by discouraging abuse of free services by those who do not really need or want them; and they can act to raise the status of service users by providing them with a feeling that they are paying for services and thus can expect these to be delivered effectively to them. On the other hand, charges, even nominal charges, can act to discourage genuinely needy, and often vulnerable, users from gaining access to services; and they are likely to impact particularly harshly on poor users who cannot afford to pay charges out of their limited incomes.

The problem of the impact of charges on poor service users can be mitigated by the introduction of rebates from charges for those with low, or no, incomes. Rebates may remove the charge altogether or reduce it according to the level of income received by the user. Rebates are widely used both by central and local government to mitigate the impact of charges on poor users. For instance, NHS prescription charges are removed for children, pensioners and some people on low incomes; and most local authorities operate rebate schemes to reduce or remove the charges for education and social services for certain groups of poor people. One of the problems with such rebate schemes, however, is that they introduce a further layer of complexity into the provision of welfare services: users have to identify their right to the service, understand the nature of the charge, and then recognise and apply for any possible rebate. This can accentuate the already problematic issue of ensuring access to welfare services, a point to which we will return in Chapter 18; it can also lead to many people failing to identify and take up their entitlement to rebates. Fees, charges and rebates can therefore have negative as well as positive effects on the provision of social policy.

Charity

The other area of funding identified by Glennerster (1997) is giving, or charity. Charitable actions and gifts are probably the oldest form of welfare funding, and there is a view amongst some supporters of state welfare services that reliance upon charity for welfare is anachronistic in a modern welfare state. However, as our discussion of the voluntary sector of welfare provision in Chapter 10 revealed, giving remains a central feature of the modern welfare mix, and, although state support for the voluntary sector is often now an essential part of the resourcing of voluntary and community organisations, most of these still rely very largely upon the time and money donated to them by voluntary activists or by the public at large. Furthermore, it is not just voluntary sector organisations that benefit from charitable sources: gifts may also be made to public service providers perhaps through bequests in wills, which is quite common in education. Volunteer time is also utilised by public service providers. For example, volunteers of all ages, including school children, are used by local social service departments to work with vulnerable clients.

Charity and gift-giving also take a variety of forms across the voluntary, private and public sectors. Volunteer time is obviously of particular importance as a resource for voluntary organisations, although time can also include skills (for instance, lawyers or accountants may have much to offer to voluntary agencies by way of unpaid professional advice and assistance). Gifts may also be made in kind: for instance, the provision of equipment, or computer software, or the use of a telephone or fax line. Such gifts in kind are made by individuals but they are often a form of corporate support for voluntary agencies provided by commercial companies in the private sector. Gifts like this may even take the form of 'sponsorship', where a commercial company provides goods or services in return for their name being publicised as a supporter of the voluntary welfare agency.

Of course, most such sponsorship arrangements take the form of cash donations made in return for publicity for the corporate, or individual, donor. Cash donations themselves take a wide variety of forms, including regular donations, one-off gifts and contributions to street collections, charity fairs, jumble sales or charity shops. Such support is encouraged by government through the granting of exemptions from liability for direct taxation for money made as charitable donations by companies or individuals (although, perhaps, this should more accurately be seen as a form of state subsidy that operates in addition to any corporate or private decision to give).

The very nature of charity, however – its unorganised and voluntary structure – can cause problems for welfare provision. It may prevent some from giving because in practice they have not been asked, and it may lead others to feel uncomfortable about this form of moral pressure to support welfare. What is more, different people may give different levels of support at different times and in different areas, and usually this bears little relation to individual income differentials. The moral pressure may also apply in reverse to the recipients of gifts: users of charitable services may not feel that they have the rights and entitlements that the users of public services, or the purchasers of private welfare, can command, and thus may not use them so readily. Charitable support for welfare is thus inevitably uneven in nature, both over time and across place. However, the services which rely on such inequitable and uneven support require some level of consistency over time and equality across different places both to employ workers and to guarantee services to all users. Paying for welfare on a voluntary basis, therefore, cannot always operate to support regular service provision in the way that public taxation or private market fees can. As a result, charitable funding is often used to supplement other sources of support, in particular state funding, or to provide very specific, and adaptable, local services where flexibility and fluctuation in activity are not a limitation on provision (and may even, of course, be a virtue).

* * *

The funding of welfare in Britain, therefore, operates in practice on a mixed economy model with state, private and voluntary funding overlapping across the sectors and areas of provision. Although state funding through taxation dominates funding regimes in many areas (such as education, health and social security), throughout both state and non-state welfare varying mixtures of funding can be found. Thus the picture presented by a study of the means of paying for welfare is a complex one, and it is also a dynamic one. Differing forms of funding and the balance between these in different sectors of welfare provision are constantly changing. In the latter part of the last century the role of direct state funding was transformed in some areas into indirect state subsidy through tax allowances and quasi-markets, and by a greater reliance on market-based fees and user charges. In the early years of the new century public spending on welfare, in particular health and education, has once again begun to rise. Such changes affect the overall structure and delivery of welfare provision. However, the delivery of welfare is also affected by a wide range of factors beyond money, and it is to these that we turn in Chapter 18.

QUESTIONS: COMPREHENSION

- What are 'hypothecated' taxes, and what are the advantages and disadvantages of using them to fund welfare services?
- What are the advantages and disadvantages of the use of charges for public services?
- What are the problems of charitable funding as a source of income for the providers of welfare services?

QUESTION: REFLECTION

- Why do you think that hostility to the payment of taxes is apparently so widespread in Britain?

FURTHER READING

Glennerster's text, last re-written in 1997, provides the best guide to the issues and sources of funding for welfare. His new book (Glennerster, 2003) updates this and covers also the broader theoretical economic literature on the subject. Hills (1993) is still the best guide to the issues underlying the public funding of welfare. Falkingham and Hills (1995) contains a range of papers on the redistribution of welfare resources over people's lifetimes. Statistical data on UK population and spending patterns can be found at **www.statistics.gov.uk**.

Delivering
Welfare

SUMMARY OF KEY POINTS

- Provision of welfare services is made on both *universal* and *selective* bases.
- Social policy analysis has tended to concentrate upon the *providers* of welfare services rather than the *users* of these.
- Access to welfare services is 'rationed' by a range of formal and informal mechanisms.
- The bureaucratic and paternalistic nature of many public services has tended to exclude users from exercising much control over these services.
- New Public Management practices have imported business management methods into public service delivery and have resulted in an enhanced role for management within welfare services.
- Performance management has led to a focus upon *inputs* and *outputs* within public services, rather than the *outcomes* of these.
- Independent audit and inspection of service providers has developed as a more effective means of ensuring public accountability of services than reliance upon individual complaints or appeals.
- Modernisation of public services has led to new commitments to partnership working, local targeting and the promotion of community participation in service development.
- The replacement of government with *governance* involves a shift from electoral to 'deliberative' democracy, but this will only be effective if it leads to a shift in power from the providers to the users of welfare services.

Access to welfare

It is a common assumption, shared especially by the protagonists of state welfare, that the provision of social services will mean that the benefits of such services will be enjoyed by all those who are the intended recipients of them: if health services, for instance, are provided free at the point of demand, those who need health care will go and use them. As a result of this, attention paid to the development, and the study, of social policy has concentrated predominantly on the structure and the funding of welfare provision rather than on the access to and use of the services themselves. The focus has thus been rather more on the *producers* than the *consumers* of welfare, a distinction to which we shall return below.

This producer domination is understandable. It reflects both the powerful influence of major service providers within social policy and, at the same time, the predominant concern of social policy analysts to influence service provision. However, it is in practice only a part of the picture of social policy; and it has not prevented some commentators questioning whether service provision is in itself a guarantee of service use or benefit (this is a concern that began to attract growing attention within social policy towards the end of the last century). What is more, there is an increasing body of evidence to suggest that the provision of welfare – including, in particular, public services provided through the state – does not in reality mean that all do benefit from these services, or benefit equally from them.

Most social policy commentators make a distinction between two contrasting approaches to access to welfare services:

1. *Universal* services are intended to be used by, and equally available to, all who need, or expect, to benefit from them. State education up to the age of 16 and most NHS services are universal, and so too are some social security benefits, notably child benefit. It is argued by some that in providing for all they are in practice wasting limited resources on many users who could afford to pay for such services privately. However, universal access should mean that publicity about services can be easily disseminated and that there is no stigma attached to those using them.
2. *Selective* services restrict access to those identified as having particular needs that could only be provided for by direct access to particular services. Selection can be made in a number of ways: for instance, by focusing service provision on a specific geographical area or on a designated social group. Such geographical or social methods of targeting are widely used both by central and local government and by private and voluntary sector providers. However, perhaps the most common form of selectivity in service allocation is the use of *means-testing* to target resources on to those who have undergone some test of their inability to provide for themselves. This ensures that resources are targeted on those most in need, but also requires these claimants to come forward and demonstrate their need and may therefore lead to negative stigma from becoming associated with 'dependency' upon such provision.

There are problems with access to both universal and selective benefits, in part associated with their different strengths and weaknesses. As we saw in Chapter 16, some social divisions may mean that universal services that are in theory are provided equally to all are not in practice equally available to, or appropriate for, all social groups. There is also the evidence from Le Grand's (1982) study of the use of education and health services, which revealed that in practice better-off sections of society were more likely to use and benefit from these, because despite the principle of universal access the better-off were more informed about service provision and more able to negotiate with professionals and other service providers. Conversely, although means-tested benefits are ostensibly targeted at the poorest groups in society, as we saw in Chapter 2, there is considerable evidence that not all those who might be entitled to social security benefits do in fact take up their rights. This non-take-up of selective benefits may be in part a product of the stigma associated with benefits 'for the poor'; but it is also a product of the fact that many potential consumers do not know about their rights or do not know how best to pursue these.

Whether services are provided on a universal or selective basis, therefore, there are problems of potential users of those services failing to recognise their right to use them and so not getting the services that they may need. This ignorance or misunderstanding is in effect operating as a significant barrier to effective service delivery and, more importantly, to the meeting of acknowledged social needs. However, there are other barriers which also operate to restrict access to public services operating within service provision itself. Some of these barriers are an intrinsic feature of service provision, working in effect as a form of 'rationing' device to reduce demand on service providers (see Foster, 1983), although others may be less formal or intentional in their operation and in their effect on potential service users.

At the more formal level any procedures that are used to administer the delivery of services can act in effect to ration access to them. For example, reception procedures in health care practices may be used to determine, and to prioritise, appointments with medical staff. Here the receptionist is operating as a kind of *gate-keeper*, restricting the use of professional resources. Professionals may also operate as gate-keepers themselves, both to their own services – putting off some clients and encouraging others – and to the services offered by others. Doctors in general practice act as important gate-keepers to a wide range of NHS services and, as we have seen, social workers also now operate a significant gate-keeping role over both public and private service provision.

Gate-keeping describes an organised and relatively well-planned way of using the process of application as a means of rationing access to welfare. However, procedural factors operate to ration access much more widely than this, and sometimes in ways that may not have been intended, or predicted, by service providers. Most obviously, the physical location of service delivery points and their structural design may exclude many. For instance, the town centre location of the local social services or housing department may mean that it is out of reach for those whose mobility is restricted by disability or those who simply cannot afford to travel a long distance to make an appointment. Even where it does not keep people at home, physical disability may prevent them from entering certain buildings if appropriate access points are not provided (the grand staircase up to the Town Hall doors, for instance, is a barrier to all people in wheelchairs).

Working practices, as well as physical design, can exclude potential service users. Where there is a relatively high demand for enquiries or problems about services, many organisations operate queuing systems for potential clients. The experience of waiting in seemingly never-ending queues has often been a common one associated with access to services such as hospitals, housing departments and social security offices. Queuing alone may deter some from pursuing potential access but it is particularly problematic where the time spent queuing is preventing someone meeting other needs or is taking them away from paid employment. It is sometimes said that 'time is money', and this is perhaps most keenly felt by the self-employed or by those in insecure and poorly protected employment where absence from work means direct deduction of wages for time lost. This is a problem that is compounded by service offices and access points which are only open during the working day on a Monday to Friday, and which therefore effectively exclude all those who work these hours and cannot negotiate, or afford, time off.

Trips to offices may be avoided by use of telephone access. Telephone enquiries to call centres are now increasingly used as the first point of contact for those enquiring about potential service use and to provide advice and assistance, or even to process formal applications over the telephone (for example, the health service line *NHS Direct*). Advice, assistance and applications for some services can also be pursued through webpages on the Internet, and much information about national welfare services is now provided on government websites. However, even telephone and Internet contact are not available to those who do not have access to a telephone or computer, or cannot afford to use one.

Furthermore, telephone and Internet access – and indeed most written information and application procedures, too – are also generally only provided in *English*. Those who have difficulty with spoken or written English are likely to be excluded from services by such a language barrier. And evidence suggests that language does operate as a barrier: for example, it excludes many members of ethnic minority communities from essential services such as social security (Law, 1996, ch.2). Thus language, location, design and working practices all operate in practice to restrict, and so to ration, access to welfare services; yet these barriers are often unplanned and generally unintended, and their effects are not monitored or considered by service providers. They tend to reflect a lack of concern within the planning and delivery of welfare services for the circumstances of the users of those services; and this is an absence that has been challenged in recent years by a wide range of critics of what has come to be called a 'provider culture' within social policy.

Whose welfare?

The design and implementation of most public services has largely been based on the assumption that both the producers and the consumers of those services would have a coinciding interest in their development and delivery.

For instance, teachers would want to teach children useful and important knowledge and children would want to learn everything that teachers had to tell them. To some extent of course this is true; but, as all of us no doubt found during our own school education, this process of teaching and learning is not without its frustrations and conflicts. More recently, critics from both the right and left wing of the ideological spectrum have begun to challenge the assumed coterminous interests of the producers and consumers of public welfare services, and to suggest that the conflicts which sometimes occur here may in fact represent contradictory tensions within the whole process of delivery between the power and control of providers and the needs and rights of users.

Challenges to the alleged producer control in public welfare were a major feature of New Right criticisms of state welfare services in the 1980s and 1990s (Green, 1988; Barry, 1990). As we discussed in Chapter 12, the essence of the New Right argument was that market provision of services, including welfare services, was preferable to state provision, because markets provide for choice for consumers and, through the exercise of choice in the market, consumers can acquire sovereignty over providers; whereas within state services most providers are monopolies and are under no pressure to respond to consumer demands or preferences.

However, criticisms of a provider culture within state welfare provision have not only come from right-wing supporters of private markets; social policy academics have also pointed out that users of public services have often been 'unequal partners' in the development and delivery of those services (see Barnes *et al.*, 1999), and organisations representing service users have also sought to challenge provider control over welfare services and to seek to influence the processes of social policy planning and delivery (Croft and Beresford, 1992; Beresford, 2001). In a review of some of the issues involved in *Consuming Public Services*, Deakin and Wright (1990, p.1) commented on the failure of many providers to recognise the need to develop services *for* the public rather than delivering services *to* them, as exemplified in the creation of 'bleak, unresponsive and inefficient bureaucracies'.

The *bureaucratic* structure of state welfare services is of course to some extent an inevitable consequence of the development and maintenance of national standards and the need to secure economies of scale through the organisation of service delivery on a large-scale basis. However, as Weber's classic discussion of bureaucracy in the early twentieth century first revealed (Weber, 1968), bureaucratic organisations eventually acquire their own logic; and the internal logic of the bureaucracy can sometimes come to overbalance the external demand for use of its services. For instance, social security claimants or local authority housing tenants seeking to challenge – or even to find out about – the processing of their cases have often experienced immense difficulties in understanding and negotiating the bureaucratic procedures that the officers dealing with them seem to be trapped within. It may seem to the users of these services – perhaps with some justification – that this bureaucracy is often presented as an *excuse* for inaction ('your file has been sent to another section') rather than as an *explanation* of what is – or is not – being done.

It is not just the process of bureaucracy that alienates consumers and perpetuates the power of producers, however. These bureaucracies employ workers whose job it is to deliver services within the procedures laid down; and these workers thus acquire a vested interest in maintaining their employment, and so indirectly in maintaining the bureaucratic structures and procedures within which they work. Public sector services workers are able to protect their work, and their working practices, in this way through membership of trade unions and through negotiation with their public sector employers. And on some occasions at least these employers (the departments of central and local government) have been forced into meeting the demands of their workers, even where these may be in conflict with the needs of potential service users: for example, in maintaining nine-to-five office hours or in keeping on workers and working practices even where service demand has lessened.

It is not just the front line workers and their trade unions that have subverted consumer interest within public services, however. The activities of the *professionals* in public service delivery have also had the effect of disempowering the consumers of professional services. Professional power can be seen most clearly in the work of the medical profession: doctors and hospital consultants think they know what their patients need and they expect patients to follow the recommendations they make without question. In fact, of course, doctors may not always know best what is in the interests of their patients' health; and in some cases patients do challenge the opinions of doctors (for example, women who wish to choose their own method of childbirth). In the case of some other welfare professionals the assumption that they always know what is in the best interests of their clients is more obviously open to question. For instance, there have been examples of social workers in residential homes deciding what time residents should go to bed or eat their meals, and of housing officers in local authority departments deciding whether to permit council tenants to put up greenhouses in their gardens.

These professionals are in most cases not acting in their own self-interest in making such judgements about their clients' needs, of course, or indeed in most cases are other workers who seek to defend the procedures and structures within which they work. The problem is not one of self-interest, rather it is one of *paternalism*: that is, the assumption that the professionals or the bureaucrats know best, and therefore that the clients, or the users, should accept what they have to offer. It is this paternalism that is behind many of the problems of the provider culture within welfare services because, to adopt the terminology of the American critic, Hirschman (1970), such services do not give their users the rights of 'exit' or 'voice'.

There is no right of *exit* for public service users because such services are in most cases a monopoly. The state provides services universally to all (in theory at least); but it is also the only provider of such services. Potential consumers are thus left with a 'take it or leave it' choice to engage with the bureaucracy and follow the professional advice, or to go without. In these circumstances people cannot take their business, or their needs, anywhere else (that is, exit); and so, if they are unable or unwilling to use the state services available, they will fail to secure the welfare services which they need, and to which indeed in theory they are entitled.

It is this lack of exit that was behind many of the right-wing criticisms of state welfare services in the 1980s and 1990s and which led to the encouragement by the Conservative governments of private market alternatives to state services and the introduction of quasi-markets to introduce some element of choice into remaining monopoly services. Since 1997 it has also been a feature of the Labour government's support for a mixed economy of service providers in some areas of welfare provision, with private and voluntary sector providers operating alongside state agencies.

The lack of a right of exit from such monopoly state services might be more acceptable if there was nevertheless a right for consumers to have a *voice* within them; in other words, if the users of these services were able to influence service provision to ensure that their needs were met in ways that they experienced as appropriate and accessible. However, the paternalism of many state services has militated against the development of any mechanisms for a consumer voice, because of the belief that it is professionals and service providers who know best what potential users need. In paternalistic monopolies it is the producers, and not the consumers, who hold the power to determine the structure of service provision.

This lack of voice has been taken up by the Labour government since 1997, and in particular by the Prime Minister, Tony Blair. Blair has often accompanied his statements about the need to support and invest in public services with a commitment also to challenge the provider culture within those services to offer more control (and choice) to service users. For instance, he has talked of the anachronistic nature of the monopoly public services of the post-war era and the need to replace the paternalistic relationship between the state and the individual within these with 'choice, equality, opportunity and autonomy' (Blair, 2002). More generally the government has referred to this challenge to the provider culture as the *modernisation* of public services (Department of Health, 1998; HM Treasury, 1998, Cabinet Office, 1999; and see Powell, 1999, ch.1).

There is much more to this modernisation agenda, however, than just the extension of a voice to users within the planning and delivery of public services. Over the last two decades or so there have been a number of significant changes to the administration and management of public services which have sought to alter the balance of decision making and to make services more accountable both to those who use them and those who pay for them (generally taxpayers through the government); and these have been taken up and developed with particular vigour by the Labour government since 1997. The result has been a broadening of the involvement of a range of different interests in the delivery of welfare services.

QUESTIONS: COMPREHENSION

■ What is 'gate-keeping', and why is it widely used to ration access to welfare services?

■ Why do the critics of the 'provider culture' of public welfare services argue that the problem with such services is the lack of *exit* and *voice* for users?

QUESTION: REFLECTION

■ How should control over welfare services be transferred to users?

New Public Management

Underlying many of the changes that have taken place in the delivery of social policy over the last two decades has been the influence of management, or managerialism, on public service delivery. In simple terms this can be characterised as a shift from the administration of public services to the management of public services, now widely referred to as the 'New Public Management', or NPM (Pollitt, 1990; Ferlie *et al.*, 1996):

1. *Administration* is concerned with the operation of established procedures which ensure that users know how services operate and that professionals are able to provide the services which they judge their clients need. Power over services lies primarily with professionals, and administrators operate to service them.
2. *Management* is concerned with the effective delivery of services; it requires the establishment of clear goals which service providers are then made accountable for meeting. The setting of goals is determined by the needs of consumers, but also by the need for accountability to funders who need to be assured that resources are being used efficiently. Managers are responsible for delivering these assurances and making sure that the professionals delivering the services are working towards them. Power over services lies primarily with the managers who direct the work of professionals.

In part this shift to management was based upon an attempt to import into public service delivery ideas that were judged to have been effective in private sector management in commercial settings. This was particularly attractive to the New Right critics of bureaucratic state welfare who argued that competition in markets was the best way to ensure improved standards, and that where private markets could not be established directly then private market ideas should still be taken on. In an influential book written in the early 1990s two American authors (Osborne and Gaebler, 1992) argued that the introduction of 'entrepreneurial spirit' was transforming the nature of the public sector. Much of the theory and practice of NPM was developed in the USA; but it was also embraced in the UK by the Thatcher governments of the 1980s with the Secretary of State, Michael Heseltine, saying as early as 1980 that: 'Efficient management is a key to the [national] revival ... And the management ethos must run right through our public life' (quoted in Pollitt, 1990, p.3).

Other supporters of NPM argued that it was based upon a concern to promote the 'three Es': economy, efficiency and effectiveness. Services should be effective in meeting the needs of citizens for which they were established, but they should also meet these needs in the most efficient way and at the least cost to public funders. These goals challenged the ideals, and the practices, of some public service professionals and bureaucrats, and it was the job of the new public service managers to ensure that where appropriate these practices changed. Not surprisingly therefore NPM was not always popular with existing public service providers, and to some extent the introduction of NPM ideas and personnel led to power struggles between professionals and managers (for instance, hospital consultants and trust managers in the NHS).

These conflicts were part of a broad cultural shift within public services which has been examined in some detail by academic commentators (see Clarke, Cochrane and McLaughlin, 1994; Clarke and Newman, 1997). Some of these commentators have been critical of some of the effects of this 'new managerialism'. For a start the influence of powerful managers seeking economy and efficiency led to reductions in the work of some professionals and in the services they were providing to users, in particular those services which were not directly specified in the legislation or guidance which provided the statutory basis for the service. More generally, however, managerialism imposed a concern with rationalisation and productivity on public service provision, sometimes referred to as *neo-Taylorism* (Newman and Clarke, 1994). In such an approach the concern is with *inputs* (what is done) and *outputs* (whether is has been done), rather than *outcomes* (whether service provision has actually improved citizens' lives).

This rather mechanistic orientation to service delivery reached a particular peak in the use of 'performance management' to monitor and control service practices. Here the concern with the goals of service provision is translated into a set of targets for the delivery of predetermined outputs (numbers of clients interviewed or waiting time for appointments), perhaps also with 'milestones' to be reached in a move towards those targets (40 minutes' waiting in six months, 20 minutes' in a year's time). Achievement of performance in reaching these targets is then reported to managers, whose job it is to ensure that they are met. Performance management has become widespread across all aspects of public service delivery at the beginning of the new century, with both new initiatives and established services being expected to set, and meet, milestones and targets.

Of course, this raises questions about the appropriateness of these targets and about who sets them, and how. It can also have other worrying consequences for service delivery, however. The setting and monitoring of targets itself consumes time and resources which cannot then be spent on direct service delivery, so performance management can be expensive. More significant still, targets and milestones can become substitutes for more direct and ongoing assessment of citizens' needs and professional expertise. At it crudest this can restrict service delivery to a concern only with meeting targets (when the waiting time is down to 20 minutes then the job is done), and can encourage the setting of (soft) targets which providers know are actually easy to achieve. More generally, however, it can stifle innovation and change, especially where this comes from professionals and other providers rather than managers.

Despite some of these perverse, and perhaps unintended, consequences, however, the principles behind performance management, and NPM more generally, have become widely accepted, and even welcomed, by many concerned with the development and delivery of public services. It is important, if not essential, to have established goals for service provision and to monitor the extent to which these goals are being met; and this can lead from performance management being seen as a bureaucratic imposition towards a recognition of all public bodies as 'learning organisations'. In this context managers can play a critical role in ensuring that services are run efficiently and effectively since few professionals have the skills or training to make good managers. However, ensuring that public services are effective in meeting individual and social needs involves more than just good management, as we shall return to discuss shortly; and it is not only public service managers who are now involved in monitoring the effectiveness of many public services.

Audit and inspection

The concern of the proponents of NPM that public services should meet the three objectives of economy, efficiency and effectiveness meant that the responsibility for delivering this would fall upon the new managers of those services. However, making this the responsibility of public service managers was not in itself a guarantee that it would be achieved in all cases. If these objectives were important to public service provision, and services were to be held accountable for their achievement of them, then some independent assessment of their achievement was also arguably needed. This pressure led to the growth of a range of agencies concerned to assure users and citizens, service providers themselves, and the government, that service delivery was meeting the requirements set for it by its managers and paymasters.

Of course, users and citizens themselves are able to make independent judgements about the effectiveness of public services, and can act on these when problems occur. For a start citizens can use the democratic process to register their approval (or not) by voting out those governments or local authorities that are not delivering on their promises to provide acceptable public services. But this is a rather general response to particular service problems, and one infrequently accessible; citizens might need more than the occasional use of the ballot box to hold providers to account.

People can complain direct to service providers when problems occur, and many do of course do this. Informal complaints can lead to changes in service provision and even to redress for complainants. However, more formal procedures are often also made available to service users and these can lead to a formal response recommending service improvements and/or compensation for aggrieved users. The *Citizen's Charters* established by the Major government in the 1990s provided such a procedure for complaints to be made about public service provision, requiring public service providers to publish details of service provision and giving individual citizens a right of redress when these were not met: for instance, financial compensation where train services were delayed for more than a minimum period. Such formal procedures extend to appeals and legal actions too. Claimants have a right of appeal against decisions taken by benefits officers denying them entitlement; and users of services such as education and health can sue where they have suffered loss as a result of faulty service provision.

Bringing a legal action is expensive and time consuming, however, and requires a significant commitment on the part of the aggrieved service user. Not all users have the resources to pursue such avenues of redress, and many may find that even following through with a formal complaint seems more trouble to them than it is worth. Furthermore, in many cases service users may not be aware that mistakes have even been made. In many areas of service provision the practices and procedures of providers are complex, detailed and specialist – for instance, social security regulations and medical diagnoses – and individual users may not always understand these. It is partly for this reason that an independent source of support for individual complaints was established with the creation of government *ombudsmen* (though they may sometimes be women). The ombudsman's task is to explore complaints about maladministration reported by service users. They do not have the power to enforce action by, or changes in, service providers; but their reports are published and can carry significant weight in creating pressure for change.

The ombudsman model has been much developed and extended in recent times, however, as a result of concern by government to introduce a further-reaching independent review of the management and delivery of public services, and one not reliant solely upon the initiative of individual service users. These new review procedures are based upon the audit and inspection of public service providers; and underlying them is the assumption that, as the funders and users of such services, the public, through the government, has a right to some independent assessment of the effectiveness of these services in meeting agreed goals.

Audit is not quite the same as inspection. It involves in particular a financial, or accountancy, assessment of the proper use of public funds, exemplified by the work of the National Audit Office in its auditing of the accounts of government departments. Judgement of the proper use of public funds can extend beyond simply ensuring that account ledgers are accurate, however; it can also involve assessment of the economy, efficiency and effectiveness of those providing public services. With the establishment of the *Audit Commission* in 1982 to investigate and report on the provision by local authorities of services such as education and social services, this broader auditing role became more established. The Audit Commission has wide-ranging powers to investigate and report on local authority service provision and has developed the use of these powers in a number of major reports (see Clarke *et al.*, 2000b). Its role is as a kind of guardian of the public interest and as such its reports may often be of interest to the public. In practice, however, it is largely the government which directs the work of the Commission, and so its reports are mainly directed at government and local government service providers, suggesting how improvements in services might be made, especially where these will lead to greater economy and efficiency.

Inspection of public services has a rather broader remit than this, and a rather broader public appeal. The idea behind inspection is the presumption that the achievement of service targets by public service providers should be subject to independent verification. Thus service requirements are established for providers (for example, the national curriculum for school pupils), and regular inspections are carried out by government-appointed visitors to ensure that these requirements are being met (for example, in schools by OFSTED, the Office for Standards in Education). OFSTED was established in 1992, and was followed by the Social Services Inspectorate (SSI) in social services. There are other similar bodies with responsibility for other areas of public service, such as the Commission for Health Improvement in the NHS and the Quality Assurance Agency (QAA) in higher education. OFSTED is perhaps the most well known, however; its regular inspections have become an established feature of education service culture and its reports, posted on its website, are available for all pupils, parents and other citizens to see.

The supporters of audit and inspection argue that in principle it is right that those responsible for delivering services to the public and spending public resources should be independently assessed on their discharge of these responsibilities. They also argue that in practice audit and inspection reporting has led to improvements in overall standards of public service delivery and to the dissemination of good practice. These views are shared by the Labour government, which has embraced the agencies established by its predecessors and has extended the scope of auditing and inspection within public policy. Such inspections not without their critics, however, including those who argue that what is going on here is something of a power struggle between the providers of public services (who are those who deal directly with users and citizens) and the managers and auditors (who are in most cases appointments made by government drawn from the ranks of other professional groups); and that whether or not this top-down process of accountability is likely to lead to genuine improvements in service provision is debatable (see Clarke, Gewirtz and McLaughlin, 2000a).

QUESTIONS: COMPREHENSION

- What is 'performance management', and how has it affected the management and delivery of public services?
- What are the advantages and disadvantages of complaints and appeals procedures as a means of ensuring accountability of providers to the users of their services?
- How do auditing and inspection procedures aim to ensure that service providers are meeting public welfare needs?

QUESTION: REFLECTION

- To what extent do you think that 'managerialism' is in contradiction to the public service ethos of welfare provision?

Modernisation and governance

The Labour government in power in Britain since 1997 has embraced and extended managerialism within welfare and the role of audit and inspection. As we suggested earlier, however, these are part of a broader review by Labour of the delivery of public services carried out under the banner of modernisation. Modernisation is an interesting concept for the government to adopt, especially in what some commentators refer to as 'postmodern' times (see Chapter 12); and Blair himself has referred to the need to develop services into a post-Fordist mould (Blair, 2002). Whatever the terminology however, the key feature of the review of public service provision is the alleged need to move beyond the provider culture of the monopoly services of the national welfare reforms of the post-war era.

This includes managerialism and inspection, but it also extends to more general 'reinvention' of the public domain, which includes also new forms of partnership and collaboration in service delivery, a more active engagement with users and citizens, and a rethinking of the role of democracy in policy planning (Clarke and Newman, 1997, ch.7). More generally it has been characterised as a move from government to governance (see Newman, 2001).

Partnership is one critical element of the government's modernisation agenda. One of the widely endorsed criticisms of the state welfare services of the last century was the claim that the departmental structures set up to administer those services had led to a departmental culture in the way services were provided (sometimes referred to as a 'silo mentality'). Officers were employed by their department (the local health authority or SSD) to deliver their services, and this they did without any knowledge of, or contact with, other providers within the area. By contrast citizens and communities often made use of a number of these local services, sometimes for similar and interrelated needs: notably, for instance, for care needs in hospitals or at home in the community. The experience of citizens was one of having to liaise between different officers in different departments with different procedures and practices, most of whom did not understand anything about the work of others. At best this was a frustrating experience; at worst it meant that needs were met by neither. To use the phrase coined by the government, it meant that service provision was not *joined-up*; and part of the commitment to modernising services was a commitment to join-up service providers.

Joining-up is achieved in large part by encouraging, or requiring, service providers to work in partnership. As we discussed in Chapter 6, such partnership planning is now required of health and social service agencies in the community care field. However, partnership working extends much beyond this to include, for instance, social and economic development, education and pre-school care, health promotion, and others. Partnership planning also extends beyond public sector agencies to include also voluntary sector and private providers in joint planning and delivery of activity across a range of service areas (see Glendinning, Powell and Rummery, 2002).

In particular partnership is expected to take place at local level, with local authorities being expected to work as enabling bodies developing partnerships with other local agencies, as discussed in Chapter 15. Such local partnership working has been a central feature of another Labour innovation in public service development, area-based initiatives (ABIs). ABIs are not in fact a new, or New Labour, idea; local action to promote economic development and combat local deprivation can be traced back to the 1960s and 1970s and was a feature of the local government anti-poverty activity of the late twentieth century (see Chapter 15 above, and Alcock *et al.*, 1995). However, Labour has much expanded local social and economic development activity and provided direct support for it through a number of national programmes such as the Single Regeneration Budget (actually inherited from the Major government),

Education and Health Action Zones, Sure Start (local projects for pre-school children), the New Deal for Communities, and many others. The government website dedicated to ABIs listed 50 different programmes in 2003.

The existence of all of these various programmes has in itself created something of a joining-up problem, however. In particular in areas of high deprivation, where there are a number of different projects running under different programmes, local people are yet again having to deal with a number of different public service providers; and furthermore optimum coordinated planning of activities may not be taking place. In response to this a government review of ABIs in 2002 led to some reductions and mergers of existing initiatives. In addition the government required all those authorities in the areas of highest deprivation (and so in receipt of the new coordinated Neighbourhood Renewal Fund) to establish Local Strategic Partnerships (LSPs) to bring public, voluntary and private sector agencies together in a formal body to coordinate economic and social development activity in the area.

LSPs are a tangible example of the government's commitment to the joining-up of public service planning and to the focusing of innovations in service development and delivery on areas of highest need. The hope is that they will ensure both that general standards are met in all services locally (referred to by government as 'floor targets'), and that service delivery is geared to the particular circumstances, resources and needs of particular local areas. They are also, however, evidence of the continuing problems of coordinating the delivery of public services, especially (as is now recognised and even encouraged) as this includes also providers in the voluntary and private sectors. Yet LSPs are charged with a further function in addition to this, and that is to ensure the participation in service planning of local citizens and communities. In addition to the government commitments to partnership are commitments to participation too.

The importance of *participation* in policy planning is evidence that government does recognise some of the problems of paternalism and provider control within past welfare practice, including a lack of 'voice' for users and citizens. In order to address this policy planners are enjoined to seek out the views of citizens and communities: for instance, the government's action plan for neighbourhood renewal starkly states that, 'Effective engagement with the community is one of the most important aspect's of LSP's work and they will have failed if they do not deliver this' (Social Exclusion Unit, 2001, p.51). Encouraging participation is not the same as delivering it, however; and LSPs and other public policy agencies are likely to find it difficult to reverse the legacy of paternalism and exclusion within many welfare services.

The government does appear to recognise that participation will require empowerment of individuals and communities, and that this will require proactive intervention by policy makers and others. However, this may prove to be a greater, and a longer, task than some policy makers, and politicians, realise. There is a long history of community development work, which has seen the development of the professional skills and expertise needed to work towards the empowerment of citizens and communities (see Craig and Mayo, 1995). One of the most widely shared conclusions of this is that achieving such change requires investment and takes time. It is far from clear that all of the agencies now seeking to promote participation within the policy process have made significant investment in such community development work, or that the politicians in local and central government who have made promises to deliver it have realised how long they may have to wait for results.

Participation in policy development is being encouraged by government in order to combat the lack of voice that users and citizens are now recognised to have in service delivery. This involves not just an acceptance of the failures of past policy providers, but also recognition of the limitations within existing mechanisms for citizens to voice their concerns. In particular it involves recognition of the limitations of electoral democracy as a means of engaging with the views of citizens. In part this is the result of the increasingly low turn-out in local, and even national, elections; but it is also the result of a feeling of 'democratic deficit' within policy planning, especially where many decisions about both development and delivery are taken in quasi-independent bodies (quangos) such as health trusts or regional development agencies.

Representative democracy cannot challenge this democratic deficit; indeed, the shift in the locus of decision making makes this less and less feasible. Rather, proponents of participation have argued, it is to 'deliberative' (or 'associative') democracy that we should look to provide a effective voice for citizens within the policy-making process (Hirst, 1994). This means establishing ways for citizens to engage directly with politicians and policy makers over issues which concern them, and requiring policy makers to establish and respond to such association. A wide range of such ways has in fact been developed within welfare services over recent years, including surveys and questionnaires, users' fora, local focus groups and citizens' juries (panels of local people consulted on key policy issues). Some have provided a new forum for local people to establish direct contact with decision makers. However, many also experience the problems of combating distrust and apathy amongst users and citizens that are the legacy of bureaucracy and paternalism, which the other attempts to encourage participation discussed above have also encountered. Such fora also have to avoid the accusation of tokenism which some attempts at engagement have encountered in the past: local citizens get invited to meetings but they are then swamped with incomprehensible paperwork and jargon by service providers and find that the agenda has been set by those who already hold most of the power and information. There is more to deliberative democracy than sitting round a table with policy makers.

For deliberative democracy to work of course it must lead to a real shift in the power over decision making moving away from politicians and government policy makers and towards service users and local communities. And the real problem with this is that power is what economists call a 'positional good': it cannot be expanded, as there is only so much available, and for some to have more others must have less. In other words power cannot be *extended*, it must be *transferred*; and it is not clear that either government politicians or social policy makers have recognised the full implications of this. It involves not just a change in the nature of service development and delivery, but a change in the very nature of government itself.

As we discussed in Chapter 15, some political scientists have explored this change in the structure of government. It is captured in the talk of a move from government to *governance*, which according to Rhodes (1997, p.46) involves a 'new method' of governing society. As Newman (2001) discusses, this move to governance has been a central element of the Labour government's strategy for the modernisation of public services at the beginning of the new century. It includes many of the features of joining-up, partnership, participation and empowerment outlined above; and the move towards public agencies as *enablers* rather than providers within a mixed economy of welfare services which we have discussed earlier in Chapter 15 and Part I.

Some commentators, drawing on a boating analogy, have referred to governance as a move from 'rowing to steering'; others talk of a 'hollowing out' of the state in which less and less is decided at government level (see Newman, 2001, ch.1). It means that state agencies must recognise that they cannot do everything themselves, as the monopoly and paternalist state services of the post-war era perhaps sought to do. Instead the task of such agencies – and indeed of government itself – is to coordinate different providers meeting different needs to engage with citizens and communities in policy planning, and more generally to act as power brokers rather than decision takers. Whether such governance can work in practice to shift power within the policy-making process, and whether this is in any event likely to lead to improved services for those who need and use them, is of course far from guaranteed. What it does involve, however, is commitment in principle at least to challenge many of the criticisms made of the delivery (or non-delivery) of welfare services in the latter part of the last century; and this may have significant consequences for the future development of these in the new one.

QUESTIONS: COMPREHENSION

- What is 'joining-up', and to what extent has it transformed the delivery of public welfare services?
- What are 'area-based initiatives', and why have they grown in prominence since 1997?
- What is the difference between *government* and *governance*, and what are the implications of a shift to the latter for the development of policy making and service delivery in social policy?

QUESTION: REFLECTION

- To what extent do you think that the government's 'modernisation' agenda for public services will lead to genuine improvements in welfare provision in the UK?

FURTHER READING

Deakin and Wright's (1990) collection remains a seminal review of the need to recognise the role of the consumers of welfare services, and Butcher (2002) provides an updated and broader discussion of the issues involved in delivering welfare.

Clarke and Newman (1997) provide a critical introduction to managerialism in welfare policy planning, and Clarke, Gewirtz and McLaughlin (2000a) is a useful collection of papers on different aspects of this under Labour. Newman (2001) is a comprehensive guide to the broader issues of government and governance under Labour. Information about ABIs and other issues in regional and local policy making can be found on the departmental website at **www.odpm.gov.uk**.

The Future of Social Policy

SUMMARY OF KEY POINTS

- The last century saw the establishment of state welfare in Britain and the transformation of the country into a 'welfare capitalist' economy.
- Social policy provision extends beyond state welfare and is best described as a *welfare mix*.
- In the future of social policy must embrace the diversity of social groups and social needs.
- The development of social policy is affected by the political, ideological and economic contexts in which it is located.
- A new consensus on the desirability of public welfare is emerging in Britain in the early years of the new century.

Past achievements

The story of the development of social policy in Britain in the twentieth century was the story of the development of the welfare state. At the beginning of the century academics and campaigners such as the Fabian Society were arguing that state welfare was needed to combat the social problems created within an inequitable and exploitative capitalist economy. Throughout the early part of the century a range of measures was introduced to extend public provision of welfare, culminating in the wide-ranging reforms of the post-war period characterised by many at the time, and since, as the establishment of a welfare state in the country. In the latter part of the century these reforms were taken further as services were expanded and new forms of protection introduced. Existing services were also subject to critical appraisal and review, however; and in the 1980s in particular the sustainability, and desirability, of state welfare services were called into question by a government which was seeking to control and contain public expenditure on welfare and to encourage alternative forms of protection on the private market or through voluntary provision.

The reforms of the 1980s did not significantly reverse the broad commitments to public welfare provision developed in earlier decades, however; and at the end of the century the establishment of state welfare in Britain remained as the outstanding policy achievement of the previous hundred years. Commentators have even argued that it led to a transformation of the social and economic structure of the country to create a new 'welfare capitalist society'. This was a development that was not confined to Britain: similar transformations had taken place in most other Western European countries, and in the advanced industrial nations of North America and Australasia. Public welfare reform was also rapidly being pursued in the growing capitalist economies of the Far East and former communist nations of Eastern Europe. State welfare had become a global phenomenon.

There is also no doubt that the public welfare reforms of the last century have transformed the lives of the citizens of Britain, and other countries. Social security protection, the NHS and free public education, for instance, have lengthened and enriched the lifetimes of all, and have expanded the expectations that we hold both of ourselves and the society in which we live. Nevertheless it is now recognised that state welfare services have only ever been a part of welfare provision within Britain and other welfare capitalist countries. As we saw in Part II, private markets have provided welfare on a commercial basis, for some at least; and such market-based provision has in practice expanded, not declined, since state services became established. Voluntary sector activity has also continued, and continued to grow. Informal welfare support, through families and communities, has consistently been the basis upon which many of the most basic of social and individual needs have been provided for. As we stressed in Chapter 1, therefore, it might now be more accurate to refer to public welfare provision constituting a *welfare mix* rather than a *welfare state*, and social policy analysis has increasingly begun to recognise and respond to this.

Identification of a welfare mix has also directed attention to the different means by which service provision is paid for and supported. The assumption that social services are provided out of public expenditure, drawn from direct taxation, has always been a very partial picture of the complex and interlocking ways in which public and private funding for welfare operate together, and of the different ways in which resources are both collected and distributed. Paying for welfare encompasses financial and non-financial contributions from a wide range of sources and involves a mixture of fees, charges, contributions and rebates that in practice govern access to services in both public and private sectors. What is more, in recent years this complex mixture of funding sources and models of resource distribution has become still more complicated as market principles have been imported into the state sector and independent providers have grown in scale.

The focus on the redistribution of public resources through state welfare services as the main feature of social policy is also, in another sense, a narrow one. It has sometimes led students and policy makers to identify the *redistribution* of resources as the main goal of social policy activity, either through the payment of benefits to people or through the provision of services to them (the 'social wage'). Recognition of the economic and social context of individual needs, on the other hand, focuses our attention also on the role that policy may play in influencing the initial *distribution* of resources from which many individual needs flow, and on the *production* of the resources which may be available to meet such needs. When we focus on these, too, the policy field broadens to include the control of wages and employment protection, and the control of wealth holding and capital movement; and analysis is extended to include economic trends and investment decisions affecting the growth and development of the wider economy.

As we have seen in Chapter 18, concern within social policy planning and analysis has also been extended to include the management and delivery of services to users and citizens, as well as the structure and funding of them. It is now widely accepted that we need to ensure that the policies that have been developed do deliver the benefits which are intended within them, and that we need to develop effective mechanisms of audit and inspection to ensure that this is the case. It is also no longer possible to examine welfare provision only from the perspective of the providers of services. Academic analysis and policy practice must focus also upon the experiences, and the opinions, of users. At the end of the last century therefore the concern of much analysis and policy planning in social policy had shifted from a focus upon *what* we do to *how* we do it.

As the chapters in Part I reveal, however, the range and scale of social policy provision in Britain is extensive, and ever changing. Even the inevitably limited coverage that could be included here tells a story of expansion, refinement and continuing reform; and under the new Labour administration of the twenty-first century the government has committed itself to wide-ranging process of 'modernisation' which is leading to further change across all services. At the beginning of the new century, therefore, social policy has achieved even higher political prominence than it enjoyed in the last. Public expenditure on welfare is reaching ever higher levels, both in real terms and as a proportion of national wealth; and the range of service activity is widening further.

Future prospects

In the new century the future development of social policy is likely to be affected by a number of important changes in the political, ideological and economic context of British society. For a start political and constitutional change is altering the formal processes through which policy making and policy delivery take place. Devolution of powers to the separate administrations in Scotland, Wales and Northern Ireland means that it is no longer really possible to talk about the development of British social policy as a single process. This fragmentation is likely to be taken further as regional devolution develops in England too, and as the changing structures of local governance bring about new fora for debate about, and determination of, local policy practice.

The global context of the British economy means that policy development will be increasingly affected by what happens outside the country as well. We can already see examples of international influences through the transfer of policy initiatives developed in other welfare capitalist countries. More general influences on the direction of policy are now being provided by the new global agencies discussed in Chapter 14. And, of course, in the UK our membership of the EU will mean that the growing social policy agenda of the Union will provide more far-reaching pressures for policy coordination across the member nations and for the implementation of policy programmes on an EU-wide basis. Globalism is not an irresistible force, of course, and there are limits to the policy capabilities of the EU. The decisions of the British government will continue to be critical in deciding the shape of future policy development in the country; but they cannot be taken without an appreciation of the broader international context.

Ideological debates are also altering the way that we conceive of the achievements and the prospects of welfare policy. It is now clear that there are very different, and contrasting, perspectives on the appropriate role of different aspects of social policy development. There are also different experiences of current provisions and different demands and expectations of future development. These changing perspectives have resulted in a range of new issues entering social policy debate, and social policy practice, at the beginning of the new century. Their overall message is the need to embrace diversity in policy planning and delivery. Whatever our aspirations for comprehensive or universal policy provision, we can no longer expect that the 'one size fits all' approach will be sufficient to meet the different needs and circumstances of the diverse social groups which constitute British society.

As we saw in Chapter 12, some postmodernist theorists have suggested that such social, and theoretical, diversity means that it is no longer possible even to discuss social structures or social policies as single – and comprehensible – entities. They argue that embracing diversity inevitably means abandoning any expectation of conceptual unity. This is a controversial view, of course, and there are many who argue that recognition of diversity need not (and should not) lead us to move away from the commitment to coordinated policy planning, even though there will continue to be disagreement about what should be the priorities and limits of this.

Indeed at the beginning of the new century there is some evidence of elements of new political and ideological consensus on the future of welfare policy. After the sharp political differences of the 1980s, when the Thatcher government's policies of privatisation and public expenditure control resulted in ideological attacks upon public welfare and led to conflict with Labour-controlled local authorities over the proper role of government in welfare policy planning, there is now much shared political ground over the future direction of public planning and the provision of welfare. Whatever the theoretical and practical limitations of the much vaunted 'Third Way', it has displaced much of past New Right and New Left (now the *old* left) criticism of state welfare, and left the focus of policy debate upon the priorities for public spending and the best means of delivering services to meet welfare needs. Perhaps there has even been a return here to the *what* and the *how* questions of the social administration tradition discussed in Chapter 1, albeit within a very different, and more diverse, social and ideological context.

The new government concerns with the practicalities of delivering effective welfare services – captured in its intention to establish 'what works' – also mean that policy makers are embracing more directly the need to engage with academic research and analysis of policy practice. Academic social policy researchers are now acting as advisers to government in a number of key areas; and academic research on policy programmes is being commissioned on a more widespread basis than ever before. It is common practice now for new social policy initiatives and programmes to be accompanied by independent evaluation carried out by social policy researchers. The *prescriptive* nature of the study of social policy is therefore stronger than at any time over the previous hundred years.

As we discussed in Chapter 13, however, social policy development is also linked to the outcomes of economic policy planning. Economic and social policy planning are inextricably intertwined, as the recent developments in education, employment and social security policy reveal. Successful social policies can lead to successful economic development. The links operate both ways, however: the future development of social policy also depends upon the success of policies to manage and direct economic growth. Growth is needed to pay the taxes which will underpin public expenditure on welfare, to create the employment for people to escape poverty, and to provide the returns on investment to sustain future commitments to pensions, housing, social care and other long-term welfare needs. It is the responsibility of government to aim to secure appropriate and sustainable economic development, but it is far from clear that they are entirely in control of future economic trends, in particular where these are subject to global economic changes. What happens on the New York stock market may seem a long way from the classrooms of the local school, but there are links between the fortunes of both; and it is for policy makers in the UK to make sure that those links are managed positively.

We cannot predict future economic, political and ideological developments; and students and practitioners of social policy may say, with some justification, that they cannot be expected to embrace such broader uncertainties in seeking to focus upon the development of particular welfare needs or welfare services.

The study and practice of social policy inevitably requires some practical compromise between contextual understanding and practical policy action. Securing and managing this balance is what drives much of political debate about the future prospects of social policy. The readers of this book will now appreciate that this the foundation of individual study too.

QUESTIONS: REFLECTION

- Do you think that there is a political consensus about the desirability of public provision to meet welfare needs?
- What would be your main priority for the expansion of social policy provision over the next five years?

References

Abbott, P 2000, 'Gender', in G Payne (ed.), *Social Divisions*, Palgrave.

Abbott, P and Wallace, C 1997, *An Introduction to Sociology. Feminist Perspectives*, Routledge.

Abel-Smith, B and Townsend, P 1965, *The Poor and the Poorest*, G Bell & Sons.

Acheson Report 1998, *Independent Inquiry into Inequalities and Health*, Stationery Office.

Adams, J and Robinson, P (eds) 2002, *Devolution in Practice: Public Policy Differences within the UK*, Institute for Public Policy Research (IPPR).

Adams, R 1996, *The Personal Social Services*, Longman.

Addison, P 1975, *The Road to 1945: British Politics and the Second World War*, Jonathan Cape.

Alcock, P 1997, *Understanding Poverty* (2nd edn), Palgrave.

Alcock, P 1999, 'Poverty and social security', in R Page and R Silburn (eds), *British Social Welfare in the Twentieth Century*, Macmillan.

Alcock, P 2001, 'The Comparative Context', in P Alcock and G Craig (eds), *International Social Policy: Welfare Regimes in the Developed World*, Palgrave.

Alcock, P, Beatty, C, Fothergill, S, Macmillan, R and Yeandle, S 2003, *Work to Welfare: How Men become Detached from the Labour Market*, Cambridge University Press.

Alcock, P and Craig, G (eds) 2001, *International Social Policy: Welfare Regimes in the Developed World*, Palgrave.

Alcock, P, Craig, G, Dalgleish, K and Pearson, S 1995, *Combating Local Poverty: The Management of Anti-Poverty Strategies by Local Government*, Local Government Management Board.

Alcock, P, Erskine, A and May, M (eds) 2003, *The Student's Companion to Social Policy* (2nd edn), Basil Blackwell.

Alcock, P, Glennerster, H, Oakley, A and Sinfield, A (eds) 2001, *Welfare and Wellbeing: Richard Titmuss's Contribution to Social Policy*, Policy Press.

Alcock, P, Harrow, J, Macmillan, R, Vincent, J and Pearson, S 1999, *Making Funding Work: Funding Regimes and Local Voluntary Organisations*, Joseph Rowntree Foundation.

Anheier, H, Carlson, L and Kendall, J (eds) 2001, *Third Sector Policy at the Crossroads: An International Nonprofit Analysis*, Routledge.

Armstrong, H 1998, 'Principles for a new housing policy', *Housing Today*, 83.

Atkinson, A 1990, *A National Minimum? A History of Ambiguity in the Determination of Benefit Scales in Britain*, WSP/47, STICERD, LSE.

Bacon, R and Eltis, W 1976, *Britain's Economic Problem: Too Few Producers*, Macmillan.

Baggott, R 2000, *Public Health: Policy and Politics*, Palgrave.

Baggott, R 2002, *Health and Health Care in Britain* (3rd edn), Palgrave.

Balchin, P and Rhodes, M 2002, *Housing Policy: An Introduction* (4th edn), Routledge.

Baldock, J 2003, 'The Personal Social Services and Community Care', in P Alcock, A Erskine and M May (eds), *The Student's Companion to Social Policy* (2nd edn), Basil Blackwell.

Baldock, J, Manning, N, Miller, S and Vickerstaff, S (eds) 1999, *Social Policy*, Oxford University Press.

Baldwin, P 1990, *The Politics of Social Solidarity*, Cambridge University Press.

Ball, S 1896, *The Moral Aspects of Socialism*, Fabian Tract No. 72.

Balloch, S and Jones, B 1990, *Poverty and Anti-Poverty Strategy: The Local Government Response*, Association of Metropolitan Authorities.

Balls, E and O'Donnell, G (eds) 2002, *Reforming Britain's Economic and Social Policy*, Palgrave.

Barclay Report 1982, *Social Workers: Their Role and Tasks*, Bedford Press.

Barnes, M, Harrison, S, Mort, M and Shardlow, P 1999, *Unequal Partners: User Groups and Community Care*, Policy Press.

Barry, N 1987, *The New Right*, Croom Helm.

Barry, N 1990, *Welfare*, Open University Press.

Bartlett, W 1993, 'Quasi-Markets and Educational Reforms', in J Le Grand and W Bartlett (eds), *Quasi-Markets and Social Policy*, Macmillan.

Bartlett, W, Roberts, J and Le Grand, J 1998, *A Revolution in Social Policy: Quasi-Market Reforms in the 1990s*, Policy Press.

Beatty, C, Fothergill, S, Gore, T and Green, A 2002, *The Real Level of Unemployment 2002*, Sheffield Hallam University.

Beresford, P 2001, 'Service Users, Social Policy and the Future of Welfare', *Critical Social Policy*, 21(4).

Beveridge, Sir W 1942, *Report on Social Insurance and Allied Services*, Cmd. 6404, HMSO.

Beveridge, Sir W 1944, *Full Employment in a Free Society*, George Allen & Unwin.

Beveridge, Sir W 1948, *Voluntary Action*, Allen & Unwin.

Billis, D 1989, *The Theory of the Voluntary Sector: Implications for Policy and Practice*, Centre for Voluntary Organisation, LSE.

Billis, D and Glennerster, H 1998, 'Human Services and the Voluntary Sector: Towards a Theory of Comparative Advantage', *Journal of Social Policy*, 27(1).

Billis, D and Harris, M (eds) 1996, *Voluntary Agencies: Challenges of Organisation and Management*, Macmillan.

Black Report 1980, *Inequalities and Health*, Department of Health and Social Security.

Blair, T 1998, *The Third Way*, Fabian Society.

Blair, T 2002, *The Courage of our Convictions: Why Reform of Public Services is the Route to Social Justice*, Fabian Society.

Blane, D and Drever, F 1998, 'Inequality amongst Men in Standardised Years of Life Lost 1970–93', *British Medical Journal*, 317.

Blunkett, D and Green, G 1983, *Building from the Bottom: The Sheffield Experience*, Fabian Society No. 491.

Blunkett, D and Jackson, K 1987, *Democracy in Crisis: The Town Halls Respond*, Hogarth Press.

Bochel, C and Bochel, H 2003, *Social Policy: Process and Practice*, Palgrave.

Boddy, M and Fudge, C (eds) 1984, *Local Socialism? Labour Councils and New Left Alternatives*, Macmillan.

Bonoli, G 2000, *The Politics of Pension Reform: Institutions and Policy Change in Western Europe*, Cambridge University Press.

Bonoli, G, George, V and Taylor-Gooby, P 2000, *European Welfare Futures: Towards a Theory of Retrenchment*, Polity Press.

Booth, C 1889, *The Life and Labour of the People*, Williams & Northgate.

Borrie Commission 1994, *Social Justice: Strategies for National Renewal – The Report of the Commission on Social Justice*, Vintage.

Bowlby, J 1963, *Child Care and the Growth of Love*, Penguin.

Boyson, R 1971, *Down with the Poor*, Churchill.

Brenton, M 1985, *The Voluntary Sector in British Social Services*, Longman.

Brewster, I and Teague, P 1989, *European Community Social Policy – Its Impact on the United Kingdom*, Institute of Personnel Management.

Buchanan, J 1986, *Liberty, Market and the State*, Harvester Wheatsheaf.

Bulmer, M, Lewis, J and Piachaud, D (eds) 1989, *The Goals of Social Policy*, Unwin Hyman.

Burchardt, T and Hills, J 1999, 'Public Expenditure and the Public/Private Mix', in M Powell (ed.), *New Labour, New Welfare State? The 'Third Way' in British Social Policy*, Policy Press.

Burnett, J 1985, *A Social History of Housing 1815–1985* (2nd edn), David & Charles.

Butcher, T 2002, *Delivering Welfare* (2nd edn), Open University Press.

Cabinet Office 1999, *Modernising Government*, Cm. 4310, Stationery Office.

Cahill, M 2001, *The Environment and Social Policy*, Routledge.

Callaghan, J 1987, *Time and Chance*, Collins.

Callender, C 1996, 'Women and Employment', in C Hallett (ed.), *Women and Social Policy: An Introduction*, Prentice Hall.

Campbell, J and Oliver, M 1996, *Disability Politics: Understanding our Past, Changing our Future*, Routledge.

Castles, F 1998, *Comparative Public Policy: Patterns of Post War Transformation*, Edward Elgar.

Castles, F and Mitchell, D 1991, *Three Worlds of Welfare Capitalism or Four?*, Discussion Paper 21, Australian National University.

Chanan, G 1992, *Out of the Shadows: Local Community Action and the European Community*, European Foundation for the Improvement of Living and Working Conditions (Dublin).

Clarke, J, Cochrane, A and McLaughlin, E (eds) 1994, *Managing Social Policy*, Sage.

Clarke, J, Gewirtz, S and McLaughlin, E (eds) 2000a, *New Managerialism New Welfare?*, Sage.

Clarke, J, Gewirtz, S, Hughes, G and Humphrey, J 2000b, 'Guarding the Public Interest? Auditing Public Services', in J Clarke, S Gewirtz and E McLaughlin (eds), *New Managerialism New Welfare?*, Sage.

Clarke, J and Newman, J 1997, *The Managerial State*, Sage.

Clarke, M and Stewart, J 1988, *The Enabling Council*, Local Government Management Board.

Clarke, M and Stewart, J 1999, *Community Governance, Community Leadership and the New Local Government*, Joseph Rowntree Foundation.

Clasen, J (ed.) 1999, *Comparative Social Policy: Concepts, Theories and Methods*, Basil Blackwell.

Cochrane, A 1993, *Whatever Happened to Local Government?*, Open University Press.

Cockburn, C 1977, *The Local State*, Pluto Press.

Cole, I and Furbey, R 1994, *The Eclipse of Council Housing*, Routledge.

Colton, M, Sanders, R and Williams, M 2001, *An Introduction to Working with Children: A Guide for Social Workers*, Palgrave.

Coxall, B and Robins, C 1998, *Contemporary British Politics* (3rd edn), Palgrave.

Craig, G and Mayo, M (eds) 1995, *Community Empowerment: A Reader in Participation and Development*, Zed Books.

Craig, G, Taylor, M, Wilkinson, M and Monro, S 2002, *Contract or Trust? The Role of Compacts in Local Governance*, Policy Press.

Croft, S and Beresford, P 1992, 'The Politics of Participation', *Critical Social Policy 35*, 12(2).

Crompton, R 1998, *Class and Stratification: An Introduction to Current Debates* (2nd edn), Polity Press.

Crompton, R (ed.) 1999, *Restructuring Gender Relations and Employment: The Decline of the Male Breadwinner*, Oxford University Press.

Crosland, C A R 1956, *The Future of Socialism*, Jonathan Cape.

Cutler, T, Williams, K and Williams, J 1986, *Keynes, Beveridge and Beyond*, Routledge & Kegan Paul.

Dale, J and Foster, P 1986, *Feminists and State Welfare*, Routledge and Kegan Paul.

Dalley, G (ed.) 1991, *Disability and Social Policy*, Policy Studies Institute.

Davis Smith, J 2001, 'Volunteers: Making a Difference?', in M Harris and C Rochester (eds), *Voluntary Organisations and Social Policy in Britain: Perspectives on Change and Choice*, Palgrave.

Davis Smith, J, Rochester, C and Hedley, R (eds) 1995, *An Introduction to the Voluntary Sector*, Routledge.

Deacon, A 1976, *In Search of the Scrounger: The Administration of Unemployment Insurance in Britain 1920–31*, Bell & Sons.

Deacon, A 2000, 'Learning from the USA? The Influence of American Ideas on New Labour Thinking on Welfare Reform', *Policy and Politics*, 20(1).

Deacon, A 2002, *Perspectives on Welfare: Ideas, Ideologies and Policy Debates*, Open University Press.

Deacon, A and Bradshaw, J 1983, *Reserved for the Poor: The Means-Test in British Social Policy*, Basil Blackwell and Martin Robertson.

Deacon, B 2003, 'Supranational Agencies and Social Policy', in P Alcock, A Erskine and M May (eds), *The Student's Companion to Social Policy* (2nd edn), Basil Blackwell.

Deacon, B, Castle-Kanerova, M, Manning, N, Millard, F, Orosz, E and Szalai, J 1992, *The New Eastern Europe: Social Policy Past, Present and Future*, Sage.

Deacon B, with Hulse, M and Stubbs, P 1997, *Global Social Policy: International Organisations and the Future of Welfare*, Sage.

Deakin Commission 1996, *Meeting the Challenge of Change: Voluntary Action into the 21st Century*, Report of the Commission on the Future of the Voluntary Sector in England, NCVO Publications.

Deakin, N 1994, *The Politics of Welfare: Continuities and Change*, Harvester Wheatsheaf.

Deakin, N 2000, *The Treasury and Social Policy: The Contest for Control of Welfare Strategy*, Palgrave.

Deakin, N 2001, *In Search of Civil Society*, Palgrave.

Deakin, N and Wright, A (eds) (1990) *Consuming Public Services*, Routledge.

Dean, H 1996, *Welfare Law and Citizenship*, Prentice Hall.

Demaine, J 2001, *Education Policy and Contemporary Politics*, Palgrave.

Denney, D 1998, *Social Policy and Social Work*, Oxford University Press.

Department of Education and Science (DES) 1985, *Education for All. The Report of the Committee of Inquiry into the Education of Children from Ethnic Minority Groups*, HMSO.

Department of Environment, Transport and the Regions 1998, *Modern Local Government: In Touch with the People*, Stationery Office.

Department of Health (DoH) 1989, *Working for Patients*, HMSO.

Department of Health (DoH) 1992, *The Health of the Nation*, Cm. 1986, HMSO.

Department of Health (DoH) 1997, *The New NHS. Modern. Dependable*, Stationery Office.

Department of Health (DoH) 1998, *Modernising Social Services: Promoting Independence, Improving Protection, Raising Standards*, Cm. 4169, Stationery Office.

Department of Health (DoH) 1999, *Saving Lives: Our Healthier Nation*, Stationery Office.

Department of Health (DoH) 2000, *The NHS Plan: A Plan for Investment, a Plan for Reform*, Cm. 4818, Stationery Office.

Department of Health (DoH) 2002a, *The Government's Expenditure Plans 2001–2. Department Report*, **www.doh.gov.uk**.

Department of Health (DoH) 2002b, *Statistical Bulletin – Personal Social Services Current Expenditure in England: 1999–2000*, **www.doh.gov.uk**.

Department of Social Security (DSS) 1993, *The Growth of Social Security*, HMSO.

Department of Social Security (DSS) 1998a, *New Ambitions for our Country: A New Contract for Welfare*, Green Paper, Cm. 3805, Stationery Office.

Department of Social Security (DSS) 1998b, *A New Contract for Welfare: Partnership in Pensions*, Cm. 4179, Stationery Office.

Department of Social Security (DSS) 1999, *Opportunity for All: Tackling Poverty and Social Exclusion*, First Annual Report, Cm. 4445, Stationery Office.

Department of Social Security (DSS) 2000a, *The Changing Welfare State: Social Security Spending*, Stationery Office.

Department of Social Security (DSS) 2000b, *Income Related Benefits: Estimates of Take-up in 1998/99*, Stationery Office.

Department of Transport, Local Government and the Regions (DTLR) 2002, *Housing Statistics Postcard*, **www.dtlr.gov.uk**.

Ditch, J (ed.) 1999, *Introduction to Social Security: Policies, Benefits and Poverty*, Routledge.

Doling, J 1997, *Comparative Housing Policy: Government and Housing in Advanced Industrial Countries*, Macmillan.

Dolowitz, D 1998, *Learning from America: Policy Transfer and the Development of the British Workfare State*, Sussex Academic Press.

Dolowitz, D with Hulme, R, Nellis, M and O'Neill, F 2000, *Policy Transfer and British Social Policy: Learning from the USA*, Open University Press.

Dolowitz, D and Marsh, D 1996, 'Who Learns What from Whom? A Review of the Policy Transfer Literature', *Political Studies*, 44.

Donnison, D 1994, 'Social Policy Studies in Britain: Retrospect and Prospect', in J Ferris and R Page (eds), *Social Policy in Transition*, Avebury.

Donzelot, J 1980, *The Policing of Families: Welfare versus the State*, Hutchinson.

Drakeford, M 1999, *Privatisation and Social Policy*, Longman.

Driver, S and Martell, L 1998, *New Labour: Politics after Thatcherism*, Polity Press.

Dunleavy, P 1984, 'The Limits of Local Government', in M Boddy and C Fudge (eds), *Local Socialism? Labour Councils and New Left Alternatives*, Macmillan.

Dunleavy, P and Husbands, C 1985, *British Democracy at the Crossroads*, Allen & Unwin.

Dutton, D 1991, *British Politics Since 1945: The Rise and Fall of Consensus*, Basil Blackwell.

Elcock, H 1982, *Local Government: Politicians, Professionals and the Public in Local Authorities* (2nd edn), Methuen.

Ellison, N and Pierson, C (eds) 2003, *Developments in British Social Policy 2*, Palgrave.

Enthoven, A 1985, *Reflections on the Management of the NHS*, Nuffield Provincial Hospitals Trusts.

Esping-Andersen, G 1985, *Politics against Markets: The Social Democratic Road to Power*, University of Harvard Press.

Esping-Andersen, G 1990, *The Three Worlds of Welfare Capitalism*, Polity Press.

Esping-Andersen, G (ed.) 1996, *Welfare States in Transition: National Adaptations in Global Economies*, Sage.

Etzioni, A 1995, *The Spirit of Community: Rights and Responsibilities and the Communitarian Agenda*, Fontana Press.

Etzioni, A 2000, *The Third Way to a Good Society*, Demos.

European Commission 1993, *Growth, Competitiveness, Employment: The Challenges and Ways Forward into the 21st Century*, COM (93) 700, European Commission.

European Commission 1994, *European Social Policy: A Way Forward for the Union*, COM (94) 333, European Commission.

Falkingham, J and Hills, J (eds) 1995, *The Dynamic of Welfare: The Welfare State and the Life Cycle*, Prentice Hall.

Ferlie, E, Ashburner, L, Fitzgerald, L and Pettigrew, A 1996, *The New Public Management in Action*, Oxford University Press.

Ferrera, M. 1996, 'The "Southern Model" of Welfare in Social Europe', *Journal of European Social Policy*, 6(1).

Fimister, G 1986, *Welfare Rights Work in Social Services*, Macmillan.

Finch, J 1984, *Education as Social Policy*, Longman.

Finch, J 1989, *Family Obligations and Social Change*, Polity Press.

Finch, J and Groves, D (eds) 1983, *A Labour of Love: Women, Work and Caring*, Routledge & Kegan Paul.

Finlayson, G 1994, *Citizen, State and Social Welfare in Britain 1830–1990*, Clarendon Press.

Finn, D 2001, 'Welfare to Work? New Labour and the Unemployed', in S Savage and R Atkinson (eds), *Public Policy under Blair*, Palgrave.

Fitzpatrick, T 2001, *Welfare Theory: An Introduction*, Palgrave.

Fitzpatrick, T 2003, 'Postmodernism and New Directions', in P Alcock, A Erskine and M May (eds), *The Student's Companion to Social Policy* (2nd edn), Basil Blackwell.

Foster, P 1983, *Access to Welfare: An Introduction to Welfare Rationing*, Macmillan.

Foucault, M 1977, *Discipline and Punish: The Birth of the Prison*, Allen Lane.

Foucault, M 1979, *The History of Sexuality*, Allen Lane.

Frankenberg, R 1966, *Communities in Britain*, Penguin.

Fraser, D 2003, *The Evolution of the British Welfare State* (3rd edn), Palgrave.

Friedman, M 1962 *Capitalism and Freedom*, University of Chicago Press.

Gamble, A 1994, *Britain in Decline* (4th edn), Macmillan.

George, V and Page, R (eds) 1995, *Modern Thinkers on Welfare*, Harvester Wheatsheaf.

George, V and Taylor-Gooby, P (eds) 1996, *European Welfare Policy: Squaring the Circle*, Macmillan.

George, V and Wilding, P 1976 *Ideology and Social Welfare*, Routledge & Kegan Paul.

George, V and Wilding, P 1994 *Welfare and Ideology*, Harvester Wheatsheaf.

Geyer, R 2000, *Exploring European Social Policy*, Polity Press.

Giddens, A 1998, *The Third Way*, Polity Press.

Gilmour, I 1978, *Inside Right*, Quartet.

Ginsburg, N 1979, *Class, Capital and Social Policy*, Macmillan.

Glendinning, C 1992, *The Costs of Informal Care: Looking Inside the Household*, HMSO.

Glendinning, C and Millar, J (eds) 1992, *Women and Poverty in Britain: The 1990s*, Harvester Wheatsheaf.

Glendinning, C, Powell, M and Rummery, K (eds) 2002, *Partnerships: New Labour and the Governance of Welfare*, Policy Press.

Glennerster, H 1988, 'Requiem for the Social Administration Association', *Journal of Social Policy*, 17(1).

Glennerster, H 1997, *Paying for Welfare: Towards 2000* (3rd end), Prentice Hall.

Glennerster, H 2000, *British Politics since 1945* (2nd edn), Basil Blackwell.

Glennerster, H 2003, *Understanding the Finance of Social Policy*, Policy Press.

Glennerster, H and Hills, J (eds) 1998, *The State of Welfare: The Economics of Social Spending* (2nd edn), Oxford University Press.

Goldthorpe, J and Hope, K 1974, *The Social Grading of Occupations: A New Approach and Scale*, Clarendon Press.

Goodin, R, Headey, B, Muffels, R and Dirven, H 1999, *The Real Worlds of Welfare Capitalism*, Cambridge University Press.

Gordon, D, Shaw, M, Dorling, D and Davey Smith, G (eds) 1999, *Inequalities in Health: The Evidence Presented to the Independent Inquiry into Inequalities in Health, chaired by Sir Donald Acheson*, Policy Press.

Gordon, D, Adelman, L, Ashworth, K, Bradshaw, J, Levitas, R, Middleton, S, Pantazis, C, Patsios, D, Payne, S, Townsend, P and Williams, J 2000, *Poverty and Social Exclusion in Britain*, Joseph Rowntree Foundation.

Gordon, P and Newnham, A 1985, *Passport to Benefits: Racism in Social Security*, CPAG/Runnymede Trust.

Gorz, A 1982, *Farewell to the Working Class*, Pluto Press.

Gough, I 1979, *The Political Economy of the Welfare State*, Macmillan.

Grahl, J and Teague, P 1990, *1992 – The Big Market: The Future of the European Community*, Lawrence & Wishart.

Green, D 1987, *The New Right: The Counter Revolution in Political, Economic and Social Thought*, Wheatsheaf.

Green, D 1988, *Everyone a Private Patient*, Institute of Economic Affairs.

Green Paper 1977, *Education in Schools: A Consultative Document*, Cmnd. 6869, HMSO.

Griffiths Report 1983, *NHS Management Inquiry*, Department of Health and Social Security.

Hadley, R and Hatch, S 1981, *Social Welfare and the Failure of the State: Centralised Services and Participatory Alternatives*, George Allen & Unwin.

Hallett, C (ed.) 1996, *Women and Social Policy: An Introduction*, Prentice Hall.

Halsey, A H, Lauder, H, Brown, P and Wells, A S (eds) 1997, *Education: Culture, Economy and Society*, Oxford University Press.

Ham, C 1999, *Health Policy in Britain* (4th edn), Palgrave.

Hantrais, L 2000, *Social Policy in the European Community* (2nd edn), Palgrave.

Harris, J 1989, 'The Webbs, The Charity Organisation Society and the Ratan Tata Foundation: Social Policy from the Perspective of 1912', in M Bulmer, J Lewis and D Piachaud (eds), *The Goals of Social Policy*, Unwin Hyman.

Harris, M and Rochester, C (eds) 2001, *Voluntary Organisations and Social Policy in Britain: Perspectives on Change and Choice*, Palgrave.

Hayek, F 1944, *The Road to Serfdom*, Routledge & Kegan Paul.

Hayek, F 1960, *The Constitution of Liberty*, Routledge & Kegan Paul.

Hayek, F 1982, *Law, Legislation and Liberty*, Routledge & Kegan Paul.

Headlam, S 1892, *Christian Socialism*, Fabian Tract No. 42.

Hedley, R and Davis Smith, J (eds) 1992, *Volunteering and Society: Principles and Practice*, NCVO Publications.

Henderson, J and Karn, V 1987, *Race, Class and State Housing*, Gower.

Hills, J 1993, *The Future of Welfare: A Guide to the Debate*, Joseph Rowntree Foundation.

Hills, J 2000, *Taxation for the Enabling State*, CASE paper 41, London School of Economics.

Hills, J 2003, 'The Distribution of Welfare', in P Alcock, A Erskine and M May (eds), *The Student's Companion to Social Policy* (2nd edn), Basil Blackwell.

Hills, J, with Karen Gardner and the LSE Welfare Programme 1997, *The Future of Welfare: A Guide to the Debate*, Joseph Rowntree Foundation.

Hirschman, A 1970, *Exit, Voice and Loyalty: Responses to Decline in Firms, Organisations and States*, Harvard University Press.

Hirst, P 1994, *Associative Democracy*, Polity Press.

HM Treasury 1998, *Modern Public Services for Britain: Investing in reform*, Cm. 4011, Stationery Office.

HM Treasury 2002, *The Role of the Voluntary and Community Sector in Service Delivery: A Cross Cutting Review*, Stationery Office.

Holman, B 1990, *Good Old George*, Lion.

Home Office 1998, *Compact on Relations between Government and the Voluntary and Community Sector in England*, Cm. 4100, Stationery Office.

Howard, M, Garnham, A, Fimister, G and Veit-Wilson, J 2001, *Poverty; The Facts* (4th edn), Child Poverty Action Group.

Huby, M 1998, *Social Policy and the Environment*, Open University Press.

Humphries, R 1995, *Sin, Organised Charity and the Poor Law in Victorian England*, Macmillan.

Hutton, W 1995, *The State We're In*, Jonathan Cape.

James, S 1998, 'Labour Markets and Social Policy in Europe: The Case of the EU', in R Sykes and P Alcock (eds), *Developments in European Social Policy: Convergence and Diversity*, Policy Press.

Johnson, N 1987, *The Welfare State in Transition: The Theory and Practice of Welfare Pluralism*, Wheatsheaf.

Johnson, N 1990, *Reconstructing the Welfare State: A Decade of Change 1980–1990*, Harvester Wheatsheaf.

Johnson, N (ed.) 1995, *Private Markets in Health and Welfare: An International Perspective*, Oxford/Providence.

Johnson, N 1999, *Mixed Economies of Welfare: A Comparative Perspective*, Prentice Hall.

Jones, C 1993, 'The Pacific Challenge: Confucian Welfare States', in C Jones (ed.), *New Perspectives on the Welfare State in Europe*, Routledge.

Jones, C and Novak, T 1999, *Poverty, Welfare and the Disciplinary State*, Routledge.

Jones, K 2002, *British Education 1944–2001*, Polity Press.

Jones, K and Fowles, A 1984, *Ideas on Institutions: Analysing the Literature of Long Term Care and Custody*, Routledge & Kegan Paul.

Jordan, B 1998, *The Politics of Welfare*, Sage.

Joshi, H 1988, *The Cash Opportunity Costs of Childbearing*, Discussion Paper 208, Centre for Economic Policy Research.

Joshi, H 1992, 'The Cost of Caring', in C Glendinning and J Millar (eds), *Women and Poverty in Britain: The 1990s*, Harvester Wheatsheaf.

Kautto, M, Fritzell, J, Hvinden, B, Kvist, J and Uusitalo, H 2001, *Nordic Welfare States in the European Context*, Routledge.

Kemp Commission 1997, *Heart and Hand, Report of the Commission on the Future of the Voluntary Sector in Scotland*, Scottish Council for Voluntary Organisations Publications.

Kemp, P, Wilcox, S and Rhodes, D 2002, *Housing Benefit Reform: Next Steps*, Joseph Rowntree Foundation.

Kendall, J and Knapp, M 1995, 'A Loose and Baggy Monster: Boundaries, Definitions and Typologies', in J Davis Smith, C Rochester and R Hedley (eds), *An Introduction to the Voluntary Sector*, Routledge.

Kendall, J and Knapp, M 1996, *The Voluntary Sector in the UK*, Manchester University Press.

Kennedy Report 1998, *The Learning Age: Further Education for the New Millennium*, DfEE.

Kenway, P and Palmer, G 2002, 'What do the Poverty Numbers Really Show?', *Policy Analysis 3*, New Policy Institute.

Keynes, J M 1936, *The General Theory of Employment, Interest and Money*, Macmillan.

King, D 1987, *The New Right: Politics, Markets and Citizenship*, Macmillan.

King, D and Stoker, G (eds) 1996, *Rethinking Local Democracy*, Macmillan.

Kirton, D 1999, 'The Care and Protection of Children', in J Baldock, N Manning, S Miller and S Vickerstaff (eds), *Social Policy*, Oxford University Press.

Klein, R 2001, *New Politics of the NHS* (4th edn), Prentice Hall.

Kleinman, M 2002, *A European Welfare State? European Union Social Policy in Context*, Palgrave.

Korpi, W 1983, *The Democratic Class Struggle*, Routledge & Kegan Paul.

Kramer, R 1990, *Voluntary Organisations in the Welfare State: On the Threshold of the 1990s*, Centre for Voluntary Organisation, LSE.

Large, P 1991, 'Paying for the Additional Costs of Disability', in G Dalley (ed.), *Disability and Social Policy*, Policy Studies Institute.

Lavalette, M and Pratt, A (eds) 2001, *Social Policy: A Conceptual and Theoretical Introduction* (2nd edn), Sage.

Law, I 1996, *Racism, Ethnicity and Social Policy*, Prentice Hall.

Le Grand, J 1982, *The Strategy of Equality*, Allen & Unwin.

Le Grand, J 1990, 'Equity Versus Efficiency: The Elusive Trade-off', *Ethics*, 100.

Le Grand, J 1993, 'Paying for or Providing Welfare', in N Deakin and R Page (eds), *The Costs of Welfare*, Avebury.

Le Grand, J and Bartlett, W (eds) 1993, *Quasi-Markets and Social Policy*, Macmillan.

Leach, R and Percy-Smith, J 2001, *Local Governance in Britain*, Palgrave.

Lee, P and Raban, C 1988, *Welfare Theory and Social Policy: Reform or Revolution*, Sage.

Leibfried, S 1993, 'Towards a European Welfare State?', in C Jones (ed.), *New Perspectives on the Welfare State in Europe*, Routledge.

Leonard, P 1997, *Postmodern Welfare: Reconstructing an Emancipatory Project*, Sage.

Lewis, G, Gewitz, S and Clarke, J (eds) 2000, *Rethinking Social Policy*, Sage.

Lewis, J 1992, 'Gender and the Development of Welfare Regimes', *Journal of European Social Policy*, 2(3).

Lewis, J 1995, *The Voluntary Sector, the State and Social Work in Britain*, Edward Elgar.

Lewis, J 2003, 'Feminist Perspectives', in P Alcock, A Erskine and M May (eds), *The Student's Companion to Social Policy* (2nd edn), Basil Blackwell.

Lipset, S 1963, *Political Man*, Heinemann.

Lodemel, I and Trickey, H, (eds) 2001, *'An Offer you can't Refuse': Workfare in International Perspective*, Policy Press.

Lowe, R 1990, 'The Second World War: Consensus and the Foundations of the Welfare State', *Twentieth Century British History*, 1(2).

Lowe, R 1999, *The Welfare State in Britain since 1945* (2nd edn), Macmillan.

Lund, B 1996, *Housing Problems and Housing Policy*, Longman.

Lyotard, J-F 1984, *The Postmodern Condition*, Manchester University Press.

Macmillan, H 1938, *The Middle Way*, Macmillan.

Macnicol, J 1980, *The Movement for Family Allowances 1918–1945; A Study in Social Policy Development*, Heinemann.

Malpass, P and Murie, A 1999, *Housing Policy and Practice* (5th edn), Palgrave.

Marshall, T H 1950, *Citizenship and Social Class*, Cambridge University Press.

Marx, K 1970, *Capital*, Vol. 1, Progress Press.

Maud Committee 1967, *Report of the Committee on the Management of Local Government*, Vol. 1, HMSO.

May, M and Brunsdon, E 2004, *Private and Occupational Welfare: In the Shadow of the State*, Open University Press (forthcoming).

Mayo, M 1994, *Communities and Caring: The Mixed Economy of Welfare*, Macmillan.

McDonald, G and Williamson, E 2002, *Against the Odds: An Evaluation of Children and Family Support Services*, National Children's Bureau.

McGlone, F 1992, *Disability and Dependency in Old Age: A Demographic and Social Audit*, Family Policy Studies Centre.

McKay, S and Rowlingson, K 1999, *Social Security in Britain*, Macmillan.

Means, R and Smith, R 2003, *Community Care: Policy and Practice* (3rd edn), Palgrave.

Merrett, S 1979, *State Housing in Britain*, Routledge.

Millar, J 2000, *Keeping Track of Welfare Reform: The New Deal Programmes*, Joseph Rowntree Foundation.

Millar, J (ed.) 2003, *Understanding Social Security: Issues for Policy and Practice*, Policy Press.

Mishra, R 1984, *The Welfare State in Crisis*, Wheatsheaf.

Mishra, R 1989, 'The academic tradition in social policy: The Titmuss years', in M Bulmer, J Lewis and D Piachaud (eds), *The Goals of Social Policy*, Unwin Hyman.

Mishra, R 1990, *The Welfare State in Capitalist Society*, Harvester Wheatsheaf.

Mishra, R 1999, *Globalisation and the Welfare State*, Edward Elgar.

Moore, R and Wallace, T 1975, *Slamming the Door*, Martin Robertson.

Morris, L 1994, *Dangerous Classes: The Underclass and Social Citizenship*, Routledge.

Mullins, D and Murie, A 2003, *Housing Policy in Britain*, Palgrave.

Muncie, J, Hughes, G and Mclaughlin, E (eds) 2002, *Youth Justice: Critical Readings*, Sage.

Murray, C 1984, *Losing Ground: American Social Policy 1950–1980*, Basic Books.

Murray, C 1996, *Charles Murray and the Underclass: The Developing Debate*, Institute of Economic Affairs.

National Council for Voluntary Organisations 2002, *The UK Voluntary Sector Almanac 2002*, NCVO Publications.

Newman, J 2001, *Modernising Governance: New Labour, Policy and Society*, Sage.

Newman, J and Clarke, J 1994, 'Going about Our Business? The Managerialization of Public Services', in J Clarke, A Cochrane and E McLaughlin (eds), *Managing Social Policy*, Sage.

O'Brien, M and Penna, S 1998, *Theorising Welfare*, Sage.

O'Connor, J 1973, *The Fiscal Crisis of the State*, St Martin's Press.

Office of National Statistics 2002, *Statbase*, **www.ons.gov.uk**.

Okun, A 1975, *Equality and Efficiency: The Big Trade-Off*, Brookings Institute.

Oliver, M 1996, *Understanding Disability: From Theory to Practice*, Macmillan.

Osborne, D and Gaebler, T 1992, *Reinventing Government: How the Entrepreneurial Spirit is Transforming the Public Sector*, Addison-Wesley.

Page, R and Silburn, R (eds) 1999, *British Social Welfare in the Twentieth Century*, Macmillan.

Pahl, J 1989, *Money and Marriage*, Macmillan.

Parker, G 1990, *With Due Care and Attention: A Review of Research on Informal Care*, Family Policy Studies Centre.

Parrott, L 2002, *Social Work and Social Care* (2nd edn), Routledge.

Parry, R 2003, 'Social Policy within the United Kingdom', in P Alcock, A Erskine and M May (eds), *The Student's Companion to Social Policy* (2nd edn), Basil Blackwell.

Pascall, G 1997, *Social Policy: A New Feminist Analysis*, Routledge.

Payne, G (ed.) 2000, *Social Divisions*, Palgrave.

Peden, G 1985, *British Economic and Social Policy: Lloyd George to Margaret Thatcher* (2nd edn), Philip Allan.

Phillipson, C and Walker, A (eds) 1986, *Ageing and Social Policy: A Critical Assessment*, Gower.

Philpott, J (ed.) 1997, *Working for Full Employment*, Routledge.

Pierson, P 1998, *Beyond the Welfare State: The New Political Economy of Welfare* (2nd edn), Polity Press.

Pierson, P 2000, *The New Politics of the Welfare State*, Oxford University Press.

Pitts, J 1999, *Working with Young Offenders* (2nd edn), Palgrave.

Plant, R 1988, *Citizenship, Rights and Socialism*, Fabian Society No. 531.

Platt, A 1969, *The Childsavers: The Invention of Delinquency*, University of Chicago Press.

Pollitt, C 1990, *Managerialism and the Public Services*, Basil Blackwell.

Powell, M (ed.) 1999, *New Labour, New Welfare State? The 'Third Way' in British Social Policy*, Policy Press.

Powell, M (ed.) 2002, *Evaluating New Labour's Welfare Reforms*, Policy Press.

Powell, M 2003, 'The Third Way', in P Alcock, A Erskine and M May (eds), *The Student's Companion to Social Policy* (2nd edn), Basil Blackwell.

Powell, M and Hewitt, M 2002, *Welfare State and Welfare Change*, Open University Press.

Putnam, R 1993, *Making Democracy Work*, Princeton University Press, USA.

Putnam, R 2000, *Bowling Alone*, Simon & Schuster, USA.

Qureshi, H and Walker, A 1989, *The Caring Relationship: Elderly People and their Families*, Macmillan.

Rhodes, R 1997, *Understanding Governance*, Open University Press.

Rochester, C 2001, 'Regulation: The Impact on Local Voluntary Action', in M Harris and C Rochester (eds), *Voluntary Organisations and Social Policy in Britain: Perspectives on Change and Choice*, Palgrave.

Rossiter, C and Wicks, M 1982, *Crisis or Challenge? Family Care, Elderly People and Social Policy*, Family Policy Studies Centre.

Rowntree, B S 1901, *Poverty: A Study of Town Life*, Macmillan.

Rowntree, B S 1941, *Poverty and Progress: A Second Social Survey of York*, Longman.

Russell, L and Scott, D 1997, *Very Active Citizens? The Impact of Contracts on Volunteers*, University of Manchester Press.

Ryan, P 1978, 'Poplarism 1893–1930', in P Thane (ed.), *The Origins of British Social Policy*, Croom Helm.

Sainsbury, R 1998, 'Putting Fraud into Perspective', *Benefits*, 21.

Salamon, L and Anheier, H 1996, *The Emerging Nonprofit Sector*, University of Manchester Press.

Sanderson, M 1999, 'Education', in R Page and R Silburn (eds), *British Social Welfare in the Twentieth Century*, Macmillan.

Saraga, E (ed.) 1998, *Embodying the Social: Constructions of Difference*, Routledge.

Sarre, P 1989, 'Recompostition of the Class Structure', in C Hamnett, L McDowell and P Sarre (eds), *Restructuring Britain: The Changing Social Structure*, Sage.

Saville, J 1983, 'The Origins of the Welfare State', in M Loney, D Boswell and J Clarke (eds), *Social Policy and Social Welfare*, Open University Press.

Schwartzmantel, J 1994, *The State in Contemporary Society: An Introduction*, Harvester Wheatsheaf.

Seebohm Report 1968, *Report of the Committee on Local Authority and Allied Personal Social Services*, Cmnd. 3703, HMSO.

Shaw, M, Dorling, D, Gordon, D and Davey Smith, G 1999, *The Widening Gap: Health Inequalities and Policy in Britain*, Policy Press.

Smith, A 1776, *An Enquiry into the Nature and Causes of the Wealth of Nations*, Adam & Charles Black.

Smith, D (ed.) 1992, *Understanding the Underclass*, Policy Studies Institute.

Smith, G 1988, 'A Paen for the Social Policy Association: A Response to Glennerster', *Journal of Social Policy*, 17(3).

Social Exclusion Unit (SEU) 2001, *A New Commitment to Neighbourhood Renewal: National Strategy Action Plan*, Stationery Office.

Solomos, J 1989, *Race and Racism in Contemporary Britain*, Macmillan.

Stoker, G 1991, *The Politics of Local Government* (2nd edn), Macmillan.

Sullivan, M 1992, *The Politics of Social Policy*, Harvester Wheatsheaf.

Sullivan, M 2003, 'Social Democracy', in P Alcock, A Erskine and M May (eds), *The Student's Companion to Social Policy* (2nd edn), Basil Blackwell.

Summerfield, C and Babb, P 2003, *Social Trends 33*, Stationery Office.

Sutherland Commission 1999, *With Respect to Old Age: Long Term Care Rights and Responsibilities*, Report by the Royal Commission on Long Term Care, Cm. 4192, Stationery Office.

Sykes, R, Palier, B and Prior, P (eds) 2001, *Globalisation and European Welfare States: Challenges and Change*, Palgrave.

Tawney, R H 1931, *Equality*, Allen & Unwin.

Taylor-Gooby, P 1991 *Social Change, Social Welfare and Social Science*, Harvester Wheatsheaf.

Taylor-Gooby, P 1994, 'Postmodernism and Social Policy: a great leap backwards?', *Journal of Social Policy*, 23(3).

Taylor-Gooby, P 1999, 'The Future of Social Policy', in J Baldock, N Manning, S Miller and S Vickerstaff (eds), *Social Policy*, Oxford University Press.

Taylor-Gooby, P and Dale, J 1981, *Social Theory and Social Welfare*, Edward Arnold.

Thane, P 1996, *The Foundations of the Welfare State* (4th edn), Longman.

Therborn, G and Roebroek, J 1986, 'The Irreversible Welfare State', *International Journal of the Health Services*, 16(3).

Thomas, I and Balloch, S 1994, 'Local Authorities and the Expansion of Credit Unions 1991–3', *Local Economy*, 9(2).

Thomas, R 2001, 'Economic Policy: The Conservative Legacy and New Labour's Third Way', in S Savage and R Atkinson (eds), *Public Policy under Blair*, Palgrave.

Thompson, A and Dobson, R 1995, 'Death of an ideal', *Community Care*, 6–12 July, pp.20–1.

Timmins, N 2001, *The Five Giants: A Biography of the Welfare State* (new edn), HarperCollins.

Titmuss, R 1955, *The Social Division of Welfare: Some Reflections on the Search for Equity*, Liverpool University Press.

Titmuss, R 1958, *Essays on 'the Welfare State'*, Allen & Unwin.

Titmuss, R 1970, *The Gift Relationship*, Pelican, and reprinted 1997, LSE books.

Titmuss, R 1974, *Social Policy: An Introduction*, Unwin Hyman.

Tomlinson, S 2001, *Education in a Post-Welfare Society*, Open University Press.

Townsend, P 1962, *The Last Refuge: A Survey of Residential Institutions and Homes of Old People*, Routledge & Kegan Paul.

Townsend, P 1979, *Poverty in the United Kingdom: A Survey of Household Resources and Standards of Living*, Penguin.

Townsend, P, Davidson, N and Whitehead, M (eds) 1988, *Inequalities in Health: The Black Report and the Health Divide*, Penguin.

Trades Union Congress (TUC) 2000, *The Employment Relations Act: A TUC Guide*, TUC.

Twigg, J 1989, 'Models of Carers: How do Social Care Agencies Conceptualise their Relationship with Informal Carers?', *Journal of Social Policy*, 18(1).

Twigg, J 1999, 'Social Care', in J Baldock, N Manning, S Miller and S Vickerstaff (eds), *Social Policy*, Basil Blackwell.

Twigg, J and Atkin, K 1994, *Carers Perceived: Policy and Practice in Informal Care*, Open University Press.

Ungerson, C 1987, *Policy is Personal. Sex, Gender and Informal Care*, Tavistock.

Van Oorschot, W 1995, *Realising Rights: A Multi-Level Approach to the Non-Take-Up of Means-Tested Benefits*, Avebury.

Veit-Wilson, J 1998, *Setting Adequacy Standards: How Governments Define Minimum Incomes*, Policy Press.

Walker, A and Walker, L 1991, 'Disability and Financial Need – the Failure of the Social Security System', in G Dalley (ed.), *Disability and Social Policy*, Policy Studies Institute.

Wall, A and Owen, B 2002, *Health Policy* (2nd edn), Routledge.

Wanless Report 2002, *Securing our Future Health: Taking a Long Term View*, HM Treasury.

Watson, S and Doyal, L (eds) 1999, *Engendering Social Policy*, Open University Press.

Weber, M 1968, *Economy and Society*, Bedminster Press.

White Paper 1944, *Employment Policy*, Cmd. 6527, HMSO.

Williams, C 1996, 'The New Barter Economy: An Appraisal of Local Exchange and Trading Schemes (LETS)', *Journal of Public Policy*, 16.

Williams, F 1989, *Social Policy: A Critical Introduction*, Polity Press.

Williams, F 2000, 'Principles of Recognition and Respect in Welfare', in G Lewis, S Gewitz and J Clarke (eds) *Rethinking Social Policy*, Sage.

Willmott, P 1984, *Community in Social Policy*, Policy Studies Institute.

Wilson, D and Game, C 2002, *Local Government in the United Kingdom* (3rd edn), Palgrave.

Wilson, E 1977, *Women and the Welfare State*, Tavistock.

Wolfenden Report 1977, *The Future of Voluntary Organisations*, Croom Helm.

Woods, K 2002, 'Health Policy and the NHS in the UK 1997–2002', in J Adams and P Robinson (eds), *Devolution in Practice: Public Policy Differences within the UK*, Institute for Public Policy Research (IPPR).

Wright, E O 1985, *Classes*, Verso.

Wright, E O (ed.) 1989, *The Debate on Classes*, Verso.

Wright, K 1987, *The Economics of Informal Care of the Elderly*, Centre for Health Economics, University of York.

Index